Louisiana Stories

Louisiana Stories

Edited by Ben Forkner

PELICAN PUBLISHING COMPANY
GRETNA 1990

Library of Congress Cataloging-in-Publication Data
Louisiana Stories / edited by Ben Forkner.
    p.   cm.
   ISBN 0-88289-784-5. — ISBN 0-88289-737-3 (pbk.)
   1. Louisiana—Fiction. 2. Short stories, American—
Louisiana. I. Forkner, Ben.
PS558.L8S56   1990
813'.010832763—dc20   89-25575
                                              CIP

Cover illustration and design by Tracey Clements

Manufactured in the United States of America
Published by Pelican Publishing Company, Inc.
1101 Monroe Street, Gretna, Louisiana 70053

To my brother John

Contents

Acknowledgments 9

Introduction
    Ben Forkner 13

The Indefatigable Bear Hunter
    Madison Tensas [Henry Clay Lewis] 35

Posson Jone'
    George Washington Cable 45

Chita: A Memory of Last Island
    Lafcadio Hearn..65

Bayou L'Ombre
    Grace King...133

Athénaïse: A Story of a Temperament
    Kate Chopin 167

The Kingdom of God
    William Faulkner 199

Cane River
    Lyle Saxon...205

A Summer Tragedy
    Arna Wendell Bontemps 221

Father Watson
    Zora Neale Hurston 233

Canker
    E. P. O'Donnell...243

Joshua
Shirley Ann Grau 259

The Sky Is Gray
Ernest Gaines 287

Goodbye
Andre Dubus...............................317

The Convict
James Lee Burke 329

Two Girls Wearing Perfume in the Summer
Robb Forman Dew...............................345

Pleadings
John William Corrington 365

About the Editor 400

Acknowledgments

A number of people have generously assisted me in the making of this book: my wife, Nadine, who shares my love of Louisiana, and who skillfully read every word of the manuscript; my son, Benjamin; my parents, Mrs. and Mr. O.C. Peterson; J. Gerald Kennedy; Michel Leterme; John Paine; Patrick Samway; the entire amiable and competent staff at Pelican Publishing Company, with a special word of thanks to its President and Publisher, Dr. Milburn Calhoun, who welcomed the proposal from the beginning, and for my editors, Dean Shapiro and Nina Kooij, who have followed the collection with care through every stage of preparation. Finally, the dedication is a very small gesture of appreciation and love for my brother, John F.D. Peterson, bayou guide *par excellence*.

Louisiana Stories

Introduction

I HAD BEEN READING LOUISIANA WRITERS for many years before it slowly dawned on me that Louisiana had a literary history, and that the driving force behind that history was a remarkable succession of powerful and original short stories. Almost all the major Louisiana writers, from the early moderns George Washington Cable and Kate Chopin, and on through the current contemporary figures Ernest Gaines and Andre Dubus, have done some of their strongest work in the short story. And one of the simple, but I hope compelling aims of *Louisiana Stories* is to make available the best of their stories in a single, fully representative volume.

But *Louisiana Stories* has other aims as well, and not the least of them is the perhaps surprising claim that these same native Louisiana stories manage to announce the central themes of modern Southern fiction more emphatically, and earlier, than the writing of any other single Southern region. Especially in the decades immediately following the Civil War, the Louisiana story, in the hands of Cable, King, and Chopin, achieved a combination of historical insight and dramatic power that would be matched in the rest of the South only during the first wave of the Southern revival after World War I.

The reasons behind this early pioneering show of strength are not that difficult to identify. No one needs to be reminded that the Civil War and the Confederate defeat shattered the old certitudes and thrust the South into a long, bitter era of lost hopes, divided loyalties, and bewildering change. Only a few Southern writers were able or willing to confront this confused new world. The great majority drifted off into a nostalgic mood of evasion and imaginative retreat. Novel after novel and story after story closed their eyes on the present in order to more easily look back and celebrate the faded glories of the old plantation South "befo' the war." Northern and Southern readers alike were understandably tempted to relax into a pastoral dream of racial harmony, civilized good will, and the occasional flaring out of honorable high spirits, but obviously this was the sort of dream that censored far more than it revealed.

Other Southern writers stayed closer to the world they had actually lived in, but tended to isolate only the most exotic sights and sounds they remembered, crowding their stories with every odd note of local speech, and every archaic Southern rite or superstition. At least these local colorists, such as Joel Chandler Harris in Georgia, and Mary Noailles Murfree in Tennessee, were writing about communities that did exist, no matter how foreign and fabled they appeared to the Northern reader. And by retelling the shrewd old animal tales of the Southern blacks, or describing the wild independent musical grace of the mountain clans, Harris and Murfree, among others, helped discover two of the deepest creative currents of the modern South.

But of course even the genuine skill of the best of the local colorists could hardly do justice to the general Southern condition after the war, not when their chosen focus was so narrowly aimed at the outlying, and the inward-turned. In this respect, most local color stories, faithful or not, often shared with the genteel legends of antebellum times an all too obvious failure of completeness. They both could only rarely suggest the full human drama of the stricken South.

Here, the Louisiana writer had a clear advantage over his Southern contemporaries. He had no trouble packing his pages with enough out-of-the-ordinary characters and stories to more than satisfy the national appetite for the homegrown exotic. After all, no other state in the country had such a flamboyant history of diverse cultures and races living side by side as native citizens. By the outbreak of the Civil War, Louisiana had been an American possession for little more than half a century. But beyond those fifty years lay a lively, highly unlikely colonial society founded, and for the most part fashioned—even during the interruption of Spanish control at the end of the 18th century—by a long line of French settlers and administrators.

As George Washington Cable was the first to realize, the old Creole community, up and down the social scale, from planter to slave, from French priest to French-speaking quadroon, gave him all he needed in the way of local color. But Cable realized too that the turbulent rise and fall of the Creoles had also left him, on his own doorstep as it were, a ghostly but complete human drama whose tragic implications for the wider South could not be missed.

For sheer everyday display of human variety, Cable and the Louisiana writer of the 19th century also had the advantage of a prodigal port city whose size, activity, and importance placed it above all the other Southern ports, a fact not lost on the Union leaders, who considered its capture a key element in the winning of the war. New Orleans in the middle of the century was still a strikingly foreign city, a national enigma, and a brimming source of fascination for the visitor and the journalist. I have always enjoyed Frederick Law Olmsted's half-comic account of his arrival there on a trip he took a few years before the war began:

> There was a sign, "Café du Faubourg," and, putting my head out of the window, I saw that we must have arrived at New Orleans. We reached the terminus, which was surrounded with *fiacres*, in the style of Paris. "To the Hotel St. Charles," I said to the driver, con-fused with the loud French and quiet English of the crowd about me. "*Oui*, yer 'onor," was the reply of my Irish-born fellow-citizen.

Right up to the war, the sound of an Irish voice combining French and English in an animated subtropical street was still possible, along with a rich choice of other strange conjunctions: the old French Creole himself, dying off but still stubbornly protesting his fate, and still scornfully claiming a purebred Gallic superiority; slaves and free men of color from a multitude of African and Caribbean origins; Kentucky rivermen and Mississip-pi steamboat captains including the living legend Horace Bixby, the pilot who taught Mark Twain; Scotch-Irish preachers; German and Jewish shopkeepers; 'Cadian (later Cajun) farmers and fishermen in from the prairies and bayous; bear hunters from Arkansas and soon-to-be-ruined cotton planters who had left Virginia and the Carolinas only a generation earlier. The list could go on for paragraphs.

After the Civil War, national attention was attracted to Louisi-ana even more than before. The disorder and violence of Recon-struction seemed to be an almost daily spectacle there, with corruption following corruption in a parade that tragicomically seemed to have no end. A firsthand account of a New Orleans, or any other Louisiana scene, was a certain guarantee of success and high sales for a national magazine. It is not surprising then, that very quickly after the war, even before the local color movement became the fashion in the rest of the South, Louisiana writers were solicited by these same magazines. Cable began his career, for example, after reading a few of his unpublished stories of Creole life and manners to Edward King, a young journalist visiting New Orleans and preparing a series of articles for *Scribner's Magazine*. In one of these articles, later published in his collection *The Great South* (1875), King had pointed to Louisiana as a densely planted, but unharvested field, ripe and ready for the kind of writing the *Scribner's* editors were looking for:

> Louisiana today is Paradise Lost. In twenty years it may be Paradise Regained. It has unlimited, magnificent possibilities. Upon its bayou-penetrated soil, on its rich uplands and its vast prairies, a gigantic struggle is in progress; it is the battle of race with race, of the *picturesque* and unjust civilisation of the past with the prosaic and leveling civilisation of the present.

Impressed by Cable's stories, and by his substantial fund of New Orleans lore, King carried several of Cable's stories back to New York, and his career was launched. A few years later, Lafcadio Hearn, his own Greek and Irish background as confused and complicated as anything New Orleans had to offer, read Cable's story "Jean-ah Poquelin" and moved to New Orleans. He fell under its spell, settled there, and began writing impressionistic stories and sketches of one of the few places in his far-stepping nomadic career he ever called home. Not long afterward, Grace King and then Kate Chopin leaped to national prominence with their collections, and Louisiana, as Edward King had predicted, had soon established itself as the leading center of the new Southern fiction.

It would be a mistake to link these first Louisiana writers too closely as a group, even more so as a literary school. But no one could deny that the single most important force behind their collective success had its origins in the peculiar tragic irony of the old Creole community after the war. When Cable began writing, the Creoles were still highly visible, and even active in Louisiana affairs. But their power and influence had waned considerably.

The war had exhausted whatever fortunes they possessed, and they had fallen generally into a proud, defensive, inbred decay, clannishly conscious that their past was far more alive than their present.

Cable was the first to fully respond to the high dramatic potential of the Creole condition. As a non-Creole native of New Orleans, he lived familiarly within their midst, and had ample occasion to study their character, and to steep himself in all the details of language and culture that separated them from the rest of the South.

But these details very quickly led him to contemplate their history from a different perspective, not so much as Frenchmen who happened to be Southerners, but as Southerners who happened to be French. The distinction is slight, and easily pivotable, but it meant for Cable a deepening of his fiction that set him apart from the other Southern writers of his day. It meant he could fill his stories with romantic, old-time portraits and colorful Louisiana dialects, and thus readily please the public fashion; but it meant too that he could use these same stories to address the unfashionable subject of the fallen South.

As a former Confederate soldier, and a devoted Southerner, Cable had felt the immense shock of the war as strongly as anyone else, and was as reluctant as any other Southern writer to confront the raw spectacle of a war-torn country mourning its dead. But he could look back, with far more detachment, on an earlier spectacle of collapse in Louisiana history: that of the once dominant and once vigorous Creole society gripped in a losing struggle with the American settler and the modern world. Almost all of Cable's work concentrates on this period of Louisiana history, the transformation of Creole colonial life around the turn of the century, and the decades just afterward. For Cable, and for many of his contemporaries, it took only a small effort of the imagination to discover in the decline of the Creole world a dark portent of the recent, and far more brutal Southern upheaval.

In Cable's mind, the comparison was made all the more revealing by the ironic fact that the sons of the old Creole had now become models of the new Confederacy. They had developed into a regional type as emblematically Southern as the aristocratic Virginians: scions of a proud, conservative planter class ruled by an inflexible code of honor, and founded on a rigid caste system with black slavery at the bottom. Here was the Creole legacy that

Cable met in the streets of New Orleans after the war, and that fascinated and troubled him. And here was the legacy that finally forced him to reconsider the moral foundations of his own Southern allegiances once he began writing.

Cable found many qualities to admire in the old Creole character: courage, loyalty, and a combination of natural courtesy and social ease that he felt was one of the highest virtues of the antebellum South. Many of the stories in his first collection, *Old Creole Days* (1879), attest to these same qualities. But in his historical researches into the Creole regime he had discovered too the cruelties of the Black Code of 1724, in which the categorical French spelled out in no uncertain terms an astonishing catalogue of punishments and mutilations for the offending slave. Cable's first story, "Bibi," never published separately, but later incorporated as the "Bras-Coupé" episode of his novel *The Grandissimes* (1880), was written, he explained, in a state of shock and indignation after reading the Code Noir for the first time.

The more he thought and wrote about the Louisiana Creole, the more he was forced to admit that the stark reality of slavery, no matter what historical circumstances could be cited to explain it, remained, even after it had been abolished, a tremendous, inescapable tragic flaw. It had condemned old Louisiana; it had condemned the Confederate South; and it threatened, in a new form, to condemn the South again and again. Of course, as Cable's subsequent career demonstrated, these were risky conclusions for a Southern writer to even hint at in Reconstruction days, and even riskier in the years immediately afterwards. When he turned from the indirections of fiction to straightforward reformist essays and public speeches, it did him little good to defend his right to examine and question, as a former Confederate himself, his own country. The Creole press and New Orleans society responded angrily with a vengeance, and made him so unwelcome in his own home that he finally decided to take his family and move North, not far from the other outspoken Southern maverick, Mark Twain.

In reading Cable's early stories today, his criticism of the Creole seems muted enough. If anything, despite his genuine skills of compact dramatization and his mastery of convincing dialect, his half-humorous portraits lean far more toward the sentimental than the surgical. Yet it would be hard to exaggerate his importance in the history of the Louisiana short story, and of modern

Southern literature in general. He introduced a healthy dose of skeptical realism in a period too often trapped between the alternatives of certitude and reverie. He reaffirmed the sacred role of the serious writer to expose vanities where he found them, even in his front yard, and to probe the contradictions behind the beliefs of his characters, even if those same beliefs betrayed larger failures of the society as a whole. And perhaps most important of all, he set a standard of artistic honesty in his treatment of Louisiana matter that every Louisiana writer who followed him was forced to acknowledge and encouraged to match. Even when they disagreed with his interpretations—certainly the case for Grace King—they could not fault the range and depth of his cultural knowledge. He knew Louisiana as few other natives knew it, not just the high-toned Creole, but also the rural Acadian, and every variety of Louisiana black. In fact, with Joel Chandler Harris of Georgia, Cable was one of the first writers anywhere to fully appreciate the traditions and arts of the Southern black. He knew their songs and dances, and an essay he wrote in 1886, "Creole Slave Songs," in which he discusses the songs of the African Creole—the slaves, and their descendants, of Creole masters— still stands today as a model of original scholarship.

Largely thanks to Cable's artistic influence, then, and his moral fire, Louisiana writing at the end of the 19th century reached a level of literary skill and independence that placed it far above and far ahead of any other Southern region. Unfortunately, Cable's own writing after he left New Orleans and turned to professional reforming suffered greatly, and he never wrote anything as substantial as *Old Creole Days* and *The Grandissimes* (although I have always been fond of his "Cajun" story, "Carancro," first published in 1887). Still, there can be no question that Cable was the founding father of the modern Louisiana story, and if I have insisted on his importance at some length, it is because the tradition of superior short stories *Louisiana Stories* represents would be difficult to imagine without his original example.

The question of why Cable and so many other Louisiana writers were able to address their region with the complexity it deserved, and why they excelled in the short story above all other forms, can only be answered, I think, by first considering a rather odd pattern in the first great age of the Louisiana story—the age of Cable, King, Hearn, and Chopin.

To begin with, not one of these writers considered himself a full-blooded member of Louisiana's French community. Cable and King were natives, but non-Creole natives, of New Orleans. Kate Chopin married into a native Louisiana family, and on her mother's side could trace her origins back to early French settlers, but her father was an O'Flaherty from Ireland, and she was raised in St. Louis. Hearn, of course, had the most tenuous links of all with long-standing Louisiana birthrights. But each one of these writers lived at home among the French-speaking natives, and each one spoke the French language well. This knowledge alone gave them a special entry into Louisiana's culture denied to even the most perceptive non-French-speaking observer.

In varying degrees, all four writers found themselves bound up in an implausible marriage of cultures, with Louisiana French making up a half, but only a half, of the united couple. The other half depended on the individual writer himself. For Cable, King, and Chopin, it involved a highly personal version of the American South; for Hearn, not even Hearn himself could ever be sure which one of his multiple selves prevailed.

The metaphor of marriage, as I want to use it here, implies an intimate knowledge of the other, at the very least, but never a blending of identities. All four writers were able to observe the society they lived in from the inside, but with a detachment not easily achieved by the Creole himself. And this sense of inner displacement, this slightly skewed combination of the foreign and the familiar, may help explain why the short story was the favorite and most successful form for the Louisiana writer of Cable's generation.

Theories of the short story should not be taken too seriously. There are too many of them, and most are easily forgettable once the reading of the stories themselves begins. But it has always seemed to me that one of the genuine distinctions of the short story form lies in its ability to thrust sharp, sudden insights into a long-established society a bit too overconfident or overpowering in its public assumptions. Certainly the modern short story very often concentrates on the single individual either denying or losing himself in one of the roles his society demands of him. Some sense of private identity in conflict with public seems to be the vital element in most short stories. V.S. Pritchett, one of the finest writers of short stories in English, and a convincing theorist of the form, has suggested that the short story writer himself must have a sort of foreign mind within his own country, a permanent feeling of being "a man living on the other side of a frontier."

The Louisiana writer would seem to fit this description well enough. Growing up in a South whose general condition was that of a society under siege, challenged to its very roots, he was naturally primed to ask questions and to write stories about individual fate—especially as he observed it in the even more conservative French Creole society where the public role came to be more and more the only life the individual seemed to possess.

The French Creoles were not much given to writing stories about themselves, short or otherwise, and certainly not stories in a realistic, reflective mode. As a steadily declining colonial society, they were ready to defend their conviction of racial and cultural superiority, but not to question it.

To some visitors to Louisiana, such as Frederick Olmsted, the Louisiana Creoles exaggerated their ancestral origins to such an extent that they often seemed more French than the French themselves. They had a name for everything, another way of saying that everything had its rightful and not-to-be-budged place. The Black Code of 1724 was a model of French clarity and completeness. It gives the impression of addressing every possible legal problem slavery could present, except of course the legal problem of slavery itself. The Creole followed that same spirit of exactness in everything he described. During Olmsted's visit to New Orleans before the Civil War, he noted with fascination the names for racial mixtures current throughout Louisiana:

> The various grades of the coloured people are desig-
> nated by the French as follows, according to the greater
> or less predominance of negro blood:
>
> | | |
> |---|---|
> | Sacatra | griffe and negress |
> | Griffe | negro and mulatto |
> | Marabon | mulatto and griffe |
> | Mulatto | white and negro |
> | Quateron | white and mulatto |
> | Metif | white and quateron |
> | Meamelouc | white and metif |
> | Quateron | white and meamelouc |
> | Sang-mele | white and quateron |
>
> And all these, with sub-varieties of them, French Spanish,
> English, and Indian, and the sub-sub-varieties, such as

Anglo-Indian mulatto, I believe experts pretend to be able to distinguish.

The experts were able to distinguish, and did so constantly. The entire social hierarchy of the Creole world depended on such distinctions. What the experts were unable to identify, however, was the private drama hidden behind the official categories. This was the realm of the imaginative writer, the realm of Cable, King, Hearn, and Chopin, whose stories were particularly effective in revealing the individual life—white, black, or mixed—shining through, even if only momentarily, the public role.

As long as I am propounding theories, I wonder if the character of New Orleans itself might help explain the special affinity of the early Louisiana writer for the short story. New Orleans was not, and is not, all of Louisiana, by any means, but it has always been a powerful element in assessing Louisiana identity. All the early writers—Cable, King, Hearn, and even Chopin—were baptized into Louisiana society first of all in the big port city. Cable and King were born and raised there; Hearn came straight to New Orleans and hardly moved for ten years; Chopin as a young bride spent almost ten years there herself before moving with her husband and children to Cloutierville in north-central Louisiana.

All four writers would have discovered in New Orleans a large Southern city unlike any other comparable city in the old South, not just in its racial and cultural diversity, but, again, in the peculiar nature of its public life. New Orleans was a wide-open, sociable, but theatrical city, a city whose very architecture, at least in the old center, made public behavior conspicuous, and readily separable from the private. The other large Southern ports, Charleston and Savannah, were both cities where public life was an extension of the private home itself. The characteristic Charleston dwelling is the "single house," whose long, informal piazza leads directly onto intimate alleys and sidestreets, allowing the casual passerby an easy view of the whole family. In Savannah, the many small public squares, shaded by large, reassuring live oaks, are placed in such a way that they can be thought of as extra front yards for the houses around them. In New Orleans, though, the Creole townhouses are turned around, the way they often are in France, with the gardens and courtyards completely hidden from view. Anything could happen there, and probably did.

Once outside in the New Orleans streets, the individual entered
onto a central stage where the roles were abundant, but socially
fixed, and where one's ability to play according to type was what
counted most of all. To write that New Orleans was both wide-
open and filled with fixed roles seems to affirm a paradox. But as
many a New Orleans resident demonstrated, playing an artificial
role was often the best excuse in the world for casting aside a
private scruple. Not for nothing was the *bal masqué*, the masked
ball, the favorite Creole form of New Orleans entertainment. The
more common temptation, especially among the blacks and mixed
blood quadroons, was to protect or hide the individual self by
disappearing into the public role entirely, gratifying the slightest
expectation of what one should do or say. Rarer and riskier was
the wild temptation to exaggerate the role into obvious caricature,
twisting it into a form of social protest. At any rate, New Orleans
society encouraged a special alternating current between private
and public identities. When tension was felt, more often than not
it was resolved in favor of the ruling social standard. But from
time to time, and herein lie the links between New Orleans and
the short story, an emphatic shout of suppressed individual life
could make itself heard in unexpected ways.

Not that every outburst was an invariable cry of protest against
public authority. There were good reasons to protest, but the
isolated New Orleans shout or song could spring from many
motives, including sheer self-exuberance in standing out from the
crowd. And here too the short story is not too far-fetchable for my
purpose. Even more than the *bal masqué*, which was, after all,
reserved for the select few, the public procession has always been
the most popular New Orleans celebration. Funerals and Mardi
Gras come immediately to mind, but any occasion was good
enough to set in motion an impromptu parade. All processions
depend on some measure of repetition, even imitation. And an
article of clothing or accessory is sometimes enough for that. In
1817 there was an ordinance adopted in New Orleans that forbade slaves "to walk with canes on the streets unless on account of
infirmity." There must have been many canes to make such an
ordinance necessary, and the mind strains at the lost vision of a
thousand canes flashing in unison on Rampart Street. Not just in
New Orleans, but all over Louisiana, a like-minded group could
make a procession and create an instant audience. Frederick

Olmsted, once again, described the following sight on his pre-Civil War visit to the South:

> At Lake Charles we had seen a troop of Alabamas, riding through the town with baskets and dressed deer-skins for sale. They were decked with feathers, and dressed more showily than the Choctaws, but in calico: and over their heads, on horseback—curious progress of manners—all carried open, black cotton *umbrellas.*

Canes and umbrellas: perhaps not the best way to theorize about the short story, and I have now even drifted from New Orleans to Lake Charles. But a procession, even a small procession, is a product of social, collective, public identity, whether it exists in time or in space. A long line of people and events would seem to call for a long narrative, the genealogical or panoramic novel. The short story loves the singular, and avoids the plural, and in a procession—now we are back in New Orleans—the great event is the sudden exalted individual, acting out against his processional role to surprise everyone with a fit of unexpected hidden genius. It may be going too far to say that New Orleans jazz is a short story, but it is too late to stop me now.

Reckless conjectures on the short story have their genuine attractions, at least to me, whatever their ultimate worth. But admitting that, I must also admit that literary history has guided my selections in *Louisiana Stories* far more than literary theory. One of my initial aims was to present the full range of Louisiana's best short fiction, from Cable and his generation after the Civil War up through the remarkable crop of Louisiana writers in our time, many of whom are still active. By following the simple principle of choosing the best stories I could find, one story per author, three distinct groups, in rough chronological order, emerged: Cable, Hearn, King, and Chopin from the late 19th century; Saxon, Bontemps, Hurston, and O'Donnell from the 1920s and 30s; and, finally, a large group of writers whose reputations were made after World War II.

The first story in *Louisiana Stories,* however, "The Indefatigable Bear Hunter" by Henry Clay Lewis, belongs to none of these groups, and takes us back to an earlier mode of Southern fiction, the "Southwestern" humorist school. Southwestern refers to those Southern states just west of the old coastal settlements, and includes middle Georgia, Tennessee, Kentucky, Alabama, Mississippi, Arkansas, and the bayous, prairies, and forests of Louisiana. The Southwestern humorists—Augustus Baldwin Longstreet, George Washington Harris, Johnson Jones Hooper, among others— flourished in the decades just before the Civil War. They specialized in stories and tall tales describing the rough manners and ripe idioms of the independent, uncivilizable, backcountry Southerner whose extravagant exploits apparently had no known bounds. As a form of popular entertainment published mainly in sporting magazines such as William T. Porter's *Spirit of the Times,* these stories have not always received the attention they deserve. They were admired and praised by Edgar Allen Poe and Mark Twain for their high realism and low humor, but critics and scholars for a long time tended to undervalue them simply because they were so popular and so difficult to classify as "literary" works of art.

It is best not to worry too much about classifications, but if we must have a category, we might call them "bear stories." Not all of them were about bears and bear-hunting, but many of them were, and that is the way they were known in the 1850s when my favorite Louisiana visitor, Frederick Olmsted, was given a big book of "bear stories" to read one night when stopping at an isolated home near the Sabine River. In that bed-side book Olmsted might have found printed, or pasted-in, two of the best bear stories ever written by Southerners, "The Big Bear of Arkansas" by Thomas Bangs Thorpe, and "The Indefatigable Bear Hunter" by Henry Clay Lewis. Both stories come at the beginning of a long line of Southern hunting fiction that culminates in William Faulkner's 20th century masterpiece, "The Bear."

Both Thorpe and Lewis had strong attachments to Louisiana before the Civil War. Though Thorpe was born in New England, he lived for almost twenty years in Louisiana and wrote many sketches and newspaper articles for the local and national press. Despite its title, and the fact that the main story is placed in Arkansas, "The Big Bear of Arkansas" could be included, legitimately, and without too much special pleading, in a Louisiana anthology. The Arkansas hunter tells his story on a steamboat just out of New Orleans, and the mixed audience and sophisticated setting help give the raw tale itself a greater power and impact. But I have always preferred the Henry Clay Lewis story. It has the advantage, at least for this anthology, of being set fully within Louisiana. It also has the virtue of a sympathetic and outrageous storyteller, Mik-hoo-tah, who is one of the most original characters in American fiction. Lewis was only 25 years old when he drowned in a bayou accident, but Mik-hoo-tah and the little else we have by Lewis in his only book, *Odd Leaves From the Life of a Louisiana Swamp Doctor* (1850), show that he was a remarkably gifted writer who had only just begun to suggest his full promise.

Turning from Lewis to the Cable era of Louisiana fiction, serious readers should find little to surprise them in my choice of stories from Cable, Hearn, King, and Chopin. They would be found in almost any list of these writers' major work. Chopin's "Athénaïse: a Story of a Temperament" is the latest in date of the group, and the most polished and accomplished of them all. Now recognized, after a long period of neglect, as one of the strong, original writers of her time, Chopin has been praised for her realistic descriptions of Louisiana rural life, and for her convincing portraits of young women struggling to redefine themselves when faced with the unforeseen constraints of marriage. Her best-known work is the novel, *The Awakening* (1899), but "Athénaïse" deserves to be ranked right alongside the more famous novel, and to my mind shows a surer grasp of the sort of unobtrusive symbolic naturalism that Chopin worked hard to achieve.

As for my choice of "Posson Jone'" by Cable, I had little trouble making a final decision, even though I did hesitate between it and two other stories, the more sober-minded, less melodramatic portrait, "Jean-ah Poquelin," and the long Civil War piece, "Carancro." But "Posson Jone'" has long been one of Cable's most popular stories, and for good reasons. It illustrates his skill at juggling and comically opposing conventional types, and his equal skill at making the compressed dramatic form of the short story suddenly thrust these same types into an unexpected dimension of individual character. And it provides a showcase for Cable's celebrated musical ear for local dialects, a quality that Mark Twain singled out for special praise in *Life on the Mississippi* (1883), and that inspired Twain in his own revolutionary use of Southern speech in *The Adventures of Huckleberry Finn* (1884).

The Hearn and King stories, "Chita: A Memory of Last Island" and "Bayou l'Ombre," are two outstanding examples of the early Louisiana writers' natural gifts for romantic irony. Hearn had first been attracted to New Orleans by his reading of Cable's "Jean-ah Poquelin," and on arriving there in 1877 he quickly immersed himself in all manner of local Creole legend and language. He wrote a number of short newspaper sketches and articles on New Orleans, but his most remarkable Louisiana work is the long story "Chita," based on an account he had heard concerning a child rescued during the great hurricane of 1856. As a lyrical adventure story in the spirit of his contemporary, Robert Lewis Stevenson, "Chita" proves Hearn as much a master of dialects as Cable, and a powerfully impressionistic artist of the non-human, elemental forces of nature.

Grace King's "Bayou l'Ombre" is an astonishing work for its time. Based on her own experiences during the Civil War, it demonstrates King's conviction that irony was the only means of doing justice to the Southern condition. She herself was deeply sympathetic to the Southern cause, and remained so until her death, but she could never bring herself to forgive Southern men for committing themselves to a war they could not win.

"Bayou l'Ombre" is a Civil War story in which the war itself figures as a remote dream whose basis in reality is only barely confirmed by fragments of news from the outside world. When the war does intrude, it does so as a confused comic play of reversals and mistaken identities completely upsetting the far more down-to-earth, everyday, even tedious world of the isolated plantation. King's lush style sometimes gets the better of the plot, but the plot itself is not all that important, and her real literary gifts are better displayed in this story than in anything else she wrote. The slow-moving, painterly descriptions of domestic chores, the wholly convincing treatment of the white girls' romanticism, and of the black women's blind faith: these are scenes that stay in the mind, and that look forward to such a work as Faulkner's *The Unvanquished* (1938). King herself best defined her aspirations in "Bayou l'Ombre" when she gave the following answer to a question she was asked about influence on her work:

> Charles Gayarré influenced me in my writing and so did Lafcadio Hearn, but no one else. I am not a romanticist. I am a realist à la mode de Nouvelle Orleans. I have never written a line that was not realistic— but our life, our circumstances, the heroism of the men and women that surrounded my early horizon—all that was romantic. I had a mind very sensitive to romantic impressions, but critical as to their expression.

With the selections from Saxon, Bontemps, Hurston, and

O'Donnell, *Louisiana Stories* moves decisively into the 20th century, and it would take an even more mulish anthologist than I am to insist too stubbornly on collective themes and subjects. One thing is certain, however; despite the shock of World War I, and all the other convulsive jolts to what was left of old Louisiana, there remained enough permanent inheritances to give the best of the native writing a peculiar, unmodern pungency and flair. In fact, the powerful changes of the new century were largely responsible for some of these inheritances finding their way into the literature at all. This is especially true for the Louisiana black and the poor rural white, both of whom had expressive gifts in vigorous untapped abundance. These four stories—Saxon's "Cane River," Bontemps' "A Summer Tragedy," Hurston's "Father Watson," and O'Donnell's "Canker," are all noteworthy, then, for introducing certain Louisiana realities that had been acknowledged by the earlier writers, especially Cable, but that had seldom been allowed an individual literary voice. The religious fatalism, hard times, and general racial suffering of these widely varied natives were not new, of course, even if they were only now being heard as fully and as clearly as they deserved. "Ain't no first blues," an old New Orleans jazzman once answered when asked to name the first blues song ever sung. "Blues has always been."

All four stories belong to what might be called documentary fiction, a style of writing that is usually associated with the bitter Depression years of the 1930s, and a term that helps me explain my reasons for including Hurston's "Father Watson." There is nothing bitter or depressing in her vivid picture of voodoo ceremony, but her manner of presentation derives from a powerful documentary imagination deeply influenced by the fiction of her times. Hurston was not a native of Louisiana. She was born in Florida and had travelled widely in the North before coming back to Florida and then to Louisiana to work on her book of black folklore, *Mules and Men* (1935). "Father Watson" comes from that book, and I include it in *Louisiana Stories* despite the fact that, on principle, only native writers or writers long attached to Louisiana were eligible, and despite the fact—again, on principle—that only independent works of fiction should be considered. But no anthology is worth much if it does not contest its own principles. And, at least in my appreciation, Hurston wrote about the Louisiana voodoo world with an understanding that surpasses any other writer; and this inner knowledge, combined with her dramatic impulse to turn everything she experienced into complete stories, fully justifies her presence.

This brings me, awkwardly I admit, to the story by William Faulkner, "The Kingdom of God." The same principles whose bending allowed me to include Zora Neale Hurston are bent again for Faulkner, but for different reasons. Of all the Mississippi writers who have written good stories about Louisiana, and there are many, Faulkner and his beginnings as a serious writer are so vitally bound to his neighboring state that to have left him out of *Louisiana Stories* would have been an injustice to everybody. Faulkner lived in New Orleans for several months in 1924 and 25, and fell in with a loose but lively circle of journalists, artists, and writers. These included the well-known Northern exile Sherwood Anderson, and a wide-ranging group of lesser known, but rising, Louisiana natives and assorted Southerners: Lyle Saxon, Hamilton Basso, Roark Bradford, and others.

Faulkner wrote his first novel, *Soldier's Pay* (1926), while living in New Orleans, and based his second, *Mosquitoes* (1927), on his various New Orleans companions and their escapades. Both novels are obvious apprentice works, but later, in 1939, Faulkner published *The Wild Palms*, arguably his most original novel. With its realistic scenes of New Orleans, and with its great, otherworldly, mythopoetic episode of the Cajun and the Convict, *The Wild Palms* must be considered one of the best Louisiana novels ever written.

"The Kingdom of God" was first published as one of a series of newspaper sketches for the *Times-Picayune* in 1925. Like "The Indefatigable Bear Hunter" by Henry Clay Lewis, it can not be made to fit in any of the three groups of stories I have gathered. Chronologically, at least, it should be placed with the "documentary" stories of the 1920s and 30s, and perhaps, too, as a reminder that Faulkner himself made an ironic bow towards the documentary school by placing all his New Orleans sketches under the general rubric of "Mirrors of Chartres Street." But "The Kingdom of God" is finally best appreciated apart from any group, and as a strange, independent anticipation of the magnificent idiot portraits of Benji Compson in *The Sound and the Fury* (1929), and of Ike Snopes in *The Hamlet* (1940).

After World War II, even a reckless anthologist has to admit that the generalities should stop for good, and let the individual stories of Grau, Gaines, Dubus, Burke, Dew, and Corrington speak for themselves. For one thing, other forms of imaginative writing begin to make an impact in Louisiana during the 1940s and 50s, and the short story no longer dominates as it did in the earlier periods. It continues to attract most of the best writers, however, and almost every active Louisiana writer today has a collection or two of stories to his credit.

Ernest Gaines and Andre Dubus are the best-known nationally, and deservedly so. They have both published stories now widely acknowledged as modern classics, and Dubus seems well on his way towards becoming one of the most highly respected craftsmen of the genre America has produced in recent years. Ernest Gaines' 1968 collection, *Bloodline*, from which "The Sky is Gray" is taken, belongs in the same company as Joyce's *Dubliners* (1914), or, closer to home, Faulkner's *Go Down, Moses* (1942). *Bloodline* is a short story cycle of five masterpieces, and each one of these stories confirms Gaines' belief that the short story still derives its vital narrative power from an active, energetic oral tradition, in this case the active, energetic tradition of the Louisiana black community not far from Gaines' hometown of New Roads.

But together with these major stories, there are other Louisiana works of distinction, even greatness, in drama, in poetry, and especially in the contemporary novel. Recently, the brilliant, reflective moral comedies by Walker Percy have placed Louisiana firmly at the forefront of the best writing being done in the English language today. My one stinging regret in compiling this anthology is that Percy has not written, and apparently has no intention of writing, a single short story.

It is gratifying to see in much of this new Louisiana writing unmistakable signs that outside the monstrous shopping malls and the self-breeding highways, Louisiana somehow manages to hold on to its differences, and to proclaim, even at the end of the 20th century, an amiable independence from the rest of the United States. The old odd marriage between French and American culture that marked Louisiana at the beginning of the 19th century has unexpectedly revived today in the wide-awake creative will of the Cajun, and the black Creole communities. Far more original, and less Europeanized than the now-vanished Creole planter, the descendants of the Cajun farmers, and along with them the descendants of the French-speaking slaves, have given new life—especially in their music—to a unique Louisiana French culture whose genius for joining free-spirited individual bravado with popular tradition is one of the miracles of modern America.

No less gratifying in this recent writing is the new vision of the old sensual spectacle of Louisiana's landscapes and wildlife. The unrealistic scenes of the early local colorists, the romance-tinted, cypress-haunted waterland of alligator, blue heron, and feu follet, are still actually there, and still just as difficult to believe. But we now have, in addition, the ordinary mysteries of the faintly reeking Louisiana rural road at night:

> I must try to tell you what, in July, in Louisiana,
> Night is. No moon, but stars whitely outrageous in
> Blackness of velvet, the long lane ahead
> Whiter than snow, wheels soundless in deep dust, dust
> Pluming whitely behind, and ahead all
> The laneside hedges and weed-growth
> Long since powdered whiter than star-dust, or frost, but air
> Hot. The night pants hot like a dog, it breathes
> Off the blossoming bayou like the expensive whiff
> Of floral tributes at a gangster's funeral in N.O.,
> It breathes the smell love makes in darkness, and far off,
> In the great swamp, an owl cries,
> And does not stop. At the sharp right turn,
> Hedge-blind, which you take too fast,
> There it is: death-trap.

The reader will have to find out what happens by reading the poem itself, the only short story set in Louisiana Robert Penn Warren has written. I end this Introduction with Warren out of admiration for his entire career, but especially as a reminder of the important role he played in the history of the modern Louisiana short story even though he himself did not write one, at least not in prose. He did write, of course, one of the few lasting political novels of the century, *All the King's Men* (1946), based on the life and death of the Louisiana "Kingfish," Huey Long. But I mention Warren here because of *The Southern Review,* the farsighted journal he and Cleanth Brooks founded in 1934 at Louisiana State University.

After Cable, *The Southern Review* must be singled out as the second great force in the development of the short story in

Louisiana. The *Review* has never limited itself to Louisiana writing alone, of course, nor even to writing by Southerners in general. Its policy from the start, guided by the esthetic judgment and critical intelligence of Warren and Brooks, has been the publication of the best short fiction, poetry, and essays it could find, by the known and the unknown around the world. A major outpost against the universal tyranny of bad art, the *Review*'s presence in Louisiana as a local institution with a far-flung international reputation has deeply influenced every good Louisiana writer. Even if these writers have not necessarily published their stories in its pages, they could not, and can not, help but be inspired by its superior standards. If the short history of the Louisiana story may be said to have begun with George Washington Cable, the long history began with Warren and Brooks' first issue of *The Southern Review*. And if the editor of *Louisiana Stories* owes them all an unpayable debt, at least he can make the small gesture of an emphatic terminal salute.

Ben Forkner
Angers, France

Madison Tensas
[Henry Clay Lewis]

Madison Tensas [Henry Clay Lewis] (1825-1850)

Madison Tensas was the pseudonym of Henry Clay Lewis, who was born in Charleston, South Carolina. His father was French, and his mother was a native of Charleston. He moved to Cincinnati when he was four years old. At 16 he was apprenticed to a doctor, and in 1846 he received his medical degree from the Louisville Medical Institute. He then moved to Louisiana to practice in small towns and remote bayou settlements. Returning home exhausted after battling a cholera epidemic, he died in a drowning accident. "The Indefatigable Bear Hunter" is taken from his only book, Odd Leaves from the Life of a Louisiana Swamp Doctor *(1850)*.

THE INDEFATIGABLE
BEAR HUNTER

IN MY ROUND OF PRACTICE, I occasionally meet with men whose peculiarities stamp them as belonging to a class composed only of themselves. So different are they in appearance, habit, and taste from the majority of mankind that it is impossible to classify them, and you have therefore to set them down as queer birds of a feather that none resemble sufficiently to associate with.

I had a patient once who was one of these queer ones—gigantic in stature, uneducated, fearless of real danger yet timorous as a child of superstitious perils, born literally in the woods, never having been in a city in his life and his idea of one being that it was a place where people met together to make whiskey and form plans for swindling country folks. To view him at one time, you would think him only a whiskey-drinking, bear-fat-loving mortal. At other moments he would give vent to ideas proving that beneath his rough exterior there ran a fiery current of high enthusiastic ambition.

It is a favorite theory of mine—and one that I am fond of consoling myself with for my own insignificance—that there is no man born who is not capable of attaining distinction and no occupation that does not contain a path leading to fame. To bide our time is all that is necessary. I had expressed this view in the hearing of Mik-hoo-tah, for so was the subject of this sketch called, and it seemed to chime in with his feelings exactly. Born in the woods and losing his parents early, he had forgotten his real name, and the bent of his genius inclining him to the slaying of bears, he had been given when a youth the name of Mik-hoo-tah signifying "the grave of bears" by his Indian associates and admirers.

To glance in and around his cabin, you would have thought that the place had been selected for ages past by the bear tribe to yield up their spirits in, so numerous were the relics. Little chance, I ween, had the cold air to whistle through that hut, so thickly it was tapestried with the soft, downy hides, the darkness of the surface relieved occasionally by the skin of a tender fawn or the short-haired irascible panther. From the joists depended bear hams and tongues innumerable, and the ground outside was literally white with bones. Ay, he was a bear hunter in its most comprehensive sense—the chief of that vigorous band, whose occupation is nearly gone, crushed beneath the advancing strides of romance-

destroying civilization. When his horn sounded—so tradition ran—
the bears began to draw lots to see who should die that day, for
painful experience had told them the uselessness of all endeavoring
to escape. The "Big Bear of Arkansas" would not have given him
an hour's extra work or raised a fresh wrinkle on his already
care-corrugated brow. But, though almost daily imbruing his
hands in the blood of Bruin, Mik-hoo-tah had not become an
impious or cruel-hearted man. Such was his piety that he never
killed a bear without getting down on his knees—to skin it—and
praying to be d—ned if it "warn't a buster." Such was his softness
of heart that he often wept when he, by mistake, had killed a
suckling bear, depriving her poor offspring of a mother's care,
and found her too poor to be eaten. So indefatigable had he
become in his pursuit that the bears bid fair to disappear from
the face of the swamp and be known to posterity only through the
one mentioned in Scripture that assisted Elisha to punish the
impertinent children, when an accident occurred to the hunter
which raised their hopes of not being entirely exterminated.

One day Mik happened to come unfortunately in contact with a
stray grizzly fellow who, doubtless in the indulgence of an adven-
turous spirit, had wandered away from the Rocky Mountains and
formed a league for mutual protection with his black and more
effeminate brethren of the swamp. Mik saluted him as he approached
with an ounce ball in the forehead to avenge half a dozen of his
best dogs who lay in fragments around. The bullet flattened upon
his impenetrable skull, merely infuriating the monster, and before
Mik could reload it was upon him. Seizing him by the leg, it bore
him to the ground and ground the limb to atoms. But before it
could attack a more vital part, the knife of the dauntless hunter
had cloven its heart, and it dropped dead upon the bleeding form
of its slayer in which condition they were shortly found by Mik's
comrades. Making a litter of branches, they placed Mik upon it
and proceeded with all haste to their camp, sending one of the
company by a near cut for me as I was the nearest physician.
When I reached their temporary shelter I found Mik doing better
than I could have expected, with the exception of his wounded
leg, and that, from its crushed and mutilated condition, I saw
would have to be amputated immediately, of which I informed
Mik. As I expected, he opposed it vehemently, but I convinced
him of the impossibility of saving it, assuring him if it were not
amputated he would certainly die, and appealed to his good sense

to grant permission, which he did at last. The next difficulty was to procure amputating instruments, the rarity of surgical operations and the generally slender purse of the Swamp Doctor not justifying him in purchasing expensive instruments. A couple of bowie knives, one ingeniously hacked and filed into a saw, a tourniquet made of a belt and piece of stick, a gun screw converted for the time into a tenaculum, and some buckskin slips for ligatures completed my case of instruments for amputation. The city physician may smile at this recital, but I assure him many a more difficult operation than the amputation of a leg has been performed by his humble brother in the swamp with far more simple means than those I have mentioned. The preparations being completed, Mik refused to have his arms bound and commenced singing a bear song, and throughout the whole operation which was necessarily tedious he never uttered a groan or missed a single stave. The next day I had him conveyed by easy stages to his pre-emption, and with my tending assiduously in the course of a few weeks he had recovered sufficiently for me to cease attentions. I made him a wooden leg which answered a good purpose, and with a sigh of regret for the spoiling of such a good hunter I struck him from my list of patients.

A few months passed over and I heard nothing more of him. Newer but not brighter stars were in the ascendant, filling with their deeds the clanging trump of bear-killing fame, and, but for the quantity of bear blankets in the neighboring cabins and the painful absence of his usual present of bear hams, Mik-hoo-tah bid fair to suffer that fate most terrible to aspiring ambitionists— forgetfulness during life.

The sun, in despair at the stern necessity which compelled him to yield up his tender offspring, day, to the gloomy cave of darkness, had stretched forth his long arms, and, with the tenacity of a drowning man clinging to a straw, had clutched the tender whispering straw-like topmost branches of the trees—in other words it was near sunset—when I arrived at home from a long wearisome semi-ride-and-swim through the swamp. Receiving a negative to my inquiry whether there were any new calls, I was felicitating myself upon a quiet night beside my tidy bachelor hearth, undisturbed by crying children, babbling women, or amo-rous cats—the usual accompaniments of married life—when, like a poor henpecked Benedick crying for peace when there is no peace, I was doomed to disappointment. Hearing the splash of a paddle in the bayou running before the door, I turned my head towards the bank and soon beheld, first the tail of a coon, next his body, a human face, and, the top of the bank being gained, a full-proportioned form clad in the garments which better than any printed label wrote him down raftsman, trapper, bear hunter. He was a messenger from the indefatigable bear hunter, Mik-hoo-tah. Asking him what was the matter, as soon as he could get the knots untied which two-thirds drunkenness had made in his tongue, he informed me, to my sincere regret, that Mik went out that morning on a bear hunt and in a fight with one had got his leg "broke all to flinders" if possible worse than the other and that he wanted me to come quickly. Getting into the canoe which awaited me, I wrapped myself in my blanket and yielding to my fatigue was soon fast asleep. I did not awaken until the canoe striking against the bank as it landed at Mik's pre-emption nearly threw me in the bayou and entirely succeeded with regard to my half-drunken paddler, who—like the sailor who circumnavigated the world and then was drowned in a puddle hole in his own garden—had escaped all the perils of the tortuous bayou to be pitched overboard when there was nothing to do but step out and tie the dugout. Assisting him out of the water, we proceeded to the house when to my indignation I learnt that the drunken messenger had given me the long trip for nothing, Mik only wanting me to make him a new wooden leg, the old one having been completely demolished that morning.

Relieving myself by a satisfactory oath, I would have returned that night, but the distance was too great for one fatigued as I was. I had to content myself with such accommodations as Mik's cabin afforded, which, to one blessed like myself with the happy faculty of ready adaptations to circumstances, was not a very difficult task.

I was surprised to perceive the change in Mik's appearance. From nearly a giant, he had wasted to a mere huge bony frame-work. The skin of his face clung tightly to the bones and showed nothing of those laughter-moving features that were wont to adorn his visage. Only his eye remained unchanged, and it had lost none of its brilliancy—the flint had lost none of its fire.

"What on earth is the matter with you, Mik? I have never seen anyone fall off so fast. You have wasted to a skeleton—surely you must have the consumption."

"Do you think so, Doc? I'll soon show you whether the old bellows has lost any of its force!" Hopping to the door which he threw wide open, he gave a death-hug rally to his dogs in such a loud and piercing tone that I imagined a steam whistle was being discharged in my ear and for several moments could hear nothing distinctly.

"That will do! Stop!" I yelled, as I saw Mik drawing in his breath preparatory to another effort to his vocal strength. "I am satisfied you have not got consumption, but what has wasted you so, Mik? Surely, you ain't in love?"

"Love! h-ll! you don't suppose, Doc, even if I was 'tarmined to make a cussed fool of myself that there is any girl in the swamp that could stand that hug, do you?" and catching up a huge bulldog who lay basking himself by the fire, he gave him such a squeeze that the animal yelled with pain and for a few moments appeared dead. "No, Doc, it's grief, pure sorrur, sorrur, Doc! When I looks at what I is now and what I used to be! Jes think, Doc, of the fust hunter in the swamp having his sport spilte like bar meat in summer without salt! Jes think of a man standin' up one day and blessing old Master for having put bar in creation and the next cussing high heaven and low h-ll 'cause he couldn't 'sist in puttin' them out! Warn't it enough to bring tears to the eyes of an Injun tater, much less take the fat off a bar hunter? Doc, I fell off like 'simmons arter frost, and folks as doubted me needn't had asked whether I war 'ceitful or not for they could have seed plum threw me! The bar and painter got so saucy that they'd cum to the t'other side of the bayou and see which could talk the impudentest! 'Don't you want some bar meat or painter blanket?' they'd ask. 'Bars is monstrous fat and painter's hide is mighty warm!' Oh! Doc, I was a miserable man! The sky warn't blue for me, the sun war always cloudy, and the shade trees gin no shade for me. Even the dogs forgot me, and the little children quit coming and asking, 'Please, Mr. Bar-Grave, cotch me a young bar or a painter kitten.' Doc, the tears would cum in my eyes and the hot blood would cum biling up from my heart when I'd hobble out of a sundown and hear the boys tell, as they went by, of the sport they'd had that day, and how the bar fit 'fore he was killed, and how fat he war arter he was slayed. Long arter they was gone and the whippoorwill had eat up their voices, I would sit out there on the old stump and think of the things that used to hold the biggest place in my mind when I was a boy, and p'raps sense I've bin a man.

"I'd heard tell of distinction and fame and people's names never dying and how Washington and Franklin and Clay and Jackson and a heap of political dicshunary folks would live when their big hearts had crumbled down to a rifle charge of dust. And I begun, too, to think, Doc, what a pleasant thing it would be to know folks a million years off would talk of me like them, and it made me 'tarmine to 'stinguish myself and have my name put in a book with a yaller kiver. I warn't a genus, Doc, I nude that, nor I warn't dicshunary. So I detarmined to strike out in a new track for glory and 'title myself to be called the 'bear hunter of Ameriky.' Doc, my heart jumpt up, and I belted my hunting shirt tigher for fear it would lepe out when I fust spoke them words out loud.

"'The bar hunter of Ameriky!' Doc, you know whether I war ernin' the name when I war ruined. There is not a child—white, black, Injun, or nigger—from the Arkansas line to the Trinity but what has heard of me, and I were happy when"—here a tremor of his voice and a tear glistening in the glare of the fire told the old fellow's emotion—"when—but les take a drink—Doc, I found I was dying—I war gettin' weaker and weaker—I nude your truck warn't what I needed, or I'd sent for you. A bar hunt war the medsin that my systum required, a fust class bar hunt—the music of the dogs, the fellers a-screaming, the cane poppin', the rifles crackin', the bar growlin', the fight hand to hand, slap goes his paw, and a dog's hide hangs on one cane and his body on another, the knife glistenin' and then goin' plump up to the handle in his heart! Oh! Doc, this was what I needed, and I swore, since death were huggin' me anyhow, I mite as well feel his last grip in a bar hunt.

"I seed the boys goin' long one day and haled them to wait awhile as I believed I would go along too. I war frade if I kept out of a hunt much longer I wood get outen practis. They laughed at me, thinkin' I war jokin', for wat cood a sick, old, one-legged man do in a bar hunt? How could he get threw the swamp, and vines, and canes, and back-water? And s'pose he mist the bar, how war he to get outen the way?

"But I war 'tarmined on goin'. My dander was up, and I swore I wood go, tellin' them if I coodent travel 'bout much I could take a stand. Seein' it war no use tryin' to 'swade me, they saddled my poney and off we started. I felt better right off. I knew I cuddent do much in the chase, so I told the fellers I would go to the cross path stand and wate for the bar as he would be sarten to cum by thar. You have never seed the cross path stand, Doc. It's the singularest place in the swamp. It's rite in the middle of a canebrake, thicker than har on a barhide, down in a deep sink that looks like the devil had cummenst diggin' a skylite for his pre-emption. I knew it war a dangersome place for a well man to go in, much less a one-leg cripple, but I war 'tarmined that time to give a deal on the dead wood and play my hand out. The boys gin me time to get to the stand and then cummenst the drive. The bar seemed 'tarmined on disappinting me, for the fust thing I heard of the dogs and bar they was outen hearing. Everything got quiet, and I got so wrathy at not being able to foller up the chase that I cust till the trees cummenst shedding their leaves and small branches, when I herd them lumbrin' back and I nude they war makin' to me. I primed old 'bar death' fresh and rubbed the frizin, for it war no time for rifle to get to snappin'. Thinks I, if I happen to miss, I'll try what virtue there is in a knife—when, Doc, my knife war gone. H-ll! bar, for God's sake have a soft head, and die easy, for I *can't* run!

"Doc, you've hearn a bar bustin' threw a canebrake and know how near to a harrycane it is. I almost cummenst dodgin' the trees, thinkin' it war the best-in-the-shop one a-comin'—for it beat the loudest thunder ever I heard, that ole bar did—comin' to get his death from an ole, one-legged cripple what had slayed more of his brethren than his nigger foot had ever made trax in the mud. Doc, he heerd a *monstrus long ways ahead of the dogs*. I warn't skeered, but I must own, as I had but one shot an' no knife, I wud have prefurd they had been closer. But here he cum! He-bar—big as a bull—boys off h-llwards—dogs nowhar—no knife—but one shot—*and only one leg that cood run!*

"The bar 'peered s'prised to see me standin' ready for him in the openin'—for it war currently reported 'mong his brethren that I war either dead or no use for bar. I thought fust he war skeered, and, Doc, I b'leve he war till he cotch a sight of my wooden leg and that toch his pride for he knew he would be hist outen every she-bear's company ef he run from a poor, sickly, one-legged cripple. So on he cum, a small river of slobber pourin' from his mouth and the blue smoke curlin' outen his ears. I tuck good aim at his left and let drive. The ball struck him on the eyebrow and glanced off, only stunnin' him for a moment, jes givin' me time to club my rifle, an' on he kum as fierce as old grizzly. As he got in reach, I gin him a lick 'cross the temples, brakin' the stock in fifty pieces an' knockin' him senseless. I struv to foller up the lick when, Doc, I war fast—my timber-toe had run inter the ground and I cuddent git out though I jerked hard enuf almost to bring my thigh out of joint. I stuped to unscrew the infurnal thing when the bar cum to and cum at me agen. Vim! I tuck him over the head, and cochunk, he keeled over. H-ll! but I cavorted and pitched. Thar war my wust enemy waitin' for me to give him a

finisher an' I *cuddent* git at him. I'd cummense unscrewin' leg—
here cum bar—vim—cochunk—he'd fall out of reach—and, Doc, *I
cuddent git to him.* I kept workin' my body round so as to unscrew
the leg and keep the bar off till I cood 'complish it, when jes as I
tuck the last turn and got loose from the d—d thing, here cum
bar more venimous than ever, and I nude thar war death to one
out and comin' shortly. I let him get close an' then cum down with
a perfect tornado on his head, as I thought. But the old villain
had learnt the dodge—the barrel jes struck him on the side of the
head and glanst off, slinging itself out of my hands 'bout twenty
feet 'mongst the thick cane, and thar I war in a fix sure. Bar but
little hurt—no gun—no knife—no dogs—no frens—no chance to
climb—*an' only one leg that cood run.* Doc, I jes cummenst makin'
'pologies to ole Master when an idee struck me. Doc, did you ever
see a piney woods nigger pullin' at a sassafras root, or a suckin' pig
in a tater patch arter the big yams? You has! Well, you can 'magin
how I jurkt at that wudden leg, for it war the last of pea time with
me, sure, if I didn't rise 'fore bar did. At last, they both cum up,
'bout the same time, and I braced myself for a death struggle.

"We fit all round that holler! Fust I'd foller bar and then bar
would chase me! I'd make a lick—he'd fend off and showin' a set
of teeth that no doctor 'cept natur had ever wurkt at, cum tearin'
at me! We both 'gan to git tired. I heard the boys and dogs cumin,
so did bar, and we were both anxshus to bring the thing to a close
'fore they cum up, though I wuddent thought they were intrudin'
ef they had cum up some time afore.

"I'd worn the old leg pretty well off to the second jint, when,
jest 'fore I made a lick, the noise of the boys and the dogs
cummin' sorter confused bar and he made a stumble, and bein' off
his guard I got a fair lick! The way that bar's flesh giv in to the
soft impresshuns of that leg war an honor to the mederkal perfeshun
for having invented sich a weepun! I hollered—but you have heered
me holler an' I won't describe it. I had whipped a bar in a fair hand
to hand fight—me, an old, sickly, one-legged bar hunter! The boys
cum up and when they seed the ground we had fit over, they swore
they would have thought 'stead of a bar fight that I had been cuttin'
cane and deadenin' timber for a corn patch, the sile war so worked
up. They then handed me a knife to finish the work.

"Doc, les licker. It's a dry talk. When will you make me another
leg? Bar meat is not over plenty in the cabin and I feel like tryin'
another!"

George Washington Cable (1844-1925)

Born in New Orleans, Cable was forced to stop school at the age of 14, after his father's death. He fought in the Confederate Army, and after the war he began a long literary career—first as a journalist, then as a well-known local colorist, and, more and more, as a Southern reformist against racial injustice. His collection of stories, Old Creole Days *(1879), and his novel,* The Grandissimes *(1880, revised 1884), gave him a national reputation as one of the best Southern writers of his day. His reformist writings and speeches made him unpopular in New Orleans, and he finally decided to make his home in New England, where he continued to write and give public readings. Among his other books are* Madame Delphine *(1881),* The Creoles of Louisiana *(1884),* Dr. Sevier *(1884),* The Silent South *(1885),* John March, Southerner *(1894),* Kincaid's Battery *(1908), and* Lovers of Louisiana *(1918). "Posson Jone'" is taken from* Old Creole Days.

POSSON JONE'

To JULES ST.-ANGE—ELEGANT LITTLE HEATHEN—there yet remained at manhood a remembrance of having been to school, and of having been taught by a stony-headed Capuchin that the world is round—for example, like a cheese. This round world is a cheese to be eaten through, and Jules had nibbled quite into his cheese-world already at twenty-two.

He realized this as he idled about one Sunday morning where the intersection of Royal and Conti Streets some seventy years ago formed a central corner of New Orleans. Yes, yes, the trouble was he had been wasteful and honest. He discussed the matter with that faithful friend and confidant, Baptiste, his yellow body-servant. They concluded that, papa's patience and *tante's* pin-money having been gnawed away quite to the rind, there were left open only these few easily enumerated resorts: to go to work—they shuddered; to join Major Innerarity's filibustering expedition; or else—why not?—to try some games of confidence. At twenty-two one must begin to be something. Nothing else tempted; could that avail? One could but try. It is noble to try; and, besides, they were hungry. If one could "make the friendship" of some person from the country, for instance, with money, not expert at cards or dice, but, as one would say, willing to learn, one might find cause to say some "Hail Marys."

The sun broke through a clearing sky, and Baptiste pronounced it good for luck. There had been a hurricane in the night. The weed-grown tile-roofs were still dripping, and from lofty brick and low adobe walls a rising steam responded to the summer sunlight. Up-street, and across the Rue du Canal, one could get glimpses of the gardens in Faubourg Ste-Marie standing in silent wretchedness, so many tearful Lucretias, tattered victims of the storm. Short remnants of the wind now and then came down the narrow street in erratic puffs heavily laden with odors of broken boughs and torn flowers, skimmed the little pools of rain-water in the deep ruts of the unpaved street, and suddenly went away to nothing, like a juggler's butterflies or a young man's money.

It was very picturesque, the Rue Royale. The rich and poor met together. The locksmith's swinging key creaked next door to the bank; across the way, crouching, mendicant-like, in the shadow of a great importing-house, was the mud laboratory of the mender of broken combs. Light balconies overhung the rows of showy shops and stores open for trade this Sunday morning, and pretty Latin faces of the higher class glanced over their savagely pronged railings upon the passers below. At some windows hung lace curtains, flannel duds at some, and at others only the scraping and sighing one-hinged shutter groaning towards Paris after its neglectful master.

M. St.-Ange stood looking up and down the street for nearly an hour. But few ladies, only the inveterate mass-goers, were out. About the entrance of the frequent *cafés* the masculine gentility stood leaning on canes, with which now one and now another beckoned to Jules, some even adding pantomimic hints of the social cup.

M. St.-Ange remarked to his servant without turning his head that somehow he felt sure he should soon return those *bons* that the mulatto had lent him.

"What will you do with them?"

"Me!" said Baptiste quickly; "I will go and see the bull-fight in the Place Congo."

"There is to be a bull-fight? But where is M. Cayetano?"

"Ah, got all his affairs wet in the tornado. Instead of his circus, they are to have a bull-fight—not an ordinary bull-fight with sick horses, but a buffalo-and-tiger fight. I would not miss it—"

Two or three persons ran to the opposite corner, and commenced striking at something with their canes. Others followed, Can M. St.-Ange and servant, who hasten forward—can the Creoles, Cubans, Spaniards, St. Domingo refugees, and other loungers—can they hope it is a fight? They hurry forward. Is a man in a fit? The crowd pours in from the sidestreets. Have they killed a so-long snake? Bareheaded shopmen leave their wives, who stand upon chairs. The crowd huddles and packs. Those on the outside make little leaps into the air, trying to be tall.

"What is the matter?"

"Have they caught a real live rat?"

"Who is hurt?" asks some one in English.

"*Personne*," replies a shopkeeper; "a man's hat blow' in the gutter; but he has it now. Jules pick it. See, that is the man, head and shoulders on top the res'."

"He is the homespun?" asks a second shopkeeper. "Humph! an *Américain*—a West-Floridian; bah!"

"But wait; 'st! he is speaking; listen!"

"To who is he speak—?"

"Sh-sh-sh! to Jules."

"Jules who?"

"Silence, you! To Jules St.-Ange, what howe me a bill since long time. Sh-sh-sh!"

Then the voice was heard.

Its owner was a man of giant stature, with a slight stoop in his shoulders, as if he was making a constant, good-natured attempt to accommodate himself to ordinary doors and ceilings. His bones were those of an ox. His face was marked more by weather than age, and his narrow brow was bald and smooth. He had instantaneously formed an opinion of Jules St.-Ange, and the multitude of words, most of them lingual curiosities, with which he was rasping the wide-open ears of his listeners, signified, in short, that, as sure as his name was Parson Jones, the little Creole was a "plum gentleman."

M. St.-Ange bowed and smiled, and was about to call attention, by both gesture and speech, to a singular object on top of the still uncovered head, when the nervous motion of the *Américain* anticipated him, as, throwing up an immense hand, he drew down a large roll of bank-notes. The crowd laughed, the West-Floridian joining, and began to disperse.

"Why, that money belongs to the Smyrny Church," said the giant.

"You are very dengerous to make your money expose like that, Misty Posson Jone'," said St.-Ange, counting it with his eyes.

The countryman gave a start and smile of surprise.

"How d'dyou know my name was Jones?" he asked; but, without pausing for the Creole's answer, furnished in his reckless way some further specimens of West-Floridian English; and the conciseness with which he presented full intelligence of his home, family, calling, lodging-house, and present and future plans, might have passed for consummate art, had it not been the most run-wild nature. "And I've done been to Mobile, you know, on busi*ness* for Bethesdy Church. It's the on'yest time I ever been from home; now you wouldn't of believed that, would you? But I admire to have saw you, that's so. You've got to come and eat with me. Me and my boy ain't been fed yit. What might one call yo' name? Jools? Come on, Jools. Come on, Colossus. That's my niggah—his name's Colossus of Rhodes. Is that yo' yallah boy, Jools? Fetch him along, Colossus. It seems like a special provi*dence.*—Jools, do you believe in a special provi*dence?*"

Jules said he did.

The new-made friends moved briskly off, followed by Baptiste and a short, square old negro, very black and grotesque, who had introduced himself to the mulatto, with many glittering and cavernous smiles, as "d'body-sarvant of d'Rev'n' Mr. Jones."

Both pairs enlivened their walk with conversation. Parson Jones descanted upon the doctrine he had mentioned, as illustrated in the perplexities of cotton-growing, and concluded that there would always be "a special provi*dence* again' cotton untell folks quits a-pressin' of it and haulin' of it on Sundays!"

"*Je dis,*" said St.-Ange, in response, "I thing you is juz right. I believe, me, strong-strong in the improvidence, yes. You know my papa he hown a sugah-plantation, you know. 'Jules, me son,' he say one time to me, 'I goin' to make one baril sugah to fedge the moze high price in New Orleanz.' Well, he take his bez baril sugah—I nevah see a so careful man like me papa always to make a so beautiful sugah *et sirop.* 'Jules, go at Father Pierre an' ged this lill pitcher fill with holy-water, an' tell him sen' his tin bucket, and I will make it fill with *quitte.*' I ged the holy-water; my papa sprinkle it over the baril, an' make one cross on the 'ead of the baril."

"Why, Jools," said Parson Jones, "that didn't do no good."

"Din do no good! Id broughd the so great value! You can strike me dead if thad baril sugah din fedge the more high cost than any other in the city. *Parce-que,* the man what buy that baril sugah he make a mistake of one hundred pound"—falling back—"*Mais certainlee!*"

"And you think that was growin' out of the holy-water?" asked the parson.

"*Mais,* what could make it else? Id could not be the *quitte,* because my papa keep the bucket, an' forget to sen' the *quitte* to Father Pierre."

Parson Jones was disappointed.

"Well, now, Jools, you know, I don't think that was right. I reckon you must be a plum Catholic."

M. St.-Ange shrugged. He would not deny his faith.

"I am a *Catholique, mais*"—brightening as he hoped to recommend himself anew—"not a good one."

"Well, you know," said Jones—"where's Colossus? Oh! all right.

Colossus strayed off a minute in Mobile, and I plum lost him for
two days. Here's the place; come in. Colossus and this boy can go
to the kitchen.—Now, Colossus, what *air* you a-beckonin' at me
faw?"

He let his servant draw him aside and address him in a whisper.

"Oh, go 'way!" said the parson with a jerk. "Who's goin' to
throw me? What? Speak louder. Why, Colossus, you shayn't talk
so, saw. 'Pon my soul, you're the mightiest fool I ever taken up
with. Jest you go down that alley-way with this yalla boy, and don't
show yo' face untell yo' called!"

The negro begged; the master wrathily insisted.

"Colossus, will you do ez I tell you, or shell I hev' to strike you,
saw?"

"O Mahs Jimmy, I—I's gwine; but"—he ventured nearer—"don't
on no account drink nothin', Mahs Jimmy."

Such was the negro's earnestness that he put one foot in the
gutter, and fell heavily against his master. The parson threw him
off angrily.

"Thar, now! Why, Colossus, you most of been dosted with
sumthin'; yo' plum crazy.—Humph, come on, Jools, let's eat!
Humph! to tell me that when I never taken a drop, exceptin' for
chills, in my life—which he knows so as well as me!"

The two masters began to ascend a stair.

"*Mais*, he is a sassy; I would sell him, me," said the young
Creole.

"No, I wouldn't do that," replied the parson; "though there is
people in Bethesdy who says he is a rascal. He's a powerful smart
fool. Why, that boy's got money, Jools; more money than religion,
I reckon. I'm shore he fallen into mighty bad company"—they
passed beyond earshot.

Baptiste and Colossus, instead of going to the tavern kitchen,
passed to the next door and entered the dark rear corner of a low
grocery, where, the law notwithstanding, liquor was covertly sold
to slaves. There, in the quiet company of Baptiste and the grocer,
the colloquial powers of Colossus, which were simply prodigious,
began very soon to show themselves.

"For whilst," said he, "Mahs Jimmy has eddication, you know—
whilst he has eddication, I has 'scretion. He has eddication and I
has 'scretion, an' so we gits along."

He drew a black bottle down the counter, and, laying half his
length upon the damp board, continued:

"As a p'inciple I discredits de imbimin' of awjus liquors. De imbimin' of awjus liquors, de wiolution of de Sabbaf, de playin' of de fiddle, and de usin' of by-words, dey is de fo' sins of de conscience; an' if any man sin de fo' sins of de conscience, de debble done sharp his fork fo' dat man.—Ain't that so, boss?"

The grocer was sure it was so.

"Neberdeless, mind you"—here the orator brimmed his glass from the bottle and swallowed the contents with a dry eye—"mind you, a roytious man, sech as ministers of de gospel and dere body-sarvants, can take a *leetle* for de weak stomach."

But the fascinations of Colossus's eloquence must not mislead us: this is the story of a true Christian; to wit, Parson Jones.

The parson and his new friend ate. But the coffee M. St.-Ange declared he could not touch; it was too wretchedly bad. At the French Market, near by, there was some noble coffee. This, however, would have to be bought, and Parson Jones had scruples.

"You see, Jools, every man has his conscience to guide him, which it does so in—"

"Oh, yes!" cried St.-Ange, "conscien'; thad is the bez, Posson Jone'. Certainlee! I am a *Catholique,* you is a *schismatique;* you thing it is wrong to dring some coffee—well, then, it *is* wrong; you thing it is wrong to make the sugah to ged the so large price—well, then, it *is* wrong; I thing it is right—well, then, it *is* right; it is all 'abit; *c'est tout.* What a man thing is right, *is right;* 'tis all 'abit. A man muz nod go again' his conscien'. My faith! do you thing I would go again' my conscien'? *Mais allons,* led us go and get some coffee."

"Jools."

"W'at?"

"Jools, it ain't the drinkin' of coffee, but the buyin' of it on a Sabbath. You must really excuse me, Jools, it's again' conscience, you know."

"Ah!" said St.-Ange, "*c'est* very true. For you it would be a sin, *mais* for me it is only 'abit. Rilligion is a very strange; I know a man one time, he thing it was wrong to go to cock-fight Sunday evening. I thing it is all 'abit. *Mais,* come, Posson Jone'; I have got one friend, Miguel; led us go at his house and ged some coffee. Come; Miguel have no familie; only him and Joe—always like to see friend; *allons,* led us come yonder."

"Why, Jools, my dear friend, you know," said the shamefaced parson, "I never visit on Sundays."

"Never w'at?" asked the astounded Creole.

"No," said Jones, smiling awkwardly.

"Never visite?"

"Exceptin' sometimes amongst church-members," said Parson Jones.

"*Mais,*" said the seductive St.-Ange, "Miguel and Joe is church-member'—certainlee! They love to talk about rilligion. Come at Miguel and talk about some rilligion. I am nearly expire for me coffee."

Parson Jones took his hat from beneath his chair and rose up.

"Jools," said the weak giant, "I ought to be in church right now."

"*Mais,* the church is right yonder at Miguel, yes. Ah!" continued St.-Ange, as they descended the stairs, "I thing every man muz have the rilligion he like the bez—me, I like the *Catholique* rilligion the bez—for me it *is* the bez. Every man will sure go to heaven if he likes his rilligion the bez."

"Jools," said the West-Floridian, laying his great hand tenderly upon the Creole's shoulder, as they stepped out upon the *banquette,* "do you think you have any shore hopes of heaven?"

"Yass!" replied St.-Ange; "I am sure-sure. I thing everybody will go to heaven. I thing you will go, *et* I thing Miguel will go, *et* Joe—everybody, I thing—*mais,* hof course, not if they not have been christen'. Even I thing some niggers will go."

"Jools," said the parson, stopping in his walk—"Jools, I *don't* want to lose my niggah."

"You will not loose him. With Baptiste he *cannot* ged loose."

But Colossus's master was not reassured.

"Now," said he, still tarrying, "this is jest the way; had I of gone to church—"

"Posson Jone'," said Jules.

"What?"

"I tell you. We goin' to church!"

"Will you?" asked Jones joyously.

"*Allons,* come along," said Jules taking his elbow.

They walked down the Rue Chartres, passed several corners, and by and by turned into a cross street. The parson stopped an instant as they were turning, and looked back up the street.

"W'at you lookin'?" asked his companion.

"I thought I saw Colossus," answered the parson, with an anxious face; "I reckon 'twa' n't him, though." And they went on.

The street they now entered was a very quiet one. The eye of any chance passer would have been at once drawn to a broad, heavy white brick edifice on the lower side of the way, with a flag-pole standing out like a bowsprit from one of its great windows, and a pair of lamps hanging before a large closed entrance. It was a theatre, honey-combed with gambling-dens. At this morning hour all was still, and the only sign of life was a knot of little barefoot girls gathered within its narrow shade, and each carrying an infant relative. Into this place the parson and M. St.-Ange entered, the little nurses jumping up from the sills to let them pass in.

A half-hour may have passed. At the end of that time the whole juvenile company were laying alternate eyes and ears to the chinks, to gather what they could of an interesting quarrel going on within.

"I did not, saw! I given you no cause of offence, saw! It's not so, saw! Mister Jools simply mistaken the house, thinkin' it was a Sabbath-school. No such thing, saw; I *ain't* bound to bet! Yes, I kin git out! Yes, without bettin'! I hev a right to my opinion; I reckon I'm a *white man*, saw! No, saw! I on'y said I didn't think you could get the game on them cards. 'Sno such thing, saw! I do *not* know how to play! I wouldn't hev a rascal's money ef I should win it! Shoot, ef you dare! You can kill me, but you can't scare me! No, I shayn't bet! I'll die first! Yes, saw; Mr. Jools can bet for me if he admires to; I ain't his mostah."

Here the speaker seemed to direct his words to St.-Ange.

"Saw, I don't understand you, saw. I never said I'd loan you money to bet on me. I didn't suspicion this from you, saw. No, I won't take any more lemonade; it's the most notorious stuff I ever drank, saw!"

M. St.-Ange's replies were in *falsetto* and not without effect; for presently the parson's indignation and anger began to melt. "Don't ask me, Jools, I can't help you. It's no use; it's a matter of conscience with me, Jools."

"*Mais oui!* 'tis a matt' of conscien' wid me, the same."

"But, Jools, the money's none o' mine, nohow; it belongs to Smyrny, you know."

"If I could make jus *one* bet," said the persuasive St.-Ange, "I would leave this place, fas'-fas', yes. If I had thing—*mais* I did not soupspicion this from you, Posson Jone'—"

"Don't, Jools, don't."

"No! Posson Jone'."

"You're bound to win?" said the parson, wavering.

"*Mais certainement!* But it is not to win that I want; 'tis me conscien'—me honor!"

"Well, Jools, I hope I'm not a-doin' no wrong. I'll loan you some of this money if you say you'll come right out 'thout takin' your winnin's."

All was still. The peeping children could see the parson as he lifted his hand to his breast-pocket. There it paused a moment in bewilderment, then plunged to the bottom. It came back empty, and fell lifelessly at his side. His head dropped upon his breast, his eyes were for a moment closed, his broad palms were lifted and pressed against his forehead, a tremor seized him, and he fell all in a lump to the floor. The children ran off with their infant-loads, leaving Jules St.-Ange swearing by all his deceased relatives, first to Miguel and Joe, and then to the lifted parson, that he did not know what had become of the money "except if" the black man had got it.

In the rear of ancient New Orleans, beyond the sites of the old rampart, a trio of Spanish forts, where the town has since sprung up and grown old, green with all the luxuriance of the wild Creole summer, lay the Congo Plains. Here stretched the canvas of the historic Cayetano, who Sunday after Sunday sowed the sawdust for his circus-ring.

But to-day the great showman had fallen short of his printed promise. The hurricane had come by night, and with one fell swash had made an irretrievable sop of everything. The circus trailed away its bedraggled magnificence, and the ring was cleared for the bull.

Then the sun seemed to come out and work for the people. "See," said the Spaniards, looking up at the glorious sky with its great, white fleets drawn off upon the horizon—"see—heaven smiles upon the bullfight!"

In the high upper seats of the rude amphitheatre sat the gayly decked wives and daughters of the Gascons, from the *métairies* along the Ridge, and the chattering Spanish women of the Market, their shining hair unbonneted to the sun. Next below were their husbands and lovers in Sunday blouses, milkmen, butchers, bakers, black-bearded fishermen, Sicilian fruiterers, swarthy Portuguese sailors, in little woollen caps, and strangers of the graver sort; mariners of England, Germany, and Holland. The lowest seats were full of trappers, smugglers, Canadian *voyageurs*, drinking and singing; *Américains*, too—more's the shame—from the upper rivers—who will not keep their seats—who ply the bottle, and who will get home by and by and tell how wicked Sodom is; broad-brimmed, silver-braided Mexicans, too, with their copper cheeks and bat's eyes, and their tinkling spurred heels. Yonder, in that quieter section, are the quadroon women in their black lace shawls—and there is Baptiste; and below them are the turbaned black women, and there is—but he vanishes—Colossus.

The afternoon is advancing, yet the sport, though loudly demanded, does not begin. The *Américains* grow derisive and find pastime in gibes and raillery. They mock the various Latins with their national inflections, and answer their scowls with laughter. Some of the more aggressive shout pretty French greetings to the women of Gascony, and one barge-man, amid peals of applause, stands on a seat and hurls a kiss to the quadroons. The mariners of England, Germany, and Holland, as spectators, like the fun, while the Spaniards look back and cast defiant imprecations upon their persecutors. Some Gascons, with timely caution, pick their women out and depart, running a terrible fire of gallantries.

In hope of truce, a new call is raised for the bull: "The bull, the bull!—hush!"

In a tier near the ground a man is standing and calling—standing head and shoulders above the rest—calling in the *Américaine* tongue. Another man, big and red, named Joe, and a handsome little Creole, in elegant dress and full of laughter, wish to stop him, but the flat-boatmen, ha-ha-ing and cheering, will not suffer it. Ah, through some shameful knavery of the men, into whose hands he has fallen, he is drunk! Even the women can see that; and now he throws his arms wildly and raises his voice until the whole great circle hears it. He is preaching!

Ah! kind Lord, for a special providence now! The men of his own nation—men from the land of the open English Bible and temperance cup and song are cheering him on to mad disgrace. And now another call for the appointed sport is drowned by the flat-boatmen singing the ancient tune of Mear. You can hear the words—

"Old Grimes is dead, that good old soul"

—from ribald lips and throats turned brazen with laughter, from singers who toss their hats aloft and roll in their seats; the chorus swells to the accompaniment of a thousand brogans—

> "He used to wear an old gray coat
> All buttoned down before."

A ribboned man in the arena is trying to be heard, and the Latins raise one mighty cry for silence. The big red man gets a hand over the parson's mouth, and the ribboned man seizes his moment.

"They have been endeavoring for hours," he says, "to draw the terrible animals from their dens, but such is their strength and fierceness, that—"

His voice is drowned. Enough has been heard to warrant the inference that the beasts cannot be whipped out of the storm-drenched cages to which menagerie-life and long starvation have attached them, and from the roar of indignation the man of ribbons flies. The noise increases. Men are standing up by hundreds, and women are imploring to be let out of the turmoil. All at once, like the bursting of a dam, the whole mass pours down into the ring. They sweep across the arena and over the showman's barriers. Miguel gets a frightful trampling. Who cares for gates or doors? They tear the beasts' houses bar from bar, and, laying hold of the gaunt buffalo, drag him forth by feet, ears, and tail; and in the midst of the *mêlée*, still head and shoulders above all, wilder, with the cup of the wicked, than any beast, is the man of God from the Florida parishes!

In his arms he bore—and all the people shouted at once when they saw it—the tiger. He had lifted it high up with its back to his breast, his arms clasped under its shoulders; the wretched brute had curled up caterpillar-wise, with its long tail against its belly, and through its filed teeth grinned a fixed and impotent wrath. And Parson Jones was shouting:

"The tiger and the buffler *shell* lay down together! You dah to say they shayn't and I'll comb you with this varmint from head to foot! The tiger and buffler *shell* lay down together. They *shell!* Now, you, Joe! Behold! I am here to see it done. The lion and the buffler *shell* lay down together!"

Mouthing these words again and again, the parson forced his way through the surge in the wake of the buffalo. This creature the Latins had secured by a lariat over his head, and were dragging across the old rampart and into a street of the city.

The northern races were trying to prevent, and there was pommelling and knocking down, cursing and knife-drawing until Jules St.-Ange was quite carried away with the fun, laughed, clapped his hands, and swore with delight, and ever kept close to the gallant parson.

Joe, contrariwise, counted all this child's-play an interruption. He had come to find Colossus and the money. In an unlucky moment he made bold to lay hold of the parson, but a piece of the broken barriers in the hands of the flat-boatman felled him to the sod, the terrible crowd swept over him, the lariat was cut, and the giant parson hurled the tiger upon the buffalo's back. In another instant both brutes were dead at the hands of the mob; Jones was lifted from his feet, and prating of Scripture and the millennium, of Paul at Ephesus and Daniel in the "buffler's" den, was borne aloft upon the shoulders of the huzzaing *Américains*. Half an hour later he was sleeping heavily on the floor of a cell in the *calaboza*.

When Parson Jones awoke, a bell was somewhere tolling for midnight. Somebody was at the door of his cell with a key. The lock grated, the door swung, the turnkey looked in and stepped back, and a ray of moonlight fell upon M. Jules St.-Ange. The prisoner sat upon the empty shackles and ring-bolt in the centre of the floor.

"Misty Posson Jone'," said the visitor, softly.

"O Jools!"

"*Mais*, w'at de matter, Posson Jone'?"

"My sins, Jools, my sins!"

"Ah! Posson Jone', is that something to cry, because a man get sometime a litt' bit intoxicate? *Mais*, if a man keep *all the time* intoxicate, I think that is again' the conscien'."

"Jools, Jools, your eyes is darkened—oh! Jools, where's my pore old niggah?"

"Posson Jone', never min'; he is wid Baptiste."

"Where?"

"I don't know w'ere—*mais* he is wid Baptiste. Baptiste is a beautiful to take care of somebody."

"Is he as good as you, Jools?'" asked Parson Jones sincerely.

Jools was slightly staggered.

"'You know, Posson Jone', you know, a nigger cannot be good as a w'ite man—*mais* Baptiste is a good nigger."

The parson moaned and dropped his chin into his hands.

"I was to of left for home to-morrow, sun-up, on the Isabella schooner. Pore Smyrny!" He deeply sighed.

"Posson Jone'," said Jules, leaning against the wall and smiling, "I swear you is the moz funny man I ever see. If I was you, I would say, me, 'Ah! 'ow I am lucky! the money I los', it was not mine, anyhow!' My faith! shall a man make hisse'f to be the more sorry because the money he los' is not his? Me, I would say, 'it is a specious providence.'

"Ah! Misty Posson Jone'," he continued, "you make a so droll sermon ad the bull-ring. Ha! ha! I swear I thing you can make money to preach thad sermon many time ad the theatre St. Philippe. Hah! you is the moz brave dat I never see, *mais* ad the same time the moz rilligious man. Where I'm goin' to fin' one priest to make like dat? *Mais*, why you can't cheer up an' be 'appy? Me, if I should be miserabl' like that I would kill meself."

The countryman only shook his head.

"*Bien*, Posson Jone', I have the so good news for you."

The prisoner looked up with eager inquiry.

"Las' evening when they lock' you, I come right off at M. De Blanc's house to get you let out of de calaboose; M. De Blanc he is the judge. So soon I was entering—'Ah! Jules, me boy, juz the man to make complete the game!' Posson Jone', it was a specious providence! I win in t'ree hours more dan six hundred dollah! Look." He produced a mass of banknotes, *bons*, and due-bills.

"And you got the pass?" asked the parson, regarding the money with a sadness incomprehensible to Jules.

"It is here; it take the effect so soon the daylight."

"Jools, my friend, your kindness is in vain."

The Creole's face became a perfect blank.

"Because," said the parson, "for two reasons: firstly, I have broken the laws, and ought to stand the penalty; and secondly— you must really excuse me, Jools, you know, but the pass has been got onfairly, I'm afeerd. You told the judge I was innocent; and in neither case it don't become a Christian (which I hope I can still say I am one) to 'do evil that good may come.' I muss stay."

M. St.-Ange stood up aghast, and for a moment speechless, at this exhibition of moral heroism; but an artifice was presently hit upon. "*Mais*, Posson Jone'!"—in his old *falsetto*—"de order—you cannot read it, it is in French—compel you to go hout, sir!"

"Is that so?" cried the parson, bounding up with radiant face— "is that so, Jools?"

The young man nodded, smiling; but, though he smiled, the fountain of his tenderness was opened. He made the sign of the cross as the parson knelt in prayer, and even whispered "Hail Mary," etc., quite through, twice over.

Morning broke in summer glory upon a cluster of villas behind the city, nestled under live-oaks and magnolias on the banks of a deep bayou, and known as Suburb St. Jean.

With the first beam came the West-Floridian and the Creole out upon the bank below the village. Upon the parson's arm hung a pair of antique saddle-bags. Baptiste limped wearily behind; both his eyes were encircled with broad blue rings, and one cheek-bone bore the official impress of every knuckle of Colossus's left hand. The "beautiful to take care of somebody" had lost his charge. At mention of the negro he became wild, and, half in English, half in the "gumbo" dialect, said murderous things. Intimidated by Jules to calmness, he became able to speak confidently on one point; he could, would, and did swear that Colossus had gone home to the Florida parishes; he was almost certain; in fact, he thought so.

There was a clicking of pulleys as the three appeared upon the bayou's margin, and Baptiste pointed out, in the deep shadow of a great oak, the Isabella, moored among the bulrushes, and just spreading her sails for departure. Moving down to where she lay, the parson and his friend paused on the bank, loath to say farewell.

"O Jools!" said the parson, "supposin' Colossus ain't gone home! O Jools, if you'll look him out for me, I'll never forget you—I'll never forget you, nohow, Jools. No, Jools, I never will believe he taken that money. Yes, I know all niggahs will steal"—he set foot upon the gang-plank—"but Colossus wouldn't steal from me. Good-by."

"Misty Posson Jone'," said St.-Ange, putting his hand on the parson's arm with genuine affection, "hol' on. You see dis money— w'at I win las' night? Well, I win' it by a specious providence, ain't it?"

"There's no tellin'," said the humbled Jones. "Providence

'Moves in a mysterious way
His wonders to perform.'"

"Ah!' cried the Creole, "c'est very true. I ged this money in the mysterieuze way. Mais, if I keep dis money, you know where it goin' be to-night?"

"I really can't say," replied the parson.

"Goin' to the dev'," said the sweetly smiling young man.

The schooner-captain, leaning against the shrouds, and even Baptiste, laughed outright.

"O Jools, you mustn't!"

"Well, den, w'at I shall do wid *it?*"

"Anything!" answered the parson; "better donate it away to some poor man—"

"Ah! Misty Posson Jone', dat is w'at I want. You los' five hondred dollar'—'t was me fault."

"No, it wa'n't, Jools."

"*Mais,* it was!"

"No!"

"It *was* me fault! I *swear* it was me fault! *Mais,* here is five hondred dollar'; I wish you shall take it. Here! I don't got no use for money.—Oh, my faith! Posson Jone', you must not begin to cry some more."

Parson Jones was choked with tears. When he found voice he said:

"O Jools, Jools, Jools! my pore, noble, dear, misguidened friend! ef you hed of hed a Christian raisin'! May the Lord show you your errors better 'n I kin, and bless you for your good intentions—oh no! I cayn't touch that money with a ten-foot pole; it wa'n't rightly got; you must really excuse me, my dear friend, but I cayn't touch it."

St.-Ange was petrified.

"Good-by, dear Jools," continued the parson. "I'm in the Lord's haynds, and he's very merciful, which I hope and trust you'll find it out. Good-by!"—the schooner swung slowly off before the breeze—"good-by!"

St.-Ange roused himself.

"Posson Jone'! make me hany'ow *dis* promise: you never, never, *never* will come back to New Orleans."

"Ah, Jools, the Lord willin', I'll never leave home again!"

"All right!" cried the Creole; "I thing he's willin'. Adieu, Posson Jone'. My faith'! you are the so fighting an' moz rilligious man as I never saw! Adieu! Adieu!"

Baptiste uttered a cry and presently ran by his master toward the schooner, his hands full of clods.

St.-Ange looked just in time to see the sable form of Colossus of

Rhodes emerge from the vessel's hold, and the pastor of Smyrna and Bethesda seize him in his embrace.

"O Colossus! you outlandish old nigger! Thank the Lord! Thank the Lord!"

The little Creole almost wept. He ran down the tow-path, laughing and swearing, and making confused allusion to the entire *personnel* and furniture of the lower regions.

By odd fortune, at the moment that St.-Ange further demonstrated his delight by tripping his mulatto into a bog, the schooner came brushing along the reedy bank with a graceful curve, the sails flapped, and the crew fell to poling her slowly along.

Parson Jones was on the deck, kneeling once more in prayer. His hat had fallen before him; behind him knelt his slave. In thundering tones he was confessing himself "a plum fool," from whom "the conceit had been jolted out," and who had been made to see that even his "nigger had the longest head of the two."

Colossus clasped his hands and groaned.

The parson prayed for a contrite heart.

"Oh, yes!" cried Colossus.

The master acknowledged countless mercies.

"Dat's so!" cried the slave.

The master prayed that they might still be "piled on."

"Glory!" cried the black man, clapping his hands; "pile on!"

"An' now," continued the parson, "bring this pore, backslidin' jackace of a parson and this pore ole fool nigger back to thar home in peace!"

"Pray fo' de money!" called Colossus.

But the parson prayed for Jules.

"Pray fo' de *money!*" repeated the negro.

"And oh, give thy servant back that there lost money!"

Colossus rose stealthily, and tiptoed by his still shouting master. St.-Ange, the captain, the crew, gazed in silent wonder at the strategist. Pausing but an instant over the master's hat to grin an acknowledgement of his beholders' speechless interest, he softly placed in it the faithfully mourned and honestly prayed for Smyrna fund; then, saluted by the gesticulative, silent applause of St.-Ange and the schooner-men, he resumed his first attitude behind his roaring master.

"Amen!" cried Colossus, meaning to bring him to a close.

"Onworthy though I be—" cried Jones.

"*Amen!*" reiterated the negro.

"A-a-amen!" said Parson Jones.

He rose to his feet, and, stooping to take up his hat, beheld the well-known roll. As one stunned he gazed for a moment upon his slave, who still knelt with clasped hands and rolling eyeballs; but when he became aware of the laughter and cheers that greeted him from both deck and shore, he lifted eyes and hands to heaven, and cried like the veriest babe. And when he looked at the roll again, and hugged and kissed it, St.-Ange tried to raise a second shout, but choked, and the crew fell to their poles.

And now up runs Baptiste, covered with slime, and prepares to cast his projectiles. The first one fell wide of the mark; the schooner swung round into a long reach of water, where the breeze was in her favor; another shout of laughter drowned the maledictions of the muddy man; the sails filled; Colossus of Rhodes, smiling and bowing as hero of the moment, ducked as the main boom swept round, and the schooner, leaning slightly to the pleasant influence, rustled a moment over the bulrushes, and then sped far away down the rippling bayou.

M. Jules St.-Ange stood long, gazing at the receding vessel as it now disappeared, now re-appeared beyond the tops of the high undergrowth; but, when an arm of the forest hid it finally from sight, he turned townward, followed by that fagged-out spaniel, his servant, saying, as he turned, "Baptiste."

"*Miché?*"

"You know w'at I goin' do wid dis money?"

"*Non, m'sieur.*"

"Well, you can strike me dead if I don't goin' to pay hall my debts! *Allons!*"

He began a merry little song to the effect that his sweetheart was a wine-bottle, and master and man, leaving care behind, returned to the picturesque Rue Royale. The ways of Providence are indeed strange. In all Parson Jones's after-life, amid the many painful reminiscences of his visit to the City of the Plain, the sweet knowledge was withheld from him that by the light of the Christian virtue that shone from him even in his great fall, Jules St.-Ange arose, and went to his father an honest man.

Lafcadio Hearn (1850—1904)

Hearn was born on a Greek island. His father was an Irish surgeon in the British army and his mother was a native of Greece. He attended schools in Ireland, England, and France. At the age of 19 he emigrated to the United States, lived and worked as a journalist in Cincinnati, and moved to New Orleans in 1877. After a severe period of near-starvation, he began contributing regular articles to the Item, *and later to the* Times-Democrat. *He wrote numerous pieces on the food, music, language, and history of the Creoles, and became, with Cable, a local authority on New Orleans. In 1890 he moved to Japan, married into a Japanese family, assumed the name of Yakimo Koisumi, and became a professor of English literature at Kyoto University. His various works include* Stray Leaves from Strange Literature *(1884),* La Cuisine Créole *(1885),* "Gombo Zhebes": A Little Dictionary of Creole Proverbs *(1885),* Two Years in the French West Indies *(1890),* Out of the East: Reveries and Studies in New Japan *(1895), and* In Ghostly Japan *(1899).* "Chita: A Memory of Last Island" *is taken from* Harper's New Monthly Magazine, April 1888.

CHITA:
A Memory of Last Island

But Nature whistled with all her winds,
Did as she pleased, and went her way.

EMERSON

> *Je suis la vaste mêlée—*
> *Reptile, étant l'onde; ailée,*
>   *Étant le vent—*
> *Force et fuite, haine et vie,*
> *Houle immense, poursuivie*
>   *Et poursuivant.*

VICTOR HUGO

PART I
The Legend of L'Île Dernière

I

TRAVELING SOUTH FROM NEW ORLEANS to the islands, you pass through a strange land into a strange sea, by various winding waterways. You can journey to the Gulf by lugger if you please; but the trip may be made much more rapidly and agreeably on some one of those light, narrow steamers, built especially for bayou-travel, which usually receive passengers at a point not far from the foot of old Saint Louis Street, hard by the sugar-landing, where there is ever a pushing and flocking of steam-craft—all striving for place to rest their white breasts against the levee, side by side—like great weary swans. But the miniature steamboat on which you engage passage to the Gulf never lingers long in the Mississippi: she crosses the river, slips into some canal-mouth, labors along the artificial channel awhile, and then leaves it with a scream of joy, to puff her free way down many a league of heavily shadowed bayou. Perhaps thereafter she may bear you through the immense silence of drenched rice-fields, where the yellow-green level is broken at long intervals by the black silhouette of some irrigating machine; —but, whichever of the five different routes be pursued, you will find yourself more than once floating through sombre mazes of swamp-forest—past assemblages of cypresses all hoary with the parasitic tillandsia, and grotesque as gatherings of fetich-gods. Ever from river or from lakelet the steamer glides again into canal or bayou—from bayou or canal once more into lake or bay; and sometimes the swamp-forest visibly thins away from these shores into wastes of reedy morass where, even of breathless nights, the quaggy soil trembles to a sound like thunder of breakers on a coast: the storm-roar of billions of reptile voices chanting in cadence—rhythmically surging in stupendous crescendo and diminuendo—a monstrous and appalling chorus of frogs!...

Panting, screaming, scraping her bottom over the sand-bars—all day the little steamer strives to reach the grand blaze of blue open water below the marsh-lands; and perhaps she may be fortunate enough to enter the Gulf about the time of sunset. For the sake of passengers, she travels by day only; but there are other vessels which make the journey also by night—threading the bayou-labyrinths winter and summer: sometimes steering by the North Star—sometimes feeling the way with poles in the white season of fogs—sometimes, again, steering by that Star of Evening which in our sky glows like another moon, and drops over the silent lakes as she passes a quivering trail of silver fire.

Shadows lengthen; and at last the woods dwindle away behind you into thin bluish lines;—land and water alike take more luminous color;—bayous open into broad passes;—lakes link themselves with sea-bays;—and the ocean-wind bursts upon you—keen, cool, and full of light. For the first time the vessel begins to swing—rocking to the great living pulse of the tides. And gazing from the deck around you, with no forest walls to break the view, it will seem to you that the low land must have once been rent asunder by the sea, and strewn about the Gulf in fantastic tatters....

Sometimes above a waste of wind-blown prairie-cane you see an oasis emerging—a ridge or hillock heavily umbraged with the rounded foliage of evergreen oaks:—a *chénière*. And from the shining flood also kindred green knolls arise—pretty islets, each with its beach-girdle of dazzling sand and shells, yellow-white—and all radiant with semi-tropical foliage, myrtle and palmetto, orange and magnolia. Under their emerald shadows curious little villages of palmetto huts are drowsing, where dwell a swarthy population of Orientals—Malay fishermen, who speak the Spanish-Creole of the Philippines as well as their own Tagal, and perpetuate in Louisiana the Catholic traditions of the Indies. There are girls in those unfamiliar villages worthy to inspire any statuary—beautiful with the beauty of ruddy bronze—gracile as the palmettoes that sway above them. . . . Farther seaward you may also pass a Chinese settlement: some queer camp of wooden dwellings clustering around a vast platform that stands above the water upon a thousand piles;—over the miniature wharf you can scarcely fail to observe a white sign-board painted with crimson ideographs. The great platform is used for drying fish in the sun; and the fantastic characters of the sign, literally translated, mean: "Heap—Shrimp—Plenty." . . . And finally all the land melts down into desolations of sea-marsh, whose stillness is seldom broken, except by the melancholy cry of long-legged birds, and in wild seasons by that sound which shakes all shores when the weird Musician of the Sea touches the bass keys of his mighty organ. . . .

II

Beyond the sea-marshes a curious archipelago lies. If you travel by steamer to the sea-islands to-day, you are tolerably certain to enter the Gulf by Grande Pass—skirting Grande Terre, the most familiar island of all, not so much because of its proximity as because of its great crumbling fort and its graceful pharos: the stationary White-Light of Barataria. Otherwise the place is bleakly uninteresting: a wilderness of wind-swept grasses and sinewy weeds waving away from a thin beach ever speckled with drift and decaying things—worm-riddled timbers, dead porpoises. Eastward the russet level is broken by the columnar silhouette of the lighthouse, and again, beyond it, by some puny scrub timber, above which rises the angular ruddy mass of the old brick fort, whose ditches swarm with crabs, and whose sluiceways are half choked by obsolete cannon-shot, now thickly covered with incrustation of oyster shells. . . . Around all the gray circling of a shark-haunted sea. . . .

Sometimes of autumn evenings there, when the hollow of heaven flames like the interior of a chalice, and waves and clouds are flying in one wild rout of broken gold—you may see the tawny grasses all covered with something like husks—wheat-colored husks—large, flat, and disposed evenly along the lee-side of each swaying stalk, so as to present only their edges to the wind. But, if you approach, those pale husks all break open to display strange splendors of scarlet and seal-brown, with arabesque mottlings in white and black: they change into wondrous living blossoms, which detach themselves before your eyes and rise in air, and flutter away by thousands to settle down farther off, and turn into wheat-colored husks once more...a whirling flower-drift of sleepy butterflies!

Southwest, across the pass, gleams beautiful Grande Isle: primitively a wilderness of palmetto (*latanier*);—then drained, diked, and cultivated by Spanish sugar-planters; and now familiar chiefly as a bathing-resort. Since the war the ocean reclaimed its own; —the cane-fields have degenerated into sandy plains, over which tramways wind to the smooth beach;—the plantation-residences have been converted into rustic hotels, and the Negro-quarters remodeled into villages of cozy cottages for the reception of guests. But with its imposing groves of oak, its golden wealth of orange-trees, its odorous lanes of oleander, its broad grazing-meadows yellow-starred with wild camomile, Grande Isle remains the prettiest island of the Gulf; and its loveliness is exceptional. For the bleakness of Grande Terre is reiterated by most of the other islands—Caillou, Cassetête, Calumet, Wine Island, the twin Timbaliers, Gull Island, and the many islets haunted by the gray pelican—all of which are little more than sand-bars covered with wiry grasses, prairie-cane, and scrub timber. Last Island (L'Île Dernière)—well worthy a long visit in other years, in spite of its remoteness, is now a ghastly desolation twenty-five miles long. Lying nearly forty miles west of Grande Isle, it was nevertheless far more populated a generation ago: it was not only the most celebrated island of the group, but also the most fashionable watering-place of the aristocratic South;—to-day it is visited by fishermen only, at long intervals. Its admirable beach in many respects resembled that of Grande Isle to-day; the accommodations also were much similar, although finer: a charming village of cottages facing the Gulf near the western end. The hotel itself was a massive two-story construction of timber, containing many apartments, together with a large dining-room and dancing-hall. In rear of the hotel was a bayou, where passengers landed—"Village Bayou" it is still called by seamen;—but the deep channel which now cuts the island in two a little eastwardly did not exist while the village remained. The sea tore it out in one night—the same night when trees, fields, dwellings, all vanished into the Gulf, leaving no vestige of former human habitation except a few of those strong brick props and foundations upon which the frame houses and cisterns had been raised. One living creature was found there after the cataclysm—a cow! But how that solitary cow survived the fury of a storm-flood that actually rent the island in twain has ever remained a mystery....

III

On the gulf side of these islands you may observe that the trees—when there are any trees—all bend away from the sea; and, even of bright, hot days when the wind sleeps, there is something grotesquely pathetic in their look of agonized terror. A group of oaks at Grande Isle I remember as especially suggestive: five stooping silhouettes in line against the horizon, like fleeing women with streaming garments and wind-blown hair—bowing grievously and thrusting out arms desperately northward as to save themselves from falling. And they are being pursued indeed;—for the sea is devouring the land. Many and many a mile of ground has yielded to the tireless charging of Ocean's cavalry: far out you can see, through a good glass, the porpoises at play where of old the sugar-cane shook out its million bannerets; and shark-fins now seam deep water above a site where pigeons used to coo. Men build dikes; but the besieging tides bring up their battering-rams—whole forests of drift—huge trunks of water-oak and weighty cypress. Forever the yellow Mississippi strives to build; forever the sea struggles to destroy;—and amid their eternal strife the islands and the promontories change shape, more slowly, but not less fantastically, than the clouds of heaven.

And worthy of study are those wan battle-grounds where the woods made their last brave stand against the irresistible invasion —usually at some long point of sea-marsh, widely fringed with billowing sand. Just where the waves curl beyond such a point you may discern a multitude of blackened, snaggy shapes protruding above the water—some high enough to resemble ruined chimneys, others bearing a startling likeness to enormous skeleton-feet and skeleton-hands—with crustaceous white growths clinging to them here and there like remnants of integument. These are bodies and limbs of drowned oaks—so long drowned that the shell-scurf is inch-thick upon parts of them. Farther in upon the beach immense trunks lie overthrown. Some look like vast broken columns; some suggest colossal torsos embedded, and seem to reach out mutilated stumps in despair from their deepening graves;—and beside these are others which have kept their feet with astounding obstinacy, although the barbarian tides have been charging them for twenty years, and gradually torn away the soil above and beneath their roots. The sand around—soft beneath and thinly crusted upon the surface—is everywhere pierced with holes made by a beautifully mottled and semi-diaphanous crab, with hairy legs, big staring eyes, and milk-white claws;—while in the green sedges beyond there is a perpetual rustling, as of some strong wind beating among reeds: a marvelous creeping of "fiddlers," which the inexperienced visitor might at first mistake for so many peculiar beetles, as they run about sideways, each with his huge single claw folded upon his body like a wing-case. Year by year that rustling strip of green land grows narrower; the sand spreads and sinks, shuddering and wrinkling like a living brown skin; and the last standing corpses of the oaks, ever clinging with naked, dead feet to the sliding beach, lean more and more out of the perpendicular. As the sands subside, the stumps appear to creep; their intertwisted masses of snakish roots seem to crawl, to writhe—like the reaching arms of cephalopods. . . .

. . . Grande Terre is going: the sea mines her fort, and will before many years carry the ramparts by storm. Grande Isle is going—slowly but surely: the Gulf has eaten three miles into her meadowed land. Last Island has gone! How it went I first heard from the lips of a veteran pilot, while we sat one evening together on the trunk of a drifted cypress which some high tide had pressed deeply into the Grande Isle beach. The day had been tropically warm; we had sought the shore for a breath of living air. Sunset came, and with it the ponderous heat lifted—a sudden breeze blew—lightnings flickered in the darkening horizon—wind and water began to strive together—and soon all the low coast boomed. Then my companion began his story; perhaps the coming of the storm inspired him to speak! And as I listened to him, listening also to the clamoring of the coast, there flashed back to me recollection of a singular Breton fancy: that the Voice of the Sea is never one voice, but a tumult of many voices—voices of drowned men—the muttering of multitudinous dead—the moaning of innumerable ghosts, all rising, to rage against the living, at the great Witch-call of storms. . . .

IV

The charm of a single summer day on these island shores is something impossible to express, never to be forgotten. Rarely, in the paler zones, do earth and heaven take such luminosity: those will best understand me who have seen the splendor of a West Indian sky. And yet there is a tenderness of tint, a caress of color, in these Gulf days which is not of the Antilles—a spirituality, as of eternal tropical spring. It must have been to even such a sky that Xenophanes lifted up his eyes of old when he vowed the Infinite Blue was God;—it was indeed under such a sky that De Soto named the vastest and grandest of Southern havens *Espiritu Santo*— the Bay of the Holy Ghost. There is a something unutterable in this bright Gulf-air that compels awe—something vital, something holy, something pantheistic: and reverentially the mind asks itself if what the eye beholds is not the Πνεῦμα indeed, the Infinite Breath, the Divine Ghost, the great Blue Soul of the Unknown. All, all is blue in the calm—save the low land under your feet, which you almost forget, since it seems only as a tiny green flake afloat in the liquid eternity of day. Then slowly, caressingly, irresistibly, the witchery of the Infinite grows upon you: out of Time and Space you begin to dream with open eyes—to drift into delicious oblivion of facts—to forget the past, the present, the substantial—to comprehend nothing but the existence of that infinite Blue Ghost as something into which you would wish to melt utterly away forever....

And this day-magic of azure endures sometimes for months together. Cloudlessly the dawn reddens up through a violet east: there is no speck upon the blossoming of its Mystical Rose—unless it be the silhouette of some passing gull, whirling his sickle-wings against the crimsoning. Ever, as the sun floats higher, the flood shifts its color. Sometimes smooth and gray, yet flickering with the morning gold, it is the vision of John—the apocalyptic Sea of Glass mixed with fire;—again, with the growing breeze, it takes that incredible purple tint familiar mostly to painters of West Indian scenery;—once more, under the blaze of noon, it changes to a waste of broken emerald. With evening, the horizon assumes tints of inexpressible sweetness—pearl-lights, opaline colors of milk and fire; and in the west are topaz-glowings and wondrous flushings as of nacre. Then, if the sea sleeps, it dreams of all these—faintly, weirdly—shadowing them even to the verge of heaven.

Beautiful, too, are those white phantasmagoria which, at the approach of equinoctial days, mark the coming of the winds. Over the rim of the sea a bright cloud gently pushes up its head. It rises; and others rise with it, to right and left—slowly at first; then more swiftly. All are brilliantly white and flocculent, like loose new cotton. Gradually they mount in enormous line high above the Gulf, rolling and wreathing into an arch that expands and advances—bending from horizon to horizon. A clear, cold breath accompanies its coming. Reaching the zenith, it seems there to hang poised awhile—a ghostly bridge arching the empyrean—upreaching its measureless span from either underside of the world. Then the colossal phantom begins to turn, as on a pivot of air—always preserving its curvilinear symmetry, but moving its unseen ends beyond and below the sky-circle. And at last it floats away unbroken beyond the blue sweep of the world, with a wind following after. Day after day, almost at the same hour, the white arc rises, wheels, and passes....

...Never a glimpse of rock on these low shores;—only long sloping beaches and bars of smooth tawny sand. Sand and sea teem with vitality;—over all the dunes there is a constant susurration, a blattering and swarming of crustacea;—through all the sea there is a ceaseless play of silver lightning—flashing of myriad fish. Sometimes the shallows are thickened with minute, transparent, crab-like organisms—all colorless as gelatine. There are days also when countless medusae drift in—beautiful veined creatures that throb like hearts, with perpetual systole and diastole of their diaphanous envelops: some, of translucent azure or rose, seem in the flood the shadows or ghosts of huge campanulate flowers;—others have the semblance of strange living vegetables—great milky tubers, just beginning to sprout. But woe to the human skin grazed by those shadowy sproutings and spectral stamens!—the touch of glowing iron is not more painful.... Within an hour or two after their appearance all these tremulous jellies vanish mysteriously as they came.

Perhaps, if a bold swimmer, you may venture out along a long way—once! Not twice!—even in company. As the water deepens beneath you, and you feel those ascending wave-currents of coldness arising which bespeak profundity, you will also begin to feel innumerable touches, as of groping fingers—touches of the bodies of fish, innumerable fish, fleeing toward shore. The farther you advance, the more thickly you will feel them come; and above you and around you, to right and left, others will leap and fall so swiftly as to daze the sight, like intercrossing fountain-jets of fluid silver. The gulls fly lower about you, circling with sinister squeaking cries;—perhaps for an instant your feet touch in the deep something heavy, swift, lithe, that rushes past with a swirling shock. Then the fear of the Abyss, the vast and voiceless Nightmare of the Sea, will come upon you; the silent panic of all those opaline millions that flee glimmering by will enter into you also....

From what do they flee thus perpetually? Is it from the giant sawfish or the ravening shark?—from the herds of the porpoises, or from the *grande-écaille*—that splendid monster whom no net may hold—all helmed and armored in argent plate-mail?—or from the hideous devil-fish of the Gulf—gigantic, flat-bodied, black, with immense side-fins ever outspread like the pinions of a bat—the terror of luggermen, the uprooter of anchors? From all these, perhaps, and from other monsters likewise—goblin shapes evolved by Nature as destroyers, as equilibrists, as counterchecks to that prodigious fecundity, which, unhindered, would thicken the deep into one measureless and waveless ferment of being....But when there are many bathers these perils are forgotten—numbers give courage—one can abandon one's self, without fear of the invisible, to the long, quivering, electrical caresses of the sea....

V

Thirty years ago, Last Island lay steeped in the enormous light of even such magical days. July was dying;—for weeks no fleck of cloud had broken the heaven's blue dream of eternity; winds held their breath; slow wavelets caressed the bland brown beach with a sound as of kisses and whispers. To one who found himself alone, beyond the limits of the village and beyond the hearing of its voices—the vast silence, the vast light, seemed full of weirdness. And these hushes, these transparencies, do not always inspire a causeless apprehension: they are omens sometimes—omens of coming tempest. Nature—incomprehensible Sphinx!—before her mightiest bursts of rage, ever puts forth her divinest witchery, makes more manifest her awful beauty....

But in that forgotten summer the witchery lasted many long days—days born in rose-light, buried in gold. It was the height of the season. The long myrtle-shadowed village was thronged with its summer population;—the big hotel could hardly accommodate all its guests;—the bathing-houses were too few for the crowds who flocked to the water morning and evening. There were diversions for all—hunting and fishing parties, yachting excursions, rides, music, games, promenades. Carriage wheels whirled flickering along the beach, seaming its smoothness noiselessly, as if muffled. Love wrote its dreams upon the sand....

... Then one great noon, when the blue abyss of day seemed to yawn over the world more deeply than ever before, a sudden change touched the quicksilver smoothness of the waters—the swaying shadow of a vast motion. First the whole sea-circle appeared to rise up bodily at the sky; the horizon-curve lifted to a straight line; the line darkened and approached—a monstrous wrinkle, an immeasurable fold of green water, moving swift as a cloud-shadow pursued by sunlight. But it had looked formidable only by startling contrast with the previous placidity of the open: it was scarcely two feet high;—it curled slowly as it neared the beach, and combed itself out in sheets of wooly foam with a low, rich roll of whispered thunder. Swift in pursuit another followed—a third—a feebler fourth; then the sea only swayed a little, and stilled again. Minutes passed, and the immeasurable heaving recommenced— one, two, three, four... seven long swells this time;—and the Gulf smoothed itself once more. Irregularly the phenomenon continued to repeat itself, each time with heavier billowing and briefer intervals of quiet—until at last the whole sea grew restless and shifted color and flickered green;—the swells became shorter and changed form. Then from horizon to shore ran one uninterrupted heaving—one vast green swarming of snaky shapes, rolling in to hiss and flatten upon the sand. Yet no single cirrus-speck revealed itself through all the violet heights: there was no wind!—you might have fancied the sea had been upheaved from beneath....

And indeed the fancy of a seismic origin for a windless surge would not appear in these latitudes to be utterly without foundation. On the fairest days a southeast breeze may bear you an odor singular enough to startle you from sleep—a strong, sharp smell as of fish-oil; and gazing at the sea you might be still more startled at the sudden apparition of great oleaginous patches spreading over the water, sheeting over the swells. That is, if you had never heard of the mysterious submarine oil-wells, the volcanic fountains, unexplored, that well up with the eternal pulsing of the Gulf Stream....

But the pleasure-seekers of Last Island knew there must have been a "great blow" somewhere that day. Still the sea swelled; and a splendid surf made the evening bath delightful. Then, just at sundown, a beautiful cloud-bridge grew up and arched the sky with a single span of cottony pink vapor, that changed and deepened color with the dying of the iridescent day. And the cloud-bridge approached, stretched, strained, and swung round at last to make way for the coming of the gale—even as the light bridges that traverse the dreamy Têche swing open when luggermen sound through their conch-shells the long, bellowing signal of approach.

Then the wind began to blow, with the passing of July. It blew from the northeast, clear, cool. It blew in enormous sighs, dying away at regular intervals, as if pausing to draw breath. All night it blew; and in each pause could be heard the answering moan of the rising surf—as if the rhythm of the sea moulded itself after the rhythm of the air—as if the waving of the water responded precisely to the waving of the wind—a billow for every puff, a surge for every sigh.

The August morning broke in a bright sky;—the breeze still came cool and clear from the northeast. The waves were running now at a sharp angle to the shore: they began to carry fleeces, an innumerable flock of vague green shapes, wind-driven to be despoiled of their ghostly wool. Far as the eye could follow the line of the beach, all the slope was white with the great shearing of them. Clouds came, flew as in a panic against the face of the sun, and passed. All that day and through the night and into the morning again the breeze continued from the northeast, blowing like an equinoctial gale....

Then day by day the vast breath freshened steadily, and the waters heightened. A week later sea-bathing had become perilous: colossal breakers were herding in, like moving leviathan-backs, twice the height of a man. Still the gale grew, and the billowing waxed mightier, and faster and faster overhead flew the tatters of torn cloud. The gray morning of the 9th wanly lighted a surf that appalled the best swimmers: the sea was one wild agony of foam, the gale was rending off the heads of the waves and veiling the horizon with a fog of salt spray. Shadowless and gray the day remained; there were mad bursts of lashing rain. Evening brought with it a sinister apparition, looming through a cloud-rent in the west—a scarlet sun in a green sky. His sanguine disk, enormously magnified, seemed barred like the body of a belted planet. A moment, and the crimson spectre vanished; and the moonless night came.

Then the Wind grew weird. It ceased being a breath; it became a Voice moaning across the world—hooting—uttering nightmare sounds—*Whoo!—whoo!—whoo!*—and with each stupendous owl-cry the mooing of the waters seemed to deepen, more and more abysmally, through all the hours of darkness. From the northwest the breakers of the bay began to roll high over the sandy slope, into the salines;—the village bayou broadened to a bellowing flood.... So the tumult swelled and the turmoil heightened until morning—a morning of gray gloom and whistling rain. Rain of bursting clouds and rain of windblown brine from the great spuming agony of the sea.

The steamer *Star* was due from Saint Mary's that fearful morning. Could she come? No one really believed it—no one. And nevertheless men struggled to the roaring beach to look for her, because hope is stronger than reason....

Even to-day, in these Creole islands, the advent of the steamer is the great event of the week. There are no telegraph lines, no telephones: the mail-packet is the only trustworthy medium of communication with the outer world, bringing friends, news, letters. The magic of steam has placed New Orleans nearer to New York than to the Timbaliers, nearer to Washington than to Wine Island, nearer to Chicago than to Barataria Bay. And even during the deepest sleep of waves and winds there will come betimes to sojourners in this unfamiliar archipelago a feeling of lonesomeness that is a fear, a feeling of isolation from the world of men—totally unlike that sense of solitude which haunts one in the silence of mountain-heights, or amid the eternal tumult of lofty granitic coasts: a sense of helpless insecurity. The land seems but an undulation of the sea-bed: its highest ridges do not rise more than the height of a man above the salines on either side;—the salines themselves lie almost level with the level of the flood-tides;—the tides are variable, treacherous, mysterious. But when all around and above these ever-changing shores the twin vastnesses of heaven and sea begin to utter the tremendous revelation of themselves as infinite forces in contention, then indeed this sense of separation from humanity appals.... Perhaps it was such a feeling which forced men, on the tenth day of August, eighteen hundred and fifty-six, to hope against hope for the coming of the *Star,* and to strain their eyes towards far-off

Terrebonne. "It was a wind you could lie down on," said my friend the pilot.

... "Great God!" shrieked a voice above the shouting of the storm—"*she is coming!*"... It was true. Down the Atchafalaya, and thence through strange mazes of bayou, lakelet, and pass, by a rear route familiar only to the best of pilots, the frail river-craft had toiled into Caillou Bay, running close to the main shore;—and now she was heading right for the island, with the wind aft, over the monstrous sea. On she came, swaying, rocking, plunging—with a great whiteness wrapping her about like a cloud, and moving with her moving—a tempest-whirl of spray;—ghost-white and like a ghost she came, for her smoke-stacks exhaled no visible smoke—the wind devoured it! The excitement on shore became wild;—men shouted themselves hoarse; women laughed and cried. Every telescope and opera-glass was directed upon the coming apparition; all wondered how the pilot kept his feet; all marveled at the madness of the captain.

But Captain Abraham Smith was not mad. A veteran American sailor, he had learned to know the great Gulf as scholars know deep books by heart: he knew the birthplace of its tempests, the mystery of its tides, the omens of its hurricanes. While lying at Brashear City he felt the storm had not yet reached its highest, vaguely foresaw a mighty peril, and resolved to wait no longer for a lull. "Boys," he said, "we've got to take her out in spite of Hell!" And they "took her out." Through all the peril, his men stayed by him and obeyed him. By mid-morning the wind had deepened to a roar—lowering sometimes to a rumble, sometimes bursting upon the ears like a measureless and deafening crash. Then the captain knew the *Star* was running a race with Death. "She'll win it," he muttered;—"she'll stand it.... Perhaps they'll have need of me to-night."

She won! With a sonorous steam-chant of triumph the brave little vessel rode at last into the bayou, and anchored hard by her accustomed resting-place, in full view of the hotel, though not near enough to shore to lower her gang-plank.... But she had sung her swan-song. Gathering in from the northeast, the waters of the bay were already marbling over the salines and half across the island; and still the wind increased its paroxysmal power.

Cottages began to rock. Some slid away from the solid props upon which they rested. A chimney tumbled. Shutters were wrenched off; verandas demolished. Light roofs lifted, dropped again, and flapped into ruin. Trees bent their heads to the earth. And still the storm grew louder and blacker with every passing hour.

The *Star* rose with the rising of the waters, dragging her anchor. Two more anchors were put out, and still she dragged— dragged in with the flood—twisting, shuddering, careening in her agony. Evening fell; the sand began to move with the wind, stinging faces like a continuous fire of fine shot; and frenzied blasts came to buffet the steamer forward, sideward. Then one of her hog-chains parted with a clang like the boom of a big bell. Then another!... Then the captain bade his men to cut away all her upper works, clean to the deck. Overboard into the seething went her stacks, her pilot-house, her cabins—and whirled away. And the naked hull of the *Star*, still dragging her three anchors, labored on through the darkness, nearer and nearer to the immense silhouette of the hotel, whose hundred windows were now all aflame. The vast timber building seemed to defy the storm. The wind, roaring round its broad verandas—hissing through every crevice with the sound and force of steam—appeared to waste its rage. And in the half-lull between two terrible gusts there came to the captain's ears a sound that seemed strange in that night of multitudinous terrors... a sound of music!

VI

... Almost every evening throughout the season there had been dancing in the great hall;—there was dancing that night also. The population of the hotel had been augmented by the advent of families from other parts of the island, who found their summer cottages insecure places of shelter: there were nearly four hundred guests assembled. Perhaps it was for this reason that the entertainment had been prepared upon a grander plan than usual, that it assumed the form of a fashionable ball. And all those pleasure-seekers—representing the wealth and beauty of the Creole parishes—whether from Ascension or Assumption, Saint Mary's or Saint Landry's, Iberville or Terrebonne, whether inhabitants of the multi-colored and many-balconied Creole quarter of the quaint metropolis, or dwellers in the dreamy paradises of the Têche— mingled joyously, knowing each other, feeling in some sort akin— whether affiliated by blood, connaturalized by caste, or simply interassociated by traditional sympathies of class sentiment and class interest. Perhaps in the more than ordinary merriment of that evening something of nervous exaltation might have been discerned—something like a feverish resolve to oppose apprehension with gayety, to combat uneasiness by diversion. But the hours passed in mirthfulness; the first general feeling of depression began to weigh less and less upon the guests; they had found reason to confide in the solidity of the massive building; there were no positive terrors, no outspoken fears; and the new conviction of all had found expression in the words of the host himself— *"Il n'y a rien de mieux à faire que de s'amuser!"* Of what avail to lament the prospective devastation of cane-fields—to discuss the possible ruin of crops? Better to seek solace in choreographic harmonies, in the rhythm of gracious motion and of perfect melody, than hearken to the discords of the wild orchestra of storms;—wiser to admire the grace of Parisian toilettes, the eddy of trailing robes with its fairy-foam of lace, the ivorine loveliness of glossy shoulders and jewelled throats, the glimmering of satin-slippered feet—than to watch the raging of the flood without, or the flying of the wrack....

So the music and the mirth went on: they made joy for themselves— those elegant guests;—they jested and sipped rich wines;—they pledged, and hoped, and loved, and promised, with never a thought of the morrow, on the night of the tenth of August, eighteen hundred and fifty-six. Observant parents were there, planning for the future bliss of their nearest and dearest;—mothers and fathers of handsome lads, lithe and elegant as young pines, and fresh from the polish of foreign university training;—mothers and fathers of splendid girls whose simplest attitudes were witcheries. Young cheeks flushed, young hearts fluttered with an emotion more puissant than the excitement of the dance;—young eyes betrayed the happy secret discreeter lips would have preserved. Slave-servants circled through the aristocratic press, bearing dainties and wines, praying permission to pass in terms at once humble and officious—always in the excellent French which well-trained house-servants were taught to use on such occasions.

...Night wore on: still the shining floor palpitated to the feet of the dancers; still the piano-forte pealed, and still the violins sang—and the sound of their singing shrilled through the darkness, in gaps of the gale, to the ears of Captain Smith, as he strove to keep his footing on the spray-drenched deck of the *Star*.

"Christ!" he muttered—"a dance! If that wind whips round

south, there'll be another dance!...But I guess the *Star* will stay."...

Half an hour might have passed; still the lights flamed calmly, and the violins trilled, and the perfumed whirl went on....And suddenly the wind veered!

Again the *Star* reeled, and shuddered, and turned, and began to drag all her anchors. But she now dragged away from the great building and its lights—away from the voluptuous thunder of the grand piano—even at that moment outpouring the great joy of Weber's melody orchestrated by Berlioz: "*L'Invitation à la Valse*" —with its marvelous musical swing!

"Waltzing!" cried the captain. "God help them!—God help us all now!...*The Wind waltzes tonight, with the Sea for his partner!*"...

O the stupendous Valse-Tourbillon! O the mighty Dancer! One— two—three! From northeast to east, from east to southeast, from southeast to south: then from the south he came, whirling the Sea in his arms...

...Some one shrieked in the midst of the revels;—some girl who found her pretty slippers wet. What could it be? Thin streams of water were spreading over the level planking—curling about the feet of the dancers....What could it be? All the land had begun to quake, even as, but a moment before, the polished floor was trembling to the pressure of circling steps;—all the building shook now; every beam uttered its groan. What could it be?...

There was a clamor, a panic, a rush to the windy night. Infinite darkness above and beyond; but the lantern-beams danced far out over an unbroken circle of heaving and swirling black water. Stealthily, swiftly, the measureless sea-flood was rising.

"*Monsieurs—mesdames, ce n'est rien.* Nothing serious, ladies, I assure you....*Mais nous en avons vu bien souvent, les inondations comme celle-ci; ça passe vite!* The water will go down in a few hours, ladies;—it never rises higher than this; *il n'y a pas le moindre danger, je vous dis! Allons! il n'y a*—My God! what is that?"...

For a moment there was a ghastly hush of voices. And through that hush there burst upon the ears of all a fearful and unfamiliar sound, as of a colossal cannonade—rolling up from the south, with volleying lightnings. Vastly and swiftly, nearer and nearer it came—a ponderous and unbroken thunder roll, terrible as the long muttering of an earthquake.

The nearest mainland—across mad Caillou Bay to the sea-marshes—lay twelve miles north; west, by the Gulf, the nearest solid ground was twenty miles distant. There were boats, yes!—but the stoutest swimmer might never reach them now!...

Then rose a frightful cry—the hoarse, hideous, indescribable cry of hopeless fear—the despairing animal-cry man utters when suddenly brought face to face with Nothingness, without preparation, without consolation, without possibility of respite.... *Sauve qui peut!* Some wrenched down the doors; some clung to the heavy banquet-tables, to the sofas, to the billiard-tables:—during one terrible instant—against fruitless heroisms, against futile generosities—raged all the frenzy of selfishness, all the brutalities of panic. And then—then came, thundering through the blackness, the giant swells, boom on boom!... One crash!—the huge frame building rocks like a cradle, seesaws, crackles. What are human shrieks now?—the tornado is shrieking! Another!—chandeliers splinter; lights are dashed out; a sweeping cataract hurls in: the immense hall rises—oscillates—twirls as upon a pivot—crepitates—crumbles into ruin. Crash again!—the swirling wreck dissolves into the wallowing of another monster billow; and a hundred cottages overturn, spin in sudden eddies; quiver, disjoint and melt into the seething.

...So the hurricane passed—tearing off the heads of the prodigious waves, to hurl them a hundred feet in air—heaping up the ocean against the land—upturning the woods. Bays and passes were swollen to abysses; rivers regorged; the sea-marshes were changed to raging wastes of water. Before New Orleans the flood of the mile-broad Mississippi rose six feet above highest watermark. One hundred and ten miles away, Donaldsonville trembled at the towering tide of the Lafourche. Lakes strove to burst their boundaries. Far-off river steamers tugged wildly at their cables—shivering like tethered creatures that hear by night the approaching howl of destroyers. Smokestacks were hurled overboard, pilot-houses torn away, cabins blown to fragments.

And over roaring Kaimbuck Pass—over the agony of Caillou Bay—the billowing tide rushed unresisted from the Gulf—tearing and swallowing the land in its course—ploughing out deep-sea channels where sleek herds had been grazing but a few hours before—rending islands in twain—and ever bearing with it, through the night, enormous vortex of wreck and vast wan drift of corpses....

* * *

But the *Star* remained. And Captain Abraham Smith, with a long, good rope about his waist, dashed again and again into that awful surging to snatch victims from death—clutching at passing hands, heads, garments, in the cataract-sweep of the seas—saving, aiding, cheering, though blinded by spray and battered by drifting wreck, until his strength failed in the unequal struggle at last, and his men drew him aboard senseless, with some beautiful half-drowned girl safe in his arms. But well-nigh twoscore souls had been rescued by him; and the *Star* stayed on through it all.

Long years after, the weed-grown ribs of her graceful skeleton could still be seen curving up from the sand-dunes of Last Island, in valiant witness of how well she stayed.

VII

Day breaks through the flying wrack, over the infinite heaving of the sea, over the low land made vast with desolation. It is a spectral dawn: a wan light, like the light of a dying sun.

The wind has waned and veered; the flood sinks slowly back to its abysses—abandoning its plunder—scattering its piteous waifs over bar and dune, over shoal and marsh, among the silences of the mango-swamps, over the long low reaches of sand-grasses and drowned weeds, for more than a hundred miles. From the shell-reefs of Pointe-au-Fer to the shallows of Pelto Bay the dead lie mingled with the high-heaped drift;—from their cypress groves the vultures rise to dispute a share of the feast with the shrieking frigate-birds and squeaking gulls. And as the tremendous tide withdraws its plunging waters, all the pirates of air follow the great white-gleaming retreat: a storm of billowing wings and screaming throats.

And swift in the wake of gull and frigate-bird the Wreckers come, the Spoilers of the dead—savage skimmers of the sea—hurricane-riders wont to spread their canvas-pinions in the face of storms; Sicilian and Corsican outlaws, Manila-men from the marshes, deserters from many navies, Lascars, marooners, refugees of a hundred nationalities—fishers and shrimpers by name, smugglers by opportunity—wild channel-finders from obscure bayous and unfamiliar chénières, all skilled in the mysteries of these mysterious waters beyond the comprehension of the oldest licensed pilot....

There is plunder for all—birds and men. There are drowned sheep in multitude, heaped carcasses of kine. There are casks of claret and kegs of brandy and legions of bottles bobbing in the surf. There are billiard-tables overturned upon the sand;—there are sofas, pianos, footstools and music-stools, luxurious chairs, lounges of bamboo. There are chests of cedar, and toilet-tables of rosewood, and trunks of fine stamped leather stored with precious apparel. There are *objets de luxe* innumerable. There are children's playthings: French dolls in marvelous toilettes, and toy carts, and wooden horses, and wooden spades, and brave little wooden ships that rode out the gale in which the great Nautilus went down. There is money in notes and in coin—in purses, in pocketbooks, and in pockets: plenty of it! There are silks, satins, laces, and fine linen to be stripped from the bodies of the drowned—and necklaces, bracelets, watches, finger-rings and fine chains, brooches and trinkets.... *"Chi bidizza!—Oh! chi bedda mughieri! Eccu, la bidizza!"* That ball-dress was made in Paris by—But you never heard of him, Sicilian Vicenzu.... *"Che bella sposina!"* Her betrothal ring will not come off, Giuseppe; but the delicate bone snaps easily: your oyster-knife can sever the tendon.... *"Guardate! chi bedda picciota!"* Over her heart you will find it, Valentino— the locket held by that fine Swiss chain of woven hair—*"Caya manan!"* And it is not your quadroon bondsmaid, sweet lady, who now disrobes you so roughly; those Malay hands are less deft than hers—but she slumbers very far away from you, and may not be aroused from her sleep. *"Na quita mo! dalaga!—na quita maganda!"* ... Juan, the fastenings of those diamond ear-drops are much too complicated for your peon fingers: tear them out!—*"Dispense, chulita!"* ...

...Suddenly a long, mighty silver trilling fills the ears of all: there is a wild hurrying and scurrying; swiftly, one after another, the overburdened luggers spread wings and flutter away.

Thrice the great cry rings rippling through the gray air, and over the green sea, and over the far-flooded shell-reefs, where the huge white flashes are—sheet-lightning of breakers—and over the weird wash of corpses coming in.

It is the steam-call of the relief-boat, hastening to rescue the living, to gather in the dead.

The tremendous tragedy is over!

PART II

Out of the Sea's Strength

I

There are regions of Louisiana coast whose aspect seems not of the present, but of the immemorial past—of that epoch when low flat reaches of primordial continent first rose into form above a Silurian Sea. To indulge this geologic dream, any fervid and breezeless day there, it is only necessary to ignore the evolutional protests of a few blue asters or a few composite flowers of the coryopsis sort, which contrive to display their rare flashes of color through the general waving of cat-heads, blood-weeds, wild cane, and marsh grasses. For, at a hasty glance, the general appearance of this marsh verdure is vague enough, as it ranges away towards the sand, to convey the idea of amphibious vegetation—a primitive flora as yet undecided whether to retain marine habits and forms, or to assume terrestrial ones;—and the occasional inspection of surprising shapes might strengthen this fancy. Queer flat-lying and many-branching things, which resemble sea-weeds in juiciness and color and consistency, crackle under your feet from time to time; the moist and weighty air seems heated rather from below than from above—less by the sun than by the radiation of a cooling world; and the mists of morning or evening appear to simulate the vapory exhalation of volcanic forces—latent, but only dozing, and uncomfortably close to the surface. And indeed geologists have actually averred that those rare elevations of the soil—which, with their heavy coronets of evergreen foliage, not only look like islands, but are so called in the French nomenclature of the coast—have been prominences created by ancient mud volcanoes.

The family of a Spanish fisherman, Feliu Viosca, once occupied and gave its name to such an islet, quite close to the Gulf-shore—the loftiest bit of land along fourteen miles of just such marshy coast as I have spoken of. Landward, it dominated a desolation that wearied the eye to look at, a wilderness of reedy sloughs, patched at intervals with ranges of bitterweed, tufts of elbow-bushes, and broad reaches of saw-grass, stretching away to a bluish-green line of woods that closed the horizon, and imperfectly drained in the driest season by a slimy little bayou that continually vomited foul water into the sea. The point had been much discussed by geologists; it proved a godsend to United States surveyors weary of attempting to take observations among quag-mires, moccasins, and arborescent weeds from fifteen to twenty feet high. Savage fishermen, at some unrecorded time, had heaped upon the eminence a hill of clam-shells—refuse of a million feasts; earth again had been formed over these, perhaps by the blind agency of worms working through centuries unnumbered; and the new soil had given birth to a luxuriant vegetation. Millennial oaks interknotted their roots below its surface, and vouchsafed protection to many a frailer growth of shrub or tree—wild orange, water-willow, palmetto, locust, pomegranate, and many trailing tendrilled things, both green and gray. Then—perhaps about half a century ago—a few white fishermen cleared a place for them-selves in this grove, and built a few palmetto cottages, with boat-houses and a wharf, facing the bayou. Later on this tempo-rary fishing station became a permanent settlement: homes constructed of heavy timber and plaster mixed with the trailing moss of the oaks and cypresses took the places of the frail and fragrant huts of palmetto. Still the population itself retained a floating character: it ebbed and came, according to season and circumstances, according to luck or loss in the tilling of the sea. Viosca, the founder of the settlement, always remained; he always managed to do well. He owned several luggers and sloops, which were hired out upon excellent terms; he could make large and profitable contracts with New Orleans fish-dealers; and he was vaguely suspected of possessing more occult resources. There were some confused stories current about his having once been a daring smuggler, and having only been reformed by the pleadings of his wife Carmen—a little brown woman who had followed him from Barcelona to share his fortunes in the western world.

On hot days, when the shade was full of thin sweet scents, the place had a tropical charm, a drowsy peace. Nothing except the peculiar appearance of the line of oaks facing the Gulf could have conveyed to the visitor any suggestion of days in which the trilling of crickets and the fluting of birds had ceased, of nights when the voices of the marsh had been hushed for fear. In one enormous rank the veteran trees stood shoulder to shoulder, but in the attitude of giants overmastered—forced backward toward the marsh—made to recoil by the might of the ghostly enemy with whom they had striven a thousand years—the Shrieker, the Sky-Sweeper, the awful Sea-Wind!

Never had he given them so terrible a wrestle as on the night of the tenth of August, eighteen hundred and fifty-six. All the waves of the excited Gulf thronged in as if to see, and lifted up their voices, and pushed, and roared, until the chénière was islanded by such a billowing as no white man's eyes had ever looked upon before. Grandly the oaks bore themselves, but every fibre of their knotted thews was strained in the unequal contest and two of the giants were overthrown, upturning, as they fell, roots coiled and huge as the serpent-limbs of Titans. Moved to its entrails, all the islet trembled, while the sea magnified its menace, and reached out whitely to the prostrate trees; but the rest of the oaks stood on, and strove in line, and saved the habitations defended by them....

II

Before a little waxen image of the mother and child—an odd little Virgin with an Indian face, brought home by Feliu as a gift after one of his Mexican voyages—Carmen Viosca had burned candles and prayed; sometimes telling her beads; sometimes murmuring the litanies she knew by heart; sometimes also reading from a prayer-book worn and greasy as a long-used pack of cards. It was particularly stained at one page, a page on which her tears had fallen many a lonely night—a page with a clumsy wood-cut representing a celestial lamp, a symbolic radiance, shining through darkness, and on either side a kneeling angel with folded wings. And beneath this rudely wrought symbol of the Perpetual Calm appeared in big, coarse type the title of a prayer that has been offered up through many a century, doubtless, by wives of Spanish mariners—"*Contra las Tempestades.*"

Once she became very much frightened. After a partial lull the storm had suddenly redoubled its force: the ground shook; the house quivered and creaked; the wind brayed and screamed and pushed and scuffled at the door; and the water, which had been whipping in through every crevice, all at once rose over the threshold and flooded the dwelling. Carmen dipped her finger in the water and tasted it. It was salt!

And none of Feliu's boats had yet come in;—doubtless they had been driven into some far-away bayous by the storm. The only boat at the settlement, the *Carmencita,* had been almost wrecked by running upon a snag three days before;—there was at least a fortnight's work for the ship-carpenter of Dead Cypress Point. And Feliu was sleeping as if nothing unusual had happened—the heavy sleep of a sailor, heedless of commotions and voices. And his men, Miguel and Mateo, were at the other end of the chénière.

With a scream Carmen aroused Feliu. He raised himself upon his elbow, rubbed his eyes, and asked her, with exasperating calmness, "*Que tienes? que tienes?*" (What ails thee?)

"Oh, Feliu! the sea is coming upon us!" she answered, in the same tongue. But she screamed out a word inspired by her fear: she did not cry, "*Se nos viene el mar encima!*" but "*Se nos viene La Altura!*"—the name that conveys the terrible thought of depth swallowed up in height—the height of the *high sea.*

"*No lo creo!*" muttered Feliu, looking at the floor; then in a quiet, deep voice he said, pointing to an oar in the corner of the room, "*Echame ese remo.*"

She gave it to him. Still reclining upon one elbow, Feliu measured the depth of the water with his thumb-nail upon the blade of the oar, and then bade Carmen light his pipe for him. His calmness reassured her. For half an hour more, undismayed by the clamoring of the wind or the calling of the sea, Feliu silently smoked his pipe and watched his oar. The water rose a little higher, and he made another mark;—then it climbed a little more, but not so rapidly; and he smiled at Carmen as he made a third mark. "*Como creia!*" he exclaimed, "*no hay porque asustarse: el agua baja!*" And as Carmen would have continued to pray, he rebuked her fears, and bade her try to obtain some rest: "*Basta ya de plegarias, querida!—vete y duerme.*" His tone, though kindly, was imperative; and Carmen, accustomed to obey him, laid herself down by his side, and soon, for very weariness, slept.

It was a feverish sleep, nevertheless, shattered at brief intervals by terrible sounds—sounds magnified by her nervous condition—a sleep visited by dreams that mingled in a strange way with the impressions of the storm, and more than once made her heart stop, and start again at its own stopping. One of these fancies she never could forget—a dream about little Concha—Conchita, her first-born, who now slept far away in the old churchyard at Barcelona. She had tried to become resigned—not to think. But the child would come back night after night, though the earth lay heavy upon her—night after night, through long distances of Time and Space. Oh! the fancied clinging of infant-lips!—the thrilling touch of little ghostly hands!—those phantom-caresses that torture mothers' hearts!...Night after night, through many a month of pain. Then for a time the gentle presence ceased to haunt her—seemed to have lain down to sleep forever under the high bright grass and yellow flowers. Why did it return, that night of all nights, to kiss her, to cling to her, to nestle in her arms?...

For in her dream she thought herself still kneeling before the waxen Image, while the terrors of the tempest were ever deepening about her—raving of winds and booming of waters and a shaking of the land. And before her, even as she prayed her dream-prayer, the waxen Virgin became tall as a woman, and taller—rising to the roof and smiling as she grew. Then Carmen would have cried out for fear, but that something smothered her voice—paralyzed her tongue. And the Virgin silently stooped above her, and placed in her arms the Child—the brown Child with the Indian face. And the Child whitened in her hands and changed—seeming as it changed to send a sharp pain through her heart: an old pain linked somehow with memories of bright windy Spanish hills, and summer-scent of olive groves, and all the luminous Past;—it looked into her face with the soft dark gaze, with the unforgotten smile of...dead Conchita!

And Carmen wished to thank the smiling Virgin for that priceless bliss, and lifted up her eyes; but the sickness of ghostly fear returned upon her when she looked; for now the Mother seemed as a woman long dead, and the smile was the smile of fleshlessness, and the places of the eyes were voids and dark-nesses....And the sea sent up so vast a roar that the dwelling rocked.

Carmen started from sleep to find her heart throbbing so that the couch shook with it. Night was growing gray; the door had just been opened and slammed again. Through the rain-whipped panes she discerned the passing shape of Feliu, making for the beach—a broad and bearded silhouette, bending against the wind. Still the waxed Virgin smiled her Mexican smile—but now she was only seven inches high; and her bead-glass eyes seemed to twinkle with kindliness while the flame of the last expiring taper struggled for life in the earthen socket at her feet.

III

Rain and a blind sky and a bursting sea. Feliu and his men, Miguel and Mateo, looked out upon the thundering and flashing of the monstrous tide. The wind had fallen, and the gray air was full of gulls. Behind the chénière, back to the cloudy line of low woods many miles away, stretched a wash of lead-colored water, with a green point piercing it here and there—elbow-bushes or wild cane tall enough to keep their heads above the flood. But the inundation was visibly decreasing;—with the passing of each hour more and more green patches and points had been showing themselves: by degrees the course of the bayou had become defined—two parallel winding lines of dwarf-timber and bushy shrubs traversing the water toward the distant cypress-swamps. Before the chénière all the shell-beach slope was piled with wreck—uptorn trees with the foliage still fresh upon them, splintered timbers of mysterious origin, and logs in multitude, scarred with gashes of the axe. Feliu and his comrades had saved wood enough to build a little town—working up to their waists in the surf, with ropes, poles, and boat-hooks. The whole sea was full of flotsam. *Voto a Cristo!*—what a wrecking there must have been! And to think the *Carmencita* could not be taken out!

They had seen other luggers making eastward during the morning—could recognize some by their sails, others by their gait—exaggerated in their struggle with the pitching of the sea: the *San Pablo*, the *Gasparina*, the *Enriqueta*, the *Agueda*, the *Constanza*. Ugly water, yes!—but what a chance for wreckers!...Some great ship must have gone to pieces;—scores of casks were rolling in the trough—casks of wine. Perhaps it was the *Manila*—perhaps the *Nautilus!*

A dead cow floated near enough for Mateo to throw his rope over one horn; and they all helped to get it out. It was a milch cow of some expensive breed; and the owner's brand had been burned upon the horns:—a monographic combination of the letters "A" and "P." Feliu said he knew that brand: Old-man Preaulx, of Belle-Isle, who kept a sort of dairy at Last Island during the summer season, used to mark all his cows that way. Strange!

But, as they worked on, they began to see stranger things—white dead faces and dead hands, which did not look like the hands or the faces of drowned sailors: the ebb was beginning to run strongly, and these were passing out with it on the other side of the mouth of the bayou;—perhaps they had been washed into the marsh during the night, when the great rush of the sea came. Then the three men left the water, and retired to higher ground to scan the furrowed Gulf;—their practiced eyes began to search the courses of the sea-currents—keen as the gaze of birds that watch the wake of the plough. And soon the casks and the drift were forgotten; for it seemed to them that the tide was heavy with human dead—passing out, processionally, to the great open. Very far, where the huge pitching of the swells was diminished by distance into a mere fluttering of ripples, the water appeared as if sprinkled with them;—they vanished and became visible again at irregular intervals, here and there—floating most thickly eastward—tossing, swaying patches of white or pink or blue or black, each with its tiny speck of flesh-color showing as the sea lifted or lowered the body. Nearer to shore there were few; but of these two were close enough to be almost recognizable: Miguel first discerned them. They were rising and falling where the water was deepest—well out in front of the mouth of the bayou, beyond the flooded sand-bars, and moving toward the shell-reef westward. They were drifting almost side by side. One was that of a Negro, apparently well attired, and wearing a white apron;—the other seemed to be a young colored girl, clad in a blue dress; she was floating upon her face; they could observe that she had nearly straight hair, braided and tied with a red ribbon. These were evidently house-servants—slaves. But from whence? Nothing could be learned until the luggers should return; and none of them was yet in sight. Still Feliu was not anxious as to the fate of his boats, manned by the best sailors of the coast. Rarely are these Louisiana fishermen lost in sudden storms; even when to other eyes the appearances are most pacific and the skies most splendidly blue, they divine some far-off danger, like the gulls; and like the gulls also, you see their light vessels fleeing landward. These men seem living barometers, exquisitely sensitive to all the invisible changes of atmospheric expansion and compression; they are not easily caught in those awful dead calms which suddenly paralyze the wings of a bark, and hold her helpless in their charmed circle, as in a nightmare, until the blackness overtakes her, and the long-sleeping sea leaps up foaming to devour her.

"*Carajo!*"

The word all at once bursts from Feliu's mouth, with that

peculiar guttural snarl of the "r" betokening strong excitement—
while he points to something rocking in the ebb, beyond the
foaming of the shell-reef, under a circling of gulls. More dead?
Yes—but something too that lives and moves, like a quivering
speck of gold; and Mateo also perceives it, a gleam of bright
hair—and Miguel likewise, after a moment's gazing. A living
child;—a lifeless mother. *Pobrecita!* No boat within reach, and only
a mighty surf-wrestler could hope to swim thither and return!

But already, without a word, brown Feliu has stripped for the
struggle;—another second, and he is shooting through the surf,
head and hands tunnelling the foam-hills.... One—two—three
lines passed!—four!—that is where they first begin to crumble
white from the summit—five!—that he can ride fearlessly!... Then
swiftly, easily, he advances, with a long, powerful breast-stroke—
keeping his bearded head well up to watch for drift—seeming to
slide with a swing from swell to swell—ascending, sinking—alternately
presenting breast or shoulder to the wave; always diminishing
more and more to the eyes of Mateo and Miguel—till he becomes
a moving speck, occasionally hard to follow through the confusion
of heaping waters.... You are not afraid of the sharks, Feliu!—no:
they are afraid of you; right and left they slunk away from your
coming that morning you swam for life in West-Indian waters, with
your knife in your teeth, while the balls of the Cuban coast-guard
were purring all around you. That day the swarming sea was
warm—warm like soup—and clear, with an emerald flash in every
ripple—not opaque and clamorous like the Gulf to-day.... Miguel
and his comrade are anxious. Ropes are unrolled and interknotted
into a line. Miguel remains on the beach; but Mateo, bearing the end
of the line, fights his way out—swimming and wading by turns, to
the farther sand-bar, where the water is shallow enough to stand
in—if you know how to jump when the breaker comes.

But Feliu, nearing the flooded shell-bank, watches the white
flashings—knows when the time comes to keep flat and take a
long, long breath. One heavy volleying of foam—darkness and
hissing as of a steam-burst; a vibrant lifting up; a rush into
light—and again the volleying and the seething darkness. Once
more—and the fight is won! He feels the upcoming chill of
deeper water—sees before him the green quaking of unbroken
swells—and far beyond him Mateo leaping on the bar—and beside
him, almost within arm's-reach, a great billiard-table swaying, and
a dead woman clinging there, and ... the child.

A moment more, and Feliu has lifted himself beside the waifs.... How fast the dead woman clings, as if with the one power which is strong as death—the desperate force of love! Not in vain; for the frail creature bound to the mother's corpse with a silken scarf has still the strength to cry out: *"Maman! maman!"* But time is life now; and the tiny hands must be pulled away from the fair dead neck, and the scarf taken to bind the infant firmly to Feliu's broad shoulders—quickly, roughly; for the ebb will not wait....

And now Feliu has a burden; but his style of swimming has totally changed;—he rises from the water like a Triton, and his powerful arms seem to spin in circles, like the spokes of a flying wheel. For now is the wrestle indeed!—after each passing swell comes a prodigious pulling from beneath—the sea clutching for its prey. But the reef is gained, is passed;—the wild horses of the deep seem to know the swimmer who has learned to ride them so well. And still the brown arms spin in an ever-nearing mist of spray; and the outer sand-bar is not far off—and there is shouting Mateo, leaping in the surf, swinging something about his head, as a vaquero swings his noose!... Sough! splash!—it struggles in the trough beside Feliu, and the sinewy hand descends upon it. *Tiene!—tíra, Miguel!* And their feet touch land again!...

She is very cold, the child, and very still, with eyes closed.

"Esta muerta, Feliu?" asks Mateo.

"No!" the panting swimmer makes answer, emerging, while the waves reach whitely up the sand as in pursuit—*"no; vive!—respira todavía!"*

Behind him the deep lifts up its million hands, and thunders as in acclaim.

IV

"Madre de Dios!—mi sueño!" screamed Carmen, abandoning her preparations for the morning meal, as Feliu, nude, like a marine god, rushed in and held out to her a dripping and gasping baby-girl—"Mother of God! my dream!" But there was no time then to tell of dreams; the child might die. In one instant Carmen's quick, deft hands had stripped the slender little body; and while Mateo and Feliu were finding dry clothing and stimulants, and Miguel telling how it all happened—quickly, passionately, with furious gesture—the kind and vigorous woman exerted all her skill to revive the flickering life. Soon Feliu came to aid her,

while his men set to work completing the interrupted preparation of the breakfast. Flannels were heated for the friction of the frail limbs; and brandy-and-water warmed, which Carmen administered by the spoonful, skillfully as any physician—until, at last, the little creature opened her eyes and began to sob. Sobbing still, she was laid in Carmen's warm feather-bed, well swathed in woollen wrappings. The immediate danger, at least, was over; and Feliu smiled with pride and pleasure.

Then Carmen first ventured to relate her dream; and his face became grave again. Husband and wife gazed a moment into each other's eyes, feeling together the same strange thrill—that mysterious faint creeping, as of a wind passing, which is the awe of the Unknowable. Then they looked at the child, lying there, pink-cheeked with the flush of the blood returning; and such a sudden tenderness touched them as they had known long years before, while together bending above the slumbering loveliness of lost Conchita.

"*Que ojos!*" murmured Feliu, as he turned away—feigning hunger.... (He was not hungry; but his sight had grown a little dim, as with a mist.) *Que ojos!* They were singular eyes, large, dark, and wonderfully fringed. The child's hair was yellow—it was the flash of it that had saved her; yet her eyes and brows were beautifully black. She was comely, but with such a curious, delicate comeliness—totally unlike the robust beauty of Concha.... At intervals she would moan a little between her sobs; and at last cried out, with a thin, shrill cry: "*Maman!—oh! maman!*" Then Carmen lifted her from the bed to her lap, and caressed her, and rocked her gently to and fro, as she had done many a night for Concha—murmuring—"*Yo seré tu madre, angel mio, dulzura mia; —seré tu madrecita, palomita mia!*" (I will be thy mother, my angel, my sweet;—I will be thy little mother, my doveling.) And the long silk fringes of the child's eyes overlapped, shadowed her little cheeks; and she slept—just as Conchita had slept long ago—with her head on Carmen's bosom.

Feliu re-appeared at the inner door: at a sign, he approached cautiously, without noise, and looked.

"She can talk," whispered Carmen in Spanish: "she called her mother"—*ha llamado a su madre.*

"*Y Dios tambien la ha llamado,*" responded Feliu, with rude pathos;—"*And God also called her.*"

"But the Virgin sent us the child, Feliu—sent us the child for Concha's sake."

He did not answer at once; he seemed to be thinking very deeply;—Carmen anxiously scanned his impassive face.

"Who knows?" he answered, at last;—"who knows? Perhaps she has ceased to belong to anyone else." ...

One after another, Feliu's luggers fluttered in—bearing with them news of the immense calamity. And all the fishermen, in turn, looked at the child. Not one had ever seen her before.

V

Ten days later, a lugger full of armed men entered the bayou, and moored at Viosca's wharf. The visitors were, for the most part, country gentlemen—residents of Franklin and neighboring towns, or planters from the Têche country—forming one of the numerous expeditions organized for the purpose of finding the bodies of relatives or friends lost in the great hurricane, and of punishing the robbers of the dead. They had searched number-less nooks of the coast, had given sepulture to many corpses, had recovered a large amount of jewelry, and—as Feliu afterward learned—had summarily tried and executed several of the most abandoned class of wreckers found with ill-gotten valuables in their possession, and convicted of having mutilated the drowned. But they came to Viosca's landing only to obtain information;—he was too well known and liked to be a subject for suspicion; and, moreover, he had one good friend in the crowd—Captain Harris of New Orleans, a veteran steamboat man and a market-contractor, to whom he had disposed of many a cargo of fresh pompano, sheep's-head, and Spanish-mackerel. ... Harris was the first to step to land;—some ten of the party followed him. Nearly all had lost some relative or friend in the great catastrophe;—the gather-ing was serious, silent—almost grim—which formed about Feliu.

Mateo, who had come to the country while a boy, spoke English better than the rest of the chéniere people;—he acted as inter-preter whenever Feliu found any difficulty in comprehending or answering questions; and he told them of the child rescued that wild morning, and of Feliu's swim. His recital evoked a murmur of interest and excitement, followed by a confusion of questions. Well, they could see for themselves, Feliu said; but he hoped they would have a little patience;—the child was still weak;—it might be dangerous to startle her. "We'll arrange it just as you like," responded the captain;—"go ahead, Feliu!" . . .

All proceeded to the house, under the great trees; Feliu and Captain Harris leading the way. It was sultry and bright;—even the sea-breeze was warm; there were pleasant odors in the shade, and a soporific murmur made of leaf-speech and the hum of gnats. Only the captain entered the house with Feliu; the rest remained without—some taking seats on a rude plank bench under the oaks—others flinging themselves down upon the weeds—a few stood still, leaning upon their rifles. Then Carmen came out to them with gourds and a bucket of fresh water, which all were glad to drink.

They waited many minutes. Perhaps it was the cool peace of the place that made them all feel how hot and tired they were: conversation flagged; and the general languor finally betrayed itself in a silence so absolute that every leaf-whisper seemed to become separately audible.

It was broken at last by the guttural voice of the old captain emerging from the cottage, leading the child by the hand, and followed by Carmen and Feliu. All who had been resting rose up and looked at the child.

Standing in a lighted space, with one tiny hand enveloped by the captain's great brown fist, she looked so lovely that a general exclamation of surprise went up. Her bright hair, loose and steeped in the sun-flame, illuminated her like a halo; and her large dark eyes, gentle and melancholy as a deer's, watched the strange faces before her with shy curiosity. She wore the same dress in which Feliu had found her—a soft white fabric of muslin, with trimmings of ribbon that had once been blue; and the now discolored silken scarf, which had twice done her such brave service, was thrown over her shoulders. Carmen had washed and repaired the dress very creditably; but the tiny slim feet were bare—the brine-soaked shoes she wore that fearful night had fallen into shreds at the first attempt to remove them.

"Gentlemen," said Captain Harris—"we can find no clue to the identity of this child. There is no mark upon her clothing; and she wore nothing in the shape of jewelry—except this string of coral beads. We are nearly all Americans here; and she does not speak any English.... Does any one here know anything about her?"

Carmen felt a great sinking at her heart: was her new-found darling to be taken so soon from her? But no answer came to the captain's query. No one of the expedition had ever seen that child before. The coral beads were passed from hand to hand; the scarf was minutely scrutinized without avail. Somebody asked if the child could not talk German or Italian.

"*Italiano?* No!" said Feliu, shaking his head.... One of his luggermen, Gioachino Sparicio, who, though a Sicilian, could speak several Italian idioms besides his own, had already essayed.

"She speaks something or other," answered the captain—"but no English. I couldn't make her understand me; and Feliu, who talks nearly all the infernal languages spoken down this way, says he can't make her understand him. Suppose some of you who know French talk to her a bit.... Laroussel, why don't you try?"

The young man addressed did not at first seem to notice the captain's suggestion. He was a tall, lithe fellow, with a dark, positive face: he had never removed his black gaze from the child since the moment of her appearance. Her eyes, too, seemed to be all for him—to return his scrutiny with a sort of vague pleasure, a half-savage confidence.... Was it the first embryonic feeling of race-affinity quickening in the little brain?—some intuitive, inexplicable sense of kindred? She shrank from Dr. Hecker, who addressed her in German, shook her head at Lawyer Solari, who tried to make her answer in Italian; and her look always went back plaintively to the dark, sinister face of Laroussel—Laroussel who had calmly taken a human life, a wicked human life, only the evening before.

"Laroussel, you're the only Creole in this crowd," said the captain: "talk to her! Talk gumbo to her!... I've no doubt this child knows German very well, and Italian too"—he added, maliciously—"but not in the way you gentlemen pronounce it!"

Laroussel handed his rifle to a friend, crouched down before the little girl, and looked into her face, and smiled. Her great sweet orbs shone into his one moment, seriously, as if searching; and then... she returned his smile. It seemed to touch something latent within the man, something rare; for his whole expression changed; and there was a caress in his look and voice none of the men could have believed possible—as he exclaimed:

"*Fais moin bo, piti.*"

She pouted up her pretty lips and kissed his black moustache. He spoke to her again:

"*Dis moin to nom, piti;—dis moin to nom, chère.*"

Then, for the first time, she spoke, answering in her argent treble: "*Zouzoune.*"

All held their breath. Captain Harris lifted his finger to his lips to command silence.

"*Zouzoune? Zouzoune qui, chère?*"

"*Zouzoune, ça c'est moin, Lili!*"

"*C'est pas tout to nom, Lili;—dis moin, chère, to laut nom.*"

"*Mo pas connin laut nom.*"

"*Commente yé té pélé to maman, piti?*"

"*Maman—maman 'Dèle.*"

"*Et comment yé té pélé to papa, chère?*"

"*Papa Zulien.*"

"*Bon! Et comment to maman té pélé to papa?—dis ça à moin, chère?*"

The child looked down, put a finger in her mouth, thought a moment, and replied:

"*Li pélé li, 'Chéri'; li pélé li, 'Papoute'.*"

"*Aïe, aïe!—c'est tout, ça?—to maman té jamain pélé li daut' chose?*"

"*Mo pas connin, moin.*"

She began to play with some trinkets attached to his watch chain;—a very small gold compass especially impressed her fancy by the trembling and flashing of its tiny needle, and she murmured, coaxingly:

"*Mo oulé ça! Donnin ça à moin.*"

He took all possible advantage of the situation, and replied at once:

"*Oui! mo va donnin toi ça si to di moin to laut nom.*"

The splendid bribe evidently impressed her greatly; for tears rose to the brown eyes as she answered:

"*Mo pas capab di' ca;—mo pas capab di' laut nom. . . . Mo oulé; mo pas capab!*"

Laroussel explained. The child's name was Lili—perhaps a contraction of Eulalie; and her pet Creole name Zouzoune. He thought she must be the daughter of wealthy people; but she could not, for some reason or other, tell her family name. Perhaps she could not pronounce it well, and was afraid of being laughed at: some of the old French names were very hard for Creole children to pronounce, so long as the little ones were indulged in the habit of talking the patois; and after a certain age their mispronunciations would be made fun of in order to accustom them to abandon the idiom of the slave-nurses, and to speak only

French. Perhaps, again, she was really unable to recall the name: certain memories might have been blurred in the delicate brain by the shock of that terrible night. She said her mother's name was Adèle, and her father's Julien; but these were very common names in Louisiana—and could afford scarcely any better clue than the innocent statement that her mother used to address her father as "dear" (*Chéri*)—or with Creole diminutive "little papa" (*Papoute*). Then Laroussel tried to reach a clue in other ways, without success. He asked her about where she lived—what the place was like; and she told him about fig-trees in a court, and galleries, and *banquettes,* and spoke of a *faubou'*—without being able to name any street. He asked her what her father used to do, and was assured that he did everything—that there was nothing he could not do. Divine absurdity of childish faith!—infinite artlessness of childish love!... Probably the little girls's parents had been residents of New Orleans—dwellers of the old colonial quarter—the *faubourg,* the *faubou'.*

"Well, gentlemen," said Captain Harris, as Laroussel abandoned his cross-examination in despair—"all we can do now is to make inquiries. I suppose we'd better leave the child here. She is very weak yet, and in no condition to be taken to the city, right in the middle of the hot season; and nobody could care for her any better than she's being cared for here. Then, again, seems to me that as Feliu saved her life—and that at the risk of his own—he's got the prior claim, anyhow; and his wife is just crazy about the child—wants to adopt her. If we can find her relatives so much the better; but I say, gentlemen, let them come right here to Feliu, themselves, and thank him as he ought to be thanked, by God! That's just what I think about it."

Carmen understood the little speech;—all the Spanish charm of her youth had faded out years before; but in the one swift look of gratitude she turned upon the captain, it seemed to blossom again;—for that quick moment, she was beautiful.

"The captain is quite right," observed Dr. Hecker: "it would be very dangerous to take the child away just now." There was no dissent.

"All correct, boys?" asked the captain.... "Well, we've got to be going. By-by, Zouzoune!"

But Zouzoune burst into tears. Laroussel was going too!

"Give her the thing, Laroussel! she gave you a kiss, anyhow—more than she'd do for me," cried the captain.

Laroussel turned, detached the little compass from his watch chain, and gave it to her. She held up her pretty face for his farewell kiss....

VI

But it seemed fated that Feliu's waif should never be identified; —diligent inquiry and printed announcements alike proved fruitless. Sea and sand had either hidden or effaced all the records of the little world they had engulfed: the annihilation of whole families, the extinction of races, had, in more than one instance, rendered vain all efforts to recognize the dead. It required the subtle perception of long intimacy to name remains tumefied and discolored by corruption and exposure, mangled and gnawed by fishes, by reptiles, and by birds;—it demanded the great courage of love to look upon the eyeless faces found sweltering in the blackness of cypress shadows, under the low palmettoes of the swamps—where gorged buzzards started from sleep, or cotton-mouths uncoiled, hissing, at the coming of the searchers. And sometimes all who had loved the lost were themselves among the missing. The full roll-call of names could never be made out; —extraordinary mistakes were committed. Men whom the world deemed dead and buried came back, like ghosts—to read their own epitaphs.

...Almost at the same hour that Laroussel was questioning the child in Creole patois, another expedition, searching for bodies along the coast, discovered on the beach of a low islet famed as a haunt of pelicans, the corpse of a child. Some locks of bright hair still adhering to the skull, a string of red beads, a white muslin dress, a handkerchief broidered with the initials "A. L. B."—were secured as clues; and the little body was interred where it had been found.

And, several days before, Captain Hotard, of the relief-boat *Estelle Brousseaux*, had found, drifting in the open Gulf (latitude 26° 43'; longitude 88° 17')—the corpse of a fair-haired woman, clinging to a table. The body was disfigured beyond recognition: even the slender bones of the hands had been stripped by the nibs of the sea-birds—except one finger, the third of the left, which seemed to have been protected by a ring of gold, as by a charm. Graven within the plain yellow circlet was a date—"JUILLET—1851"; and the names—"ADÈLE + JULIEN"—separated by a cross. The

Estelle carried coffins that day; most of them were already full; but there was one for Adèle.

Who was she?—who was her Julien?...When the *Estelle* and many other vessels had discharged their ghastly cargoes;—when the bereaved of the land had assembled as hastily as they might for the duty of identification;—when memories were strained almost to madness in research of names, dates, incidents—for the evocation of dead words, resurrection of vanished days, recollection of dear promises—then, in the confusion, it was believed and declared that the little corpse found on the pelican island was the daughter of the wearer of the wedding-ring: Adèle La Brierre, née Florane, wife of Dr. Julien La Brierre, of New Orleans, who was numbered among the missing.

And they brought dead Adèle back—up shadowy river windings, over linked brightnesses of lake and lakelet, through many a green-glimmering bayou—to the Creole city, and laid her to rest somewhere in the old Saint Louis Cemetery. And upon the tablet recording her name were also graven the words:

AUSSI À LA MÉMOIRE DE

SON MARI,

JULIEN RAYMOND LA BRIERRE,

NÉ À LA PAROISSE ST. LANDRY,

LE 29 MAI, MDCCCXXVIII;

ET DE LEUR FILLE,

EULALIE,

AGÉE DE 4 ANS ET 5 MOIS—

QUI TOUS PÉRIRENT

DANS LA GRANDE TEMPÊTE QUI

BALAYÂ L'ILE DERNIÈRE, LE

10 AOÛT, MDCCCLVI

... + ...

PRIEZ POUR EUX!

VII

Yet six months afterward the face of Julien la Brierre was seen again upon the streets of New Orleans. Men stared at the sight of him, as at a spectre standing in the sun. And nevertheless the apparition cast a shadow. People paused, approached, half extended a hand through old habit, suddenly checked themselves and passed on—wondering why they should have forgotten, asking themselves why they had so nearly made an absurd mistake.

It was a February day—one of those crystalline days of our snowless Southern winter, when the air is clear and cool, and outlines sharpen in the light as if viewed through the focus of a diamond glass;—and in that brightness Julien La Brierre perused his own brief epitaph, and gazed upon the sculptured name of drowned Adèle. Only half a year had passed since she was laid away in the high wall of tombs—in that strange colonial columbarium where the dead slept in rows, behind squared marbles lettered in black or bronze. Yet her resting-place—in the highest range—already seemed old. Under our Southern sun, the vegetation of cemeteries seems to spring into being spontaneously—to leap all suddenly into luxuriant life! Microscopic mossy growths had begun to mottle the slab that closed her in;—over its face some singular creeper was crawling, planting tiny reptile-feet into the chiseled letters of the inscription; and from the moist soil below speckled euphorbias were growing up to her—and morning-glories—and beautiful green tangled things of which he did not know the name.

And the sight of the pretty lizards, puffing their crimson pouches in the sun, or undulating athwart epitaphs, and shifting their color when approached, from emerald to ashen-gray;—the caravans of the ants, journeying to and from tiny chinks in the masonry;—the bees gathering honey from the crimson blossoms of the *crête-de-coq*, whose radicles sought sustenance, perhaps from human dust, in the decay of generations:—all that rich life of graves summoned up fancies of Resurrection, Nature's resurrection-work—wondrous transformations of flesh, marvelous transmigration of souls!... From some forgotten crevice of that tomb roof, which alone intervened between her and the vast light, a sturdy weed was growing. He knew that plant, as it quivered against the blue—the *chou-gras,* as Creole children call it: its dark berries form the mocking-bird's favorite food.... Might not its roots, exploring darkness, have found some unfamiliar nutriment within?—might it not be that something of the dead heart had risen to purple and emerald life—in the sap of translucent leaves, in the wine of the savage berries—to blend with the blood of the Wizard Singer—to lend a strange sweetness to the melody of his wooing?...

...Seldom, indeed, does it happen that a man in the prime of youth, in the possession of wealth, habituated to comforts and the elegances of life, discovers in one brief week how minute his true relation to the human aggregate—how insignificant his part as one living atom of the social organism. Seldom, at the age of twenty-eight, has one been made able to comprehend, through experience alone, that in the vast and complex Stream of Being he counts for less than a drop; and that, even as the blood loses and replaces its corpuscles, without a variance in the volume and vigor of its current, so are individual existences eliminated and replaced in the pulsing of a people's life, with never a pause in its mighty murmur. But all this, and much more, Julien had learned in seven merciless days—seven successive and terrible shocks of experience. The enormous world had not missed him; and his place therein was not void—society had simply forgotten him. So long as he had moved among them, all he knew for friends had performed their petty altruistic rôles—had discharged their small human obligations—had kept turned toward him the least selfish side of their natures—had made with him a tolerably equitable exchange of ideas and of favors; and after his disappearance from their midst, they had duly mourned for his loss—to themselves! They had played out the final act in the unimportant drama of his life: it was really asking too much to demand a repetition.... Impossible to deceive himself as to the feeling his unanticipated return had aroused:—feigned pity where he had looked for sympathetic welcome; dismay where he had expected surprised delight; and, oftener, airs of resignation, or disappointment ill disguised—always insincerity, politely masked or coldly bare. He had come back to find strangers in his home, relatives at law concerning his estate, and himself regarded as an intruder among the living—an unlucky guest, a revenant.... How hollow and selfish a world it seemed! And yet there was love in it; he had been loved in it, unselfishly, passionately, with the love of father and mother, of wife and child.... All buried!—all lost forever!...Oh! would to God the story of that stone were not a lie!—would to kind God he also were dead!...

Evening shadowed: the violet deepened and prickled itself with stars;—the sun passed below the west, leaving in his wake a momentary splendor of vermilion...our Southern day is not prolonged by gloaming. And Julien's thoughts darkened with the darkening, and as swiftly. For while there was yet light to see, he read another name that he used to know—the name of RAMIREZ.... *Nació en Cienfuegos, isla de Cuba*.... Wherefore born?—for what eternal purpose, Ramirez—in the City of a Hundred Fires? He had blown out his brains before the sepulchre of his young wife.... It was a detached double vault, shaped like a huge chest, and much dilapidated already:—under the continuous burrowing of the crawfish it had sunk greatly on one side, tilting as if about to fall. Out from its zigzag fissurings of brick and plaster, a sinister voice seemed to come: *"Go thou and do likewise!...Earth groans with her burthen even now—the burthen of Man: she holds no place for thee!"*

VIII

...That voice pursued him into the darkness of his chilly room—haunted him in the silence of his lodging. And then began within the man that ghostly struggle between courage and despair, between patient reason and mad revolt, between weakness and force, between darkness and light, which all sensitive and generous natures must wage in their own souls at least once—perhaps many times—in their lives. Memory, in such moments, plays like an electric storm;—all involuntarily he found himself reviewing his life.

Incidents long forgotten came back with singular vividness: he saw the Past as he had not seen it while it was the Present;—remembrances of home, recollections of infancy, recurred to him with terrible intensity—the artless pleasures and the trifling griefs, the little hurts and the tender pettings, the hopes and the anxieties of those who loved him, the smiles and tears of slaves.... And his first Creole pony, a present from his father the day after he had proved himself able to recite his prayers correctly in French, without one mispronunciation—without saying *crasse* for *grâce;*—and yellow Michel, who taught him to swim and to fish and to paddle a pirogue;—and the bayou, with its wonder-world of turtles and birds and creeping things;—and his German tutor, who could not pronounce the "j";—and the songs of the cane-fields—strangely pleasing, full of quaverings and long plaintive notes, like the call of the cranes.... *Tou', tou' pays blanc!*... Afterward Camanière had leased the place;—everything must have been changed; even the songs could not be the same. *Tou', tou' pays blanc!—Danié qui commandé....*

And then Paris; and the university, with its wild under-life—some debts, some follies; and the frequent fond letters from home to which he might have replied so much oftener;—Paris, where talent is mediocrity; Paris, with its thunders and its splendors and its seething of passion;—Paris, supreme focus of human endeavor, with its madnesses of art, its frenzied striving to express the Inexpressible, its spasmodic strainings to clutch the Unattainable, its soarings of soul-fire to the heaven of the Impossible....

What a rejoicing there was at his return!—how radiant and level the long Road of the Future seemed to open before him! —everywhere friends, prospects, felicitations. Then his first serious love;—and the night of the ball at Saint Martinsville—the vision of light! Gracile as a palm, and robed at once so simply, so exquisitely in white, she had seemed to him the supreme realization of all possible dreams of beauty.... And his passionate jealousy; and the slap from Laroussel; and the humiliating two-minute duel with rapiers in which he learned that he had found his master. The scar was deep. Why had not Laroussel killed him then?... Not evil-hearted, Laroussel;—they used to salute each other afterward when they met; and Laroussel's smile was kindly. Why had he refrained from returning it? Where was Laroussel now?

For the death of his generous father, who had sacrificed so much to reform him; for the death, only a short while after, of his all-forgiving mother, he had found one sweet woman to console him with her tender words, her loving lips, her delicious caress. She had given him Zouzoune, the darling link between their lives—Zouzoune, who waited each evening with black Églantine at the gate to watch for his coming, and to cry through all the house like a bird, "*Papa, lapé vini!—papa Zulien apé vini!*"... And once that she had made him very angry by upsetting the ink over a mass of business papers, and he had slapped her (could he ever forgive himself?)—she had cried, through her sobs of astonishment and pain: "*To laimin moin?—to batté moin!*" (Thou lovest me?—thou beatest me!) Next month she would have been five years old. *To laimin moin?—to batté moin!*...

A furious paroxysm of grief convulsed him, suffocated him; it seemed to him that something within must burst, must break. He flung himself down upon his bed, biting the coverings in order to stifle his outcry, to smother the sounds of his despair. What crime had he ever done, O God! that he should be made to suffer thus?—was it for this he had been permitted to live? had been rescued from the sea and carried round all the world unscathed?

Why should he live to remember, to suffer, to agonize? Was not Ramirez wiser?

How long the contest within him lasted, he never knew; but ere it was done, he had become, in more ways than one, a changed man. For the first—though not indeed for the last—time something of the deeper and nobler comprehension of human weakness and of human suffering had been revealed to him—something of that larger knowledge without which the sense of duty can never be fully acquired, nor the understanding of unselfish goodness, nor the spirit of tenderness. The suicide is not a coward; he is an egotist.

A ray of sunlight touched his wet pillow—awoke him. He rushed to the window, flung the latticed shutters apart, and looked out.

Something beautiful and ghostly filled all the vistas—frost-haze; and in some queer way the mist had momentarily caught and held the very color of the sky. An azure fog! Through it the quaint and checkered street—as yet but half illumined by the sun—took tones of impossible color; the view paled away through the faint bluish tints into transparent purples;—all the shadows were indigo. How sweet the morning!—how well life seemed worth living! Because the sun had shown his face through a fairy-veil of frost! . . .

Who was the ancient thinker?—was it Hermes? who said:

"The Sun is Laughter; for 'tis He who maketh joyous the thoughts of men, and gladdeneth the infinite world." . . .

PART III

The Shadow of the Tide

I

Carmen found that her little pet had been taught how to pray; for each night and morning when the devout woman began to make her orisons, the child would kneel beside her, with little hands joined, and in a voice sweet and clear murmur something she had learned by heart. Much as this pleased Carmen, it seemed to her that the child's prayers could not be wholly valid unless uttered in Spanish;—for Spanish was Heaven's own tongue—*la lengua de Dios, el idioma de Dios;* and she resolved to teach her to say the *Salve Maria* and the *Padre Nuestro* in Castilian—also her own favorite prayer to the Virgin, beginning with the words, "*Madre santísima, toda dulce y hermosa.*" . . .

So Conchita—for a new name had been given to her with that terrible sea-christening—received her first lessons in Spanish; and she proved a most intelligent pupil. Before long she could prattle to Feliu;—she would watch for his return of evenings, and announce his coming with "*Aqui viene mi papacito!*"—she learned, too, from Carmen, many little caresses of speech to greet him with. Feliu's was not a joyous nature; he had his dark hours, his sombre days; yet it was rarely that he felt too sullen to yield to the little one's petting, when she would leap up to reach his neck and to coax his kiss, with—"*Dame un beso, papa!—así;—y otro! otro! otro!*" He grew to love her like his own;—was she not indeed his own, since he had won her from death? And none had yet come to dispute his claim. More and more, with the passing of weeks, months, seasons, she became a portion of his life—a part of all that he wrought for. At the first, he had had a half-formed hope that the little one might be reclaimed by relatives generous and rich enough to insist upon his acceptance of a handsome compensation; and that Carmen could find some solace in a pleasant visit to Barceloneta. But now he felt that no possible generosity could requite him for her loss; and with the unconscious selfishness of affection, he commenced to dread her identification as a great calamity.

It was evident that she had been brought up nicely. She had pretty prim ways of drinking and eating, queer little fashions of sitting in company, and of addressing people. She had peculiar notions about colors in dress, about wearing her hair; and she seemed to have already imbibed a small stock of social prejudices not altogether in harmony with the republicanism of Viosca's Point. Occasional swarthy visitors—men of the Manilla settlements—she spoke of contemptuously as "*nègues-marrons*"; and once she shocked Carmen inexpressibly by stopping in the middle of her evening prayer, declaring that she wanted to say her prayers to a *white* Virgin; Carmen's Señora de Guadalupe was only a *negra!* Then, for the first time, Carmen spoke so crossly to the child as to frighten her. But the pious woman's heart smote her the next moment for that first harsh word;—and she caressed the motherless one, consoled her, cheered her, and at last explained to her—I

know not how—something very wonderful about the little figu-
rine, something that made Chita's eyes big with awe. Thereafter
she always regarded the Virgin of Wax as an object mysterious
and holy.

And, one by one, most of Chita's little eccentricities were gradually
eliminated from her developing life and thought. More rapidly
than ordinary children, because singularly intelligent, she learned
to adapt herself to all the changes of her new environment—
retaining only that indescribable something which to an experienced eye tells of hereditary refinement of habit and of mind:—a
natural grace, a thoroughbred ease and elegance of movement, a
quickness and delicacy of perception.

She became strong again and active—active enough to play a
great deal on the beach, when the sun was not too fierce; and
Carmen made a canvas bonnet to shield her head and face. Never
had she been allowed to play so much in the sun before; and it
seemed to do her good, though her little bare feet and hands
became brown as copper. At first, it must be confessed, she
worried her foster-mother a great deal by various queer misfortunes and extraordinary freaks;—getting bitten by crabs, falling
into the bayou while in pursuit of "fiddlers," or losing herself at
the conclusion of desperate efforts to run races at night with the
moon, or to walk to the "end of the world." If she could only once
get to the edge of the sky, she said, she "could climb up." She
wanted to see the stars, which were the souls of good little
children; and she knew that God would let her climb up. "Just
what I am afraid of!"—thought Carmen to herself;—"He might
let her climb up—a little ghost!" But one day naughty Chita
received a terrible lesson—a lasting lesson—which taught her the
value of obedience.

She had been particularly cautioned not to venture into a
certain part of the swamp in the rear of the grove, where the
weeds were very tall; for Carmen was afraid some snake might
bite the child. But Chita's bird-bright eye had discerned a gleam
of white in that direction; and she wanted to know what it was.
The white could only be seen from one point, behind the farthest
house, where the ground was high. "Never go there," said Carmen; "there is a Dead Man there—will bite you!" And yet, one
day, while Carmen was unusually busy, Chita went there.

In the early days of the settlement, a Spanish fisherman had
died; and his comrades had built him a little tomb with the

surplus of the same bricks and other material brought down the bayou for the construction of Viosca's cottages. But no one, except perhaps some wandering duck hunter, had approached the sepulchre for years. High weeds and grasses wrestled together all about it, and rendered it totally invisible from the surrounding level of the marsh.

Fiddlers swarmed away as Chita advanced over the moist soil, each uplifting its single huge claw as it sidled off;—the frogs began to leap before her as she reached the thicker grass;—and long-legged brown insects sprang showering to right and left as she parted the tufts of the thickening verdure. As she went on, the bitter-weeds disappeared;—jointed grasses and sinewy dark plants of a taller growth rose above her head: she was almost deafened by the storm of insect shrilling, and the mosquitoes became very wicked. All at once something long and black and heavy wriggled almost from under her naked feet—squirming so horribly that for a minute or two she could not move for fright. But it slunk away somewhere, and hid itself; the weeds it had shaken ceased to tremble in its wake; and her courage returned. She felt such an exquisite and fearful pleasure in the gratification of that naughty curiosity! Then, quite unexpectedly—oh! what a start it gave her!—the solitary white object burst upon her view, leprous and ghastly as the yawn of a cottonmouth. Tombs ruin soon in Louisiana;—the one Chita looked upon seemed ready to topple down. There was a great ragged hole at one end, where wind and rain, and perhaps also the burrowing of crawfish and of worms, had loosened the bricks, and caused them to slide out of place. It seemed very black inside; but Chita wanted to know what was there. She pushed her way through a gap in the thin and rotten line of pickets, and through some tall weeds with big coarse pink flowers;—then she crouched down on hands and knees before the black hole, and peered in. It was not so black inside as she had thought; for a sunbeam slanted down through a chink in the roof; and she could see!

A brown head—without hair, without eyes, but with teeth, ever so many teeth!—seemed to laugh at her; and close to it sat a Toad, the hugest she had ever seen; and the white skin of his throat kept puffing out and going in. And Chita screamed and screamed, and fled in wild terror—screaming all the way, till Carmen ran out to meet her and carry her home. Even when safe in her adopted mother's arms, she sobbed with fright. To the vivid fancy of the child there seemed to be some hideous relation between the staring reptile and the brown death's-head, with its empty eyes, and its nightmare-smile.

The shock brought on a fever—a fever that lasted several days, and left her very weak. But the experience taught her to obey, taught her that Carmen knew best what was for her good. It also caused her to think a great deal. Carmen had told her that the dead people never frightened good little girls who stayed at home.

"*Madrecita Carmen*," she asked, "is my mamma dead?"

"*Pobrecita!* . . . Yes, my angel. God called her to Him—your darling mother."

"*Madrecita*," she asked again—her young eyes growing vast with horror—"is my own mamma now like *That?*" . . . She pointed toward the place of the white gleam, behind the great trees.

"No, no, no! my darling!" cried Carmen, appalled herself by the ghastly question—"your mamma is with the dear, good, loving God, who lives in the beautiful sky—above the clouds, my darling, beyond the sun!"

But Carmen's kind eyes were full of tears; and the child read their meaning. He who teareth off the Mask of the Flesh had looked into her face one unutterable moment:—she had seen the brutal Truth, naked to the bone!

Yet there came to her a little thrill of consolation, caused by the words of the tender falsehood; for that which she had discerned by day could not explain to her that which she saw almost nightly in her slumber. The face, the voice, the form of her loving mother still lived somewhere—could not have utterly passed away; since the sweet presence came to her in dreams, bending and smiling over her, caressing her, speaking to her—sometimes gently chiding, but always chiding with a kiss. And then the child would laugh in her sleep, and prattle in Creole—talking to the luminous shadow, telling the dead mother all the little deeds and thoughts of the day. . . . Why would God only let her come at night?

. . . Her idea of God had been first defined by the sight of a quaint French picture of the Creation—an engraving which represented a shoreless sea under a black sky, and out of the blackness a solemn and bearded gray head emerging, and a cloudy hand through which stars glimmered. God was like old Dr. de Coulanges, who used to visit the house, and talk in a voice like a low roll of thunder. . . . At a later day, when Chita had been told that God was "everywhere at the same time"—without and within, beneath and above all things—this idea became somewhat changed. The awful bearded face, the huge shadowy hand, did not fade from her thought; but they became fantastically blended with the larger and vaguer notion of something that filled the world and reached to the stars—something diaphanous and incomprehensible like the invisible air, omnipresent and everlasting like the high blue of heaven....

II

...She began to learn the life of the coast.

With her acquisition of another tongue, there came to her also the understanding of many things relating to the world of the sea. She memorized with novel delight much that was told her day by day concerning the nature surrounding her—many secrets of the air, many of those signs of heaven which the dwellers in cities cannot comprehend because the atmosphere is thickened and made stagnant above them—cannot even watch because the horizon is hidden from their eyes by walls, and by weary avenues of trees with whitewashed trunks. She heard, by listening, by asking, by observing also, how to know the signs that foretell wild weather: —tremendous sunsets, scuddings and bridgings of cloud—sharpening and darkening of the sea-line—and the shriek of gulls flashing to land in level flight, out of a still transparent sky—and halos about the moon.

She learned where the sea-birds, with white bosoms and brown wings, made their hidden nests of sand—and where the cranes waded for their prey—and where the beautiful wild-ducks, plumaged in satiny lilac and silken green, found their food—and where the best reeds grew to furnish stems for Feliu's red-clay pipe—and where the ruddy sea-beams were most often tossed upon the shore—and how the gray pelicans fished all together, like men— moving in far-extending semi-circles, beating the flood with their wings to drive the fish before them.

And from Carmen she learned the fables and the sayings of the sea—the proverbs about its deafness, its avarice, its treachery, its terrific power—especially one that haunted her for all time thereafter: *Si quieres aprender a orar, entra en el mar* (If thou wouldst learn to pray, go to the sea). She learned why the sea is salt—how "the tears of women made the waves of the sea"—and how the sea has "no friends"—and how the cat's eyes change with the tides.

What had she lost of life by her swift translation from the dusty existence of cities to the open immensity of nature's freedom? What did she gain?

Doubtless she was saved from many of those little bitternesses and restraints and disappointments which all well-bred city children must suffer in the course of their training for the more or less factitious life of society:—obligations to remain very still with every nimble nerve quivering in dumb revolt;—the injustice of being found troublesome and being sent to bed early for the comfort of her elders;—the cruel necessity of straining her pretty eyes, for many long hours at a time, over grimy desks in gloomy school-rooms, though birds might twitter and bright winds flutter in the trees without;—the austere constraint and heavy drowsiness of warm churches, filled with the droning echoes of a voice preaching incomprehensible things;—the progressively augmenting weariness of lessons in deportment, in dancing, in music, in the impossible art of keeping her dresses unruffled and unsoiled. Perhaps she never had any reason to regret all these.

She went to sleep and awakened with the wild birds;—her life remained as unfettered by formalities as her fine feet by shoes. Excepting Carmen's old prayerbook—in which she learned to read a little—her childhood passed without books—also without pictures, without dainties, without music, without theatrical amusements. But she saw and heard and felt much of that which, though old as the heavens and the earth, is yet eternally new and eternally young with the holiness of beauty—eternally mystical and divine—eternally weird: the unveiled magnificence of Nature's moods—the perpetual poem hymned by wind and surge—the everlasting splendor of the sky.

She saw the quivering pinkness of waters curled by the breath of the morning—under the deepening of the dawn—like a far fluttering and scattering of rose-leaves of fire;—

Saw the shoreless, cloudless, marvelous double-circling azure of perfect summer days—twin glories of infinite deeps interreflected, while the Soul of the World lay still, suffused with a jewel-light, as of vaporized sapphire;—

Saw the Sea shift color—"change sheets"—when the viewless Wizard of the Wind breathed upon its face, and made it green;—

Saw the immeasurable panics—noiseless, scintillant—which silver, summer after summer, curved leagues of beach with bodies of little fish—the yearly massacre of migrating populations, na-tions of sea-trout, driven from their element by terror;—and the winnowing of shark-fins—and the rushing of porpoises—and the rising of the grande-écaille, like a pillar of flame—and the diving and pitching and fighting of the frigates and the gulls—and the armored hordes of crabs swarming out to clear the slope after the carnage and the gorging had been done;—

Saw the Dreams of the Sky—scudding mockeries of ridged foam—and shadowy stratification of capes and coasts and promontories long-drawn-out—and imageries, multicolored, of mountain frondage, and sierras whitening above sierras—and phantom islands ringed around with lagoons of glory;—

Saw the toppling and smouldering of cloud-worlds after the enormous conflagration of sunsets—incandescence ruining into darkness; and after it a moving and climbing of stars among the blacknesses—like searching lamps;—

Saw the deep kindle countless ghostly candles as for mysterious night-festival—and a luminous billowing under a black sky, and effervescences of fire, and the twirling and crawling of phosphoric foam;—

Saw the mesmerism of the Moon;—saw the enchanted tides self-heaped in muttering obeisance before her.

Often she heard the Music of the Marsh through the night: an infinity of flutings and tinklings made by tiny amphibia—like the low blowing of numberless little tin horns, the clanking of billions of little bells;—and, at intervals, profound tones, vibrant and heavy, as of a bass-viol—the orchestra of the great frogs! And interweaving with it all, one continuous shrilling—keen as the steel speech of a saw—the stridulous telegraphy of crickets.

But always—always, dreaming or awake, she heard the huge blind Sea chanting that mystic and eternal hymn, which none may hear without awe, which no musician can learn;—

Heard the hoary Preacher—*El Pregonador*—preaching the ancient Word, the word "as a fire, and as a hammer that breaketh the rock in pieces,"—the Elohim-Word of the Sea! . . .

Unknowingly she came to know the immemorial sympathy of the mind with the Soul of the World—the melancholy wrought by its moods of gray, the reverie responsive to its vagaries of mist, the exhilaration of its vast exultings—days of windy joy, hours of transfigured light.

She felt—even without knowing it—the weight of the Silences, the solemnities of sky and sea in these low regions where all things

seem to dream—waters and grasses with their momentary wavings—
woods gray-webbed with mosses that drip and drool—horizons
with their delusions of vapor—cranes meditating in their marshes
—kites floating in the high blue....Even the children were singularly
quiet; and their play less noisy—though she could not have
learned the difference—than the play of city children. Hour after
hour, the women sewed or wove in silence. And the brown
men—always barefooted, always wearing rough blue shirts—seemed,
when they lounged about the wharf on idle days, as if they had
told each other long ago all they knew or could ever know, and
had nothing more to say. They would stare at the flickering of the
current, at the drifting of clouds and buzzards—seldom looking at
each other, and always turning their black eyes again, in a weary
way, to sky or sea. Even thus one sees the horses and the cattle of
the coast, seeking the beach to escape the whizzing flies;—all
watch the long waves rolling in, and sometimes turn their heads a
moment to look at one another, but always look back to the waves
again, as if wondering at a mystery....

How often she herself had wondered—wondered at the multi-
form changes of each swell as it came in—transformations of tint,
of shape, of motion, that seemed to betoken a life infinitely more
subtle than the strange cold life of lizards and of fishes—and
sinister, and spectral. Then they all appeared to move in order—
according to one law or impulse;—each had its own voice, yet all
sang one and the same everlasting song. Vaguely, as she watched
them and listened to them, there came to her the idea of a unity
of *will* in their motion, a unity of *menace* in their utterance—the
idea of one monstrous and complex life! The sea *lived:* it could
crawl backward and forward; it could speak!—it only feigned
deafness and sightlessness for some malevolent end. Thencefor-
ward she feared to find herself alone with it. Was it not at her that
it strove to rush, muttering, and showing its white teeth...just
because it knew that she was all by herself?... *Si quieres aprender a
orar, entra en el mar!* And Concha had well learned to pray. But the
sea seemed to her the one Power which God could not make to
obey Him as He pleased. Saying the creed one day, she repeated
very slowly the opening words, *"Creo en un Dios, padre todopoderoso,
Criador del cielo y de la tierra"*—and paused and thought. *"Creator of
Heaven and Earth? "Madrecita Carmen,"* she asked—*"quien entonces
hizó el mar?"* (who then made the sea?)

"*Dios, mi querida,*" answered Carmen. "God, my darling. . . . All things were made by Him" (*todas las cosas fueron hechas por Él*).

Even the wicked Sea! And He had said unto it: "Thus far, and no farther." . . . Was that why it had not overtaken and devoured her when she ran back in fear from the sudden reaching out of its waves? *Thus far . . . ?* But there were times when it disobeyed—when it rushed further, shaking the world! Was it because God was then asleep—could not hear, did not see, until too late?

And the tumultuous ocean terrified her more and more: it filled her sleep with enormous nightmare;—it came upon her in dreams, mountain-shadowing—holding her with its spell, smothering her power of outcry, heaping itself to the stars.

Carmen became alarmed;—she feared that the nervous and delicate child might die in one of those moaning dreams out of which she had to arouse her, night after night. But Feliu, answering her anxiety with one of his favorite proverbs, suggested a heroic remedy:

"The world is like the sea: those who do not know how to swim in it are drowned;—and the sea is like the world," he added. . . . "Chita must learn to swim!"

And he found the time to teach her. Each morning, at sunrise, he took her into the water. She was less terrified the first time than Carmen thought she would be;—she seemed to feel confidence in Feliu; although she screamed piteously before her first ducking at his hands. His teaching was not gentle. He would carry her out, perched upon his shoulder, until the water rose to his own neck; and there he would throw her from him, and let her struggle to reach him again as best she could. The first few mornings she had to be pulled out almost at once; but after that Feliu showed her less mercy, and helped her only when he saw she was really in danger. He attempted no other instruction until she had learned that in order to save herself from being half choked by the salt water, she must not scream; and by the time she became habituated to these austere experiences, she had already learned by instinct alone how to keep herself afloat for a while, how to paddle a little with her hands. Then he commenced to train her to use them—to lift them well out and throw them forward as if reaching, to dip them as the blade of an oar is dipped at an angle, without loud splashing;—and he showed her also how to use her feet. She learned rapidly and astonishingly well. In less than two months Feliu felt really proud at the progress made by his tiny pupil: it was a delight to watch her lifting her slender arms above the water in swift, easy curves, with the same fine grace that marked all her other natural motions. Later on he taught her not to fear the sea even when it growled a little—how to ride a swell, how to face a breaker, how to dive. She only needed practice thereafter; and Carmen, who could also swim, finding the child's health improving marvelously under this new discipline, took good care that Chita should practice whenever the mornings were not too cold, or the water too rough.

With the first thrill of delight at finding herself able to glide over the water unassisted, the child's superstitious terror of the sea passed away. Even for the adult there are few physical joys keener than the exultation of the swimmer;—how much greater the same glee as newly felt by an imaginative child—a child, whose vivid fancy can lend unutterable value to the most insignificant trifles, can transform a weed-patch to an Eden!...Of her own accord she would ask for her morning bath, as soon as she opened her eyes;—it even required some severity to prevent her from remaining in the water too long. The sea appeared to her as something that had become tame for her sake, something that loved her in a huge rough way; a tremendous playmate, whom she no longer feared to see come bounding and barking to lick her feet. And, little by little, she also learned the wonderful healing and caressing power of the monster, whose cool embrace at once dispelled all drowsiness, feverishness, weariness—even after the sultriest nights when the air had seemed to burn, and the mosquitoes had filled the chamber with a sound as of water boiling in many kettles. And on mornings when the sea was in too wicked a humor to be played with, how she felt the loss of her loved sport, and prayed for calm! Her delicate constitution changed; —the soft, pale flesh became firm and brown, the meagre limbs rounded into robust symmetry, the thin cheeks grew peachy with richer life; for the strength of the sea had entered into her; the sharp breath of the sea had renewed and brightened her young blood....

...Thou primordial Sea, the awfulness of whose antiquity hath stricken all mythology dumb;—thou most wrinkled living Sea, the millions of whose years outnumber even the multitude of thy hoary motions;—thou omniform and most mysterious Sea, mother of the monsters and the gods—whence thine eternal youth? Still do thy waters hold the infinite thrill of that Spirit which brooded above their face in the Beginning!—still is thy quickening breath an elixir unto them that flee to thee for life—like the breath of young girls, like the breath of children, prescribed for the senescent by magicians of old—prescribed unto weazened elders in the books of the Wizards.

III

... Eighteen hundred and sixty-seven;—midsummer in the pest-smitten city of New Orleans.

Heat motionless and ponderous. The steel-blue of the sky bleached from the furnace-circle of the horizon;—the lukewarm river ran yellow and noiseless as a torrent of fluid wax. Even sounds seemed blunted by the heaviness of the air;—the rumbling of wheels, the reverberation of footsteps, fell half-toned upon the ear, like sounds that visit a dozing brain.

Daily, almost at the same hour, the continuous sense of atmospheric oppression became thickened;—a packed herd of low-bellying clouds lumbered up from the Gulf; crowded blackly against the sun; flickered, thundered, and burst in torrential rain—tepid, perpendicular—and vanished utterly away. Then, more furiously than before, the sun flamed down;—roofs and pavements steamed; the streets seemed to smoke; the air grew suffocating with vapor; and the luminous city filled with a faint, sickly odor—a stale smell, as of dead leaves suddenly disinterred from wet mould—as of grasses decomposing after a flood. Something saffron speckled the slimy water of the gutters; sulphur some called it; others feared even to give it a name! Was it only the wind-blown pollen of some innocuous plant? I do not know; but to many it seemed as if the Invisible Destruction were scattering visible seed! ... Such were the days; and each day the terror-stricken city offered up its hecatomb to death; and the faces of all the dead were yellow as flame!

"DÉCÉDÉ—"; "DÉCÉDÉ—"; "FALLECIO";—"DIED."... On the doorposts, the telegraph-poles, the pillars of verandas, the lamps—over the Government letter-boxes—everywhere glimmered the white annunciations of death. All the city was spotted with them. And lime was poured into the gutters; and huge purifying fires were kindled after sunset.

The nights began with a black heat;—there were hours when the acrid air seemed to ferment for stagnation, and to burn the bronchial tubing;—then, toward morning, it would grow chill with venomous vapors, with morbific dews—till the sun came up to lift the torpid moisture, and to fill the buildings with oven-glow. And the interminable procession of mourners and hearses and carriages again began to circulate between the centres of life and of death;—and long trains and steamships rushed from the port, with heavy burden of fugitives.

Wealth might flee; yet even in flight there was peril. Men, who might have been saved by the craft of experienced nurses at home, hurriedly departed in apparent health, unconsciously carrying in their blood the toxic principle of a malady unfamiliar to physicians of the West and North;—and they died upon their way, by the road-side, by the river-banks, in woods, in deserted stations, on the cots of quarantine hospitals. Wiser those who sought refuge in the purity of the pine forests, or in those near Gulf Islands, whence the bright sea-breath kept ever sweeping back the expanding poison into the funereal swamps, into the misty lowlands. The watering-resorts became overcrowded;—then the fishing villages were thronged—at least all which were easy to reach by steamboat or by lugger. And at last, even Viosca's Point—remote and unfamiliar as it was—had a stranger to shelter: a good old gentleman named Edwards, rather broken down in health—who came as much for quiet as for sea-air, and who had been warmly recommended to Feliu by Captain Harris. For some years he had been troubled by a disease of the heart.

Certainly the old invalid could not have found a more suitable place so far as rest and quiet were concerned. The season had early given such little promise that several men of the Point betook themselves elsewhere; and the aged visitor had two or three vacant cabins from among which to select a dwelling-place. He chose to occupy the most remote of all, which Carmen furnished for him with a cool moss bed and some necessary furniture—including a big wooden rocking-chair. It seemed to him very comfortable thus. He took his meals with the family, spent most of the day in his own quarters, spoke very little, and lived so unobtrusively and inconspicuously that his presence in the settlement was felt scarcely more than that of some dumb creature—some domestic animal—some humble pet whose relation to the family is only fully comprehended after it has failed to appear for several days in its accustomed place of patient waiting—and we know that it is dead.

IV

Persistently and furiously, at half-past two o'clock of an August morning, Sparicio rang Dr. La Brierre's night-bell. He had fifty dollars in his pocket, and a letter to deliver. He was to earn another fifty dollars—deposited in Feliu's hands—by bringing the Doctor to Viosca's Point. He had risked his life for that money—and was terribly in earnest.

Julien descended in his under-clothing, and opened the letter by the light of the hall lamp. It enclosed a check for a larger fee than he had ever before received, and contained an urgent request that he would at once accompany Sparicio to Viosca's Point—as the sender was in hourly danger of death. The letter, penned in a long, quavering hand, was signed—*"Henry Edwards."*

His father's dear old friend! Julien could not refuse to go—though he feared it was a hopeless case. *Angina pectoris*—and a third attack at seventy years of age! Would it even be possible to reach the sufferer's bedside in time? *"Dùe giorno—con vento"*—said Sparicio. Still, he must go; and at once. It was Friday morning;—might reach the Point Saturday night, with a good wind. . . . He roused his housekeeper, gave all needful instructions, prepared his little medicine-chest;—and long before the first rose-gold fire of day had flashed to the city spires, he was sleeping the sleep of exhaustion in the tiny cabin of a fishing-sloop.

. . . For eleven years Julien had devoted himself, heart and soul, to the exercise of that profession he had first studied rather as a polite accomplishment than as a future calling. In the unselfish pursuit of duty he had found the only possible consolation for his irreparable loss; and when the war came to sweep away his wealth, he entered the struggle valorously, not to strive against men, but to use his science against death. After the passing of that huge shock, which left all the imposing and splendid fabric of Southern feudalism wrecked forever, his profession stood him in good stead;—he found himself not only able to supply those personal wants he cared to satisfy, but also to alleviate the misery of many whom he had known in days of opulence;—the princely misery that never doffed its smiling mask, though living in secret, from week to week, on bread and orange-leaf tea;—the misery that affected condescension in accepting an invitation to dine—staring at the face of a watch (refused by the *Mont-de-Piété*) with eyes half blinded by starvation;—the misery which could afford but one robe for three marriageable daughters—one plain dress to be worn in turn by each of them, on visiting days;—the pretty misery—young, brave, sweet—asking for a "treat" of cakes too jocosely to have its asking answered—laughing and coquetting with its well-fed wooers, and crying for hunger after they were gone. Often and often, his heart had pleaded against his purse for such as these, and won its case in the silent courts of Self. But ever mysteriously the gift came—sometimes as if from the hand of a former slave; sometimes as from a remorseful creditor, ashamed to write his name. Only yellow Victorine knew; but the Doctor's housekeeper never opened those sphinx-lips of hers, until years after the Doctor's name had disappeared from the City Directory....

He had grown quite thin—a little gray. The epidemic had burthened him with responsibilities too multifarious and ponderous for his slender strength to bear. The continual nervous strain of abnormally protracted duty, the perpetual interruption of sleep, had almost prostrated even his will. Now he only hoped that, during this brief absence from the city, he might find renewed strength to do his terrible task.

Mosquitoes bit savagely; and the heat became thicker;—and there was yet no wind. Sparicio and his hired boy Carmelo had been walking backward and forward for hours overhead—urging the vessel yard by yard, with long poles, through the slime of canals and bayous. With every heavy push, the weary boy would sigh out—"*Santo Antonio!—Santo Antonio!*"—Sullen Sparicio himself at last burst into vociferations of ill-humor: "*Santo Antonio? —Ah! santissimu e santu diavulu!...Sacramentu poescite vegnu un asidente!—malidittu lu Signuri!*" All through the morning they walked and pushed, trudged and sighed and swore; and the minutes dragged by more wearily than the shuffling of their feet. "*Managgia Cristo co tutta a croce!*"..."*Santissimu e santu diavulu!!*"...

But as they reached at last the first of the broad bright lakes, the heat lifted, the breeze leaped up, the loose sail flapped and filled; and, bending graciously as a skater, the old *San Marco* began to shoot in a straight line over the blue flood. Then, while the boy sat at the tiller, Sparicio lighted his tiny charcoal furnace below, and prepared a simple meal—delicious yellow macaroni, flavored with goats' cheese; some fried fish, that smelled appetizingly; and rich black coffee, of Oriental fragrance and thickness. Julien ate a little, and lay down to sleep again. This time his rest was undisturbed by the mosquitoes; and when he woke, in the cooling evening, he felt almost refreshed. The *San Marco* was flying into Barataria Bay. Already the lantern in the lighthouse tower had begun to glow like a little moon; and right on the rim of the sea, a vast and vermilion sun seemed to rest his chin. Gray pelicans came flapping around the mast;—sea-birds sped hurtling by, their white bosoms rose-flushed by the western glow.... Again Sparicio's little furnace was at work—more fish, more macaroni, more black coffee; also a square-shouldered bottle of gin made its appearance. Julien ate less sparingly at this second meal; and smoked a long time on deck with Sparicio, who suddenly became very good-humored, and chatted volubly in bad Spanish, and in much worse English. Then while the boy took a few hours' sleep, the Doctor helped delightedly in maneuvering the little vessel. He had been a good yachtsman in other years; and Sparicio declared he would make a good fisherman. By midnight the *San Marco* began to run with a long, swinging gait;—she had reached deep water. Julien slept soundly; the steady rocking of the sloop seemed to soothe his nerves.

"After all," he thought to himself, as he rose from his little bunk next morning—"something like this is just what I needed."... The pleasant scent of hot coffee greeted him;—Carmelo was handing him the tin cup containing it, down through the hatchway. After drinking it he felt really hungry;—he ate more macaroni than he had ever eaten before. Then, while Sparicio slept, he aided Carmelo; and during the middle of the day he rested again. He had not had so much uninterrupted repose for many a week. He fancied he could feel himself getting strong. At supper-time it seemed to him he could not get enough to eat—although there was plenty for everybody.

All day long there had been exactly the same wave-crease distorting the white shadow of the *San Marco's* sail upon the blue water;—all day long they had been skimming over the liquid level of a world so jewel-blue that the low green ribbon-strips of marsh land, the far-off fleeing lines of pine-yellow sand beach, seemed flaws or breaks in the perfected color of the universe;—all day long had the cloudless sky revealed through all its exquisite transparency that inexpressible tenderness which no painter and no poet can ever re-image—that unutterable sweetness which no art of man may ever shadow forth, and which none may ever comprehend—though we feel it to be in some strange way akin to the luminous and unspeakable charm that makes us wonder at the eyes of a woman when she loves.

Evening came; and the great dominant celestial tone deepened; —the circling horizon filled with ghostly tints—spectral greens and grays, and pearl-lights and fish-colors.... Carmelo, as he crouched at the tiller, was singing, in a low, clear alto, some tristful little melody. Over the sea, behind them, lay, black-stretching, a long low arm of island-shore;—before them flamed the splendor of sun-death; they were sailing into a mighty glory—into a vast and awful light of gold.

Shading his vision with his fingers, Sparicio pointed to the long lean limb of land from which they were fleeing, and said to La Brierre:

"Look-a, Doct-a! Last-a Islan'!"

Julien knew it;—he only nodded his head in reply, and looked the other way—into the glory of God. Then, wishing to divert the fisherman's attention to another theme, he asked what was Carmelo singing. Sparicio at once shouted to the lad:

"Ha!...ho! Carmelo!—*Santu diavulu!*...Sing-a loud-a! Doct-a lik-a! sing-a! sing!!"..."He sing-a nicee"—added the boatman, with his peculiar dark smile. And then Carmelo sang, loud and clearly, the song he had been singing before—one of those artless Mediterranean ballads, full of caressing vowel-sounds, and young passion, and melancholy beauty:

> *M' ama ancor, beltà fulgente,*
>   *Come tu m' amasti allor;—*
> *Ascoltar non dei gente,*
>   *Solo interroga il tuo cor....*

"He sing-a nicee—mucha bueno!" murmured the fisherman. And then, suddenly—with a rich and splendid basso that seemed to thrill every fibre of the planking—Sparicio joined in the song:

> *M' ama pur d' amore eterno,*
> *Nè delítto sembri a te;*
> *T' assicuro che l' inferno*
>   *Una favola sol è....*

All the roughness of the man was gone! To Julien's startled fancy, the fishers had ceased to be;—lo! Carmelo was a princely page; Sparicio, a king! How perfectly their voices married together! —they sang with passion, with power, with truth, with that wondrous natural art which is the birthright of the rudest Italian soul. And the stars throbbed out in the heaven; and the glory died in the west; and the night opened its heart; and the splendor of the eternities fell all about them. Still they sang; and the *San Marco* sped on through the soft gloom, ever slightly swerved by the steady blowing of the southeast wind in her sail;—always wearing the same crimpling-frill of wave-spray about her prow—always accompanied by the same smooth-backed swells—always spinning out behind her the same long trail of interwoven foam. And Julien looked up. Ever the night thrilled more and more with silent twinklings;—more and more multitudinously lights pointed in the eternities;—the Evening Star quivered like a great drop of liquid white fire ready to fall;—Vega flamed as a pharos lighting the courses ethereal—to guide the sailing of the suns, and the swarming of fleets of worlds. Then the vast sweetness of that violet night entered into his blood—filled him with that awful joy, so near akin to sadness, which the sense of the Infinite brings— when one feels the poetry of the Most Ancient and Most Excellent of Poets, and then is smitten at once with the contrast-thought of the sickliness and selfishness of Man—of the blindness and brutality of cities, whereinto the divine blue light never purely comes, and the sanctification of the Silences never descends...furious cities, walled away from heaven....Oh! if one could only sail on thus always, always through such a night—through such a star-sprinkled violet night, and hear Sparicio and Carmelo sing, even though it were the same melody always, always the same song!

...."Scuza, Doct-a!—look-a out!" Julien bent down, as the big boom, loosened, swung over his head. The *San Marco* was rounding into shore—heading for her home. Sparicio lifted a huge conch-shell from the deck, put it to his lips, filled his deep lungs, and flung out into the night—thrice—a profound, mellifluent, booming horn-tone. A minute passed. Then, ghostly faint, as an echo from very far away, a triple blowing responded....

And a long purple mass loomed and swelled into sight, heightened, approached—land and trees black-shadowing, and lights that swung....The *San Marco* glided into a bayou—under a high wharfing of timbers, where a bearded fisherman waited, and a woman. Sparicio flung up a rope.

The bearded man caught it by the lantern-light, and tethered the *San Marco* to her place. Then he asked, in a deep voice:

"*Has traido al Doctor?*"

"*Si, si!*" answered Sparicio.... "*Y el viejo?*"

"*Aye! pobre!*" responded Feliu—"*hace tres dias que esta muerto.*"

Henry Edwards was dead!

He had died very suddenly, without a cry or a word, while resting in his rocking-chair—the very day after Sparicio had sailed. They had made him a grave in the marsh—among the high weeds, not far from the ruined tomb of the Spanish fisherman. But Sparicio had fairly earned his hundred dollars.

V

So there was nothing to do at Viosca's Point except to rest. Feliu and all his men were going to Barataria in the morning on business;—the Doctor could accompany them there, and take the Grand Island steamer Monday for New Orleans. With this intention Julien retired—not sorry for being able to stretch himself at full length on the good bed prepared for him, in one of the unoccupied cabins. But he woke before day with a feeling of intense prostration, a violent headache, and such an aversion for the mere idea of food that Feliu's invitation to breakfast at five o'clock gave him an internal qualm. Perhaps a touch of malaria. In any case he felt it would be both dangerous and useless to return to town unwell; and Feliu, observing his condition, himself advised against the journey. Wednesday he would have another opportunity to leave; and in the meanwhile Carmen would take good care of him.... The boats departed, and Julien slept again.

The sun was high when he rose up and dressed himself, feeling no better. He would have liked to walk about the place, but felt nervously afraid of the sun. He did not remember having ever felt so broken down before. He pulled a rocking-chair to the window, tried to smoke a cigar. It commenced to make him feel still sicker, and he flung it away. It seemed to him the cabin was swaying, as the *San Marco* swayed when she first reached the deep water.

A light rustling sound approached—a sound of quick feet treading the grass: then a shadow slanted over the threshold. In the glow of the open doorway stood a young girl—gracile, tall—with singularly splendid eyes—brown eyes peeping at him from beneath a golden riot of loose hair.

"*M'sieu-le-Docteur, maman d'mande si vous n'avez bisoin d' que' que chose?* ... She spoke the rude French of the fishing villages, where the language lives chiefly as a *baragouin,* mingled often with words and forms belonging to many other tongues. She wore a loose-falling dress of some light stuff, steel-gray in color;—boys' shoes were on her feet.

He did not reply;—and her large eyes grew larger for wonder at the strange fixed gaze of the physician, whose face had visibly bleached—blanched to corpse-pallor. Silent seconds passed; and still the eyes stared—flamed as if the life of the man had centralized and focussed within them.

His voice had risen to a cry in his throat, quivered and swelled one passionate instant, and failed—as in a dream when one strives to call, and yet can only moan.... *She!* Her unforgotten eyes, her brows, her lips!—the oval of her face!—the dawn-light of her hair!... Adèle's own poise—her own grace!—even the very turn of her neck—even the bird-tone of her speech!... Had the grave sent forth a Shadow to haunt him?—could the perfidious Sea have yielded up its dead? For one terrible fraction of a minute, memories, doubts, fears, mad fancies, went pulsing through his brain with a rush like the rhythmic throbbing of an electric stream;—then the shock passed, the Reason spoke: "Fool!—count the long years since you first saw her thus!—count the years that have gone since you looked upon her last! And Time has never halted, silly heart!—neither has Death stood still!"

..."*Plait-il?*"—the clear voice of the young girl asked. She thought he had made some response she could not distinctly hear.

Mastering himself an instant, as the heart faltered back to its duty, and the color remounted to his lips, he answered her in French:

"Pardon me!—I did not hear ... you gave me such a start!" ... But even then another extraordinary fancy flashed through his thought; —and with the *tutoiement* of a parent to a child, with an irresistible outburst of such tenderness as almost frightened her, he cried: "Oh! merciful God!—how like her! ... Tell me, darling, your name; —tell me who you are?" (*Dis-moi qui tu es, mignonne;—dis-moi ton nom.*)

... Who was it had asked her the same question, in another idiom—ever so long ago? The man with the black eyes and nose like an eagle's beak—the one who gave her the compass. Not *this* man—no!

She answered, with the timid gravity of surprise:
"Chita Viosca."

He still watched her face, and repeated the name slowly—reiterated it in a tone of wonderment: "Chita Viosca?—Chita Viosca!"

"*C'est à dire...*" she said, looking down at her feet—"Concha—Conchita." His strange solemnity made her smile—the smile of shyness that knows not what else to do. But it was the smile of dead Adèle.

"Thanks, my child," he exclaimed of a sudden—in a quick, hoarse, changed tone. (He felt that his emotion would break loose in some wild way, if he looked upon her longer.) "I would like to see your mother this evening; but I now feel too ill to go out. I am going to try to rest a little."

"Nothing I can bring you?" She asked;—"some fresh milk?"

"Nothing now, dear: if I need anything later, I will tell your mother when she comes."

"Mamma does not understand French very well."

"*No importa, Conchita;—le hablaré en Español.*"

"*Bien, entonces!*" she responded, with the same exquisite smile. "*Adios, señor!*" ...

But as she turned in going, his piercing eye discerned a little brown speck below the pretty lobe of her right ear—just in the peachy curve between neck and cheek.... His own little Zouzoune had a birthmark like that!—he remembered the faint pink trace left by his fingers above and below it the day he had slapped her for overturning his ink-bottle.... "*To laimin moin?—to batté moin!*"

"Chita!—Chita!"

She did not hear.... After all, what a mistake he might have made! Were not Nature's coincidences more wonderful than fiction? Better to wait—to question the mother first, and thus make sure.

Still—there were so many coincidences! The face, the smile, the eyes, the voice, the whole charm;—then that mark—and the fair hair. Zouzoune had always resembled Adèle so strangely! That golden hair was a Scandinavian bequest to the Florane family;—the tall daughter of a Norwegian sea-captain had once become the wife of a Florane. Viosca?—who ever knew a Viosca with such hair? Yet again, these Spanish emigrants sometimes married blonde German girls.... Might be a case of atavism, too. Who was this

Viosca? If that was his wife—the little brown Carmen—whence Chita's sunny hair?...

And this was part of that same desolate shore whither the Last Island dead had been drifted by that tremendous surge! On a clear day, with a good glass, one might discern from here the long blue streak of that ghastly coast....Somewhere—between here and there....Merciful God!...

...But again! That bivouac-night before the fight at Chancellorsville, Laroussel had begun to tell him such a singular story....Chance had brought them—the old enemies—together; made them dear friends in the face of Death. How little he had comprehended the man!—what a brave, true, simple soul went up that day to the Lord of Battles!...What was it—the story about the little Creole girl saved from Last Island—that story which was never finished?...Eh! what a pain!

Evidently he had worked too much, slept too little. A decided case of nervous prostration. He must lie down, and try to sleep. These pains in the head and back were becoming unbearable. Nothing but rest could avail him now.

He stretched himself under the mosquito curtain. It was very still, breathless, hot! The venomous insects were thick;—they filled the room with a continuous ebullient sound, as if invisible kettles were boiling overhead. A sign of storm....Still, it was strange!—he could not perspire....

Then it seemed to him that Laroussel was bending over him—Laroussel in his cavalry uniform. "*Bonjour, camarade!—nous allons avoir un bien mauvais temps, mon pauvre Julien.*" How! bad weather? —"*Comment un mauvais temps?*"...He looked in Laroussel's face. There was something so singular in his smile. Ah! yes—he remembered now: it was the wound!..."*Un vilain temps!*" whispered Laroussel. Then he was gone....Whither?

"*Chéri!*"...

The whisper roused him with a fearful start....Adèle's whisper! So she was wont to rouse him sometimes in the old sweet nights— to crave some little attention for ailing Eulalie—to make some little confidence she had forgotten to utter during the happy evening.... No, no! It was only the trees. The sky was clouding over. The wind was rising....How his heart beat! how his temples pulsed! Why, this was fever! Such pains in the back and head!

Still his skin was dry—dry as parchment—burning. He rose up; and a bursting weight of pain at the base of the skull made him reel like a drunken man. He staggered to the little mirror nailed upon the wall, and looked. How his eyes glowed;—and there was blood in his mouth! He felt his pulse—spasmodic, terribly rapid. Could it possibly—?... No: this must be some pernicious malarial fever! The Creole does not easily fall a prey to the great tropical malady—unless after a long absence in other climates. True! he had been four years in the army! But this was 1867.... He hesitated a moment; then—opening his medicine-chest, he measured out and swallowed thirty grains of quinine.

Then he lay down again. His head pained more and more;—it seemed as if the cervical vertebrae were filled with fluid iron. And still his skin remained dry as if tanned. Then the anguish grew so intense as to force a groan with almost every aspiration.... Nausea— and the stinging bitterness of quinine rising in his throat;—dizziness, and a brutal wrenching within his stomach. Everything began to look pink;—the light was rose-colored. It darkened more—kindled with deepening tint. Something kept sparkling and spinning before his sight, like a firework.... Then a burst of blood mixed with a chemical bitterness filled his mouth; the light became scarlet as claret.... This—this was ... not malaria....

VI

Carmen knew what it was; but the brave little woman was not afraid of it. Many a time before she had met it face to face, in Havanese summers; she knew how to wrestle with it;—she had torn Feliu's life away from its yellow clutch, after one of those long struggles that strain even the strength of love. Now she feared mostly for Chita. She had ordered the girl under no circumstances to approach the cabin.

Julien felt that blankets had been heaped upon him—that some gentle hand was bathing his scorching face with vinegar and water. Vaguely also there came to him the idea that it was night. He saw the shadow-shape of a woman moving against the red light upon the wall;—he saw there was a lamp burning.

Then the delirium seized him: he moaned, sobbed, cried like a child—talked wildly at intervals in French, in English, in Spanish.

"*Mentira!*—you could not be her mother.... Still, if you were— And she must not come in here—*jamas!*... Carmen, did you know Adèle—Adèle Florane? So like her—so like—God only knows how like!... Perhaps I think I know;—but I do not—do not know justly, fully—how like! ... *Si! si!—es el vómito!—yo lo conozco, Carmen!* ... She must not die twice. ... I died twice. ... I am going to die again. She only once. Till the heavens be no more she will not rise. ... *Moi, au contraire, il faut que je me lève toujours!* They need me so much;—the slate is always full; the bell will never stop. They will ring that bell for men when I am dead. ... So will I rise again!—*resurgam!* ... How could I save him?—could not save myself. It was a bad case—at seventy years! ... There! *Qui çà?*" ...

He saw Laroussel again—reaching out a hand to him through a whirl of red smoke. He tried to grasp it, and could not. ... *"N'importe, mon ami,"* said Laroussel—*"tu vas la voir bientôt."* Who was he to see soon?—*"qui donc,* Laroussel?" But Laroussel did not answer. Through the red mist he seemed to smile;—then passed.

For some hours Carmen had trusted she could save her patient—desperate as the case appeared to be. His was one of those rapid and violent attacks, such as often despatch their victims in a single day. In the Cuban hospitals she had seen many and many terrible examples: strong young men—soldiers fresh from Spain—carried panting to the fever wards at sunrise; carried to the cemeteries at sunset. Even troopers riddled with revolutionary bullets had lingered longer. ... Still, she had believed she might save Julien's life: the burning forehead once began to bead, the burning hands grew moist.

But now the wind was moaning;—the air had become lighter, thinner, cooler. A storm was gathering in the east; and to the fever-stricken man the change meant death. ... Impossible to bring the priest of the Caminada now; and there was no other within a day's sail. She could only pray; she had lost all hope in her own power to save.

Still the sick man raved; but he talked to himself at longer intervals, and with longer pauses between his words;—his voice was growing more feeble, his speech more incoherent. His thought vacillated and distorted, like flame in a wind.

Weirdly the past became confounded with the present; impressions of sight and of sound interlinked in fantastic affinity—the face of Chita Viosca, the murmur of the rising storm. Then flickers of spectral lightning passed through his eyes, through his brain, with every throb of the burning arteries; then utter darkness came—a darkness that surged and moaned, as the circumfluence of a shadowed sea. And through and over the moaning pealed one multitudinous human cry, one hideous interblending of shoutings and shriekings.... A woman's hand was locked in his own.... "Tighter," he muttered, "tighter still, darling! hold as long as you can!" It was the tenth night of August, eighteen hundred and fifty-six....

"*Chéri!*"

Again the mysterious whisper startled him to consciousness— the dim knowledge of a room filled with ruby-colored light—and the sharp odor of vinegar. The house swung round slowly;—the crimson flame of the lamp lengthened and broadened by turns; —then everything turned dizzily fast—whirled as if spinning in a vortex.... Nausea unutterable; and a frightful anguish as of teeth devouring him within—tearing more and more furiously at his breast. Then one atrocious wrenching, rending, burning—and the gush of blood burst from lips and nostrils in a smothering deluge. Again the vision of lightnings, the swaying, and the darkness of long ago. "Quick!—quick!—hold fast to the table, Adèle!—never let go!"...

...Up—up—up!—what! higher yet? Up to the red sky! Red-black-red...heated iron when its vermilion dies. So, too, the frightful flood! And noiseless. Noiseless because heavy, clammy— thick, warm, sickening...blood? Well might the land quake for the weight of such a tide!...Why did Adèle speak Spanish? Who prayed for him?...

"*Alma de Cristo santísima santifícame!*
"*Sangre de Cristo, embriágame!*
"*O buen Jesus, oye me!*"...

Out of the darkness into—such a light! An azure haze! Ah! —the delicious frost!... All the streets were filled with the sweet blue mist.... Voiceless the City and white;—crooked and weed-grown its narrow ways!... Old streets of tombs, these.... Eh! how odd a custom!—a night-bell at every door. Yes, of course!—a *night*-bell!—the Dead are Physicians of Souls: they may be summoned only by night—called up from the darkness and silence.... Yet *she?*—might he not dare to ring for her even by day?... Strange he had deemed it day!—why, it was black, starless.... And it was growing queerly cold.... How should he ever find her now? It was so black...so cold!...

"*Chéri!*"
All the dwelling quivered with the mighty whisper.

Outside, the great oaks were trembling to their roots;—all the shore shook and blanched before the calling of the sea.

And Carmen, kneeling at the feet of the dead, cried out, alone in the night:

"*O Jesus misericordioso!—tened compasion de él!*"

Grace King

Grace King (1852-1932)

Born in New Orleans, Grace King was educated at the local convent schools, even though she and her family were Presbyterian. Her father was a prominent lawyer whose fortunes and practice were permanently shattered by the Civil War. Her first story was "Monsieur Motte," written to defend her position that the Creoles deserved a more flattering image than the one presented in Cable's stories. Among her books are two collections of stories, Tales of a Time and Place *(1892) and* Balcony Stories *(1893), a novel,* The Pleasant Ways of St. Médard *(1916), a history,* New Orleans: the Place and the People *(1895), and a memoir,* Memories of a Southern Woman of Letters *(1932). "Bayou l'Ombre" is taken from* Tales of a Time and Place.

BAYOU L'OMBRE

Of course they knew all about war—soldiers, flags, music, generals on horseback brandishing swords, knights in armor escalading walls, cannons booming through clouds of smoke. They were familiarized with it pictorially and by narrative long before the alphabet made its appearance in the nursery with rudimentary accounts of the world they were born into, the simple juvenile world of primary sensations and colors. Their great men, and great women, too, were all fighters; the great events of their histories, battles; the great places of their geography, where they were fought (and generally the more bloody the battle, the more glorious the place); while their little chronology—the pink-covered one—stepped briskly over the centuries solely on the names of kings and sanguinary saliencies. Sunday added the sabbatical supplement to week-day lessons, symbolizing religion, concreting sin, incorporating evil, for their better comprehension, putting Jehovah himself in armor, to please their childish faculties—the omnipotent Intervener of the Old Testament, for whom they waved banners, sang hymns, and by the brevet title, "little *soldiers* of the cross," felt committed as by baptism to an attitude of expectant hostility. Mademoiselle Couper, their governess, eased the cross-stitching in their samplers during the evenings, after supper, with traditions of "le grand Napoléon," in whose army her grandfather was a terrible and distinguished officer, le Capitaine Césaire Paul Picquet de Montignac; and although Mademoiselle Couper was most unlovable and exacting at times, and very homely, such were their powers of sympathetic enthusiasm even then that they often went to bed envious of the possessor of so glorious an ancestor, and dreamed fairy tales of him whose gray hair, enshrined in a brooch, reposed comfortably under the folds of mademoiselle's fat chin—the hair that Napoleon had looked upon!

When a war broke out in their own country they could hardly credit their good-fortune; that is, Christine and Régina, for Lolotte was still a baby. A wonderful panorama was suddenly unfolded before them. It was their first intimation of the identity of the world they lived in with the world they learned about, their first perception of the existence of an entirely novel sentiment in their hearts—patriotism, the *amour sacré de la patrie*, over which they had seen mademoiselle shed tears as copiously as her grandfather had

133

blood. It made them and all their little companions feel very proud, this war; but it gave them a heavy sense of responsibility, turning their youthful precocity incontinently away from books, slates, and pianos toward the martial considerations that befitted the hour. State rights, Federal limits, monitors and fortresses, proclamations, Presidents, recognitions, and declarations, they acquired them all with facility, taxing, as in other lessons, their tongue to repeat the unintelligible on trust for future intelligence. As their father fired his huge after-dinner bombs, so they shot their diminutive ammunition; as he lighted brands in the great conflagration, they lighted tapers; and the two contending Presidents themselves did not get on their knees with more fervor before their colossal sphinxes than these little girls did before their doll-baby presentment of "Country." It was very hard to realize at times that histories and story-books and poetry would indeed be written about them; that little flags would mark battles all over the map of their country—the country Mademoiselle Couper despised as so hopelessly, warlessly insignificant; that men would do great things and women say them, teachers and copy-books reiterate them, and children learn them, just as they did of the Greeks and Romans, the English and French. The great advantage was having God on their side, as the children of Israel had; the next best thing was having the finest country, the most noble men, and the bravest soldiers. The only fear was that the enemy would be beaten too easily, and the war cease too soon to be glorious; for, characteristic of their sex, they demanded nothing less than that their war should be the longest, bloodiest, and most glorious of all wars ever heard of, in comparison with which even "le grand Napoleon" and his Capitaine Picquet would be effaced from memory. For this were exercised their first attempts at extempore prayer. God, the dispenser of inexhaustible supplies of munitions of war, became quite a different power, a nearer and dearer personality, than "Our Father," the giver of simple daily bread, and He did not lack reminding of the existence of the young Confederacy, nor of the hearsay exigencies they gathered from the dinner-table talk.

Titine was about thirteen, Gina twelve, and Lolotte barely eight years old, when this, to them, happy break in their lives occurred. It was easily comprehensible to them that their city should be captured, and that to escape that grim ultimatum of Mademoiselle Couper, "*passées au fil de l'épée*," they should be bundled up very hurriedly one night, carried out of their home, and journey in troublesome roundabout ways to the plantation on Bayou l'Ombre.

That was all four years ago. School and play and city life, dolls and fêtes and Santa Claus, had become the property of memory. Peace for them hovered in that obscurity which had once enveloped war, while " '61," " '62," " '63," " '64," filled immeasurable spaces in their short past. Four times had Christine and Régina changed the date in their diaries—the last token of remembrance from Mademoiselle Couper—altering the numerals with naïve solemnity, as if under the direction of the Almighty himself, closing with conventional ceremony the record of the lived-out twelve months, opening with appropriate aspirations the year to come. The laboriously careful chronicle that followed was not, however, of the growth of their bodies advancing by inches, nor the expansion of their minds, nor of the vague forms that began to people the shadow-land of their sixteen and seventeen year old hearts. Their own budding and leafing and growing was as unnoted as that of the trees and weeds about them. The progress of the war, the growth of their hatred of the enemy, the expansion of the *amour sacré* germ—these were the confidences that filled the neatly-stitched foolscap volumes. If on comparison one sister was found to have been happier in the rendition of the common sentiment, the coveted fervor and eloquence were plagiarized or imitated the next day by the other, a generous emulation thus keeping the original flame not only alight, but burning, while from assimilating each other's sentiments the two girls grew with identity of purpose into identity of mind, and effaced the slight difference of age between them.

Little Lolotte responded as well as she could to the enthusiastic exactions of her sisters. She gave her rag dolls patriotic names, obediently hated and loved as they required, and learned to recite all the war songs procurable, even to the teeming quantities of the stirring "Men of the South, our foes are up!" But as long as the squirrels gambolled on the fences, the blackbirds flocked in the fields, and the ditches filled with fish; as long as the seasons imported such constant variety of attractions—persimmons, dewberries, blackberries, acorns, wild plums, grapes, and muscadines; as long as the cows had calves, the dogs puppies, the hogs pigs, and the quarters new babies to be named; as long as the exasperating negro children needed daily subjugation, regulation, and discipline—the day's measure was too well filled and the night's slumber too short to admit of her carrying on a very vigorous warfare for a country so far away from Bayou l'Ombre—a country whose grievances she could not understand.

But—there were no soldiers, flags, music, parades, battles, or sieges. This war was altogether distinct from the wars contained in books or in Mademoiselle Couper's memory. There was an absence of the simplest requirements of war. They kept awaiting the familiar events for which they had been prepared; but after four years the only shots fired on Bayou l'Ombre were at game in the forest, the only blood shed was from the tottering herds of Texas beeves driven across the swamps to them, barely escaping by timely butchery the starvation they came to relieve, and the only heroism they had been called upon to display was still going to bed in the dark. Indeed, were it not that they knew there was a war they might have supposed that some malignant fairy had transported them from a state of wealth and luxury to the condition of those miserable Hathorns, the pariahs of their childhood, who lived just around the corner from them in the city, with whom they had never been allowed to associate. If they had not so industriously fostered the proper feelings in their hearts, they might almost have forgotten it, or, like Lolotte, been diverted from it by the generous overtures of nature all around them. But they kept on reminding each other that it was not the degrading want of money, as in the Hathorns' case, that forced them to live on salt meat, corn-bread, and sassafras tea, to dress like the negro women in the quarters, that deprived them of education and society, and imprisoned them in a swamp-encircled plantation, the prey of chills and fever; but it was for love of country, and being little women now, they loved their country more, the more they suffered for her. Disillusion might have supervened to disappointment and bitterness have quenched hope, experience might at last have sharpened their vision, but for the imagination, that ethereal parasite which fattens on the stagnant forces of youth and garnishes with tropical luxuriance the abnormal source of its nourishment. Soaring aloft, above the prosaic actualities of the present, beyond the rebutting evidence of earth, was a fanciful stage where the drama of war such as they craved was unfolded; where neither homespun, starvation, overflows, nor illness were allowed to enter; where the heroes and heroines they loved acted roles in all the conventional glitter and costume and conduct, amid the dazzling pomps and circumstances immortalized in history and romance. Their hearts would bound and leap after these phantasms, like babes in nurses' arms after the moon, and would almost burst with longing, their ripe little hearts, Pandora-boxes packed with passions and pleasures for a lifetime, ready to spring open at a touch! On moonlit nights in summer, or under the low gray clouds of winter days, in the monotony of nothingness about them, the yearning in their breasts was like that of hunting dogs howling for the unseen game. Sometimes a rumor of a battle "out in the Confederacy" would find its way across the swamps to them, and months afterwards a newspaper would be thrown to them from a passing skiff, some old, useless, tattered, disreputable, journalistic tramp, garrulous with mendacities; but it was all true to them, if to no one else in the world—the factitious triumphs, the lurid glories, the pyrotechnical promises, prophecies, calculations, and Victory with the laurel wreath always in the future, never out of sight for an instant. They would con the fraudulent evangel, entranced; their eyes would sparkle, the blood color their cheeks, their voices vibrate, and a strange strength excite and nerve their bodies. Then would follow wakeful nights and restless days; Black Margarets, Jeanne d'Arcs, Maids of Saragossa, Katherine Douglases, Charlotte Cordays, would haunt them like the goblins of a delirium; then their prayers would become imperious demands upon Heaven, their diaries would almost break into spontaneous combustion from the incendiary material enmagazined in their pages, and the South would have conquered the world then and there could their hands but have pointed the guns and their hearts have recruited the armies. They would with mingled pride and envy read all the names, barely decipherable in the travel-stained record, from the President and Generals in big print to the diminishing insignificance of smallest-type privates; and they would shed tears, when the reaction would come a few days later, at the thought that in the whole area of typography, from the officers gaining immortality to the privates losing lives, there was not one name belonging to them; and they would ask why, of all the families in the South, precisely their father and mother should have no relations, why, of all the women in the South, they should be brotherless.

There was Beau, a too notorious guerilla captain; but what glory was to be won by raiding towns, wrecking trains, plundering transports, capturing couriers, disobeying orders, defying regulations? He was almost as obnoxious to his own as to the enemy's flag.

Besides, Beau at most was only a kind of a cousin, the son of a deceased step-sister of their father's; the most they could expect from him was to keep his undisciplined crew of "'Cadians," Indians, and swampers away from Bayou l'Ombre.

"Ah, if we were only men!" But no! They who could grip daggers and shed blood, they who teemed with all the possibilities of romance or poetry, they were selected for a passive, paltry contest against their own necessities; the endurance that would have laughed a siege to scorn ebbing away in a never-ceasing wrangle with fever and ague—willow-bark tea at odds with a malarious swamp!

It was now early summer; the foliage of spring was lusty and strong, fast outgrowing tenderness and delicacy of shade, with hints of maturity already swelling the shape. The day was cloudless and warm, the dinner-hour was long past, and supper still far off. There were no appetizing varieties of menu to make meals objects of pleasant anticipation; on the contrary, they had become mournful effigies of a convivial institution of which they served at most only to recall the hours, monotonously measuring off the recurring days which passed like unlettered mileposts in a desert, with no information to give except that of transition. To-day the meal-times were so far apart as to make one believe that the sun had given up all forward motion, and intended prolonging the present into eternity. The plantation was quiet and still; not the dewy hush of early dawn trembling before the rising sun, nor the mysterious muteness of midnight, nor yet the lethargic dulness of summer when the vertical sun-rays pin sense and motion to the earth. It was the motionless, voiceless state of unnatural quietude, the oppressive consciousness of abstracted activity, which characterized those days when the whole force of Bayou l'Ombre went off into the swamps to cut timber. Days that began shortly after one midnight and lasted to the other; rare days, when neither horn nor bell was heard for summons; when not a skiff, flat-boat, nor pirogue was left at the "gunnels;" when old Uncle John alone remained to represent both master and men in the cares and responsibilities devolving upon his sex. The bayou lived and moved as usual, carrying its deceptive depths of brackish water unceasingly onward through the shadow and sunshine, rippling over the opposite low, soft banks, which seemed slowly sinking out of sight under the weight of the huge cypress-trees growing upon it. The long stretch of untilled fields back of the house, feebly kept in symmetrical proportion by crumbling fences, bared their rigid, seedless furrows in despairing barrenness to the sun, except in corner spots where a rank growth of weeds had inaugurated a reclamation in favor of barbarism. The sugar-house, superannuated and decrepit from unwholesome idleness, tottered against its own massive, smokeless chimney; the surrounding sheds, stables, and smithy looked forsaken and neglected; the old blind mule peacefully slept in the shade of his once flagellated course under the corn-mill. Afar off against the woods the huge wheel of the draining-machine rose from the underbrush in the big ditch. The patient buzzards, roosting on the branches of the gaunt, blasted gum-tree by the bayou, would raise their heads from time to time to question the loitering sun, or, slowly flapping their heavy wings, circle up into the blue sky, to fall again in lazy spirals to their watch-tower, or they would take short flights by twos and threes over the moribund plantation to see if dissolution had not yet set in, and then all would settle themselves again to brood and sleep and dream, and wait in tranquil certainty the striking of their banqueting hour.

The three girls were in the open hall-way of the plantation house, Christine reading, Régina knitting, both listlessly occupied. Like everything else, they were passively quiet, and, like everything else, their appearance advertised an unwholesome lack of vitality, an insidious anamorphosis from an unexplained dearth or constraint. Their meagre maturity and scant development clashed abnormally with the surrounding prodigality of insensible nature. Though tall, they were thin; they were fair, but sallow; their gentle deep eyes were reproachful and deprived-looking. If their secluded hearts ventured even in thought towards the plumings natural to their age, their coarse, homely, ill-fitting garments anathematized any coquettish effort or naïve expression of a desire to find favor. Like the fields, they seemed hesitating on the backward path from cultivation. Lolotte stood before the cherry-wood armoire that held the hunting and fishing tackle, the wholesome receptacle of useful odd and ends. Not old enough to have come into the war with preconceptions, Lolotte had no reconciliations or compromises to effect between the ideal and the real, no compensations to solicit from an obliging imagination, which so far never rose beyond the possibilities of perch, blackbirds, and turtle eggs. The first of these occupied her thoughts at the present moment. She had made a tryst with the negro children at the draining-machine this afternoon. If she could, unperceived, abstract enough tackle from the armoire for the crowd, and if they could slip away from the quarters, and she evade the surveillance of Uncle John, there would be a diminished number of "brim" and "goggle-eye" in the ditch out yonder, and such a notable addition to the plantation supper to-night as would crown the exploit a success, and establish for herself a reputation above all annoying recollections of recent mishaps and failures. As she tied the hooks on to the lines she saw herself surrounded by the acclaiming infantile populace, pulling the struggling perch up one after the other; she saw them strung on palmetto thongs, long strings of them; she walked home at the head of her procession; heard Peggy's exclamations of surprise, smelt them frying, and finally was sitting at the table, a plate of bones before her, the radiant hostess of an imperial feast.

"Listen!" Like wood-ducks from under the water, the three heads rose simultaneously above their abstractions. "Rowlock! Rowlock!" The eyes might become dull, the tongue inert, and the heart languid on Bayou l'Ombre, but the ears were ever assiduous, ever on duty. Quivering and nervous, they listened even through sleep for that one blessed echo of travel, the signal from another and a distant world. Faint, shadowy, delusive, the whispering forerunner of on-coming news, it overrode the rippling of the current, the hooting of the owls, the barking of dogs, the splash of the gar-fish, the grunting of the alligator, the croaking of frogs, penetrating all turmoil, silencing all other sounds. "Rowlock! Rowlock!" Slow, deliberate, hard, and strenuous, coming upstream; easy, soft, and musical, gliding down. "Rowlock! Rowlock!" Every stroke a very universe of hope, every oar frothing a sea of expectation! Was it the bayou or the secret stream of their longing that suggested the sound to-day? "Rowlock! Rowlock!" The smouldering glances brightened in their eyes, they hollowed their hands behind their ears and held their breath for greater surety. "Rowlock! Rowlock!" In clear, distinct reiteration. It resolved the moment of doubt.

"Can it be papa coming back?"

"No; it's against stream."

"It must be swampers."

"Or hunters, perhaps."

"Or Indians from the mound."

"Indians in a skiff?"

"Well, they sometimes come in a skiff."

The contingencies were soon exhausted, a cutoff leading travellers far around Bayou l'Ombre, whose snaggy, rafted, convoluted course was by universal avoidance relegated to an isolation almost insulting. The girls, listening, not to lose a single vibration, quit their places and advanced to the edge of the gallery, then out under the trees, then to the levee, then to the "gunnels," where they stretched their long, thin, white necks out of their blue and brown check gowns, and shaded their eyes and gazed downstream for the first glimpse of the skiff—their patience which had lasted months fretting now over the delay of a few moments.

"At last we shall get some news again."

"If they only leave a newspaper!"

"Or a letter," said Lolotte.

"A letter! From whom?"

"Ah, that's it!"

"What a pity papa isn't here!"

"Lolotte, don't shake the gunnels so; you are wetting our feet."

"How long is it since the last one passed?"

"I can tell you," said Lolotte—"I can tell you exactly: it was the day Lou Ann fell in the bayou and nearly got drowned."

"You mean when you both fell in."

"I didn't fall in at all; I held on to the pirogue."

The weeping-willow on the point below veiled the view; stretching straight out from the bank, it dropped its shock of long, green, pliant branches into the water, titillating and dimpling the surface. The rising bayou bore a freight of logs and drift from the swamps above; rudely pushing their way through the willow boughs, they tore and bruised the fragile tendrils that clung to the rough bark, scattering the tiny leaves which followed hopelessly after in their wake or danced up and down in the hollow eddies behind them. Each time the willow screen moved, the gunnels swayed under the forward motion of the eager bodies of the girls.

"At last!"

They turned their eyes to the shaft of sunlight that fell through the plantation clearing, bridging the stream. The skiff touched, entered, and passed through it with a marvellous revelation of form and color, the oars silvering and dripping diamonds, arrows and lances of light scintillating from polished steel, golden stars rising like dust from tassels, cordons, buttons, and epaulets, while the blue clouds themselves seemed to have fallen from their empyrean heights to uniform the rowers with their own celestial hue—blue, not gray!

"Rowlock! Rowlock!" What loud, frightful, threatening reverberations of the oars! And the bayou flowed on the same, and the cypress-trees gazed stolidly and steadfastly up to the heavens, and the heavens were serenely blue and white! But the earth was sympathetic, the ground shook and swayed under their feet; or was it the rush of thoughts that made their heads so giddy? They tried to arrest one and hold it for guidance, but on they sped, leaving only wild confusion of conjecture behind.

"Rowlock! Rowlock!" The rudder headed the bow for the gunnels.

"Titine! Gina! Will they kill us all?" whispered Lolotte, with anxious horror.

The agile Lou Ann, Lolotte's most efficient co-adjutor and Uncle John's most successful tormentor, dropped her bundle of fishing-poles (which he had carefully spread on his roof to "cure"), and while they rolled and rattled over the dry shingles she scrambled with inconceivable haste to her corner of descent. Holding to the eaves while her excited black feet searched and found the top of the window that served as a step, she dropped into the ash-hopper below. Without pausing, as usual, to efface betraying evidences of her enterprise from her person, or to cover her tracks in the wet ashes, she jumped to the ground, and ignoring all secreting offers of bush, fence, or ditch, contrary to her custom, she ran with all the speed of her thin legs down the shortest road to the quarters. They were, as she knew, deserted. The doors of the cabins were all shut, with logs of wood or chairs propped against them. The chickens and dogs were making free of the galleries, and the hogs wallowed in peaceful immunity underneath. A waking baby from a lonely imprisoned cradle sent cries for relief through an open window. Lou Ann, looking neither to the right nor the left, slackened not her steps, but passed straight on through the little avenue to the great white-oak which stood just outside the levee on the bank of the bayou.

Under the wide-spreading, moss-hung branches, upon the broad flat slope, a grand general washing of the clothes of the small community was in busy progress by the women, a proper feminine consecration of this purely feminine day. The daily irksome routine was broken, the men were all away, the sun was bright and warm, the air soft and sweet. The vague recesses of the opposite forest were dim and silent, the bayou played under the gunnels in caressing modulations. All furthered the hearkening and the yielding to a debonair mood, with disregard of concealment, license of pose, freedom of limb, hilarity, conviviality, audacities of heart and tongue, joyous indulgence in freak and impulse, banishment of thought, a return, indeed, for one brief moment to the wild, sweet ways of nature, to the festal days of ancestral golden age (a short retrogression for them), when the body still had claims, and the mind concessions, and the heart owed no allegiance, and when god and satyr eyes still might be caught peeping and glistening from leafy covert on feminine midsummer gambols. Their skirts were girt high around their broad full hips, their dark arms and necks came naked out of their low, sleeveless, white chemise bodies, and glistened with perspiration in the sun as if frosted with silver. Little clouds of steam rose from the kettles standing around them over heaps of burning chips. The splay-legged battling-boards sank firmer and firmer into the earth under the blows of the bats, pounding and thumping the wet clothes, squirting the warm suds in all directions, up into the laughing faces, down into the panting bosoms, against the shortened, clinging skirts, over the bare legs, out in frothy runnels over the soft red clay corrugated with innumerable toe-prints. Out upon the gunnels the water swished and foamed under the vigorous movements of the rinsers, endlessly bending and raising their flexible, muscular bodies, burying their arms to the shoulders in the cool, green depths, piling higher and higher the heaps of tightly-wrung clothes at their sides. The water-carriers, passing up and down the narrow, slippery plank-way, held the evenly filled pails with the ease of coronets upon their heads. The children, under compulsion of continuous threats and occasional chastisement, fed the fire with chips from distant wood-piles, squabbling for the possession of the one cane-knife to split kindlers, imitating the noise and echoing with absurd fidelity the full-throated laughter that interrupted from time to time the work around the wash-kettles.

High above the slop and tumult sat old Aunt Mary, the official sick-nurse of the plantation, commonly credited with conjuring powers. She held a corn-cob pipe between her yellow protruding teeth, and her little restless eyes travelled inquisitively from person to person as if in quest of professional information, twinkling with amusement at notable efforts of wit, and with malice at the general discomfiture expressed under their gaze. Heelen sat near, nursing her baby. She had taken off her kerchief, and leaned her uncovered head back against the trunk of the tree; the long wisps of wool, tightly wrapped in white knitting-cotton, rose from irregular sections all over her elongated narrow skull, and encircled her wrinkled, nervous, toothless face like some ghastly serpentine chevelure.

"De Yankees! de Yankees! I seed 'em—at de big house! Little

mistus she come for Uncle John. He fotched his gun—for to shoot 'em."

Lou Ann struggled to make her exhausted breath carry all her tidings. After each item she closed her mouth and swallowed violently, working her muscles until her little horns of hair rose and moved with the contortions of her face.

"An' dey locked a passel o' men up in de smoke-house—Cornfedrits."

The bats paused in the air, the women on the gunnels lifted their arms out of the water, those on the gang-plank stopped where they were; only the kettles simmered on audibly.

Lou Ann recommenced, this time finishing in one breath, with the added emphasis of raising her arm and pointing in the direction from whence she came, her voice getting shriller and shriller to the end:

"I seed 'em. Dey was Yankees. Little mistus she come for Uncle John; he fotched his gun for to shoot 'em; and they locked a passel o' men up in de smoke-house—Cornfedrits."

The Yankees! What did it mean to them? How much from the world outside had penetrated into the unlettered fastnesses of their ignorance? What did the war mean to them? Had Bayou l'Ombre indeed isolated both mind and body? Had the subtle time-spirit itself been diverted from them by the cut-off? Could their rude minds draw no inferences from the gradual loosening of authority and relaxing of discipline? Did they neither guess nor divine their share in the shock of battle out there? Could their ghost-seeing eyes not discern the martyr-spirits rising from two opposing armies, pointing at, beckoning to them? If, indeed, the water-shed of their destiny was forming without their knowledge as without their assistance, could not maternal instinct spell it out of the heart-throbs pulsing into life under their bosoms, or read from the dumb faces of the children at their breast the triumphant secret of their superiority over others born and nourished before them?

Had they, indeed, no gratifications beyond the physical, no yearnings, no secret burden of a secret prayer to God, these bonded wives and mothers? Was this careless, happy, indolent existence genuine, or only a fool's motley to disguise a tragedy of suffering? What to them was the difference between themselves and their mistresses? their condition? or their skin, that opaque black skin which hid so well the secrets of life, which could feel but not own the blush of shame, the pallor of weakness.

If their husbands had brought only rum from their stealthy midnight excursions to distant towns, how could the child repeat it so glibly—"Yankees—Cornfedrits?" The women stood still and silent, but their eyes began to creep around furtively, as if seeking degrees of complicity in a common guilt, each waiting for the other to confess comprehension, to assume the responsibility of knowledge.

The clear-headed children, profiting by the distraction of attention from them, stole away for their fishing engagement, leaving cane-knife and chips scattered on the ground behind them. The murmuring of the bayou seemed to rise louder and louder; the cries of the forsaken baby, clamorous and hoarse, fell distinctly on the air.

"My Gord A'mighty!"

The exclamation was uncompromising; it relieved the tension and encouraged rejoinder.

"My Lord!—humph!"

One bat slowly and deliberately began to beat again—Black Maria's. Her tall, straight back was to them, but, as if they saw it, they knew that her face was settling into that cold, stern rigidity of hers, the keen eyes beginning to glisten, the long, thin nostrils nervously to twitch, the lips to open over her fine white teeth—the expression they hated and feared.

"O-h! o-h! o-h!"

A long, thin, tremulous vibration, a weird, haunting note: what inspiration suggested it?

"Glo-o-ry!"

Old Aunt Mary nodded her knowing head affirmatively, as if at the fulfilment of a silent prophecy. She quietly shook the ashes out of her pipe, hunted her pocket, put it in, and rising stiffly from the root, hobbled away on her stick in the direction of her cabin.

"Glo-o-ry!"

Dead-arm Harriet stood before them, with her back to the bayou, her right arm hanging heavy at her side, her left extended, the finger pointing to the sky. A shapely arm and tapering finger; a comely, sleek, half-nude body; the moist lips, with burning red linings, barely parting to emit the sound they must have culled in uncanny practices. The heavy lids drooped over the large sleepy eyes, looking with languid passion from behind the thick black lashes.

"Glo-o-ry!" It stripped their very nerves and bared secret places of sensation! The "happy" cry of revival meetings—as if midnight were coming on, salvation and the mourners' bench before them,

Judgment-day and fiery flames behind them, and "Sister Harriet" raising her voice to call them on, on, through hand-clapping, foot-stamping, shouting, groaning, screaming, out of their sins, out of their senses, to rave in religious inebriation, and fall in religious catalepsy across the floor at the preacher's feet. With a wild rush, the hesitating emotions of the women sought the opportune outlet, their hungry blood bounding and leaping for the mid-day orgy. Obediently their bodies began the imperceptible motion right and left, and the veins in their throats to swell and stand out under their skins, while the short, fierce, intense responsive exclamations fell from their lips to relieve their own and increase the exaltation of the others.

"Sweet Christ! sweet Christ!"

"Take me, Saviour!"

"Oh, de Lamb! de Lamb!"

"I'm a-coming! I'm a-coming!"

"Hold back, Satan! we's a-catching on!"

"De blood's a-dripping! de blood's a-dripping!"

"Let me kiss dat cross! let me kiss it!"

"Sweet Master!"

"Glo-o-ry! Fre-e-dom!" It was a whisper, but it came like a crash, and transfixed them; their mouths stood open with the last words, their bodies remained bent to one side or the other, the febrile light in their eyes burning as if from their blood on fire. They could all remember the day when Dead-arm Harriet, the worst worker and most violent tongue of the gang, stood in the clearing, and raising that dead right arm over her head, cursed the overseer riding away in the distance. The wind had been blowing all day; there was a sudden loud crack above them, and a limb from a deadened tree broke, sailed, poised, and fell crashing to her shoulder, and deadening her arm forever. They looked instinctively now with a start to the oak above them, to the sky—only moss and leaves and blue and white clouds. And still Harriet's voice rose, the words faster, louder, bolder, more determined, whipping them out of their awe, driving them on again down the incline of their own passions.

"Glory! Freedom! Freedom! Glory!"

"I'm bound to see 'em! Come along!"

Heelen's wild scream rang shrill and hysterical. She jerked her breast from the sucking lips, and dropped her baby with a thud on the ground. They all followed her up the levee, pressing one after the other, slipping in the wet clay, struggling each one not to be left behind. Emmeline, the wife of little Ben, the only yellow woman on the place, was the last. Her skirt was held in a grip of iron; blinded, obtuse, she pulled forward, reaching her arms out after the others.

"You stay here!"

She turned and met the determined black face of her mother-in-law.

"You let me go!" she cried, half sobbing, half angry.

"You stay here, I tell you!" The words were muttered through clinched teeth.

"You let me go, I tell you!"

"Glory! Freedom!"

The others had already left the quarters, and were on the road. They two were alone on the bank now, except Heelen's baby, whimpering under the tree; their blazing eyes glared at each other. The singing voices grew fainter and fainter. Suddenly the yellow face grew dark with the surge of blood underneath, the brows wrinkled, and the lips protruded in a grimace of animal rage. Grasping her wet bat tightly with both hands, she turned with a furious bound, and raised it with all the force of her short muscular arms. The black woman darted to the ground; the cane-knife flashed in the air and came down pitilessly towards the soft fleshy shoulder. A wild, terrified scream burst from Emmeline's lips; the bat dropped, seizing her skirt with both hands, she pulled forward, straining her back out of reach of the knife; the homespun tore, and she fled up the bank, her yellow limbs gleaming through the rent left by the fragment in the hand of the black woman.

The prisoners were so young, so handsome, so heroic; the very incarnation of the holy spirit of patriotism in their pathetic uniform of brimless caps, ragged jackets, toeless shoes, and shrunken trousers—a veteran equipment of wretchedness out of keeping with their fresh young faces. How proud and unsubdued they walked through the hall between the file of bayonets! With what haughty, defiant eyes they returned the gaze of their insultingly resplendent conquerors! Oh, if girls' souls had been merchantable at that moment! Their hands tied behind their backs like runaway slaves! Locked up in the smoke-house! That dark, rancid, gloomy, mouldy depot of empty hogs-heads, barrels, boxes, and fetid exhalations.

They were the first soldiers in gray the girls had ever seen; their own chivalrous knights, the champions of their radiant country.

What was the story of their calamity? Treacherously entrapped? Overpowered by numbers? Where were their companions—staring with mute, cold, upturned faces from pools of blood? And were these to be led helplessly tethered into captivity, imprisoned; with ball and chain to gangrene and disgrace their strong young limbs, or was solitary confinement to starve their hearts and craze their minds, holding death in a thousand loathsome, creeping shapes ever threateningly over them?

The smoke-house looked sinister and inimical after its sudden promotion from keeper of food to keeper of men. The great square whitewashed logs seemed to settle more ponderously on the ground around them, the pointed roof to press down as if the air of heaven were an emissary to be dreaded; the hinges and locks were so ostentatiously massive and incorruptible. What artful, what vindictive security of carpenter and lock-smith to exclude thieves or immure patriots!

The two eldest girls stood against the open armoire with their chill fingers interlaced. Beyond the wrinkled back of Uncle John's copperas-dyed coat before them lay the region of brass buttons and blue cloth and hostility; but they would not look at it; they turned their heads away; the lids of their eyes refused to lift and reveal the repugnant vision to them. If their ears had only been equally sensitive!

"And so you are the uncle of the young ladies? Brother of the father or mother?" What clear, incisive, nasal tones! Thank Heaven for the difference between them of the voice at least!

The captain's left arm was in a sling, but his hand could steadily hold the note-book in which he carefully pencilled Uncle John's answers to his minute cross-examination—a dainty, fragrant, Russia-leather note-book, with monogram and letters and numbers emblazoned on the outside in national colors. It had photographs inside, also, which he would pause and admire from time to time, reading the tender dedications aloud to his companions.

"And the lady in the kitchen called mammy? She is the mother, I guess?"

"P-p-p-peggy's a nigger, and my mistresses is white," stuttered Uncle John.

"Ah, indeed! Gentlemen in my uniform find it difficult to remember these trifling distinctions of color."

What tawdry pleasantry! What hypocritical courtesy! What exquisite ceremony and dainty manual for murderous dandies!

"Ef-ef-ef-ef I hadn't done gone and forgot dem caps!"

Uncle John stood before his young mistresses erect and determined, his old double-barrel shotgun firmly clasped in his tremulous hands, his blear, bloodshot eyes fearlessly measuring the foe. If it were to be five hundred lashes on his bare back under the trees out there (terms on which he would gladly have compromised), or, his secret fear, a running noose over one of the branches, or the murderous extravagance of powder and shot for him, he had made up his mind, despite every penalty, to fulfil his duty and stand by his word to Marse John. Ever since the time the little crawling white boy used to follow the great awkward black boy around like a shadow, John had made a cult of Marse John. He had taught him as a child to fish, hunt, trap birds, to dress skins, knit gloves, and play cards on the sly, to fight cocks on Sunday, to stutter, to cut the "pigeon wing" equal to any negro in the State—and other personal accomplishments besides. He had stood by him through all his scrapes as a youth, was valet to all his frolics as a young man, and now in his old age he gardened for him, and looked after the young ladies for him, stretching or contracting his elastic moral code as occasion required; but he had never deceived him nor falsified his word to him. He knew all about the war: Marse John had told him. He knew what Marse John meant when he left the children to him, and Marse John knew what to expect from John. He would treat them civilly as long as they were civil, but his gun was loaded, both barrels with bullets, and—

"Ef-ef-ef-ef I hadn't done gone and forgot dem caps!"

There was his powder-horn under one arm, there was his shot-flask filled with the last batch of slugs under the other; but the caps were not in his right-hand coat-pocket, they were in his cupboard, hidden for safety under a pile of garden "truck."

The busy martins twittered in and out of their little lodge under the eaves of the smoke-house. Régina and Christine were powerless to prevent furtive glances in that direction. Could the *prisoners* hear it inside? Could *they* see the sun travelling westward, crack by crack, chink by chink, in the roof? Could they feel it sinking, and with it sinking all their hopes of deliverance? Or did they hope still?

Maidens had mounted donjon towers at midnight, had eluded Argus-eyed sentinels, had drugged savage blood-hounds, had crossed lightning-flashed seas, had traversed robber-infested forests; whatever maidens had done they would do, for could ever men more piteously implore release from castle keep than these gray-clad youths from the smoke-house? And did ever maiden hearts beat more valiantly than theirs? (and did ever maiden limbs tremble more cowardly?) Many a tedious day had been lightened by their rehearsal of just such a drama as this; they had prepared roles for every imaginable sanguinary circumstance, but prevision, as usual, had overlooked the unexpected. The erstwhile feasible conduct, the erstwhile feasible weapons, of a Jeanne d'Arc or Charlotte Corday, the defiant speeches, the ringing retorts—how inappropriate, inadequate, here and now! If God would only help them! but, like the bayou, the cypresses, and the blue sky, He seemed to-day eternally above such insignificant human necessities as theirs.

Without the aid of introspection or the fear of capital punishment, Lolotte found it very difficult to maintain the prolonged state of rigidity into which her sisters had frozen themselves. All the alleviations devised during a wearisome experience of compulsory attendance on plantation funerals were exhausted in the course of this protracted, hymnless, prayerless solemnity. She stood wedged in between them and the armoire which displayed all its shelves of allurements to her. There were her bird-traps just within reach; there was the fascinating bag of nux-vomica root—crow poison; there was the little old work-box filled with ammunition, which she was forbidden to touch, and all the big gar-fish lines and harpoons and decoy-ducks. There were her own perch lines, the levy she had raised in favor of her companions; they were neatly rolled, ready to tie on the rods, only needing sinkers; and there was the old Indian basket filled with odds and ends, an unfailing treasure of resource and surprise. She was just about searching in it for sinkers when this interruption occurred.

The sky was so bright over the fields! Just the evening to go fishing, whether they caught anything or not. If the enemy would only hurry and go, there might still be time; they would leave, they said, as soon as mammy cooked them something to eat. She had seen mammy chasing a chicken through the yard. She wondered how the nice, fat little round "doodles" were getting on in their tin can under the house; she never had had such a fine box of bait; she wondered if the negro children would go all the same without her; she wondered if she could see them creeping down the road. How easy she could have got away from Uncle John! Anything almost would do for sinkers—bits of iron, nails; they had to do since their father and Uncle John made their last moulding of bullets. She thought they might have left her just one real sinker simply as a matter of distinction between herself and the little darkies. Her eyes kept returning to the Indian basket, and if she stopped twisting her fingers one over the other but a moment they would take their way to rummaging among the rusty contents.

"Glory! Freedom!"

In came the negresses, Bacchantes drunk with the fumes of their own hot blood, Dead-arm Harriet, like a triumphant sorceress, leading them, waving and gesticulating with her one "live" arm, all repeating over and over again the potent magical words, oblivious of the curious looks of the men, their own exposure, the presence of their mistresses, of everything but their own ecstasy.

"Freedom! Master! Freedom!"

Christine and Régina raised their heads and looked perplexed at the furious women in the yard, and the men gazing down to them.

What was the matter with them? What did they mean? What was it all about?

"Freedom! Freedom!"

Then light broke upon them; their fingers tightened in each other's clasp, and their cheeks flushed crimson.

"How dared they? What insolence! What—"

The opposite door stood open; they rushed across the hall and closed it between them and the humiliating scene. This, this they had not thought of, this they had never read about, this their imagination in wildest flights had not ventured upon. This was not a superficial conflict to sweep the earth with cannons and mow it with sabres; this was an earthquake which had rent it asunder, exposing the quivering organs of hidden life. What a chasm was yawning before them! There was no need to listen one to the other; the circumstances could wring from the hearts of millions but one sentiment, the tongue was left no choice of words.

"Let them go! let them be driven out! never, never to see them again!"

The anger of outraged affection, betrayed confidence, abandoned trust, traitorous denial, raged within them.

These were their servants, their possessions! From generation to generation their lives had been woven together by the shuttle of destiny. How flimsy and transparent the fabric! how grotesque and absurd the tapestry, with its vaunted traditions of mutual loyalty and devotion! What a farce, what a lying, disgusting farce it had all been! Well, it was over now; that was a comfort—all over, all ended. If the hearts had intergrown, they were torn apart now.

After this there was no return, no reconciliation possible! Through the storm of their emotions a thought drifted, then another; little detached scenes flitted into memory; familiar gestures, speeches, words, one reminiscence drawing another. Thicker and thicker came little episodes of their pastoral existence together; the counter interchanges of tokens, homely presents, kind offices, loving remembrances; the mutual assistance and consolation in all the accidents of life traversed together, the sicknesses, the births, the deaths; and so many thousand trivial incidents of long, long ago—memory had not lost one—down to the fresh eggs and the pop-corn of that very morning; they were all there, falling upon their bruised hearts.

In the hearts of the women out there were only shackles and scourges. What of the long Sundays of Bible-reading and catechism, the long evenings of woodland tales; the confidences; the half-hours around the open fireplaces when supper was cooking, the potatoes under their hillocks of ashes, the thin-legged ovens of cornbread with their lids of glowing coals, the savory skillets of fried meat, the—Was it indeed all of the past, never again to be present or future? And those humble, truthful, loving eyes, which had looked up to them from the first moment of their lives: did they look with greater trust up to God Himself? It was all over, yes, all over! The color faded from their faces, the scornful resolution left their lips; they laid their faces in their hands and sobbed.

"Do you hear, Titine?" Lolotte burst into the room. "They are all going to leave, every one of them; a transport is coming to-night to take them off. They are going to bundle up their things and wait at the steamboat-landing; and they are not going to take a child, and not a single husband. The captain says the government at Washington will give them the nicest white husbands in the land; that they ought to be glad to marry them. They carried on as if they were drunk. Do you believe it, Titine? Oh, I do wish Jeff Davis would hurry up and win!"

The door opened again; it was Black Maria, still holding the cane-knife in her hand. She crossed the room with her noiseless barefooted tread, and placed herself behind them. They did not expect her to say anything; Black Maria never talked much; but they understood her, as they always did.

Her skirts were still tied up, her head-kerchief awry; they saw for the first time that the wool under it was snow-white.

Black Maria! They might have known it! They looked at her.

No! She was not! She was not negro, like the others. Who was she? What was she? Where did she come from, with her white features and white nature under her ebon skin? What was the mystery that enveloped her? Why did the brain always torture itself in surmises about her? Why did she not talk as the others did, and just for a moment uncover that coffin heart of hers? Why was she, alone of all the negroes, still an alien, a foreigner, an exile among them? Was she brooding on disgrace, outrage, revenge? Was she looking at some mirage behind her—a distant equatorial country, a princely rank, barbaric state, some inherited memory transmitted by that other Black Maria, her mother? Who was the secret black father whom no one had discovered? Was it, as the negroes said, the Prince of Darkness? Who was her own secret consort, the father of Ben? What religion had she to warrant her scornful repudiation of Christianity? What code that enabled her to walk as if she were free through slavery, to assume slavery now when others hailed freedom, to be loyal in the midst of treason?

"Look!" Lolotte came into the room, and held up a rusty, irregular piece of iron. "I found this in the old Indian basket where I was looking for sinkers. Don't you see what it is? It is the old key of the smoke-house, and I am going to let those Confederates out." She spoke quietly and decidedly. There was something else in the other hand, concealed in the folds of her dress. She produced it reluctantly. It was the gun-wrench that filled so prominent a part in her active life—always coveting it, getting possession of it, being deprived of it, and accused unfailingly for its every absence and misplacement. "You see, it is so convenient; it screws so nicely on to everything," she continued, apologetically, as she demonstrated the useful qualification by screwing it on to the key. "There! it is as good as a handle. All they've got to do is to slip away in the skiff while the others are eating. And I would like to know how they can ever be caught, without another boat on the place! But oh, girls"—her black eyes twinkled maliciously—"what fools the Yankees are!"

If the Federals, as they announced, were only going to remain long enough for the lady in the kitchen to prepare them something to eat, the length of their stay clearly rested in Peggy the cook's hands, as she understood it. She walked around her kitchen with a briskness rarely permitted by her corpulent proportions, and with an intuitive faith in the common nature of man regardless of political opinion, she exerted her culinary skill to the

utmost. She knew nothing of the wholesale quarrelling and fighting of a great war, but during her numerous marital experiments,
not counting intermittent conjugalities for twenty-five years with
Uncle John, she had seen mercy and propitiation flow more than
once after a good meal from the most irate; and a healthy
digestion aiding, she never despaired of even the most revengeful.
The enemy, in her opinion, were simply to be treated like furious
husbands, and were to be offered the best menu possible under
the trying circumstances. She worked, inspired by all the wife-lore
of past ages, the infiltrated wisdom that descends to women in the
course of a world of empirical connubiality, that traditionary
compendium to their lives by which they still hope to make
companionship with men harmonious and the earth a pleasant
abiding-place. With minute particularity Peggy set the table and
placed the dishes. The sun was now sinking, and sending almost
horizontal rays over the roof of the smoke-house, whose ugly
square frame completely blocked the view of the dining-room
window. Peggy carefully drew the red calico curtain across it, and
after a moment's rehearsal to bring her features to the conventional womanly expression of cheerful obtuseness to existing
displeasure, she opened the dining-room door.

Gina and Lolotte stood close under the window against the
dwelling, looking at the locked door of the smoke-house before
them, listening to the sounds falling from the dining-room above.
Once in the skiff, the prisoners were safe; but the little red curtain
of the window fluttering flimsily in the breeze coquetted with
their hopes and the lives of three men. If the corners would but
stay down a second! Titine and Black Maria were in front, busy
about the skiff. Peggy's culinary success appeared, from the com-
ments of the diners, to be complimentary to her judgment. But
food alone, however, does not suffice in the critical moments of
life; men are half managed when only fed. There was another
menu, the ingredients of which were not limited or stinted by
blockade of war. Peggy had prepared that also; and in addition to
the sounds of plates, knives, forks, and glasses, came the tones of
her rich voice dropping from a quick tongue the *entremets* of her
piquant imagination. The attention in the room seemed tense,
and at last the curtain hung straight and motionless.

"Now! now!" whispered Gina. "We must risk something."

Woman-like, they paused midway and looked back; a hand

stretched from the table was carelessly drawing the curtain aside, and the window stared unhindered at the jail.

Why had they waited? Why had they not rushed forward immediately? By this time their soldiers might have been free! They could hear Peggy moving around the table; they could see her bulky form push again and again across the window.

"Mammy! Mammy!"

Could she hear them? They clasped their hands and held their faces up in imploring appeal. The sun was setting fast, almost running down the west to the woods. The dinner, if good, was not long. It all depended upon Peggy now.

"Mammy! Mammy!" They raised their little voices, then lowered them in agony of apprehension. "Mammy, do something! Help us!"

But still she passed on and about, around the table, and across the window, blind to the smoke-house, deaf to them, while her easy, familiar voice recited the comical gyrations of "old Frizzly," the half-witted hen, who had set her heart against being killed and stewed, and ran and hid, and screamed and cackled, and ducked and flew, and then, after her silly head was twisted off, "just danced, as if she were at ''Cadian' ball, all over the yard."

It would soon be too late! It was, perhaps, too late now!

Black Maria had got the skiff away from the gunnels, but they might just as well give it up; they would not have time enough now.

"Mammy!" The desperate girls made a supreme effort of voice and look. The unctuous black face, the red bead ear-rings, the bandanna head-kerchief, appeared at the window with "old Frizzly's" last dying cackle. There was one flashing wink of the left eye.

Her nurslings recognized then her *pièce de résistance oratoire*—a side-splitting prank once played upon her by another nursling, her pet, her idol, the plague of her life—Beau.

Who could have heard grating lock or squeaking hinges through the boisterous mirth that followed? Who could have seen the desperate bound of the three imprisoned soldiers for liberty through that screen of sumptuous flesh—the magnificent back of Mammy that filled to overlapping the insignificant little window?

They did not wait to hear the captain's rapturous toast to Peggy in sassafras tea, nor his voluble protestations of love to her, nor could they see him in his excitement forgetting his wounded arm, bring both clinched fists with a loud bravo to the table, and then faint dead away.

"I knew it!"

"Just like him!"

"Take him in the air—quick!"

"No, sir! You take him in there, and put him on the best bed in the house." Peggy did not move from the window, but her prompt command turned the soldiers from the door in the hall, and her finger directed them to the closed bed-chamber.

Without noticing Christine standing by the open window, they dropped their doughty burden—boots, spurs, sword, epaulets, and all—on the fresh, white little bed, the feather mattress fluffing up all around as if to submerge him.

"Oh, don't bother about that; cut the sleeve off!"

"Who has a knife?"

"There."

"That's all right now."

"He's coming round."

"There's one nice coat spoiled."

"Uncle Sam has plenty more."

"Don't let it drip on the bed."

"Save it to send to Washington—trophy—wet with rebel blood."

The captain was evidently recovering.

"You stay here while I keep 'em eating," whispered Peggy, authoritatively, to Christine.

Titine trembled as if she had an ague.

"How could they help seeing the tall form of Black Maria standing in the prow of the boat out in the very middle of the bayou? Suppose she, Titine, had not been there to close the window quick as thought? Suppose instead of passing through her room she had run through the basement, as she intended, after pushing off the skiff?"

Rollicking, careless, noisy, the soldiers went back to their interrupted meal, while the boat went cautiously down the bayou to the meeting place beyond the clearing.

"How far was Black Maria now?" Titine opened the window a tiny crack. "Heavens! how slowly she paddled! lifting the oar deliberately from side to side, looking straight ahead. How clear and distinct she was in the soft evening light! Why did she not hurry? why did she not row? She could have muffled the oars. But no, no one thought of that; that was always the way—always something overlooked and forgotten. The soldiers could finish a dozen dinners before the skiff got out of sight at this rate. Without the skiff the prisoners might just as well be locked still in the smoke-house. Did he on the bed suspect something, seeing her look out this way?" She closed the window tight.

"How dark the room was! She could hardly see the wounded man. How quiet he was! Was he sleeping, or had he fainted again? In her bed! her enemy lying in her bed! his head on her pillow, her own little pillow, the feverish confidant of so many sleepless nights! How far were they now on the bayou? She must peep out again. Why, Maria had not moved! not moved an inch! Oh, if she could only scream to her! if she were only in the skiff!

"How ghastly pale he looked on the bed! his face as white as the coverlet, his hair and beard so black; how changed without his bravado and impertinence! And he was not old, either; not older than the boys in gray. She had fancied that age and ugliness alone could go with violence and wrong. How much gold! how much glitter! Why, the sun did not rise with more splendor of equipment. Costumed as if for the conquest of worlds. If the Yankees dressed their captains this way, what was the livery of their generals? How curious the sleeveless arm looked! What a horrible mark the gash made right across the soft white skin! What a scar it would leave! What a disfigurement! And this, this is what men call love of country!" ʿ

On Saturday nights sometimes, in the quarters, when rum had been smuggled in, the negroes would get to fighting and beating their wives, and her father would be sent for in a hurry to come with his gun and separate them. Hatchets, axes, cane-knives— anything they would seize, to cut and slash one another, husbands, wives, mothers, sons, sisters, brothers; but they were negroes, ignorant, uneducated, barbarous, excited; they could not help it; they could not be expected to resist all at once the momentum of centuries of ancestral ferocity. But for white men, gentlemen, thus furiously to mar and disfigure their own mother-given bodies! All the latent maternal instinct in her was roused, all the woman in her revolted against the sacrilegious violence of mutilation. "Love of country to make her childless, or only the mother of invalids! This was only one. What of the other thousands and hundreds of thousands? Are men indeed so inexhaustible? Are the pangs of maternity so cheap? Are women's hearts of no account whatever in the settlement of disputes? O God! cannot the world get along without war? But even if men want it, even if God permits it, how can the women allow it? If the man on the bed were a negro, she could do something for his arm. Many a time, early Sunday mornings, Saturday night culprits had come to her secretly, and she had washed off the thick, gummy blood, and bandaged up their cuts and bruises; they did not show so on black skin.... This man had a mother somewhere among the people she called 'enemies;' a mother sitting counting day by day the continued possession of a live son, growing gray and old before that terrible next minute ever threatening to take her boy and give her a corpse. Or perhaps, like her own, his mother might be dead. They might be friends in that kingdom which the points of the compass neither unite nor divide; together they might be looking down on this quarrelling, fighting world; mothers, even though angels, looking, looking through smoke and powder and blood and hatred after their children. Their eyes might be fixed on this lonely little spot, on this room...." She walked to the bed.

The blood was oozing up through the strips of plaster. She stanched and bathed and soothed the wound as she well knew how with her tender, agile fingers, and returned to the window. Maria had disappeared now; she could open the window with impunity. The trackless water was flowing innocently along, the cooling air was rising in mist, the cypress-trees checked the brilliant sky with the filigree and net-work of their bristly foliage. The birds twittered, the chickens loitered and dallied on their way to roost. The expectant dogs were lying on the levee waiting for the swampers, who, they ought to know, could not possibly return before midnight. And Molly was actually on time this evening, lowing for mammy to come and milk her; what was the war to her? How happy and peaceful it all was! What a jarring contrast to swords and bayonets! Thank God that Nature was impartial, and could not be drilled into partisanship! If humanity were like Nature! If—if there had been no war! She paused, shocked at her first doubt; of the great Circumstance of her life it was like saying, "If there had been no God!"

As she stood at the window and thought, all the brilliant coloring of her romantic fantasies, the stories of childhood, the perversions of education, the self-delusions, they all seemed to fade with the waning light, and with the beautiful day sink slowly and quietly into the irrevocable past. "Thank God, above all, that it is a human device to uniform people into friends and enemies! The heart (her own felt so soft and loving)—the heart repudiates such attempts of blue and gray; it still clings to Nature, and belongs to God." She thought the wound must need tending again, and returned to the bed. The patient, meanwhile, went in and out of the mazes of unconsciousness caused by weakness.

"Was that really he on this foamy bed? What a blotch his camp-battered body made down the centre of it! It was good to be on a bed once more, to look up into a mosquito-bar instead of the boughs of trees, to feel his head on a pillow. But why did they put him there? Why did they not lay him somewhere on the floor, outside on the ground, instead of soiling and crumpling this lily-white surface?"

He could observe his nurse through his half-closed lids, which fell as she approached the bed, and closed tight as she bent above him. When she stood at the window he could look full at her. "How innocent and unsuspecting she looked!" The strained rigidity had passed away from her face. Her transparent, child-like eyes were looking with all their life of expression in the direction of the bed, and then at something passing in her own mind. "Thank Heaven, the fright had all gone out of them! How horrible for a gentleman to read fear in the eyes of a woman! Her mind must be as pure and white, yes, and as impressionable, too, as her bed. Did his presence lie like a blot upon it also? How she must hate him! how she must loathe him! Would it have been different if he had come in the other uniform—if he had worn the gray? would she then have cared for him, have administered to him? How slight and frail she was! What a wan, wistful little face between him and the gloomy old bayou! He could see her more plainly now since she had opened the window and let in the cool, fragrant air. There was no joyous development of the body in her to proclaim womanhood, none of the seductive, confident beauty that follows coronation of youth; to her had only come the care and anxiety of maturity. This—this," he exclaimed to himself, "is the way women fight a war." Was she coming this way? Yes. To the bed? Hardly. Now she was pressing against it, now bending over him, now dropping a cooling dew from heaven on his burning arm, and now—oh, why so soon?—she was going away to stand and look out of the window again.

The homely little room was filled with feminine subterfuges for ornament, feminine substitutes for comfort. How simple women are! how little they require, after all! only peace and love and quiet, only the impossible in a masculine world. What was she thinking of? If he could only have seen the expression of her eyes as she bent over him! Suppose he should open his and look straight up at her? but no, he had not the courage to frighten her again. He transplanted her in his mind to other surroundings, her proper surroundings by birthright, gave her in abundance all of which this war had deprived her, presented to her assiduous courtiers, not reckless soldiers like himself, but men whom peace had guided in the lofty sphere of intellectual pursuits. He held before her the sweet invitations of youth, the consummations of life. He made her smile, laugh.

"Ah!"—he turned his face against the pillow—"had that sad face ever laughed? Could any woman laugh during a war? Could any triumph, however glorious, atone for battles that gave men death, but left the women to live? This was only one; how many, wan and silent as she, were looking at this sunset—the sunset not of a day, but a life? When it was all over, who was to make restitution to them, the women? Was any cost too great to repurchase for them simply the privilege of hoping again? What an endless chain of accusing thoughts! What a miserable conviction tearing his heart! If he could get on his knees to her, if he could kiss her feet, if he could beg pardon in the dust—he, a man for all men, of her, a woman for all women. If he could make her his country, not to fight, but to work for, it..."

She came to his side again, she bent over him, she touched him.

Impulsive, thoughtless, hot-headed, he opened his eyes full, he forgot again the wounded arm. With both hands he stayed her frightened start; he saw the expression of her eyes bending over him.

"Can you forgive me? It is a heartless, cowardly trick! I am not a Yankee; I am Beau, your cousin, the guerilla."

The door of the smoke-house opened, the escaped soldiers ran like deer between the furrows of Uncle John's vegetable garden, where the waving corn leaves could screen them; then out to the bank of the bayou—not on the levee, but close against the fence—snagging their clothes and scratching their faces and hands on the cuckleburs; Lolotte in front, with a stick in her hand, beating the bushes through habit to frighten the snakes, calling, directing, animating, in excited whispers; Régina in the rear, urging, pressing, sustaining the young soldier lagging behind, but painfully striving with stiffened limbs to keep up with the pace of his older, more vigorous companions. Ahead of them Black Maria was steadily keeping the skiff out in the current. The bayou narrowed and grew dark as it entered between the banks of serried cypress-trees, where night had already begun.

Régina looked hurriedly over her shoulder. "Had they found out yet at the house? How slowly she ran! How long it took to get to the woods! Oh, they would have time over and over again to finish their dinner and catch them. Perhaps at this very moment, as she was thinking of it, some forgotten article in the skiff was betraying them! Perhaps a gun might even now be pointing down their path! Or, now! the bullet could start and the report come too late to warn them."

She looked back again and again.

From the little cottage under the trees the curtains fluttered, but no bayonet nor smooth-bore was visible.

She met her companion's face, looking back also, but not for guns—for her. "If it had been different! If he had been a visitor, come to stay; days and evenings to be passed together!" The thought lifting the sulphurous war-clouds from her heart, primitive idyls burst into instantaneous fragrant bloom in it like spring violets. He was not only the first soldier in gray she had ever seen, but the first young man; or it seemed so to her.

Again she looked back.

"How near they were still to the house! how plainly they could yet be seen! He could be shot straight through the back, the gray jacket getting one stain, one bullet-hole, more, the country one soldier less. Would they shoot through a woman at him? Would they be able to separate them if she ran close behind him, moving this way and that way, exactly as he did? If she saw them in time she could warn him; he could lie flat down in the grass; then it would be impossible to hit him."

Increasing and narrowing the space between them at the hest of each succeeding contradictory thought, turning her head again and again to the house behind her, she lost speed. Lolotte and the two men had already entered the forest before she reached it. Coming from the fields, the swamps seemed midnight dark. Catching her companion's hand, they groped their way along, tripped by the slimy cypress knees that rose like evil gnomes to beset and entangle their feet, slipping over rolling logs, sinking in stagnant mire, noosed by the coils of heavy vines that dropped from unseen branches overhead. Invisible wings of startled birds flapped above them, the croaking of frogs ebbed and flowed around them, owls shrieked and screamed from side to side of the bayou. Lolotte had ceased her beating; swamp serpents are too sluggish to be frightened away. In the obscurity, Black Maria could be dimly seem turning the skiff to a half-submerged log, from which a turtle dropped as if ballasted with lead. A giant cypress-tree arrested them; the smooth, fluted trunk, ringed with whitish watermarks, recording floods far over their heads; where they were scrambling once swam fish and serpents. The young soldier turned and faced her, the deliverer, whose manoeuvres in the open field had not escaped him.

She had saved him from imprisonment, insult, perhaps death—the only heir of a heroic father, the only son of a widowed mother; she had restored him to a precious heritage of love and honor, replaced him in the interrupted ambitious career of patri-otic duty; she had exposed her life for him—she was beautiful. She stood before him, panting, tremulous, ardent, with dumb, open red lips, and voluble, passionate eyes, and with a long scratch in her white cheek from which the blood trickled. She had much to say to him, her gray uniformed hero; but how in one moment express four years—four long years—and the last long minutes. The words were all there, had been rushing to her lips all day; her lips were parted, but the eager, overcrowded throng were jammed on the threshold; and her heart beat so in her ears! He could not talk; he could not explain. His companions were already in the boat, his enemies still in gunshot. He bent his face to hers in the dim light to learn by heart the features he must never forget—closer, closer, leaning, knowing more and more, with the eager precocity of youth.

Bellona must have flown disgusted away with the wings of an owl, Columbia might have nodded her head as knowingly as old Aunt Mary could, when the callow hearts, learning and knowing, brought the faces closer and closer together, until the lips touched.

"I shall come again; I shall come again. Wait for me. Surely I shall come again."

"Yes! Yes!"

Black Maria pushed the skiff off. "Rowlock! Rowlock!" They were safe and away.

A vociferous group stood around the empty gunnels. Uncle John, with the daring of desperation, advanced, disarmed as he was, towards them.

"I-I-I-I don't keer ef you is de-de-de President o' de United States hisself, I ain't gwine to 'low no such cussin' an' swarin' in de hearin' o' de-de-de young ladies. Marse John he-he-he don't 'low it, and when Marse John ain't here I-I-I don't 'low it."

His remonstrance and heroic attitude had very little effect, for the loud talk went on, and chiefly by ejaculation, imprecation, and self-accusation published the whole statement of the case; understanding which, Uncle John added his voice also:

"Good Gord A'mighty! Wh-wh-what's dat you say? Dey—dey—dey Yankees, an' you Cornfedrits? Well, sir, an' are you Marse Beau—you wid your arm hurted? Go 'long! You can't fool me; Marse Beau done had more sense en dat. My Gord! an' dey wuz Yankees? You better cuss—cussin's about all you kin do now. Course de boat's gone. You'll never ketch up wid 'em in Gord's world now. Don't come along arter me about it? 'Tain't my fault. How wuz I to know? You wuz Yankees enough for me. I declar', Marse Beau, you ought to be ashamed o' yourself! You wanted to l'arn dem a lesson! I reckon dey l'arnt you one! You didn't mean 'em no harm! Humph! dey've cut dey eye-teeth, dey have! Lord! Marse Beau, I thought you done knowed us better. Did you really think we wuz a-gwine to let a passel o' Yankees take us away off our own plantation? You must done forgot us. We jes cleaned out de house for 'em, we did—clo'es, food, tobacco, rum. De young ladies 'ain't lef' a mossel for Marse John. An'—an'—an' 'fore de good Gord, my gun! Done tuck my gun away wid 'em! Wh-wh-wh-what you mean by such doin's? L-l-look here, Marse Beau, I don't like dat, nohow! Wh-wh-what! you tuck my gun and gin it to de Yankees? Dat's my gun! I done had dat gun twenty-five year an' more! Dog-gone! Yes, sir, I'll cuss—I'll cuss ef I wants to! I 'ain't got no use for gorillas, nohow! Lem me 'lone, I tell you! lem me 'lone! Marse John he'll get de law o' dat! Who's 'sponsible? Dat's all I want to know—who's 'sponsible? Ef-ef-ef-ef—No, sir; dar ain't nary boat on de place, nor hereabouts. Yes, sir; you kin cross de swamp ef you kin find de way. No, sir—no, sir; dar ain't no one to show you. I ain't gwine to leave de young ladies twell Marse John he comes back. Yes, I reckon you kin git to de cut-off by to-morrow mornin', ef you ain't shot on de way for Yankees, an' ef your company is fool enough to wait for you. No, sir, I don't know nothin' 'bout nothin'; you better wait an' arsk Marse John.... My Gord! I'm obleeged to laugh; I can't help it. Dem fool nigger wimen a-sittin' on de brink o' de byer, dey clo'es tied up in de bedquilts, an' de shotes an' de pullits all kilt, a-waitin' for freedom! I lay dey'll git freedom enough to-night when de boys come home.

Dey git white gentleman to marry 'em! Dey'll git five hundred apiece. Marse Beau, Gord'll punish you for dis—He surely will. I done tole Marse John long time ago he oughter sell dat brazen nigger Dead-arm Harriet, an' git shet o' her. Lord! Lord! Lord! Now you done gone to cussin' an' swearin' agin. Don't go tearin' off your jackets an' flingin' 'em at me. We don't want 'em; we buys our clo'es—what we don't make. Yes, Marse John 'll be comin' along pretty soon now. What's your hurry, Marse Beau? Well, so long, ef you won't stay. He ain't got much use for gorillas neither, Marse John hain't."

The young officer wrote a few hasty words on a leaf torn from the pretty Russia-leather note-book, and handed it to the old darky. "For your Marse John."

"For Marse John—yes, sir; I'll gin hit to him soon 's he comes in."

They had dejectedly commenced their weary tramp up the bayou; he called him back, and lowered his voice confidentially: "Marse Beau, when you captured dat transport and stole all dem fixin's an' finery, you didn't see no good chawin' tobacco layin' round loose, did you? Thanky! thanky, child! Now I looks good at you, you ain't so much changed sence de times Marse John used to wallop you for your tricks. Well, good-bye, Marse Beau."

On the leaf were scrawled the words:

"All's up! Lee has surrendered.—BEAU."

Kate Chopin

Kate Chopin (1851-1904)

Kate Chopin was born Katherine O'Flaherty in St. Louis. Her father was an Irishman from Galway, and her mother came from a family of early French settlers. At 19 she married Oscar Chopin, a Louisiana planter and cotton trader. She lived with him and their children, first in New Orleans, and then in Cloutierville in Natchitoches Parish. After her husband's death in 1883, Chopin returned to St. Louis and began to write. Her books include two collections of short stories, Bayou Folk (1894) and A Night in Acadia (1897), and the well-known novel, The Awakening (1899). "Athénaïse: A Story of a Temperament" is taken from A Night in Acadia.

ATHENAISE:
A Story of a Temperament
I

ATHÉNAÏSE WENT AWAY IN THE MORNING to make a visit to her parents, ten miles back on rigolet de Bon Dieu. She did not return in the evening, and Cazeau, her husband, fretted not a little. He did not worry much about Athénaïse, who, he suspected, was resting only too content in the bosom of her family; his chief solicitude was manifestly for the pony she had ridden. He felt sure those "lazy pigs," her brothers, were capable of neglecting it seriously. This misgiving Cazeau communicated to his servant, old Félicité, who waited upon him at supper.

His voice was low pitched, and even softer than Félicité's. He was tall, sinewy, swarthy, and altogether severe looking. His thick black hair waved, and it gleamed like the breast of a crow. The sweep of his mustache, which was not so black, outlined the broad contour of the mouth. Beneath the under lip grew a small tuft which he was much given to twisting, and which he permitted to grow, apparently for no other purpose. Cazeau's eyes were dark blue, narrow and over-shadowed. His hands were coarse and stiff from close acquaintance with farming tools and implements, and he handled his fork and knife clumsily. But he was distinguished looking, and succeeded in commanding a good deal of respect, and even fear sometimes.

He ate his supper alone, by the light of a single coal-oil lamp that but faintly illuminated the big room, with its bare floor and huge rafters, and its heavy pieces of furniture that loomed dimly in the gloom of the apartment. Félicité, ministering to his wants, hovered about the table like a little, bent, restless shadow.

She served him with a dish of sunfish fried crisp and brown. There was nothing else set before him beside the bread and butter and the bottle of red wine which she locked carefully in the buffet after he had poured his second glass. She was occupied with her mistress's absence, and kept reverting to it after he had expressed his solicitude about the pony.

"Dat beat me! on'y marry two mont', an' got de head turn' a'ready to go 'broad. C'est pas Chrétien, ténez!"

Cazeau shrugged his shoulders for answer, after he had drained his glass and pushed aside his plate. Félicité's opinion of the unchristianlike behavior of his wife in leaving him thus alone after two months of marriage weighed little with him. He was used to solitude, and did not mind a day or night or two of it. He had lived alone ten years, since his first wife died, and Félicité might have known better than to suppose that he cared. He told her she was a fool. It sounded like a compliment in his modulated, caressing voice. She grumbled to herself as she set about clearing the table, and Cazeau arose and walked outside on the gallery; his spur, which he had not removed upon entering the house, jangled at every step.

The night was beginning to deepen, and to gather black about the clusters of trees and shrubs that were grouped in the yard. In the beam of light from the open kitchen door a black boy stood feeding a brace of snarling, hungry dogs; further away, on the steps of a cabin, some one was playing the accordion; and in still another direction a little negro baby was crying lustily. Cazeau walked around to the front of the house, which was square, squat and one-story.

A belated wagon was driving in at the gate, and the impatient driver was swearing hoarsely at his jaded oxen. Félicité stepped out on the gallery, glass and polishing towel in hand, to investigate, and to wonder, too, who could be singing out on the river. It was a party of young people paddling around, waiting for the moon to rise, and they were singing Juanita, their voices coming tempered and melodious through the distance and the night.

Cazeau's horse was waiting, saddled, ready to be mounted, for Cazeau had many things to attend to before bedtime; so many things that there was not left to him a moment in which to think of Athénaïse. He felt her absence, though, like a dull, insistent pain.

However, before he slept that night he was visited by the thought of her, and by a vision of her fair young face with its dropping lips and sullen and averted eyes. The marriage had been a blunder; he had only to look into her eyes to feel that, to discover her growing aversion. But it was a thing not by any possibility to be undone. He was quite prepared to make the best of it, and expected no less than a like effort on her part. The less she revisited the rigolet, the better. He would find means to keep her at home hereafter.

These unpleasant reflections kept Cazeau awake far into the night, notwithstanding the craving of his whole body for rest and sleep. The moon was shining, and its pale effulgence reached dimly into the room, and with it a touch of the cool breath of the spring night. There was an unusual stillness abroad; no sound to be heard save the distant, tireless, plaintive note of the accordion.

II

Athénaïse did not return the following day, even though her husband sent her word to do so by her brother, Montéclin, who passed on his way to the village early in the morning.

On the third day Cazeau saddled his horse and went himself in search of her. She had sent no word, no message, explaining her absence, and he felt that he had good cause to be offended. It was rather awkward to have to leave his work, even though late in the afternoon—Cazeau had always so much to do; but among the many urgent calls upon him, the task of bringing his wife back to a sense of her duty seemed to him for the moment paramount.

The Michés, Athénaïse's parents, lived on the old Gotrain place. It did not belong to them; they were "running" it for a merchant in Alexandria. The house was far too big for their use. One of the lower rooms served for the storing of wood and tools; the person "occupying" the place before Miché having pulled up the flooring in despair of being able to patch it. Upstairs, the rooms were so large, so bare, that they offered a constant temptation to lovers of the dance, whose importunities Madame Miché was accustomed to meet with amiable indulgence. A dance at Miché's and a plate of Madame Miché's gumbo filé at midnight were pleasures not to be neglected or despised, unless by such serious souls as Cazeau.

Long before Cazeau reached the house his approach had been observed, for there was nothing to obstruct the view of the outer road; vegetation was not yet abundantly advanced, and there was but a patchy, straggling stand of cotton and corn in Miché's field.

Madame Miché, who had been seated on the gallery in a rocking-chair, stood up to greet him as he drew near. She was short and fat, and wore a black skirt and loose muslin sack fastened at the throat with a hair brooch. Her own hair, brown and glossy, showed but a few threads of silver. Her round pink face was cheery, and her eyes were bright and good humored. But she was plainly perturbed and ill at ease as Cazeau advanced.

Montéclin, who was there too, was not ill at ease, and made no attempt to disguise the dislike with which his brother-in-law inspired him. He was a slim, wiry fellow of twenty-five, short of stature like his mother, and resembling her in feature. He was in shirt-sleeves, half leaning, half sitting, on the insecure railing of the gallery, and fanning himself with his broad-rimmed felt hat.

"Cochon!" he muttered under his breath as Cazeau mounted the stairs, "sacré cochon!"

"Cochon" had sufficiently characterized the man who had once on a time declined to lend Montéclin money. But when this same man had had the presumption to propose marriage to his well-beloved sister, Athénaïse, and the honor to be accepted by her, Montéclin felt that a qualifying epithet was needed fully to express his estimate of Cazeau.

Miché and his oldest son were absent. They both esteemed Cazeau highly, and talked much of his qualities of head and heart, and thought much of his excellent standing with city merchants.

Athénaïse had shut herself up in her room. Cazeau had seen her rise and enter the house at perceiving him. He was a good deal mystified, but no one could have guessed it when he shook hands with Madame Miché. He had only nodded to Montéclin, with a muttered "Comment ça va?"

"Tiens! something tole me you were coming to-day!" exclaimed Madame Miché, with a little blustering appearance of being cordial and at ease, as she offered Cazeau a chair.

He ventured a short laugh as he seated himself.

"You know, nothing would do," she went on, with much gesture of her small, plump hands, "nothing would do but Athénaïse mus' stay las' night fo' a li'le dance. The boys wouldn' year to their sister leaving."

Cazeau shrugged his shoulders significantly, telling as plainly as words that he knew nothing about it.

"Comment! Montéclin didn' tell you we were going to keep Athénaïse?" Montéclin had evidently told nothing.

"An' how about the night befo'," questioned Cazeau, "an' las' night? It isn't possible you dance every night out yere on the Bon Dieu!"

Madame Miché laughed, with amiable appreciation of the sarcasm; and turning to her son, "Montéclin, my boy, go tell yo' sister that Monsieur Cazeau is yere."

Montéclin did not stir except to shift his position and settle himself more securely on the railing.

"Did you year me, Montéclin?"

"Oh yes, I yeard you plain enough," responded her son, "but

you know as well as me it's no use to tell 'Thénaïse anything. You been talkin' to her yo'se'f since Monday, an' pa's preached himse'f hoa'se on the subject, an' you even had uncle Achille down yere yesterday to reason with her. W'en 'Thénaïse said she wasn' goin' to set her foot back in Cazeau's house, she meant it."

This speech, which Montéclin delivered with thorough unconcern, threw his mother into a condition of painful but dumb embarrassment. It brought two fiery red spots to Cazeau's cheeks, and for the space of a moment he looked wicked.

What Montéclin had spoken was quite true, though his taste in the manner and choice of time and place in saying it were not of the best. Athénaïse, upon the first day of her arrival, had announced that she came to stay, having no intention of returning under Cazeau's roof. The announcement had scattered consternation, as she knew it would. She had been implored, scolded, entreated, stormed at, until she felt herself like a dragging sail that all the winds of heaven had beaten upon. Why in the name of God had she married Cazeau? Her father had lashed her with the question a dozen times. Why indeed? It was difficult now for her to understand why, unless because she supposed it was customary for girls to marry when the right opportunity came. Cazeau, she knew, would make life more comfortable for her; and again, she had liked him, and had even been rather flustered when he pressed her hands and kissed them, and kissed her lips and cheeks and eyes, when she accepted him.

Montéclin himself had taken her aside to talk the thing over. The turn of affairs was delighting him.

"Come, now, 'Thénaïse, you mus' explain to me all about it, so we can settle on a good cause, an' secu' a separation fo' you. Has he been mistreating an' abusing you, the sacré cochon?" They were alone together in her room, whither she had taken refuge from the angry domestic elements.

"You please to reserve yo' disgusting expressions, Montéclin. No, he has not abused me in any way that I can think."

"Does he drink? Come 'Thénaïse, think well over it. Does he ever get drunk?"

"Drunk! Oh, mercy, no,—Cazeau never gets drunk."

"I see; it's jus' simply you feel like me; you hate him."

"No, I don't hate him," she returned reflectively, adding with a sudden impulse, "It's jus' being married that I detes' an' despise. I hate being Mrs. Cazeau, an' would want to be Athénaïse Miché again. I can't stan' to live with a man, to have him always there, his coats an' pantaloons hanging in my room, his ugly bare feet—washing them in my tub, befo' my very eyes, ugh!" She shuddered with recollections, and resumed, with a sigh that was almost a sob: "Mon Dieu, mon Dieu! Sister Marie Angélique knew w'at she was saying; she knew me better than myse'f w'en she said God had sent me a vocation an' I was turning deaf ears. W'en I think of a blessed life in the convent, at peace! Oh, w'at was I dreaming of!" and then the tears came.

Montéclin felt disconcerted and greatly disappointed at having obtained evidence that would carry no weight with a court of justice. The day had not come when a young woman might ask the court's permission to return to her mamma on the sweeping ground of a constitutional disinclination for marriage. But if there was no way of untying this Gordian knot of marriage, there was surely a way of cutting it.

"Well, 'Thénaïse, I'm mightly durn sorry you got no better groun's 'an w'at you say. But you can count on me to stan' by you w'atever you do. God knows I don' blame you fo' not wantin' to live with Cazeau."

And now there was Cazeau himself, with the red spots flaming in his swarthy cheeks, looking and feeling as if he wanted to thrash Montéclin into some semblance of decency. He arose abruptly, and approaching the room which he had seen his wife enter, thrust open the door after a hasty preliminary knock. Athénaïse, who was standing erect at a far window, turned at his entrance.

She appeared neither angry nor frightened, but thoroughly unhappy, with an appeal in her soft dark eyes and a tremor on her lips that seemed to him expressions of unjust reproach, that wounded and maddened him at once. But whatever he might feel, Cazeau knew only one way to act toward a woman.

"Athénaïse, you are not ready?" he asked in his quiet tones. "It's getting late; we havin' any time to lose."

She knew that Montéclin had spoken out, and she had hoped for a wordy interview, a stormy scene, in which she might have held her own as she had held it for the past three days against her family, with Montéclin's aid. But she had no weapon with which to combat subtlety. Her husband's looks, his tones, his mere presence, brought to her a sudden sense of hopelessness, and instinctive realization of the futility of rebellion against a social and sacred institution.

Cazeau said nothing further, but stood waiting in the doorway. Madame Miché had walked to the far end of the gallery, and pretended to be occupied with having a chicken driven from her parterre. Montéclin stood by, exasperated, fuming, ready to burst out.

Athénaïse went and reached for her riding skirt that hung against the wall. She was rather tall, with a figure which, though not robust, seemed perfect in its fine proportions. "La fille de son père," she was often called, which was a great compliment to Miché. Her brown hair was brushed all fluffily back from her temples and low forehead, and about her features and expression lurked a softness, a prettiness, a dewiness, that were perhaps too childlike, that savored of immaturity.

She slipped the riding skirt, which was of black alpaca, over her head, and with impatient fingers hooked it at the waist over her pink linenlawn. Then she fastened on her white sunbonnet and reached for her gloves on the mantel piece.

"If you don' wan' to go, you know w'at you got to do, 'Thénaïse," fumed Montéclin. "You don' set yo' feet back on Cane River, by God, unless you want to,—not w'ile I'm alive."

Cazeau looked at him as if he were a monkey whose antics fell short of being amusing.

Athénaïse still made no reply, said not a word. She walked rapidly past her husband, past her brother, bidding good-by to no one, not even to her mother. She descended the stairs, and without assistance from any one mounted the pony, which Cazeau had ordered to be saddled upon his arrival. In this way she obtained a fair start of her husband, whose departure was far more leisurely, and for the greater part of the way she managed to keep an appreciable gap between them. She rode almost madly at first, with the wind inflating her skirt balloonlike about her knees, and her sunbonnet falling back between her shoulders.

At no time did Cazeau make an effort to overtake her until traversing an old fallow meadow that was level and hard as a table. The sight of a great solitary oak tree, with its seemingly immutable outlines, that had been a landmark for ages—or was it the odor of elderberry stealing up from the gully to the south? or what was it that brought vividly back to Cazeau, by some association of ideas, a scene of many years ago? He had passed that old live-oak hundreds of times, but it was only now that the memory of one day came back to him. He was a very small boy that day, seated before his father on horseback. They were proceeding slowly, and Black Gabe was moving on before them at a little dogtrot. Black Gabe had run away, and had been discovered back in the Gotrain swamp. They had halted beneath this big oak to enable the negro to take breath; for Cazeau's father was a kind and considerate master, and every one had agreed at the time that Black Gabe was a fool, a great idiot indeed, for wanting to run away from him.

The whole impression was for some reason hideous, and to dispel it Cazeau spurred his horse to a swift gallop. Overtaking his wife, he rode the remainder of the way at her side in silence.

It was late when they reached home. Félicité was standing on the grassy edge of the road, in the moonlight, waiting for them.

Cazeau once more ate his supper alone, for Athénaïse went to her room, and there she was crying again.

III

Athénaïse was not one to accept the inevitable with patient resignation, a talent born in the souls of many women; neither was she the one to accept it with philosophical resignation, like her husband. Her sensibilities were alive and keen and responsive. She met the pleasureable things of life with frank, open appreciation, and against distasteful conditions she rebelled. Dissimulation was as foreign to her nature as guile to the breast of a babe, and her rebellious outbreaks, by no means rare, had hitherto been quite open and aboveboard. People often said that Athénaïse would know her own mind some day, which was equivalent to saying that she was at present unacquainted with it. If she ever came to such knowledge, it would be by no intellectual research, by no subtle analyses or tracing the motives of actions to their source. It would come to her as the song to the bird, the perfume and color to the flower.

Her parents had hoped—not without reason and justice—that marriage would bring the poise, the desirable pose, so glaringly lacking in Athénaïse's character. Marriage they knew to be a wonderful and powerful agent in the development and formation of a woman's character; they had seen its effect too often to doubt it.

"And if this marriage does nothing else," exclaimed Miché in an outburst of sudden exasperation, "it will rid us of Athénaïse, for I am at the end of my patience with her! You have never had the firmness to manage her"—he was speaking to his wife—"I have not had the time, the leisure, to devote to her training; and what good we might have accomplished, that maudit Montéclin—Well, Cazeau is the one! It takes just such a steady hand to guide a disposition like Athénaïse's, a master hand, a strong will that compels obedience."

And now, when they had hoped for so much, here was Athénaïse, with gathered and fierce vehemence, beside which her former outbursts appeared mild, declaring that she would not, and she would not, and she would not continue to enact the role of wife to Cazeau. If she had had a reason! as Madame Miché lamented; but it could not be discovered that she had any sane one. He had never scolded, or called names, or deprived her of comforts, or been guilty of any of the many reprehensible acts commonly attributed to objectionable husbands. He did not slight nor neglect her. Indeed, Cazeau's chief offense seemed to be that he loved her, and Athénaïse was not the woman to be loved against her will. She called marriage a trap set for the feet of unwary and unsuspecting girls, and in round, unmeasured terms reproached her mother with treachery and deceit.

"I told you Cazeau was the man," chuckled Miché, when his wife had related the scene that had accompanied and influenced Athénaïse's departure.

Athénaïse again hoped, in the morning, that Cazeau would scold or make some sort of a scene, but he apparently did not dream of it. It was exasperating that he should take her acquiescence so for granted. It is true he had been up and over the fields and across the river and back long before she was out of bed, and he may have been thinking of something else, which was no excuse, which was even in some sense an aggravation. But he did say to her at breakfast, "That brother of yo's, that Montéclin, is unbearable."

"Montéclin? Par exemple!"

Athénaïse, seated opposite to her husband, was attired in a white morning wrapper. She wore a somewhat abused, long face, it is true—an expression of countenance familiar to some husbands—but the expression was not sufficiently pronounced to mar the charm of her youthful freshness. She had little heart to eat, only playing with the food before her, and she felt a pang of resentment at her husband's healthy appetite.

"Yes, Montéclin," he reasserted. "He's developed into a firs'-class nuisance; an' you better tell him, Athénaïse—unless you want me to tell him—to confine his energies after this to matters that concern him. I have no use fo' him or fo' his interference in w'at regards you an' me alone."

This was said with unusual asperity. It was the little breach that Athénaïse had been watching for, and she charged rapidly: "It's strange, if you detes' Montéclin so heartily, that you would desire to marry his sister." She knew it was a silly thing to say, and was not surprised when he told her so. It gave her a little foothold for further attack, however. "I don't see, anyhow, w'at reason you had to marry me, w'en there were so many others," she complained, as if accusing him of persecution and injury. "There was Marianne running after you fo' the las' five years till it was disgraceful; an' any one of the Dortrand girls would have been glad to marry you. But no, nothing would do; you mus' come out on the rigolet fo' me." Her complaint was pathetic, and at the same time so amusing that Cazeau was forced to smile.

"I can't see w'at the Dortrand girls or Marianne have to do with it," he rejoined; adding, with no trace of amusement, "I married you because I loved you; because you were the woman I wanted to marry, an' the only one. I reckon I tole you that befo'. I thought— of co'se I was a fool fo' taking things fo' granted—but I did think that I might make you happy in making things easier an' mo' comfortable fo' you. I expected—I was even that big a fool—I believed that yo' coming yere to me would be like the sun shining out of the clouds, an' that our days would be like w'at the story-books promise after the wedding. I was mistaken. But I can't imagine w'at induced you to marry me. W'atever it was, I reckon you foun' out you made a mistake, too. I don' see anything to do but make the best of a bad bargain, an' shake han's over it." He had arisen from the table, and, approaching, held out his hand to her. What he had said was commonplace enough, but it was significant, coming from Cazeau, who was not often so unreserved in expressing himself.

Athénaïse ignored the hand held out to her. She was resting her chin in her palm, and kept her eyes fixed moodily upon the table. He rested his hand, that she would not touch, upon her head of an instant, and walked away out of the room.

She heard him giving orders to workmen who had been waiting for him out on the gallery, and she heard him mount his horse and ride away. A hundred things would distract him and engage his attention during the day. She felt that he had perhaps put her and her grievance from his thoughts when he crossed the threshold; whilst she—

Old Félicité was standing there holding a shining tin pail, asking for flour and lard and eggs from the storeroom, and meal for the chicks.

Athénaïse seized the bunch of keys which hung from her belt and flung them at Félicité's feet.

"Tiens! tu vas les garder comme tu as jadis fait. Je ne veux plus de ce train là, moi!"

The old woman stooped and picked up the keys from the floor. It was really all one to her that her mistress returned them to her keeping, and refused to take further account of the ménage.

IV

It seemed now to Athénaïse that Montéclin was the only friend left to her in the world. Her father and mother had turned from her in what appeared to be her hour of need. Her friends laughed at her, and refused to take seriously the hints which she threw out—feeling her way to discover if marriage were as distasteful to other women as to herself. Montéclin alone understood her. He alone had always been ready to act for her and with her, to comfort and solace her with his sympathy and his support. Her only hope for rescue from her hateful surroundings lay in Montéclin. Of herself she felt powerless to plan, to act, even to conceive a way out of this pitfall into which the whole world seemed to have conspired to push her.

She had a great desire to see her brother and wrote asking him to come to her. But it better suited Montéclin's spirit of adventure to appoint a meeting place at the turn of the lane, where Athénaïse might appear to be walking leisurely for health and recreation, and where he might seem to be riding along, bent on some errand of business or pleasure.

There had been a shower, a sudden downpour, short as it was sudden, that had laid the dust in the road. It had freshened the pointed leaves of the live oaks, and brightened up the big fields of cotton on either side of the lane till they seemed carpeted with green, glittering gems.

Athénaïse walked along the grassy edge of the road, lifting her crisp skirts with one hand, and with the other twirling a gay sunshade over her bare head. The scent of the fields after the rain was delicious. She inhaled long breaths of their freshness and perfume, that soothed and quieted her for the moment. There were birds splashing and spluttering in the pools, pluming themselves on the fencerails, and sending out little sharp cries, twitters, and shrill rhapsodies of delight.

She saw Montéclin approaching from a great distance—almost as far away as the turn of the woods. But she could not feel sure it was he; it appeared too tall for Montéclin, but that was because he was riding a large horse. She waved her parasol to him; she was so glad to see him. She had never been so glad to see Montéclin before, not even the day when he had taken her out of the convent, against her parents' wishes, because she had expressed a desire to remain there no longer. He seemed to her, as he drew near, the embodiment of kindness, of bravery, of chivalry, even of wisdom, for she had never known Montéclin at a loss to extricate himself from a disagreeable situation.

He dismounted, and, leading his horse by the bridle, started to walk beside her, after he had kissed her affectionately and asked her what she was crying about. She protested that she was not crying, for she was laughing, though drying her eyes at the same time on her handkerchief, rolled in a soft mop for the purpose.

She took Montéclin's arm, and they strolled slowly down the lane; they could not seat themselves for a comfortable chat, as they would have liked, with the grass all sparkling and bristling wet.

Yes, she was quite as wretched as ever, she told him. The week which had gone by since she saw him had in no wise lightened the burden of her discontent. There had even been some additional provocations laid upon her, and she told Montéclin all about them—about the keys, for instance, which in a fit of temper she had returned to Félicité's keeping; and she told how Cazeau had brought them back to her as if they were something she had accidentally lost, and he had recovered; and how he had said, in that aggravating tone of his, that it was not the custom on Cane river for the Negro servants to carry the keys, when there was a mistress at the head of the household.

But Athénaïse could not tell Montéclin anything to increase the disrespect which he already entertained for his brother-in-law; and it was then he unfolded to her a plan which he had conceived and worked out for her deliverance from this galling matrimonial yoke.

It was not a plan which met with instant favor, which she was at once ready to accept, for it involved secrecy and dissimulation, hateful alternatives, both of them. But she was filled with admiration for Montéclin's resources and wonderful talent for contrivance. She accepted the plan; not with the immediate determination to act upon it, rather with the intention to sleep and to dream upon it.

Three days later she wrote to Montéclin that she had abandoned herself to his counsel. Displeasing as it might be to her sense of honesty, it would yet be less trying than to live on with a soul full of bitterness and revolt, as she had done for the past two months.

V

When Cazeau awoke, one morning at his usual very early hour, it was to find the place at his side vacant. This did not surprise him until he discovered that Athénaïse was not in the adjoining room, where he had often found her sleeping in the morning on the lounge. She had perhaps gone out for an early stroll, he reflected, for her jacket and hat were not on the rack where she had hung them the night before. But there were other things absent—a gown or two from the armoire; and there was a great gap in the piles of lingerie on the shelf; and her traveling-bag was missing, and so were her bits of jewelry from the toilet tray—and Athénaïse was gone!

But the absurdity of going during the night, as if she had been a prisoner, and he the keeper of a dungeon! So much secrecy and mystery, to go sojourning out on the Bon Dieu! Well, the Michés might keep their daughter after this. For the companionship of no woman on earth would he again undergo the humiliating sensation of baseness that had overtaken him in passing the old oak-tree in the fallow meadow.

But a terrible sense of loss overwhelmed Cazeau. It was not new or sudden; he had felt it for weeks growing upon him, and it seemed to culminate with Athénaïse's flight from home. He knew that he could again compel her return as he had done once before—compel her to return to the shelter of his roof, compel her cold and unwilling submission to his love and passionate transports; but the loss of self-respect seemed to him too dear a price to pay for a wife.

He could not comprehend why she had seemed to prefer him above others; why she had attracted him with eyes, with voice, with a hundred womanly ways, and finally distracted him with love which she seemed, in her timid, maidenly fashion, to return. The great sense of loss came from the realization of having missed a chance for happiness—a chance that would come his way again only through a miracle. He could not think of himself loving any other woman, and could not think of Athénaïse ever—even at some remote date—caring for him.

He wrote her a letter, in which he disclaimed any further intention of forcing his commands upon her. He did not desire her presence ever again in his home unless she came of her free will, uninfluenced by family or friends; unless she could be the companion he had hoped for in marrying her, and in some measure return affection and respect for the love which he continued and would always continue to feel for her. This letter he sent out to the rigolet by a messenger early in the day. But she was not out on the rigolet, and had not been there.

The family turned instinctively to Montéclin, and almost literally fell upon him for an explanation; he had been absent from home all night. There was much mystification in his answers, and a plain desire to mislead in his assurances of ignorance and innocence.

But with Cazeau there was no doubt or speculation when he accosted the young fellow. "Montéclin, w'at have you done with Athénaïse?" he questioned bluntly. They had met in the open road on horseback, just as Cazeau ascended the river bank before his house.

"W'at have you done to Athénaïse?" returned Montéclin for answer.

"I don't reckon you've considered yo' conduct by any light of decency an' propriety in encouraging yo' sister to such an action, but let me tell you—"

"Voyons! you can let me alone with yo' decency an' morality an' fiddlesticks. I know you mus' 'a' done Athénaïse pretty mean that she can't live with you; an' fo' my part, I'm mighty durn glad she had the spirit to quit you."

"I ain't in the humor to take any notice of yo' impertinence, Montéclin; but let me remine you that Athénaïse is nothing but a chile in character; besides that, she's my wife, an' I hole you responsible fo' her safety an' welfare. If any harm of any description happens to her, I'll strangle you, by God, like a rat, and fling you in Cane river, if I have to hang fo' it!" He had not lifted his voice. The only sign of anger was a savage gleam in his eyes.

"I reckon you better keep yo' big talk fo' the women, Cazeau," replied Montéclin, riding away.

But he went doubly armed after that, and intimated that the precaution was not needless, in view of the threats and menaces that were abroad touching his personal safety.

VI

Athénaïse reached her destination sound of skin and limb, but a good deal flustered, a little frightened, and altogether excited and interested by her unusual experiences.

Her destination was the house of Sylvie, on Dauphine Street, in New Orleans—a three-story gray brick, standing directly on the banquette, with three broad stone steps leading to the deep front entrance. From the second-story balcony swung a small sign, conveying to passers-by the intelligence that within were "*chambres garnies.*"

It was one morning in the last week of April that Athénaïse presented herself at the Dauphine Street house. Sylvie was expecting her, and introduced her at once to her apartment, which was in the second story of the back ell, and accessible by an open, outside gallery. There was a yard below, paved with broad stone flagging; many fragrant flowering shrubs and plants grew in a bed along the side of the opposite wall, and others were distributed about in tubs and green boxes.

It was a plain but large enough room into which Athénaïse was ushered, with matting on the floor, green shades and Nottingham lace curtains at the windows that looked out on the gallery, and furnished with a cheap walnut suite. But everything looked exquisitely clean, and the whole place smelled of cleanliness.

Athénaïse at once fell into the rocking-chair, with the air of exhaustion and intense relief of one who has come to the end of her troubles. Sylvie, entering behind her, laid the big traveling-bag on the floor and deposited the jacket on the bed.

She was a portly quadroon of fifty or thereabout, clad in an ample *volante* of the old-fashioned purple calico so much affected by her class. She wore large golden hoop-earrings, and her hair was combed plainly, with every appearance of effort to smooth out the kinks. She had broad, coarse features, with a nose that turned up, exposing the wide nostrils, and that seemed to emphasize the loftiness and command of her bearing—a dignity that in the presence of white people assumed a character of respectfulness, but never of obsequiousness. Sylvie believed firmly in maintaining the colorline, and would not suffer a white person, even a child, to call her "Madame Sylvie"—a title which she exacted religiously, however, from those of her own race.

"I hope you be please' wid yo' room, madame," she observed amiably. "Dat's de same room w'at yo' brother, M'sieur Miché, all time like w'en he come to New Orlean'. He well, M'sieur Miché? I receive' his letter las' week, an' dat same day a gent'man want I give 'im dat room. I say, 'No, dat room already ingage'.' Ev-body like dat room on 'count it so quite (quiet). M'sieur Gouvernail, dere in nax' room, you can't pay 'im! He been stay t'ree year' in dat room; but all fix' up fine wid his own furn'ture an' books, 'tel you can't see! I say to 'im plenty time', 'M'sieur Gouvernail, w'y you don't take dat t'ree-story front, now, long it's empty?' He tells me, 'Leave me 'lone, Sylvie; I know a good room w'en I fine it, me.'"

She had been moving slowly and majestically about the apartment, straightening and smoothing down bed and pillows, peering into ewer and basin, evidently casting an eye around to make sure that everything was as it should be.

"I sen' you some fresh water, Madame," she offered upon retiring from the room. "An' w'en you want an't'ing, you jus' go out on de gall'ry an' call Pousette: she year you plain—she right down dere in de kitchen."

Athénaïse was really not so exhausted as she had every reason to be after that interminable and circuitous way by which Montéclin had seen fit to have her conveyed to the city.

Would she ever forget that dark and truly dangerous midnight ride along the "coast" to the mouth of Cane river! There Montéclin had parted with her, after seeing her aboard the St. Louis and Shreveport packet which he knew would pass there before dawn.

She had received instructions to disembark at the mouth of Red river, and there transfer to the first south-bound steamer for New Orleans, all of which instructions she had followed implicitly, even to making her way at once to Sylvie's upon her arrival in the city. Montéclin had enjoined secrecy and much caution; the clandestine nature of the affair gave it a savor of adventure which was highly pleasing to him. Eloping with his sister was only a little less engaging than eloping with some one else's sister.

But Montéclin did not do the *grand seigneur* by halves. He had paid Sylvie a whole month in advance for Athénaïse's board and lodging. Part of the sum he had been forced to borrow, it is true, but he was not niggardly.

Athénaïse was to take her meals in the house, which none of the other lodgers did; the one exception being that Mr. Gouvernail was served with breakfast on Sunday mornings.

Sylvie's clientéle came chiefly from the southern parishes; for the most part, people spending but a few days in the city. She prided herself upon the quality and highly respectable character of her patrons, who came and went unobtrusively.

The large parlor opening upon the front balcony was seldom used. Her guests were permitted to entertain in this sanctuary of elegance—but they never did. She often rented it for the night to parties of respectable and discreet gentlemen desiring to enjoy a quiet game of cards outside the bosom of their families. The second-story hall also led by a long window out on the balcony. And Sylvie advised Athénaïse, when she grew weary of her back room, to go and sit on the front balcony, which was shady in the afternoon, and where she might find diversion in the sounds and sights of the street below.

Athénaïse refreshed herself with a bath, and was soon unpacking her few belongings, which she ranged neatly away in the bureau drawers and the armoire.

She had revolved certain plans in her mind during the past hour or so. Her present intention was to live on indefinitely in this big, cool clean back room on Dauphine street. She had thought seriously, for moments, of the convent, with all readiness to embrace the vows of poverty and chastity; but what about obedience? Later, she intended, in some roundabout way, to give her parents and her husband the assurance of her safety and welfare, reserving the right to remain unmolested and lost to them. To live on at the expense of Montéclin's generosity was wholly out of the question, and Athénaïse meant to look about for some suitable and agreeable employment.

The imperative thing to be done at present, however, was to go out in search of material for an inexpensive gown or two; for she found herself in the painful predicament of a young woman having almost literally nothing to wear. She decided upon pure white for one, and some sort of a sprigged muslin for the other.

VII

On Sunday morning, two days after Athénaïse's arrival in the city, she went in to breakfast somewhat later than usual, to find two covers laid at table instead of the one to which she was accustomed. She had been to mass, and did not remove her hat, but put her fan, parasol, and prayerbook aside. The dining-room was situated just beneath her own apartment, and, like all rooms of the house, was large and airy; the floor was covered with a glistening oilcloth.

The small, round table, immaculately set, was drawn near the open window. There were some tall plants in boxes on the gallery outside; and Pousette, a little, old, intensely black woman, was splashing and dashing buckets of water on the flagging, and talking loud in her Creole patois to no one in particular.

A dish piled with delicate river shrimps and crushed ice was on the table; a caraffe of crystal-clear water, a few *hors d'oeuvres*, beside a small golden-brown crusty loaf of French bread at each plate. A half-bottle of wine and the morning paper were set at the place opposite Athénaïse.

She had almost completed her breakfast when Gouvernail came in and seated himself at table. He felt annoyed at finding his cherished privacy invaded. Sylvie was removing the remains of a mutton chop from before Athénaïse, and serving her with a cup of café au lait.

"M'sieur Gouvernail," offered Sylvie in her most insinuating and impressive manner, "you please leave me make you acquaint' wid Madame Cazeau. Dat's M'sieur Miché's sister; you meet 'im two t'ree time', you rec'lec', an' been one day to de race wid 'im. Madame Cazeau, you please leave me make you acquaint' wid M'sieur Gouvernail."

Gouvernail expressed himself greatly pleased to meet the sister of Monsieur Miché, of whom he had not the slightest recollection.

He inquired after Monsieur Miché's health, and politely offered Athénaïse a part of his newspaper—the part which contained the Woman's page and the social gossip.

Athénaïse faintly remembered that Sylvie had spoken of a Monsieur Gouvernail occupying the room adjoining hers, living amid luxurious surroundings and a multitude of books. She had not thought of him further than to picture him a stout, middle-aged gentleman, with a bushy beard turning gray, wearing large gold-rimmed spectacles, and stooping somewhat from much bending over books and writing material. She had confused him in her mind with the likeness of some literary celebrity that she had run across in the advertising pages of a magazine.

Gouvernail's appearance was, in truth, in no sense striking. He looked older than thirty and younger than forty, was of medium height and weight, with a quiet, unobtrusive manner which seemed to ask that he be let alone. His hair was light brown, brushed carefully and parted in the middle. His mustache was brown, and so were his eyes, which had a mild, penetrating quality. He was neatly dressed in the fashion of the day; and his hands seemed to Athénaïse remarkably white and soft for a man's.

He had been buried in the contents of his newspaper, when he suddenly realized that some further little attention might be due to Miché's sister. He started to offer her a glass of wine, when he was surprised and relieved to find that she had quietly slipped away while he was absorbed in his own editorial on Corrupt Legislation.

Gouvernail finished his paper and smoked his cigar out on the gallery. He lounged about, gathered a rose for his buttonhole, and had his regular Sunday-morning confab with Pousette, to whom he paid a weekly stipend for brushing his shoes and clothing. He made a great pretense of haggling over the transaction, only to enjoy her uneasiness and garrulous excitement.

He worked or read in his room for a few hours, and when he quitted the house, at three in the afternoon, it was to return no more till late at night. It was his almost invariable custom to spend Sunday evenings out in the American quarter, among a congenial set of men and women—*des esprits forts,* all of them, whose lives were irreproachable, yet whose opinions would startle even the traditional "sapeur," for whom "nothing is sacred." But for all his "advanced" opinions, Gouvernail was a liberal-minded fellow; a man or woman lost nothing of his respect by being married.

When he left the house in the afternoon, Athénaïse had already ensconced herself on the front balcony. He could see her through the jalousies when he passed on his way to the front entrance. She had not yet grown lonesome or homesick; the newness of her surroundings made them sufficiently entertaining. She found it diverting to sit there on the front balcony watching people pass by, even though there was no one to talk to. And then the comforting, comfortable sense of not being married!

She watched Gouvernail walk down the street, and could find no fault with his bearing. He could hear the sound of her rocker for some little distance. He wondered what the "poor little thing" was doing in the city, and meant to ask Sylvie about her when he should happen to think of it.

VIII

The following morning, towards noon, when Gouvernail quitted his room, he was confronted by Athénaïse, exhibiting some confusion and trepidation at being forced to request a favor of him at so early a stage of their acquaintance. She stood in her doorway, and had evidently been sewing, as the thimble on her finger testified, as well as a long-threaded needle thrust in the bosom of her gown. She held a stamped but unaddressed letter in her hand.

And would Mr. Gouvernail be so kind as to address the letter to her brother, Mr. Montéclin Miché? She would hate to detain him with explanations this morning—another time, perhaps—but now she begged that he would give himself the trouble.

He assured her that it made no difference, that it was no trouble whatever; and he drew a fountain pen from his pocket and addressed the letter at her dictation, resting it on the inverted rim of his straw hat. She wondered a little at a man of his supposed erudition stumbling over the spelling of "Montéclin" and "Miché."

She demurred at overwhelming him with the additional trouble of posting it, but he succeeded in convincing her that so simple a task as the posting of a letter would not add an iota to the burden of the day. Moreover, he promised to carry it in his hand, and thus avoid any possible risk of forgetting it in his pocket.

After that, and after a second repetition of the favor, when she had told him that she had had a letter from Montéclin, and looked as if she wanted to tell him more, he felt that he knew her better. He felt that he knew her well enough to join her out on the balcony, one night, when he found her sitting there alone. He was not one who deliberately sought the society of women, but he was not wholly a bear. A little commiseration for Athénaïse's aloneness, perhaps some curiosity to know further what manner of woman she was, and the natural influence of her feminine charm were equal unconfessed factors in turning his steps towards the balcony when he discovered the shimmer of her white gown through the open hall window.

It was already quite late, but the day had been intensely hot, and neighboring balconies and doorways were occupied by chattering groups of humanity, loath to abandon the grateful freshness of the outer air. The voices about her served to reveal to Athénaïse the feeling of loneliness that was gradually coming over her. Notwithstanding certain dormant impulses, she craved human sympathy and companionship.

She shook hands impulsively with Gouvernail, and told him how glad she was to see him. He was not prepared for such an admission, but it pleased him immensely, detecting as he did that the expression was as sincere as it was outspoken. He drew a chair up within comfortable conversational distance of Athénaïse, though he had no intention of talking more than was barely necessary to encourage Madame—He had actually forgotten her name!

He leaned an elbow on the balcony rail, and would have offered an opening remark about the oppressive heat of the day, but Athénaïse did not give him the opportunity. How glad she was to talk to someone, and how she talked!

An hour later she had gone to her room, and Gouvernail stayed smoking on the balcony. He knew her quite well after that hour's talk. It was not so much what she had said as what her half saying had revealed to his quick intelligence. He knew that she adored Montéclin, and he suspected that she adored Cazeau without being herself aware of it. He had gathered that she was self-willed, impulsive, innocent, ignorant, unsatisfied, dissatisfied; for had she not complained that things seemed all wrongly arranged in this world, and no one was permitted to be happy in his own way? And he told her he was sorry she had discovered that primordial fact of existence so early in life.

He commiserated her loneliness, and scanned his bookshelves next morning for something to lend her to read, rejecting everything that offered itself to his view. Philosophy was out of the question, and so was poetry; that is, such poetry as he possessed. He had not sounded her literary tastes, and strongly suspected she had none; that she would have rejected The Duchess as readily as Mrs. Humphrey Ward. He compromised on a magazine.

It had entertained her passably, she admitted, upon returning it. A New England story had puzzled her, it was true, and a Creole tale had offended her, but the pictures had pleased her greatly, especially one which had reminded her so strongly of Montéclin after a hard day's ride that she was loath to give it up. It was one of Remington's Cowboys, and Gouvernail insisted upon her keeping it—keeping the magazine.

He spoke to her daily after that, and was always eager to render her some service or to do something towards her entertainment.

One afternoon he took her out to the lake end. She had been there once, some years before, but in winter, so the trip was comparatively new and strange to her. The large expanse of water studded with pleasure-boats, the sight of children playing merrily along the grassy palisades, the music, all enchanted her. Gouvernail thought her the most beautiful woman he had ever seen. Even her gown—the sprigged muslin—appeared to him the most charming one imaginable. Nor could anything be more becoming than the arrangement of her brown hair under the white sailor hat, all rolled back in a soft puff from her radiant face. And she carried her parasol and lifted her skirts and used her fan in ways that seemed quite unique and peculiar to herself, and which he considered almost worthy of study and imitation.

They did not dine out there at the water's edge, as they might have done, but returned early to the city to avoid the crowd. Athénaïse wanted to go home, for she said Sylvie would have dinner prepared and would be expecting her. But it was not difficult to persuade her to dine instead in the quiet little restaurant that he knew and liked, with its sanded floor, its secluded atmosphere, its delicious menu, and its obsequious waiter wanting to know what he might have the honor of serving to "monsieur et madame." No wonder he made the mistake, with Gouvernail assuming such an air of proprietorship! But Athénaïse was very tired after it all; the sparkle went out of her face, and she hung draggingly on his arm in walking home.

He was reluctant to part from her when she bade him good-night at her door and thanked him for the agreeable evening. He

had hoped she would sit outside until it was time for him to regain
the newspaper office. He knew that she would undress and get
into her peignoir and lie upon her bed; and what he wanted to
do, what he would have given much to do, was to go and sit beside
her, read to her something restful, soothe her, do her bidding,
whatever it might be. Of course there was no use in thinking of
that. But he was surprised at his growing desire to be serving her.
She gave him an opportunity sooner than he looked for.

"Mr. Gouvernail," she called from her room, "will you be so
kine as to call Pousette an' tell her she fo'got to bring my ice
water?"

He was indignant at Pousette's negligence, and called severely
to her over the banisters. He was sitting before his own door,
smoking. He knew that Athénaïse had gone to bed, for her room
was dark, and she had opened the slats of the door and windows.
Her bed was near a window.

Pousette came flopping up with the ice water, and with a
hundred excuses: "Mo pa oua vou a tab c'te lanuite, mo cri vou pé
gagni deja la-bas; parole! Vou pas cri conté ça Madame Sylvie?"
She had not seen Athénaïse at table, and thought she was gone.
She swore to this, and hoped Madame Sylvie would not be
informed of her remissness.

A little later Athénaïse lifted her voice again: "Mr. Gouvernail,
did you remark that young man sitting on the opposite side from
us, coming in, with a gray coat an' a blue ban' aroun' his hat?"

Of course Gouvernail had not noticed any such individual, but
he assured Athénaïse that he had observed the young fellow
particularly.

"Don't you think he looked something—not very much, of
co'se—but don't you think he had a little faux-air of Montéclin?"

"I think he looked strikingly like Montéclin," asserted Gouvernail,
with the one idea of prolonging the conversation. "I meant to call
your attention to the resemblance, and something drove it out of
my head."

"The same with me," returned Athénaïse. "Ah, my dear Montéclin!
I wonder w'at he is doing now?"

"Did you receive any news, any letter from him today?" asked
Gouvernail, determined that if the conversation ceased it should
not be through lack of effort on his part to sustain it.

"Not today, but yesterday. He tells me that maman was so
distracted with uneasiness that finally, to pacify her, he was fo'ced

to confess that he knew w'ere I was, but that he was boun' by a vow of secrecy not to reveal it. But Cazeau has not noticed him or spoken to him since he threaten' to throw po' Montéclin in Cane river. You know Cazeau wrote me a letter the morning I lef', thinking I had gone to the rigolet. An' maman opened it, an' said it was full of the mos' noble sentiments, an' she wanted Montéclin to sen' it to me; but Montéclin refuse' poin' blank, so he wrote to me."

Gouvernail preferred to talk of Montéclin. He pictured Cazeau as unbearable, and did not like to think of him.

A little later Athénaïse called out, "Good night, Mr. Gouvernail."

"Good night," he returned reluctantly. And when he thought that she was sleeping, he got up and went away to the midnight pandemonium of his newspaper office.

IX

Athénaïse could not have held out through the month had it not been for Gouvernail. With the need of caution and secrecy always uppermost in her mind, she made no new acquaintances, and she did not seek out persons already known to her; however, she knew so few, it required little effort to keep out of their way. As for Sylvie, almost every moment of her time was occupied in looking after her house; and, moreover, her deferential attitude towards her lodgers forbade anything like the gossipy chats in which Athénaïse might have condescended sometimes to indulge with her landlady. The transient lodgers, who came and went, she never had occasion to meet. Hence she was entirely dependent upon Gouvernail for company.

He appreciated the situation fully; and every moment that he could spare from his work he devoted to her entertainment. She liked to be out of doors, and they strolled together in the summer twilight through the mazes of the old French quarter. They went again to the lake end, and stayed for hours on the water; returning so late that the streets through which they passed were silent and deserted. On Sunday morning he arose at an unconscionable hour to take her to the French market, knowing that the sights and sounds there would interest her. And he did not join the intellectual coterie in the afternoon, as he usually did, but placed himself all day at the disposition and service of Athénaïse.

Notwithstanding all, his manner toward her was tactful, and

evinced intelligence and a deep knowledge of her character, surprising upon so brief an acquaintance. For the time he was everything to her that she would have him; he replaced home and friends. Sometimes she wondered if he had ever loved a woman. She could not fancy him loving anyone passionately, rudely, offensively, as Cazeau loved her. Once she was so naïve as to ask him outright if he had ever been in love, and he assured her promptly that he had not. She thought it an admirable trait in his character, and esteemed him greatly therefor.

He found her crying one night, not openly or violently. She was leaning over the gallery rail, watching the toads that hopped about in the moonlight, down on the damp flagstones of the courtyard. There was an oppressively sweet odor rising from the cape jessamine. Pousette was down there, mumbling and quarreling with someone, and seeming to be having it all her own way—as well she might, when her companion was only a black cat that had come in from a neighboring yard to keep her company.

Athénaïse did admit feeling heartsick, body-sick, when he questioned her; she supposed it was nothing but homesick. A letter from Montéclin had stirred her all up. She longed for her mother, for Montéclin; she was sick for a sight of the cotton fields, the scent of the ploughed earth, for the dim, mysterious charm of the woods, and the old tumble-down home on the Bon Dieu.

As Gouvernail listened to her, a wave of pity and tenderness swept through him. He took her hands and pressed them against him. He wondered what would happen if he were to put his arms around her.

He was hardly prepared for what happened, but he stood it courageously. She twined her arms around his neck and wept outright on his shoulder; the hot tears scalding his cheek and neck, and her whole body shaken in his arms. The impulse was powerful to strain her to him; the temptation was fierce to seek her lips; but he did neither.

He understood a thousand times better than she herself understood it that he was acting as substitute for Montéclin. Bitter as the conviction was, he accepted it. He was patient; he could wait. He hoped some day to hold her with a lover's arms. That she was married made no particle of difference to Gouvernail. He could not conceive or dream of it making a difference. When the time came that she wanted him—as he hoped and believed it would come—he felt he would have a right to her. So long as she did not want him, he had no right to her—no more than her husband had. It was very hard to feel her warm breath and tears upon his cheek, and her struggling bosom pressed against him and her soft arms clinging to him and his whole body and soul aching for her, and yet to make no sign.

He tried to think what Montéclin would have said and done, and to act accordingly. He stroked her hair, and held her in a gentle embrace, until the tears dried and the sobs ended. Before releasing herself she kissed him against the neck; she had to love somebody in her own way! Even that he endured like a stoic. But it was well he left her, to plunge into the thick of rapid, breathless, exacting work till nearly dawn.

Athénaïse was greatly soothed, and slept well. The touch of friendly hands and caressing arms had been very grateful. Henceforward she would not be lonely and unhappy, with Gouvernail there to comfort her.

X

The fourth week of Athénaïse's stay in the city was drawing to a close. Keeping in view the intention which she had of finding some suitable and agreeable employment, she had made a few tentatives in that direction. But with the exception of two little girls who had promised to take piano lessons at a price that would be embarrassing to mention, these attempts had been fruitless. Moreover, the homesickness kept coming back, and Gouvernail was not always there to drive it away.

She spent much of her time weeding and pottering among the flowers down in the courtyard. She tried to take an interest in the black cat, and a mockingbird that hung in a cage outside the kitchen door, and a disreputable parrot that belonged to the cook next door, and swore hoarsely all day long in bad French.

Besides, she was not well; she was not herself, as she told Sylvie. The climate of New Orleans did not agree with her. Sylvie was distressed to learn this, as she felt in some measure responsible for the health and well being of Monsieur Miché's sister; and she made it her duty to inquire closely into the nature and character of Athénaïse's malaise.

Sylvie was very wise, and Athénaïse was very ignorant. The extent of her ignorance and the depth of her subsequent enlightenment were bewildering. She stayed a long, long time quite still, quite stunned, after her interview with Sylvie, except for the short, uneven breathing that ruffled her bosom. Her whole being was steeped in a wave of ecstasy. When she finally arose from the chair in which she had been seated, and looked at herself in the mirror, a face met hers which she seemed to see for the first time, so transfigured was it with wonder and rapture.

One mood quickly followed another, in this new turmoil of her senses, and the need of action became uppermost. Her mother must know at once, and her mother must tell Montéclin. And Cazeau must know. As she thought of him, the first purely sensuous tremor of her life swept over her. She half whispered his name, and the sound of it brought red blotches into her cheeks. She spoke it over and over, as if it were some new, sweet sound born out of darkness and confusion, and reaching her for the first time. She was impatient to be with him. Her whole passionate nature was aroused as if by a miracle.

She seated herself to write to her husband. The letter he would get in the morning, and she would be with him at night. What would he say? How would he act? She knew that he would forgive her, for had he not written a letter?—and a pang of resentment toward Montéclin shot through her. What did he mean by withholding that letter? How dared he not have sent it?

Athénaïse attired herself for the street, and went out to post the letter which she had penned with a single thought, a spontaneous impulse. It would have seemed incoherent to most people, but Cazeau would understand.

She walked along the street as if she had fallen heir to some magnificent inheritance. On her face was a look of pride and satisfaction that passersby noticed and admired. She wanted to talk to some one, to tell some person; and she stopped at the corner and told the oyster-woman, who was Irish, and who God-blessed her, and wished prosperity to the race of Cazeaus for generations to come. She held the oyster-woman's fat, dirty little baby in her arms and scanned it curiously and observingly, as if a baby were a phenomenon that she encountered for the first time in life. She even kissed it!

Then what a relief it was to Athénaïse to walk the streets without dread of being seen and recognized by some chance acquaintance from Red River! No one could have said now that she did not know her own mind.

She went directly from the oyster-woman's to the office of

Harding & Offdean, her husband's merchants; and it was with such an air of partnership, almost proprietorship, that she demanded a sum of money on her husband's account, they gave it to her as unhesitatingly as they would have handed it over to Cazeau himself. When Mr. Harding, who knew her, asked politely after her health, she turned so rosy and looked so conscious, he thought it a great pity for so pretty a woman to be such a little goose.

Athénaïse entered a dry-goods store and bought all manner of things—little presents for nearly everybody she knew. She bought whole bolts of sheerest, softest, downiest white stuff; and when the clerk, in trying to meet her wishes, asked if she intended it for infant's use, she could have sunk through the floor, and wondered how he might have suspected it.

As it was Montéclin who had taken her away from her husband, she wanted it to be Montéclin who should take her back to him. So she wrote him a very curt note—in fact it was a postal card—asking that he meet her at the train on the evening following. She felt convinced that after what had gone before, Cazeau would await her at their own home; and she preferred it so.

Then there was the agreeable excitement of getting ready to leave, of packing up her things. Pousette kept coming and going, coming and going; and each time that she quitted the room it was with something that Athénaïse had given her—a handkerchief, a petticoat, a pair of stockings with two tiny holes at the toes, some broken prayer-beads, and finally a silver dollar.

Next it was Sylvie who came along bearing a gift of what she called "a set of pattern"—things of complicated design which never could have been obtained in any newfangled bazaar or pattern store, that Sylvie had acquired of a foreign lady of distinction whom she had nursed years before at the St. Charles hotel. Athénaïse accepted and handled them with reverence, fully sensible of the great compliment and favor, and laid them religiously away in the trunk which she had lately acquired.

She was greatly fatigued after the day of unusual exertion, and went early to bed and to sleep. All day long she had not once thought of Gouvernail, and only did think of him when aroused for a brief instant by the sound of his footfalls on the gallery, as he passed in going to his room. He had hoped to find her up, waiting for him.

But the next morning he knew. Some one must have told him.

There was no subject known to her which Sylvie hesitated to discuss in detail with any man of suitable years and discretion.

Athénaïse found Gouvernail waiting with a carriage to convey her to the railway station. A momentary pang visited her for having forgotten him so completely, when he said to her, "Sylvie tells me you are going away this morning."

He was kind, attentive, and amiable, as usual, but respected to the utmost the new dignity and reserve that her manner had developed since yesterday. She kept looking from the carriage window, silent, and embarrassed as Eve after losing her ignorance. He talked of the muddy streets and the murky morning, and of Montéclin. He hoped she would find everything comfortable and pleasant in the country, and trusted she would inform him whenever she came to visit the city again. He talked as if afraid or mistrustful of silence and himself.

At the station she handed him her purse, and he bought her ticket, secured for her a comfortable section, checked her trunk, and got all the bundles and things safely aboard the train. She felt very grateful. He pressed her hand warmly, lifted his hat, and left her. He was a man of intelligence, and took defeat gracefully; that was all. But as he made his way back to the carriage, he was thinking, "By heaven, it hurts, it hurts!"

XI

Athénaïse spent a day of supreme happiness and expectancy. The fair sight of the country unfolding itself before her was balm to her vision and to her soul. She was charmed with the rather unfamiliar, broad, clean sweep of the sugar plantations, with their monster sugar houses, their rows of neat cabins like little villages of a single street, and their impressive homes standing apart amid clusters of trees. There were sudden glimpses of a bayou curling between sunny, grassy banks, or creeping sluggishly out from a tangled growth of wood, and brush, and fern, and poison-vines, and palmettos. And passing through the long stretches of monotonous woodlands, she would close her eyes and taste in anticipation the moment of her meeting with Cazeau. She could think of nothing but him.

It was night when she reached her station. There was Montéclin, as she had expected, waiting for her with a two-seated buggy, to which he had hitched his own swift-footed, spirited pony. It was good, he felt, to have her back on any terms; and he had no fault to find since she came of her own choice. He more than suspected the cause of her coming; her eyes and her voice and her foolish little manner went far in revealing the secret that was brimming over in her heart. But after he had deposited her at her own gate, and as he continued his way toward the rigolet, he could not help feeling that the affair had taken a very disappointing, an ordinary, a most commonplace turn, after all. He left her in Cazeau's keeping.

Her husband lifted her out of the buggy, and neither said a word until they stood together within the shelter of the gallery. Even then they did not speak at first. But Athénaïse turned to him with an appealing gesture. As he clasped her in his arms, he felt the yielding of her whole body against him. He felt her lips for the first time respond to the passion of his own.

The country night was dark and warm and still, save for the distant notes of an accordion which some one was playing in a cabin away off. A little Negro baby was crying somewhere. As Athénaïse withdrew from her husband's embrace, the sound arrested her.

"Listen, Cazeau! How Juliette's baby is crying! Pauvre ti chou, I wonder w'at is the matter with it?"

William Faulkner (1897-1962)

  Faulkner was born in New Albany, Mississippi, and lived most of his life in nearby Oxford, Mississippi. In his own lifetime he moved from relative obscurity to international prominence, and in 1949 was awarded the Nobel Prize for Literature. While living in New Orleans in the 1920s, he met Sherwood Anderson, who encouraged him to write and helped him find a publisher. Faulkner's first novel, Soldier's Pay *(1926) was written while he was living in New Orleans, and his second,* Mosquitoes *(1927), was based on the friends he made during his New Orleans period. It should be noted that Faulkner's most notorious New Orleans production, the parody of Sherwood Anderson in* Sherwood Anderson and other Famous Creoles: A Gallery of Contemporary New Orleans *(1926), was the first published book of the fledgling Pelican Press, the ancestor of today's Pelican Publishing Company. Among Faulkner's many works, the following stand out as vital classics of American prose fiction:* The Sound and the Fury *(1929),* As I Lay Dying *(1930),* Light in August *(1932),* Absalom, Absalom! *(1936),* The Wild Palms *(1939),* The Hamlet *(1940), and* Go Down, Moses *(1942). "The Kingdom of God," first published April 26, 1925, in the* Times-Picayune, *is taken from* William Faulkner: New Orleans Sketches, *ed. Carvel Collins, 1968.*

THE KINGDOM OF GOD

(April 26, 1925)

THE CAR CAME SWIFTLY DOWN Decatur street and turning into the alleyway, stopped. Two men alighted, but the other remained in his seat. The face of the sitting man was vague and dull and loose-lipped, and his eyes were clear and blue as cornflowers, and utterly vacant of thought; he sat a shapeless, dirty lump, life without mind, an organism without intellect. Yet always in his slobbering, vacuous face were his two eyes of a heart-shaking blue, and gripped tightly in one fist was a narcissus.

The two who had got out of the car leaned within it and went swiftly to work. Soon they straightened up, and a burlap bundle rested on the door of the car. A door in the wall near at hand opened, a face appeared briefly and withdrew.

"Come on, let's get this stuff out of here," said one of the men. "I ain't scared, but there ain't no luck in making a delivery with a loony along."

"Right you are," replied the other. "Let's get done here: we got two more trips to make."

"You ain't going to take him along, are you?" asked the first speaker, motioning with his head toward the one lumped oblivious in the car.

"Sure. He won't hurt nothing. He's a kind of luck piece, anyway."

"Not for me he ain't. I been in this business a long time and I ain't been caught yet, but it ain't because I been taking no squirrel chasers for luck pieces."

"I know how you feel about him—you said so often enough. But like it was, what could I do? He never had no flower, he lost it somewheres last night, so I couldn't leave him to Jake's, going on like he was for another one; and after I got him one today I couldn't of put him out nowheres. He'd of stayed all right, till I come for him, but some bull might of got him."

"And a —— good thing," swore the other. "Dam'f I see why you lug him around when they's good homes for his kind everywheres."

"Listen. He's my brother, see? And it's my business what I do with him. And I don't need no —— that wears hair to tell me, neither."

199

"Ah, come on, come on. I wasn't trying to take him away from you. I'm just superstitious about fooling with 'em, that's all."

"Well, don't say nothing about it, then. If you don't wanta work with me, say so."

"All right, all right, keep your shirt on." He looked at the blind doorway. "Cheest, what's the matter with them birds today? Hell, we can't wait here like this: be better to drive on. Whatcher say?" As he spoke the door opened again and a voice said: "All right, boys."

The other gripped his arm, cursing. At the corner two blocks away a policeman appeared, stood a moment, then sauntered down the street toward them. "—— here comes a bull. Make it snappy now; get one of them fellows inside to help you and I'll head him off and keep him till you get unloaded." The speaker hurried off and the other, glancing hurriedly about, grasped the sack resting upon the door of the car and carried it swiftly through the doorway. He returned and leaned over the side of the car, trying to lift up the other sack onto the door. The policeman and his companion had met and were talking.

Sweat broke out on his face as he struggled with the awkward bundle, trying to disengage it from the floor of the car. It moved, but hung again despite his utmost efforts, while the body of the car thrust against his lower chest, threatened to stop his breathing. He cast another glance toward the officer. "What luck, what rotten luck!" he panted, grasping the sack again. He released one hand and grasped the idiot's shoulder. "Here, bub," he whispered, "turn around here and lend a hand, quick!" The other whimpered at his touch, and the man hauled him half about so that his vacant, pendulous face hung over the back seat. "Come on, come on, for God's sake," he repeated in a frenzy, "catch hold here and lift up, see?"

The heavenly blue eyes gazed at him without intent, drops of moisture from the drooling mouth fell upon the back of his hand. The idiot only raised his narcissus closer to his face. "Listen!" the man was near screaming, "do you wanta go to jail? Catch hold here, for God's sake!" But the idiot only stared at him in solemn detachment, and the man raised up and struck him terribly in the face. The narcissus, caught between fist and cheek, broke and hung limply over the creature's fist. He screamed, a hoarse, inarticulate bellow which his brother, standing beside the officer, heard and came leaping toward him.

The other man's rage left him and he stood in vacant and frozen despair, when vengeance struck him. The brother leaped, shrieking and cursing, upon him and they both went to the pavement. The idiot howled unceasingly, filling the street with dreadful sound.

"Hit my brother, would you, you ——," panted the man. The other, after the surprise of the assault, fought back until the policeman leaped upon them, clubbing and cursing impartially. "What in hell is this?" he demanded when they were erect and dishevelled, glaring and breathless.

"He hit my brother, the ——."

"Somebody certainly done something to him," snapped the officer. "For Pete's sake, made him stop that racket," he roared above the deafening sound. Another policeman thrust through the gathering crowd. "What you got here? Mad cow?" The idiot's voice rose and fell on waves of unbelievable sound and the second policeman, stepping to the car, shook him.

"Here, here," he began, when the brother, breaking from the grasp of his captor, leaped upon his back. They crashed against the car, and the first officer, releasing the other captive, sprang to his aid. The other man stood in amazement, bereft of power to flee, while the two officers swayed and wrestled with the brother, stretching the man, screaming and kicking, between them until he wore himself out. The second policemen had two long scratches on his cheek. "Phew!" he puffed, mopping his jaw with his handkerchief, "what a wildcat! Has the whole zoo broke out today? What's the trouble?" he roared above the magnificent sorrow of the idiot.

"I dunno exactly," his partner shouted back. "I hear that one in the car bellow out, and look around and here's these two clawing in the gutter. This one says the other one hit his brother. How about it?" he ended, shaking his captive.

The man raised his head. "Hit my brother, he did. I'll kill him for this!" he shouted in a recurrence of rage, trying to cast himself on the other prisoner, who crouched behind the other policeman. The officer struggled with him. "Come on, come on; want me to beat some sense into you? Come on, make that fellow in the car stop the howling."

The man looked at his brother for the first time. "His flower is broken, see?" he explained, "that's what he's crying about."

" 'Flower?' " repeated the law. "Say, what is this, anyway? Is your brother sick, or dead, that he's got to have a flower?"

"He ain't dead," interjected the other policeman, "and he don't sound sick to me. What is this, a show? What's going on here?" He peered into the car again and found the burlap sack. "Aha," he said. He turned swiftly. "Where's the other one? Get him quick! They've got liquor in here." He sprang toward the second man, who had not moved. "Station house for yours, boys." His companion was again struggling with the brother, and he quickly handcuffed his captive to the car, and sprang to the other's aid.

"I ain't trying to get away," the brother was shrieking. "I just want to fix his flower for him. Lemmego, I tell you!"

"Will he quit that bellowing if you fix his flower?"

"Yeh, sure; that's what he's crying for."

"Then for God's sake fix it for him."

The idiot still clutched his broken narcissus, weeping bitterly; and while the officer held his wrist the brother hunted about and found a small sliver of wood. String was volunteered by a spectator, who fetched it from a nearby shop; and under the interested eyes of the two policemen and the gathering crowd, the flower stalk was splinted. Again the poor damaged thing held its head erect, and the loud sorrow went at once from the idiot's soul. His eyes were like two scraps of April sky after a rain, and his drooling face was moonlike in ecstasy.

"Beat it, now," and the officers broke up the crowd of bystanders. "Show's all over for the day. Move on, now."

By ones and twos the crowd drifted away. And with an officer on each fender the car drew away from the curb and on down the street, and so from sight, the ineffable blue eyes of the idiot dreaming above his narcissus clenched tightly in his dirty hand.

Lyle Saxon (1891-1946)

Born in Baton Rouge, Louisiana, Saxon attended local schools and graduated from Louisiana State University with a B.A. in 1912. After working as a journalist in Chicago, he moved to New Orleans in 1918 and began a career combining newspaper work, imaginative fiction, and popular Louisiana histories. His home became a well-known center for the New Orleans literary circle, attracting, at one time or another, William Faulkner, Sherwood Anderson, and Roark Bradford. His books include Father Mississippi *(1927),* Fabulous New Orleans *(1928),* Old Louisiana *(1929),* Lafitte the Pirate *(1930),* Children of Strangers *(1937),* A Collection of Louisiana Folk Tales: Gumbo Ya-Ya *(1945), and* The Friends of Joe Gilmore *(1948). All of these books, with the exception of* Father Mississippi *and* The Friends of Joe Gilmore, *have been reprinted by Pelican Publishing Company. "Cane River" is taken from* The Dial, *March 1926.*

CANE RIVER

SUSIE WAS NOT A NATIVE of Cane River country. She came here with an old woman called Aunt Dicey, from somewhere down Bayou Lafourche way, from southwest Louisiana. She was a bad one, always—a wild nigger girl with short hair that she combed straight out; and she wore nutmegs on a string around her neck, to ward off evil spirits. She was skinny and ugly; perhaps it was her very ugliness that filled the black men with unrest, as she went flaunting by. An untamed savage, that's what she was. "Trick-nigger" they called her—little old Susie with her scrawny arms, her rolling eyes, and her barbarous ways. Why, you could hear her laughing as she went traipsing through the fields, half a mile away. "Dat's dat Susie," folks would say, as they heard the shrill scream of her laughter coming across Cane River at night, "Dat's a crazy chile!"

She and Aunt Dicey lived in a tumble-down cabin, not far from the African Baptist Church, and Aunt Dicey washed clothes two days of each week, for the white folks at Yucca Plantation. She made a little garden, too, and kept chickens. She got along with everybody.

But that Susie! Oh, she was a bad one. First one boy, and then another: that long black boy of Papa Chawlie's, and the mulatto son of Ambrose Jenks—and even Babe Johnson, bandy-legged and under-sized. But Susie favoured Big Brown. He was six feet tall, and his profile was like that of Ethiopians in Egyptian carvings. And Big Brown had a way with woman. Not that he was the marrying kind. He wasn't. He had learned city ways when he spent a year at Angola, the State Penitentiary, for shooting another negro one Christmas night...just shooting for nothing, being drunk and in a good humour.

Well, there's no stigma attached to the penitentiary, on Cane River. Many of the black boys have been in for a year or two, for bigamy, or a shooting scrape, or for some other minor offence like that—and it is rather like sending a boy off to college. Lord! Some of them are proud of it when they come back to the plantation again. Or, at least, Big Brown was that way. He came back to Cane River when Susie was fourteen, when her popularity was at its height. There was little Babe Johnson, for instance. She flouted him with her wild antics and her monkey-shines. But Babe followed her, and used to slip up to Aunt Dicey's cabin on summer nights, carrying a big watermelon for her, on his shoulder. And Susie would eat it, there on the gallery, spitting out the seeds at him and making fun of him.

Then Big Brown came slouching up. He would take her to church, or to picnics, or fish-fries. She would come running. Aunt Dicey hated Brown, and tried to make Susie behave herself. But Lord! That Susie! Might as well try to make the sun stand still.

When trouble began to brew, well—Big Brown went off somewhere into the hills, and Susie was left alone with Aunt Dicey in the cabin on the river bank.

"I tol' yer so! I tol' yer so!" Aunt Dicey said over and over, as she sat rocking her ample body back and forth. But Susie, mis-shapen and ugly, would stand looking out of the door, to where the big red moon hung low in the sky over Cane River. Sometimes she would be racked with great sobs that shook her thin body. At other times she would laugh shrilly and say: "I don' keer! I don' keer!"

A month before the baby was born she married Babe Johnson. For Babe loved her, and that was the only way he could get her. Susie didn't love him, and didn't want to marry him; but Aunt Dicey begged and argued, and talked of the disgrace, and of "gettin' read out in chu'ch"—a terrible punishment in the old woman's eyes—and Susie gave in.

That sort of thing happens oftener than one would suppose, on Cane River where we plantation negroes know less of white folks' conventions that other negroes do. Here, you do what you want to do—and usually, that's the end of it. Babe had his dreams doubtless. This bad start—well, they would get past it and Susie would make him a good wife. And he would have her all to himself then—Susie, who turned the heads of all the nigger men, ugly old Susie, with her woolly hair, that she disdained to straighten with "ointment" as the other girls did, but which she wore standing on end, like a savage woman—Susie, with her skinny, mis-shapen body, and her big bare black feet, with charms dangling on dirty strings around her ankles.

So they were married, the baby was born, and they lived in a new cabin that Mr. Guy built for them not far from Aunt Dicey's. For Babe was a favourite with Mr. Guy, who considered him the best field-hand that he had. Oh yes, Babe stood well with the white folks at Yucca Plantation, and they thought that Susie ought to thank her lucky stars that she had found a man who was willing to provide for her, who would buy her sleazy pink dresses, and plenty of cheap white lace to sew on them, or would let her buy red bandanna handkerchiefs to sew together into dresses, Cane River style.

Now Mr. Guy was not entirely pleased with Babe's marriage, because he liked Babe and considered him a fine boy. Even if he was slow in his work, his slowness was methodical; if Babe set out to do a thing he finished it. But Susie! Just one step from actual madness, with her monkey-motions and her ape-like chatterings. The mentality of a child of five. And who would have guessed that quiet, stolid Babe would be taken in by one of these trick-niggers! But the white man could never realize that the girl's very savagery was more provocative than the charms of those negresses who had taken on a veneer of civilization from the white folks. Just one bold side glance from Susie would send the black boys nudging and guffawing, as she swaggered barefoot down the dusty lane, a watermelon balanced on her head, singing as she went.

Mr. Guy's hard and fast code was: "Make your negroes work; make them respectful; try to treat them fair—but hands off in affairs among themselves, for these private things do not concern you." Mr. Guy felt that he did not understand his own race any too well, and there were things about negroes that were beyond him—although he had been born on a plantation, and there had been negroes around him all his life. The black folks liked Mr. Guy. He didn't "meddle them," as so many of the white planters did. That was the reason Mr. Guy never had labour troubles, and why there was never a vacant cabin on Yucca Plantation. And, as he always tried to play fair with them, he made no comment when Babe threw himself away on Susie. He told Babe that he could take that new cabin on the river bank, next door to Aunt Dicey's, near the lane that led to the church—a cabin built under a big Chinaberry tree, just across the river from the plantation store.

Babe and Susie got along fine for a while. The loiterers could hear her laughing in the evenings. For it was upon the store gallery that the black men gathered at night, loafing and "visitin'" together; the deserted building, tight-barred and dark, was their nightly meeting place; it was their club, their refuge from hot cabins full of squalling black children.

"Susie done quiet down," said Papa Chawlie, one night as they sat looking across the placid water to the light that glimmered in Babe's cabin.

"Babe's done bought him a 'cawdeen," commented a shapeless black shadow at his elbow.

An accordion, he meant. That was nice, too, because Susie could play upon the mouth-organ, and they heard her often, playing "blues" through the summer night. It was wrong, of course, because folks that belong to the church have no business playing the blues. It's ungodly. After you are baptized, you must give up your sinful ways, and play and sing hymn-tunes, or spirituals, or "ballots," or "jump-up" songs about folks in the Bible. Some of them are lively enough. There's that one beginning:

"Delilah wuz a woman, fine an' fair,
Pleasant-lookin' wid her coal-black hair..."

That was a grand one with its surging refrain:

"Oh, if I wuz Sampson, I'd pull dat buildin' down!"

Law! But that Susie! No ballot-tunes and jump-up songs for her.

"I got a gal, so lean an' so tall,
Her big mouf flops open like a red parasol!"

Susie would shout shrilly, all thirty verses, some of them filthy, and Babe's accordion would accompany her, with its irresponsible whine. Sometimes, Babe would sing, too, tunes he had learned in lumber camps long ago:

"Oh, I got forty dollars, an' I got it fo' to spen',
If the wimmin don' wan' it, gonna give it to de men!"

That was all of it, two lilting lines, ending in a wail. Susie liked that one and would join in with a wild shriek on the mouth-organ.

But the happiness was after all only transient, for Big Brown came back. He came slouching up to the store gallery one night, just as though he had never been away at all, and had never heard of Susie or the other girls.

"Who's dat singin' de blues, ovah de rivah?" he asked Papa Chawlie, and the old man answered: "Yo' know widdout my tellin' yo', Big Brown, dat's Susie singin'."

Brown said "Huh!" That was all, but the men on the gallery knew that his return meant unhappiness for Babe, and they were sorry, for they liked him.

And so it turned out, for Susie welcomed Big Brown with open arms. Not before Babe, of course, for Brown chose times when Babe was absent in the cotton fields; but he came to the cabin, and Aunt Dicey saw him go. She went down, herself, later, to remonstrate with Susie. But Susie just laughed and rolled her eyes. Oh, she was a bad one; no mistaking that.

It wasn't long before Babe knew, for gossip spreads rapidly.

Well, on Cane River the proper thing to do, if you can no longer ignore your wife's misdemeanors with another man, is to pick a quarrel with him on some pretext, beat him, or kill him, as you can, and then the affair is settled. And pretexts are always easy to find. So Babe brushed against Big Brown, a little too roughly, one noon on the store gallery, and the fight ensued. But, of course, Big Brown had it all his own way. He beat Babe as one would beat a mad dog, and finally grabbed him by the shoulders and pounded his head against a roll of barbed wire that lay there by the cotton scales. Mr. Guy, hearing the scuffling, came out to see what it was all about, and he was so angry to see such brutality, that he picked up a club and gave Brown a crack over the head that would have killed a man whose skull was thinner.

But Brown bore Mr. Guy no grudge. Mr. Guy had his conventions, too, and both Babe and Brown knew that it was not the thing to fight on the store gallery. After a time, some men took Babe home in a rowboat, and Susie tied up his head with a white cloth, soaked in turpentine, the only antiseptic that was handy. Brown got his senses back, after a while, and staggered off to the cabin where he lived, down the lane that led to the gin.

The fight was over, and after that, when Babe and Brown passed in the road, they spoke as before:

"Howdy, Big Brown!"

"How 'bout yo', Babe?"

That was all. And not long after, Brown began slipping to Babe's cabin again, in the day-time, when Babe was plowing out in Mr. Guy's field. And Babe knew it, and, before long, Susie knew that Babe knew it.

But Susie didn't care. She was a bad one. Reckless, too, and laughing out in her sleep at night, like a crazy woman, until the sound waked Babe, and he would lie there in the moonlight that came in through the open door, and curse his weak body....Oh, yes, Susie was a bad one, right enough, but Babe loved her. That was what hurt. For Babe knew that Big Brown didn't love her. He would lie awake until the moon set, and the grey mists hung low over the water; and he could hear the first roosters crowing, as they came fluttering down from the fig-trees by Aunt Dicey's cabin. Then, sleepless, he would rise, and wake Susie to make the coffee before he put on his overalls and hat, and went out to his day of plowing.

It was hard to find a way to get at Brown. For he wasn't employed on Yucca Plantation. He just lived there, as a good many others did. He was a trapper, that was why he went away into the hills and remained for days at a time. Sometimes, though, he made shorter trips, into the swamps a few miles back from the river bank. Bad places, those swamps, with their snakes and fevers; but Brown trapped 'possums and coons and skunks and even foxes there; and he sold the pelts. Sometimes he would be gone for a week, and would come back with a pile of hides that he sold to a man who came from New Orleans, once a month or so, to Mr. Guy's store. The man always paid in cash for the pelts, and so Brown had, nearly always, some money in hand—not commissary cheques, like the rest of us, to carry us over the periods of depression between the times when we sell our cotton, and, for a few weeks, have money to throw away with both hands.

Once Brown gave a string of beads to Susie, red beads unlike anything ever seen on Cane River before. The man who bought the pelts, brought them from New Orleans to Big Brown, in exchange for a particularly fine skin. And Susie flaunted those beads, although half a dozen negroes had seen Brown get them from the white man. Oh yes, Susie was a bad one. In spite of Aunt Dicey's prominence in the African Baptist Church, the members took a stand, and had Susie "read out."

That is supreme disgrace—and on Cane River, it means that you are barred, not only from the church itself, but from all church activities and festivities—and these festivities of church folks are the only entertainments we have. But Susie just flounced, and said she didn't care. On Sunday, she sat on the gallery before her cabin, wearing the red beads, and with the baby on her knee—Big Brown's baby—and played on her mouth-organ. Played the blues, mind you, over and over, while people were passing on the way to church. Aunt Dicey shuddered, and thought of the red hell Susie was going to.

And Babe brooded. Day by day, he grew more morose, more silent. Finally, even Susie, old foolish Susie, noticed it.

"W-what yo' studyin' bout, Babe?" she asked him, once, with something like fear in her voice.

"I'm studyin' bout Sunday," he answered. Only that. It might mean anything, but Susie asked no more. He had never asked her why she had stopped attending church, and why she had suddenly lost her old passion for shouting and singing hymns on Sunday morning.

It was just at this time that Big Brown ordered the bear trap from Mr. Guy—a brutal-looking steel trap, a trap so large that it came in a crate all by itself. For, back in the hills, miles away, where Big Brown rode, beyond the scarey woods that were full of malaria mosquitoes and bullfrogs and cotton-mouthed moccasins, he had come across bear tracks. And a bearskin, nowadays, was not to be despised. There were cubs, too. Brown had seen their tracks in the soft mud by a spring. Yes, God only knows what lies in those remote hills beyond the swamp, where no one lives, and few go, and where buzzards breed in caves on barren hillsides. "Carencro Roost" one hill is called—and from the Cane River valley, on clear days, you can see the buzzards circling high in the air, above its summit. But the buzzard hill seems as remote as the moon, although it is hardly more than ten miles away, through the swamp. On Cane River we do not wander too far away from the watercourse. The barren hills and swamps are not for us. We prefer to gather together in groups, where we can have our churches, and our social life, and where our work is waiting for us. No, the hills and swamps are not for plantation negroes, except of course for those bold and reckless spirits like Big Brown. It was along the dimly-marked trail to Carencro Roost that Brown toted the bear trap, slung over the back of a white pack mule he had borrowed from Papa Chawlie.

From the field, Babe saw him go, and bowed his head over the plow: "Git up, Mule!" he said to the beast that stood with drooping head in the simmering sun of August.

That night Babe asked Mr. Guy's permission to get Papa Chawlie to substitute for him in the field, while he went to town, twenty miles away.

"Business?" Mr. Guy smiled quizzically, and almost asked a question, but, remembering the Cane River code, merely nodded assent. Better let him go now, and get it over with—whatever it was—for next month would be cotton-picking time, and Babe couldn't be spared then, as he was a valuable man at the gin.

However, Mr. Guy did say that he hoped Babe wouldn't be gone long. The code permitted so much, at least. Babe couldn't promise, exactly. It might be a week before he got back—he had important business to attend to.

Now everybody knew that Babe had no business in town, unless it was "legal business"—and that meant only one thing. So, in the evening speculation was rife, there on the store gallery; language was guarded, but the word "divo'ce" was bandied about. It was after nine o'clock, almost time to go, when Papa Chawlie said, suddenly:

"Fo' Gawd! Look at 'er, an' lissen at 'er!"

For Susie, brazen-faced Susie, was sitting on the gallery of her cabin, sitting there in plain view, with Big Brown lolling on the floor beside her; and she was playing for him upon the mouthorgan, playing the blues. Across the narrow river, the wailing strains came, whining with slow, suggestive undulation.

The watchers in the dark said no more than "Ump!" or "Aie-Yie!" those two expressions into which the negro can pack all human emotions, scorn, love, or mere lazy comment. After a time, they saw the two forms silhouetted in the cabin doorway, against the light of the smoky oil lamp. And presently, the light went out.

Then, the men on the store gallery yawned, and said goodnight to each other; and mounting their sleepy horses, rode slowly down the moonlit road, toward the cabins, dotted along the river bank. Yes, surely, Babe was justified in getting a divorce from that woman. She was just a low-down trick-nigger. No mistaking that.

But Babe was not, as they thought, riding toward town. As soon as he was out of sight of the store, he stopped the old calico pony and looked to the right and to the left. Then he turned the animal's head into the cotton rows, and kept on through the field. Nobody was plowing to-day, and there was no cabin from which the spying eyes of a woman could see him. Presently, he drew rein at the place where the cotton rows met the woodland. And again he looked about. Only the field, simmering in the sun, and the cool shadows of the moss-covered trees before him. He sighed. Then he clucked his tongue, and the thin pony began to go forward into the woods: "Git up, Hoss!" he said.

For hours he rode, the horse picking its way through the brush, avoiding depressions and fallen logs. By looking at the westering sun, Babe was able to make the wide circle he intended. At twilight, he had reached a point some eight miles back of his own cabin, and in the heart of the swamp. It was too late to go further, so he dismounted and unsaddled his horse, tying him with a rope so the animal could graze. From a sack tied to the saddle, Babe took a can of sausage, which he opened. He ate slowly. Then he lay down under a tree, watching the rising moon, and slapping at mosquitoes that whined over him—great black swamp mosquitoes, that settled on his face and hands like a veil and remained there until brushed off dead. Finally, he put his bandanna handkerchief over his face, slipped his hands into his pockets, and lay on his back, looking at the moon through the red cloth. At last he slept.

At the first streaks of dawn, he was on horseback again. This time he rode forward, into the swamp, looking carefully to right and left. Twice he changed his course. Finally, he found the trail for which he was looking—the tracks of two horses. This was the way that Big Brown had taken the afternoon before. Yes, surely, for further along, in a marshy place, Babe found both trails, one going into the hills, one returning. Babe rode carefully now, watching the ground intently, looking for something. It was nearly ten o'clock before he found the place where Brown had dismounted and left his horses.

Before him rose a steep hill, thickly wooded, and full of little ravines, depressions which had washed out in the tropical storms of bygone years, and which were now full of a dense undergrowth. Half an hour later, he found the trap, buried in leaves and soft earth, near the mouth of a cave in the hillside. It lay in a gully, a narrow place, approachable from only one side. The bait had been partially eaten by a 'possum or a skunk, or some other small animal, too light to spring the heavy trap.

Babe examined it carefully. Certainly, it was strong enough to break the leg of a horse—or man. He worked there for an hour before he succeeded in accomplishing his purpose; but, when he had finished, the trap was covered with a light layer of earth and rotting leaves, and was fully ten yards nearer the outer end of the gully, directly in the path.

Then he went back to his horse, tethered in the woods, and rode off. He hid the old pony in a thicket, a mile away—no use to be betrayed by the whinnying of an animal—and crept back on foot, to a point not far from the trail which he knew Big Brown would follow. There Babe waited, listening, and watching the sun which shone straight down.

Hours passed. The sun drew in and heavy clouds banked up in

the south. Big raindrops came pattering down on the leaves. In the thicket, Babe smiled. All the better; no chance, now, for any one to see the tracks he had made. It seemed as though nature were working with him, for if this downpour had come yesterday, it would have been impossible for him to find the trap. He was wet through, as he sat there under the leaves. Toward twilight, the sky cleared and swarms of mosquitoes whined about him.

He began to wonder why Big Brown didn't come—and then, as his slow mind turned to possible reasons, he hung his head with shame. And the night closed around him. Sometimes he dozed; sometimes he sat motionless for hours, staring straight into the darkness; sometimes he swayed back and forth, as Aunt Dicey had done in the cabin. He slept a little, too, lightly, like an animal; waking at the slightest noise, only to stretch his body and doze again. By sun-up, he was alert, lying motionless in the wet brush, looking out through a tangle of wild grape-vines.

It was nearly nine o'clock, he reckoned by the sun, when Big Brown passed on horseback, singing as he rode, singing Babe's own song:

"Oh, I got forty dollars an' I got it fo' to spen',
 If the wimmin don' wan' it, gonna give it to de men!"

Babe heard it die away, and, peering out, saw Brown get down from his horse, and tie the animal to a branch. Then the big fellow disappeared into the woods, going toward the ravine.

A minute later Babe heard a sharp snap, and a wild cry. After a time—a great while, it seemed—he heard calls for help. At first they were sharp and frantic, then slower; finally they ceased.

It was a long way back to his horse, but Babe reached him after nightfall. From the bundle tied to the saddle, he brought out another can of sausage, ate hungrily, and when he had finished, drank from a spring, like an animal, lying flat on the ground. He brought his horse to the water and saw him drink, then tethered him where there was green, tender grass. That night Babe slept.

Shortly after daylight he crawled back to the hilltop. Brown's horse, tied to a branch, was whinnying and pawing the ground.

Hum! He'd have to do something about that old white horse. Couldn't let it stay tied there. The poor thing would starve. Must be mighty thirsty right now, too. Another thing. Suppose someone should happen to come riding by and see that horse, and investigate.

Babe took the bridle from its head, and gave the beast a smart rap with a stick. He stood watching as the horse went blundering into the brush, stopping half a hundred yards away to grasp greedily at the dewy grass. Babe followed it for half a mile or more, driving it further and further into the woods. He threw clods of earth at it, and the horse began to run, jingling the iron rings fastened to the saddle.

That afternoon Babe dozed by the spring, near his calico pony as it munched the grass. It was pleasant by the spring. Little birds came down to drink, and if you lay quiet, they came quite close.

When he crept to the gully next morning, he saw long streams of red ants in the grass, going towards the trap.

The day was unbearably hot. Babe fanned himself with a bunch of dried grass, and dozed, and woke again to fight the mosquitoes and gnats. In the afternoon, he followed the stream that ran from the spring, until he reached a place where there was a bed of white sand. Here, he undressed and lay in the water that did not cover him. However, the sand was soft, and with a little labour, he was able to scoop out a depression big enough to fit his body; and he lay there for more than an hour, watching the leaves that drifted by in the slow-moving current: long green leaves, that were like little snakes; round red berries, like Susie's red beads.

That day was hot on Cane River, too. Mr. Guy had given notice that two full hours' rest be given the men and mules at midday, instead of one, as usual, and it was nearly three o'clock in the afternoon before the plantation bell rang for the hands to go back to the fields.

Aunt Dicey, having come home in a flat-bottomed rowboat from the store, carrying a piece of salt meat in an old meal sack, turned in at the gate of Babe's cabin, deciding suddenly that she would stop and talk to Susie. Lately, she had given the girl a wide berth. But to-day, curiosity overcame distaste. She found Susie sitting listlessly beside the table, the baby in her lap. She looked—as the old woman said afterward—as though she were listening to some sound from a distance.

"What ails yo', Susie?" said Aunt Dicey, helping herself to a gourdful of water, from the pail on a shelf inside the door; "Is yo' worried becuz Babe ain't come back?"

The black girl shook her head, and the red beads clicked against the blue dish. The old woman bridled:

"It's scan'lous an' a shame," she said, "de way yo' wears dem beads, Susie. Gawd gonna strike yo' down. Yo' jus' watch!"

Instead of answering scornfully as usual, Susie raised one lanky arm and pointed to the China tree outside the door: "Look at dat leaf, Auntie!" she whispered tensely, "Oh my Gawd, jus' look at it!"

The day was airless, no breeze stirred, but in the Chinaberry tree, one leaf was waving rapidly back and forth in the mounting heat-waves.

Aunt Dicey sniffed, as she saw Susie's shaking hands: "Ef yo's lookin' for sperrits, I speck yo' gwine to see sperrits," she said. But, sensing suddenly the realness of Susie's fear, she temporized: "Ah sho did heah a squinch owl in de tree, las' night. An' I heerd de dawg howl, too!"

Susie nodded. She looked long into the older woman's face, and then she said, in a hoarse whisper: "Auntie, sump'n done happen to 'im!"

"Babe's done gone to town to get a divo'ce f'um yo', dat's wat happen to 'im!" retorted Aunt Dicey. But Susie shook her head.

"Ah don' keer, ef he do...I don' keer!"...She gulped. "Auntie, sump'n done kotch Big Brown. All las' night, an' all de night befo', seems I heah 'im callin'.... He says: 'Susie...Oh, Susie!' ovah, an' ovah. It wuz like a dyin' man, Auntie.... It wuz like a dyin' man!"

Dicey rose. "So dat's whut's wurrying yo'!" she said. "Fo' Gawd, Susie! Don' yo' know whut dey's saying' bout yo' at de sto'? Dey say, Big Brown done foun' out dat Babe's gone off to divo'ce yo', and he's lit out again....Jus' like 'e done de fust time! Ha! Dat man don' wan' yo', Susie. He's jus' bewitch yo', dat's all!" And she moved toward the door.

"Fo' Gawd's sake, don' go an' leave me, Aunt Dicey...." Susie had taken the mouth-organ from the pocket of her apron, and was twisting it over and over in her fingers. But a voice from outside interrupted the words. Papa Chawlie was passing, and seeing Aunt Dicey emerging from the door of Susie's cabin, he hailed her:

"Hey, Dicey! Sump'n done happen to Big Brown! His ol' w'ite hoss is come home widdout 'im!" There was in his voice that joy which only evil tidings can evoke, "Yonder 'e is, grazin' in de lane by de gin. Good riddance to bad rubbish, ef yo' ax me!" And he shouted the last sentence, knowing that Susie would hear.

Suddenly, despite the stifling day, Aunt Dicey shivered, and turned back into the cabin. Susie was cowering against the chimney, the mouth-organ still clenched in her hand, her eyes rolling wildly. A hoarse scream broke from her lips, and she put her arms over her face, as though to ward off a nightmare.

"W-whut yo' seein', Susie?" Aunt Dicey asked in a whisper, clutching the table's edge.

But the young black woman wheeled sharply about, and with the spring of an animal, was gone through the back door. Aunt Dicey could see her running, between the cotton rows, toward the swamp.

It stormed that night. Babe, crouched in a hollow tree, watched the blinding flashes of lightning, remembering how Susie feared it. Well, to-night, he would be back at Cane River, back with Susie, and master of his own cabin; in the morning that followed, he could return to his mules again, a peaceful man.

He dozed at intervals, despite the storm. Once, just at daylight he thought he heard screams in the woods, and lay listening, his hair tingling on his scalp, but heard no more; only the soughing of the wind, and the distant thunder.

By sunrise it was clear again; the rain had washed the air clean, and the sky was blue; the first rays of sunlight turned the dark tree-trunks to copper. Birds began calling in the thickets, and the soft moan of the wood-dove came with melancholy regularity, faint and sweet.

Shortly after the rising of the sun, Babe began his journey toward the gully. He went slowly, this morning, creeping along, keeping a sharp look-out, walking carefully in order to leave no trace. As he came near he saw a buzzard perched in a dead tree; and high in the air, another buzzard circling lower.

As his eyes descended from the tree to the path before him, he shivered and drew in his breath. For there was the print of a bare foot. Someone had walked with unerring step, directly to the trap, down into the gully.

Crouching in the bushes, he listened. Only the humming of insects came to him, and distant bird notes; the great song of the day was beginning as the sun rose. There was no other sound. Stillness, ominous silence.... Over in the gully, someone was lying in wait, spying upon him from behind the vines, for there were no returning footprints.

On hands and knees, Babe crouched, every nerve tense. Long minutes passed.

And then a thin, ghastly sound came to him—an incredible ripple, blown through reeds—music—a tuneless and discordant strain from a mouth-organ. It whined on the morning air, just one broken bar, then stopped.

A moment later, there was the rustling of leaves, and Susie appeared. She came staggering, slowly, her bare feet dragging.

She was quite close to him before she looked up, the mouth-organ against her lips, her woolly hair full of dew drops which glittered in the sunlight. She seemed incapable of controlling her eyes. He was not sure that she had seen him.

"Susie!" He moved toward her, his hand outstretched.

She started back, her eyes fixed upon him for a moment, an uncertain smile upon her face. Then, distressed and confused, she turned away from him.

"Come heah, Susie...I ain't gwine to hu't yo'...."

He advanced upon her, cautiously, as one approaches a frightened dog: "Susie...Susie...!" But she avoided him, running, floundering through the brush. Pursuing, he caught up with her in a little clearing, and came close.

"Susie, I ain't..." He grasped at her arm.

She jerked free and was off, under the trees, with a burst of loud, witless laughter. As soon as she had run a little way, she stopped and looked back at him, then raised the mouth-organ to her lips again; but as he came up, ran deeper into the woods.

In the clearing, Babe stood stupidly. From far off, an imperfect thread of melody was carried back to him—fainter and fainter—the same whimpering strain, over and over and over....

Arna Wendell Bontemps

Arna Wendell Bontemps (1902–1973)

Born in Alexandria, Louisiana, Bontemps moved to California with his family when he was three years old. He remained, however, in constant touch with his Louisiana origins through his relatives. During the 1920s he became one of the important figures of the Harlem Renaissance, and later published a wide range of anthologies and studies dealing with the life and folklore of the Southern black. Among his books are God Sends Sunday *(1931),* Black Thunder *(1936),* Drums at Dusk *(1939),* George Washington Carver *(1950),* The Book of American Negro Folklore *(1958, with Langston Hughes),* Great Slave Narratives *(1969), and a collection of short stories first published separately in the 1930s,* The Old South: A Summer Tragedy and Other Stories of the Thirties *(1973). "A Summer Tragedy" is taken from* The Old South.

A SUMMER TRAGEDY

OLD JEFF PATTON, THE BLACK SHARE FARMER, fumbled with his bow tie. His fingers trembled, and the high, stiff collar pinched his throat. A fellow loses his hand for such vanities after thirty or forty years of simple life. Once a year, or maybe twice if there's a wedding among his kin-folks, he may spruce up; but generally fancy clothes do nothing but adorn the wall of the big room and feed the moths. That had been Jeff Patton's experience. He had not worn his stiff-bosomed shirt more than a dozen times in all his married life. His swallowtailed coat lay on the bed beside him, freshly brushed and pressed, but it was as full of holes as the overalls in which he worked on week days. The moths had used it badly. Jeff twisted his mouth into a hideous toothless grimace as he contended with the obstinate bow. He stamped his good foot and decided to give up the struggle.

"Jennie," he called.

"What's that, Jeff?" His wife's shrunken voice came out of the adjoining room like an echo. It was hardly bigger than a whisper.

"I reckon you'll have to he'p me wid this heah bow tie, baby," he said meekly. "Dog if I can hitch it up."

Her answer was not strong enough to reach him, but presently the old woman came to the door, feeling her way with a stick. She had a wasted, dead-leaf appearance. Her body, as scrawny and gnarled as a stringbean, seemed less than nothing in the ocean of frayed and faded petticoats that surrounded her. These hung an inch or two above the tops of her heavy, unlaced shoes and showed little grotesque piles where the stockings had fallen down from her negligible legs.

"You oughta could do a heap mo' wid a thing like that 'n me—beingst as you got yo' good sight."

"Looks like I *oughta* could," he admitted. "But ma fingers is gone democrat on me. I get all mixed up in the looking glass an' can't tell whicha way to twist the devilish thing."

Jennie sat on the side of the bed and old Jeff Patton got down on one knee while she tied the bow knot. It was a slow and painful ordeal for each of them in this position. Jeff's bones cracked, his knee ached, and it was only after a half dozen attempts that Jennie worked a semblance of a bow into the tie.

"I got to dress maself now," the old woman whispered. "These is

221

ma old shoes an' stockings, and I ain't so much as unwrapped ma dress."

"Well, don't worry 'bout me no mo', baby," Jeff said. "That 'bout finishes me. All I gotta do now is slip on that old coat 'n ves' an' I'll be fixed to leave."

Jennie disappeared again through the dim passage into the shed room. Being blind was no handicap to her in that black hole. Jeff heard the cane placed against the wall beside the door and knew that his wife was on easy ground. He put on his coat, took a battered top hat from the bed post, and hobbled to the front door. He was ready to travel. As soon as Jennie could get on her Sunday shoes and her old black silk dress, they would start.

Outside the tiny log house the day was warm and mellow with sunshine. A host of wasps was humming with busy excitement in the trunk of a dead sycamore. Grey squirrels were searching through the grass for hickory nuts and blue jays were in the trees, hopping from branch to branch. Pine woods stretched away to the left like a black sea. Among them were scattered scores of log houses like Jeff's, houses of black share farmers. Cows and pigs wandered freely among the trees. There was no danger of loss. Each farmer knew his own stock and knew his neighbor's as well as he knew his neighbor's children.

Down the slope to the right were the cultivated acres on which the colored folks worked. They extended to the river, more than two miles away, and they were today green with the unmade cotton crop. A tiny thread of a road, which passed directly in front of Jeff's place, ran through these green fields like a pencil mark.

Jeff, standing outside the door with his absurd hat in his left hand, surveyed the wide scene tenderly. He had been forty-five years on these acres. He loved them with the unexplained affection that others have for the countries to which they belong.

The sun was hot on his head, his collar still pinched his throat, and the Sunday clothes were intolerably hot. Jeff transferred the hat to his right hand and began fanning with it. Suddenly the whisper that was Jennie's voice came out of the shed room.

"You can bring the car round front whilst you's waitin'," it said feebly. There was a tired pause; then it added, "I'll soon be fixed to go."

"A' right, baby," Jeff answered. "I'll get it in a minute."

But he didn't move. A thought struck him that made his mouth fall open. The mention of the car brought to his mind, with new intensity, the trip he and Jennie were about to take. Fear came into his eyes; excitement took his breath. Lord, Jesus!

"Jeff...Oh Jeff," the old woman's whisper called.

He awakened with a jolt. "Hunh, baby?"

"What you doin'?"

"Nuthin. Jes studyin'. I jes been turnin' things round 'n round in ma mind."

"You could be gettin' the car," she said.

"Oh yes, right away, baby."

He started round to the shed, limping heavily on his bad leg. There were three frizzly chickens in the yard. All his other chickens had been killed or stolen recently. But the frizzly chickens had been saved somehow. That was fortunate indeed, for these curious creatures had a way of devouring "poison" from the yard and in that way protecting against conjure and bad luck and spells. But even the frizzly chickens seemed now to be in a stupor. Jeff thought they had some ailment; he expected all three of them to die shortly.

The shed in which the old model-T Ford stood was only a grass roof held up by four corner poles. It had been built by tremulous hands at a time when the little rattletrap car had been regarded as a peculiar treasure. And, miraculously, despite wind and downpour, it still stood.

Jeff adjusted the crank and put his weight on it. The engine came to life with a sputter and bang that rattled the old car from radiator to tail light. Jeff hopped into the seat and put his foot on the accelerator. The sputtering and banging increased. The rattling became more violent. That was good. It was good banging, good sputtering and rattling, and it meant that the aged car was still in running condition. She could be depended on for this trip.

Again Jeff's thought halted as if paralyzed. The suggestion of the trip fell into the machinery of his mind like a wrench. He felt dazed and weak. He swung the car out into the yard, made a half turn, and drove around to the front door. When he took his hands off the wheel, he noticed that he was trembling violently. He cut off the motor and climbed to the ground to wait for Jennie.

A few moments later she was at the window, her voice rattling against the pane like a broken shutter.

"I'm ready, Jeff."

He did not answer, but limped into the house and took her by the arm. He led her slowly through the big room, down the step, and across the yard.

"You reckon I'd oughta lock the do'?" he asked softly.

They stopped and Jennie weighed the question. Finally she shook her head.

"Ne' mind the do'," she said. "I don't see no cause to lock up things."

"You right," Jeff agreed. "No cause to lock up."

Jeff opened the door and helped his wife into the car. A quick shudder passed over him. Jesus! Again he trembled.

"How come you shaking so?" Jennie whispered.

"I don't know," he said.

"You mus' be scairt, Jeff."

"No, baby, I ain't scairt."

He slammed the door after her and went around to crank up again. The motor started easily. Jeff wished that it had not been so responsive. He would have liked a few more minutes in which to turn things around in his head. As it was, with Jennie chiding him about being afraid, he had to keep going. He swung the car into the little pencil-mark road and started off toward the river, driving very slowly, very cautiously.

Chugging across the green countryside, the small, battered Ford seemed tiny indeed. Jeff felt a familiar excitement, a thrill, as they came down the first slope to the immense levels on which the cotton was growing. He could not help reflecting that the crops were good. He knew what that meant, too; he had made forty-five of them with his own hands. It was true that he had worn out nearly a dozen mules, but that was the fault of old man Stevenson, the owner of the land. Major Stevenson had the odd notion that one mule was all a share farmer needed to work a thirty-acre plot. It was an expensive notion, the way it killed mules from overwork, but the old man held to it. Jeff thought it killed a good many share farmers as well as mules, but he had no sympathy for them. He had always been strong, and he had been taught to have no patience with weakness in men. Women or children might be tolerated if they were puny, but a weak man was a curse. Of course, his own children—

Jeff's thought halted there. He and Jennie never mentioned their dead children any more. And naturally he did not wish to dwell upon them in his mind. Before he knew it, some remark would slip out of his mouth and that would make Jennie feel blue. Perhaps she would cry. A woman like Jennie could not easily throw off the grief that comes from losing five grown children within two years. Even Jeff was still staggered by the blow. His memory had not been much good recently. He frequently talked to himself. And, although he had kept it a secret, he knew that his courage had left him. He was terrified by the least unfamiliar sound at night. He was reluctant to venture far from home in the daytime. And that habit of trembling when he felt fearful was now far beyond his control. Sometimes he became afraid and trembled without knowing what had frightened him. The feeling would just come over him like a chill.

The car rattled slowly over the dusty road. Jennie sat erect and silent, with a little absurd hat pinned to her hair. Her useless eyes seemed very large and very white in their deep sockets. Suddenly Jeff heard her voice, and he inclined his head to catch the words.

"Is we passed Delia Moore's house yet?" she asked.

"Not yet," he said.

"You must be drivin' mighty slow, Jeff."

"We jes as well take our time, baby."

There was a pause. A little puff of steam was coming out of the radiator of the car. Heat wavered above the hood. Delia Moore's house was nearly half a mile away. After a moment Jennie spoke again.

"You ain't really scairt, is you, Jeff?"

"Nah, baby, I ain't scairt."

"You know how we agreed—we gotta keep on goin'."

Jewels of perspiration appeared on Jeff's forehead. His eyes rounded, blinked, became fixed on the road.

"I don't know," he said with a shiver. "I reckon it's the only thing to do."

"Hm."

A flock of guinea fowls, pecking in the road, were scattered by the passing car. Some of them took to their wings; others hid under bushes. A blue jay, swaying on a leafy twig, was annoying a roadside squirrel. Jeff held an even speed till he came near Delia's place. Then he slowed down noticeably.

Delia's house was really no house at all, but an abandoned store building converted into a dwelling. It sat near a crossroads, beneath a single black cedar tree. There Delia, a catlike old creature of Jennie's age, lived alone. She had been there more

years than anybody could remember, and long ago had won the
disfavor of such women as Jennie. For in her young days Delia
had been gayer, yellower, and saucier than seemed proper in
those parts. Her ways with menfolks had been dark and suspicious. And the fact that she had had as many husbands as
children did not help her reputation.

"Yonder's old Delia," Jeff said as they passed.

"What she doin'?"

"Jes sittin' in the do'," he said.

"She see us?"

"Hm," Jeff said. "Musta did."

That relieved Jennie. It strengthened her to know that her old
enemy had seen her pass in her best clothes. That would give the
old she-devil something to chew her gums and fret about, Jennie
thought. Wouldn't she have a fit if she didn't find out? Old evil
Delia! This would be just the thing for her. It would pay her back
for being so evil. It would also pay her, Jennie thought, for the
way she used to grin at Jeff—long ago when her teeth were good.

The road became smooth and red, and Jeff could tell by the
smell of the air that they were nearing the river. He could see the
rise where the road turned and ran along parallel to the stream.
The car chugged on monotonously. After a long silent spell,
Jennie leaned against Jeff and spoke.

"How many bale o' cotton you think we got standin'?" she said.

Jeff wrinkled his forehead as he calculated.

" 'Bout twenty-five, I reckon."

"How many you make las' year?"

"Twenty-eight," he said. "How come you ask that?"

"I's jes thinkin'," Jennie said quietly.

"It don't make a speck o' diff'ence though," Jeff reflected. "If we
get much or if we get little, we still gonna be in debt to old man
Stevenson when he gets through counting up agin us. It's took us
a long time to learn that."

Jennie was not listening to these words. She had fallen into a
trance-like meditation. Her lips twitched. She chewed her gums
and rubbed her old gnarled hands nervously. Suddenly, she leaned
forward, buried her face in the nervous hands, and burst into
tears. She cried aloud in a dry, cracked voice that suggested the
rattle of fodder on dead stalks. She cried aloud like a child, for
she had never learned to suppress a genuine sob. Her slight old

frame shook heavily and seemed hardly able to sustain such violent grief.

"What's the matter, baby?" Jeff asked awkwardly. "Why you cryin' like all that?"

"I's jes thinkin'," she said.

"So you the one what's scairt now, hunh?"

"I ain't scairt, Jeff. I's jes thinkin' 'bout leavin' eve'thing like this—eve'thing we been used to. It's right sad-like."

Jeff did not answer, and presently Jennie buried her face again and continued crying.

The sun was almost overhead. It beat down furiously on the dusty wagon path road, on the parched roadside grass, and the tiny battered car. Jeff's hands, gripping the wheel, became wet with perspiration; his forehead sparkled. Jeff's lips parted and his mouth shaped a hideous grimace. His face suggested the face of a man being burned. But the torture passed and his expression softened again.

"You mustn't cry, baby," he said to his wife. "We gotta be strong. We can't break down."

Jennie waited a few seconds, then said, "You reckon we oughta do it, Jeff? You reckon we oughta go 'head an' do it really?"

Jeff's voice choked; his eyes blurred. He was terrified to hear Jennie say the thing that had been in his mind all morning. She had egged him on when he had wanted more than anything in the world to wait, to reconsider, to think things over a little longer. Now *she* was getting cold feet. Actually, there was no need of thinking the question through again. It would only end in making the same painful decision once more. Jeff knew that. There was no need of fooling around longer.

"We jes as well to do like we planned," he said. "They ain't nuthin else for us now—it's the bes' thing."

Jeff thought of the handicaps, the near impossibility, of making another crop with his leg bothering him more and more each week. Then there was always the chance that he would have another stroke, like the one that had made him lame. Another one might kill him. The least it could do would be to leave him helpless. Jeff gasped... Lord, Jesus! He could not bear to think of being helpless, like a baby, on Jennie's hands. Frail, blind Jennie.

The little pounding motor of the car worked harder and harder. The puff of steam from the cracked radiator became larger. Jeff realized that they were climbing a little rise. A moment later the road turned abruptly and he looked down upon the face of the river.

"Jeff."

"Hunh?"

"Is that the water I hear?"

"Hm. Tha's it."

"Well, which way you goin' now?"

"Down this-a way," he answered. "The road runs 'long-side o' the water a lil piece."

She waited a while calmly. Then she said, "Drive faster."

"A'right, baby," Jeff said.

The water roared in the bed of the river. It was fifty or sixty feet below the level of the road. Between the road and the water there was a long smooth slope, sharply inclined. The slope was dry; the clay had been hardened by prolonged summer heat. The water below, roaring in a narrow channel, was noisy and wild.

"Jeff."

"Hunh?"

"How far you goin'?"

"Jes a lil piece down the road."

"You ain't scairt is you, Jeff?"

"Nah, baby," he said trembling. "I ain't scairt."

"Remember how we planned it, Jeff. We gotta do it like we said. Brave-like."

"Hm."

Jeff's brain darkened. Things suddenly seemed unreal, like figures in a dream. Thoughts swam in his mind foolishly, hysterically, like little blind fish in a pool within a dense cave. They rushed, crossed one another, jostled, collided, retreated, and rushed again. Jeff soon became dizzy. He shuddered violently and turned to his wife.

"Jennie, I can't do it. I can't." His voice broke pitifully.

She did not appear to be listening. All the grief had gone from her face. She sat erect, her unseeing eyes wide open, strained and frightful. Her glossy black skin had become dull. She seemed as thin and as sharp and bony as a starved bird. Now, having suffered and endured the sadness of tearing herself away from beloved things, she showed no anguish. She was absorbed with her own thoughts, and she didn't even hear Jeff's voice shouting in her ear.

Jeff said nothing more. For an instant there was light in his cavernous brain. That chamber was, for less than a second, peopled by characters he knew and loved. They were simple, healthy creatures, and they behaved in a manner that he could understand. They had quality. But since he had already taken leave of them long ago, the remembrance did not break his heart again. Young Jeff Patton was among them, the Jeff Patton of fifty years ago who went down to New Orleans with a crowd of country boys to the Mardi Gras doings. The gay young crowd—boys with candy-striped shirts and rouged brown girls in noisy silks—was like a picture in his head. Yet it did not make him sad. On that very trip Slim Burns had killed Joe Beasley—the crowd had been broken up. Since then Jeff Patton's world had been the Greenbrier Plantation. If there had been other Mardi Gras carnivals, he had not heard of them. Since then there had been no time; the years had fallen on him like waves. Now he was old, worn out. Another paralytic stroke like the one he had already suffered would put him on his back for keeps. In that condition, with a frail blind woman to look after him, he would be worse off than if he were dead.

Suddenly Jeff's hands became steady. He actually felt brave. He slowed down the motor of the car and carefully pulled off the road. Below, the water of the stream boomed, a soft thunder in the deep channel. Jeff ran the car onto the clay slope, pointed it directly toward the stream, and put his foot heavily on the accelerator. The little car leaped furiously down the steep incline toward the water. The movement was nearly as swift and direct as a fall. The two old black folks, sitting quietly side by side, showed no excitement. In another instant the car hit the water and dropped immediately out of sight.

A little later it lodged in the mud of a shallow place. One wheel of the crushed and upturned little Ford became visible above the rushing water.

Zora Neale Hurston

Zora Neale Hurston (1891–1960)

Born and raised in Eatonville, Florida, Hurston lived a nomadic life that took her from Florida to Washington D.C., where she attended Howard University, to New York, where she continued her studies at Barnard College. She began writing during the high tide of the Harlem Renaissance, and then went back to Florida and Louisiana, where she lived and put together material for her remarkable book of black folklore, Mules and Men *(1935). Her other books include the novels,* Jonah's Gourd Vine *(1934),* Their Eyes Were Watching God *(1937), and* Moses, Man of the Mountain *(1939), and an autobiography,* Dust Tracks on a Road *(1942). "Father Watson" is taken from* Mules and Men.

"Father Watson," by Zora Neale Hurston. Reprinted by permission of the estate of Zora Neale Hurston.

FATHER WATSON

I heard of Father Watson the "Frizzly Rooster" from afar, from people for whom he had "worked" and their friends, and from people who attended his meetings held twice a week in Myrtle Wreath Hall in New Orleans. His name is "Father" Watson, which in itself attests his Catholic leanings, though he is formally a Protestant.

On a given night I had a front seat in his hall. There were the usual camp-followers sitting upon the platform and bustling around performing chores. Two or three songs and a prayer were the preliminaries.

At last Father Watson appeared in a satin garment of royal purple, belted by a gold cord. He had the figure for wearing that sort of thing and he probably knew it. Between prayers and songs he talked, setting forth his powers. He could curse anybody he wished—and make the curse stick. He could remove curses, no matter who had laid them on whom. Hence his title The Frizzly Rooster. Many persons keep a frizzled chicken in the yard to locate and scratch up any hoodoo that may be buried for them. These chickens have, no doubt, earned this reputation by their ugly appearance—with all of their feathers set in backwards. He could "read" anybody at sight. He could "read" anyone who remained out of his sight if they but stuck two fingers inside the door. He could "read" anyone, no matter how far away, if he were given their height and color. He begged to be challenged.

He predicted the hour and the minute nineteen years hence, when he should die—without even having been ill a moment in his whole life. God had told him.

He sold some small packets of love powders before whose powers all opposition must break down. He announced some new keys that were guaranteed to unlock every door and remove every obstacle in the way of success that the world knew. These keys had been sent to him by God through a small Jew boy. The old keys had been sent through a Jew man. They were powerful as long as they did not touch the floor—but if you ever dropped them, they lost their power. These new keys at five dollars each were not affected by being dropped, and were otherwise much more powerful.

I lingered after the meeting and made an appointment with him for the next day at his home.

Before my first interview with the Frizzly Rooster was fairly begun, I could understand his great following. He had the physique of Paul Robeson with the sex appeal and hypnotic whatever-you-might-call-it of Rasputin. I could see that women would rise to flee from him but in mid-flight would whirl and end shivering at his feet. It was that way in fact.

His wife Mary knew how slight her hold was and continually planned to leave him.

"Only thing that's holding me here is this." She pointed to a large piece of brain-coral that was forever in a holy spot on the altar. "That's where his power is. If I could get me a piece, I could go start up a business all by myself. If I could only find a piece."

"It's very plentiful down in South Florida," I told her. "But if that piece is so precious, and you're his wife, I'd take it and let *him* get another piece."

"Oh my God! Naw! That would be my end. He's too powerful. I'm leaving him," she whispered this stealthily. "You get me a piece of that—you know."

The Frizzly Rooster entered and Mary was a different person at once. But every time that she was alone with me it was "That on the altar, you know. When you back in Florida, get me a piece. I'm leaving this man to his women." Then a quick hush and forced laughter at her husband's approach.

So I became the pupil of Reverend Father Joe Watson, "The Frizzly Rooster" and his wife, Mary, who assisted him in all things. She was "round the altar"; that is while he talked with the clients, and usually decided on whatever "work" was to be done, she "set" the things on the altar and in the jars. There was one jar in the kitchen filled with honey and sugar. All the "sweet" works were set in this jar. That is, the names and the thing desired were written on paper and thrust into this jar to stay. Already four or five hundred slips of paper had accumulated in the jar. There was another jar called the "break up" jar. It held vinegar with some unsweetened coffee added. Papers were left in this one also.

When finally it was agreed that I should come to study with them, I was put to running errands such as "dusting" houses, throwing pecans, rolling apples, as the case might be; but I was not told why the thing was being done. After two weeks of this I was taken off this phase and initiated. This was the first step towards the door of the mysteries.

My initiation consisted of the Pea Vine Candle Drill. I was told to remain five days without sexual intercourse. I must remain indoors all day the day before the initiation and fast. I might wet my throat when necessary, but I was not to swallow water.

When I arrived at the house the next morning a little before nine, as per instructions, six other persons were there, so that there were nine of us—all in white except Father Watson who was in his purple robe. There was no talking. We went at once to the altar room. The altar was blazing. There were three candles around the vessel of holy water, three around the sacred sand pail, and one large cream candle burning in it. A picture of St. George and a large piece of brain coral were in the center. Father Watson dressed eight long blue candles and one black one, while the rest of us sat in the chairs around the wall. Then he lit the eight blue candles one by one from the altar and set them in the pattern of a moving serpent. Then I was called to the altar and both Father Watson and his wife laid hands on me. The black candle was placed in my hand; I was told to light it from all the other candles. I lit it at number one and pinched out the flame, and re-lit it at number two and so on till it had been lit by the eighth candle. Then I held the candle in my left hand, and by my right was conducted back to the altar by Father Watson. I was led through the maze of candles beginning at number eight. We circled numbers seven, five and three. When we reached the altar he lifted me upon the step. As I stood there, he called aloud, "Spirit! She's standing here without no home and no friends. She wants you to take her in." Then we began at number one and threaded back to number eight, circling three, five and seven. Then back to the altar again. Again he lifted me and placed me upon the step of the altar. Again the spirit was addressed as before. Then he lifted me down by placing his hands in my arm-pits. This time I did not walk at all. I was carried through the maze and I was to knock down each candle as I passed it with my foot. If I missed one, I was not to try again, but to knock it down on my way back to the altar. Arrived there the third time, I was lifted up and told to pinch out my black candle. "Now," Father told me, "you are made Boss of Candles. You have the power to light candles and put out candles, and to work with the spirits anywhere on earth."

Then all of the candles on the floor were collected and one of them handed to each of the persons present. Father took the black candle himself and we formed a ring. Everybody was given two matches each. The candles were held in our left hands, matches in the right; at a signal everybody stooped at the same moment, the matches scratched in perfect time and our candles lighted in concert. Then Father Watson walked rhythmically around the person at his right. Exchanged candles with her and went back to his place. Then that person did the same to the next so that the black candle went all around the circle and back to Father. I was then seated on a stool before the altar, sprinkled lightly with holy sand and water and confirmed as a Boss of Candles.

Then conversation broke out. We went into the next room and had a breakfast that was mostly fruit and smothered chicken. Afterwards the nine candles used in the ceremony were wrapped up and given to me to keep. They were to be used for lighting other candles only, not to be just burned in the ordinary sense.

In a few days I was allowed to hold consultations on my own. I felt insecure and said so to Father Watson.

"Of course you do now," he answered me, "but you have to learn and grow. I'm right here behind you. Talk to your people first, then come see me."

Within the hour a woman came to me. A man had shot and seriously wounded her husband and was in jail.

"But, honey," she all but wept, "they say ain't a thing going to be done with him. They say he got good white folks back of him and he's going to be let loose soon as the case is tried. I want him punished. Picking a fuss with my husband just to get chance to shoot him. We needs help. Somebody that can hit a straight lick with a crooked stick."

So I went in to the Frizzly Rooster to find out what I must do and he told me, "That a low fence." He meant a difficulty that was easily overcome.

"Go back and get five dollars from her and tell her to go home and rest easy. That man will be punished. When we get through with him, white folks or no white folks, he'll find a tough jury sitting on his case." The woman paid me and left in perfect confidence of Father Watson.

So he and I went into the workroom.

"Now," he said, "when you want a person punished who is

already indicted, write his name on a slip of paper and put it in a sugar bowl or some other deep something like that. Now get your paper and pencil and write the name; alright now, you got it in the bowl. Now put in some red pepper, some black pepper—don't be skeered to put it in, it needs a lot. Put in one eightpenny nail, fifteen cents worth of ammonia and two door keys. You drop one key down in the bowl and you leave the other one against the side of the bowl. Now you got your bowl set. Go to your bowl every day at twelve o'clock and turn the key that is standing against the side of the bowl. That is to keep the man locked in jail. And every time you turn the key, add a little vinegar. Now I know this will do the job. All it needs is for you to do it in faith. I'm trusting this job to you entirely. Less see what you going to do. That can wait another minute. Come sit with me in the outside room and hear this woman out here that's waiting."

So we went outside and found a weakish woman in her early thirties that looked like somebody had dropped a sack of something soft on a chair.

The Frizzly Rooster put on his manner, looking like a brown, purple and gold throne-angel in a house.

"Good morning, sister er, er—"

"Murchison," she helped out.

"Tell me how you want to be helped, Sister Murchison."

She looked at me as if I was in the way and he read her eyes.

"She's alright, dear one. She's one of us. I brought her in with me to assist and help."

I thought still I was in her way but she told her business just the same.

"Too many women in my house. My husband's mother is there and she hates me and always puttin' my husband up to fight me. Look like I can't get her out of my house no ways I try. So I done come to you."

"We can fix that up in no time, dear one. Now go take a flat onion. If it was a man, I'd say a sharp pointed onion. Core the onion out, and write her name five times on paper and stuff it into the hole in the onion and close it back with the cutout piece of onion. Now you watch when she leaves the house and then you roll the onion behind her before anybody else crosses the door-sill. And you make a wish at the same time for her to leave your house. She won't be there two weeks more." The woman paid and left.

That night we held a ceremony in the altar room on the case. We took a red candle and burnt it just enough to consume the tip. Then it was cut into three parts and the short lengths of candle were put into a glass of holy water. Then we took the glass and went at midnight to the door of the woman's house and the Frizzly Rooster held the glass in his hands and said, "In the name of the Father, in the name of the Son, in the name of the Holy Ghost." He shook the glass three times violently up and down, and the last time he threw the glass to the ground and broke it, and said, "Dismiss this woman from this place." We scarcely paused as this was said and done and we kept going and went home by another way because that was part of the ceremony.

Somebody came against a very popular preacher. "He's getting too rich and big. I want something done to keep him down. They tell me he's 'bout to get to be a bishop. I sho' would hate for that to happen. I got forty dollars in my pocket right now for the work."

So that night the altar blazed with the blue light. We wrote the preacher's name on a slip of paper with black ink. We took a small doll and ripped open its back and put in the paper with the name along with some bitter aloes and cayenne pepper and sewed the rip up again with the black thread. The hands of the doll were tied behind it and a black veil tied over the face and knotted behind it so that the man it represented would be blind and always do the things to keep himself from progressing. The doll was then placed in a kneeling position in a dark corner where it would not be disturbed. He would be frustrated as long as the doll was not disturbed.

When several of my jobs had turned out satisfactorily to Father Watson, he said to me, "You will do well, but you need the Black Cat Bone. Sometimes you have to be able to walk invisible. Some things must be done in deep secret, so you have to walk out of the sight of man."

First I had to get ready even to try this most terrible of experiences—getting the Black Cat Bone.

First we had to wait on the weather. When a big rain started, a new receptacle was set out in the yard. It could not be put out until the rain actually started for fear the sun might shine in it. The water must be brought inside before the weather faired off for the same reason. If lightning shone on it, it was ruined.

We finally got the water for the bath and I had to fast and

"seek," shut in a room that had been purged by smoke. Twenty-four hours without food except a special wine that was fed to me every four hours. It did not make me drunk in the accepted sense of the word. I merely seemed to lose my body, my mind seemed very clear.

When dark came, we went out to catch a black cat. I must catch him with my own hands. Finding and catching black cats is hard work, unless one has been released for you to find. Then we repaired to a prepared place in the woods and a circle drawn and "protected" with nine horseshoes. Then the fire and the pot were made ready. A roomy iron pot with a lid. When the water boiled I was to toss in the terrified, trembling cat.

When he screamed, I was told to curse him. He screamed three times, the last time weak and resigned. The lid was clamped down, the fire kept vigorously alive. At midnight the lid was lifted. Here was the moment! The bones of the cat must be passed through my mouth until one tasted bitter.

Suddenly, the Rooster and Mary rushed in close to the pot and he cried, "Look out! This is liable to kill you. Hold your nerve!" They both looked fearfully around the circle. They communicated some unearthly terror to me. Maybe I went off in a trance. Great beast-like creatures thundered up to the circle from all sides. Indescribable noises, sights, feelings. Death was at hand! Seemed unavoidable! I don't know. Many things I have thought and felt, but I always have to say the same thing. I don't know. I don't know.

Before day I was home, with a small white bone for me to carry.

E. P. O'Donnell

E. P. O'Donnell (1895–1943)

Edwin Philip "Pat" O'Donnell was born in New Orleans. Both his father and his mother (an O'Brien) came from Irish families of modest means. O'Donnell worked at a wide range of odd jobs after leaving school in the fourth grade. He began writing in the late 1920s after being encouraged by Sherwood Anderson. Apart from his short stories, published separately in magazines and journals, he published two novels, Green Margins *(1936), and* The Great Big Doorstep, a Delta Comedy *(1941). "Canker" is taken from* The Yale Review, *25, 1936.*

CANKER

IN THE HOT WEATHER the oranges were half grown. Behind the levee the fruitful trees nodded drowsily in oblique ranks. Everyone along the river was contented, because a good crop of fruit means cash.

One day two brisk state inspectors left the mail boat at Belle Plume to inspect the orange orchards for disease, and to destroy any orchard found infected. They spoke neither French nor Slavonian, but both were amiable and careful to offend none of the people, whose votes had helped them get their jobs. They strolled from grove to grove indolently, keeping in the shade, casually poking among the orange leaves with their long staffs of peeled willow, followed by dark indifferent eyes. The sun was white.

Minus Dobravich discovered the inspectors in the morning. His mother had sent him for some tomato paste at Jule's. Minus and a small Negro lad named Alfred were having a dust fight. When the two strangers passed them, the boys stopped throwing, and the Negro sat on his ankle in the hot levee dust. The inspectors were eating big black figs and laughing about something. With his languid insolent stare the Negro followed the two seersucker backs receding. Then he turned to Minus and widened his eyes and flopped his puffed lips about in a dry sinister groan—"Dem's *gub*ment mens!"

"Yeah," said Minus. "Huntin' sick trees. Huntin'—"

"Bettah go tell yo' *maw*! Let's go tell ou' maws, huh Minus?"

"Ain' got no maw."

"Yo' stepmaw. Huh, Minus?"

"What my stepmaw cares?"

"Le's go tell 'um, huh Minus? You come wid me, Ah go wid you."

"Man, our trees been sprayed all over."

"Ah'm goin' tell my *maw*!"

Alfred stood up, spilling a lapful of dust and tinkling clamshell grit. Minus watched him walk away backwards, with his thick tight hair dusted gray.

"My paw ain' got no nigger trees!" Minus called.

"Y'alls' trees got de *canker*!" said Alfred.

"You crazy! Our trees prettier than anybody's."

243

The Negro walked backwards, toes after toes, with his wide vacant grin. "Neb' mind," he said mysteriously. "Might be *pretty*, but dey's got de canker *right on*! Ah *knows* dey got it! Gubment goin' 'stroy yo' *trees*!"

Minus was not bothered. Everybody knew the Dobravich orchard was the cleanest on the river. The Negro was running home. Minus reflected, then decided he would run home and tell his stepmother the inspectors were coming—to see what she would do. Minus's stepmother was a nervous wreck. Minus always enjoyed the scenes she made; particularly when, distracted by one of the minor misfortunes that were constantly befalling the family, Olga took her hair in her hands and screamed, "I could *kill* myself!"

The backyard felt sad. The garbage hamper of souring rinds and cans and shrimp heads, vocal with flies, had not yet been taken to the river. Olga Dobravich stood tall and sunlit, with long creamy arms lifted to a clothesline sagging with diapers that shone a bitter white with luminous blue holes.

"Son, take the slops to the batture, please," she said.

"Mama, them gubment mens down the road, mama!" said Minus, panting dramatically and watching her fixedly. "Expectin' the trees!"

Olga squinted down into the cruel cherubic face lifted. Minus perceived her green neurotic eyes briefly webbed with apprehension.

"Take away the slops, like a good boy, and blow your nose. As if we care about canker men! Where are they?"

"Down by the oyster wharf."

"We'll be glad to see them."

Last night, lying in bed listening to the river's innocent laughter and stroking Nick's tough slumbering fingers resting on her thigh, Olga had resolved again to banish her senseless fears, smite them as they lifted their heads, laugh them away.

The trees around her were plump and bronzed with promise. It was a day of gold. Far over her, brief as curving sparks, the man-of-war birds coasted over a bulge of wind, heavy with devoured prey. Olga, working with a clothespin in her teeth, let her mind dip into and out of some lines read last night while Nick was carving the orangewood sticks—"the voice of the turtle is heard in our land. The fig tree putteth forth her green figs, and the vines with the tender grape give a good smell."

Sure enough, the trees were proud with good fruit, each as

complete as a round green vowel! Nick had predicted a master crop of fruit this year. Nick always knew. Come spring, they would at last have enough money to visit her people in Tennessee.

Tennessee!

She was suddenly aware of sinewed oxen sleeping between the hills—the ozonic crags of home—the railroad train of a purple evening puffing inside the mountain's vast brown shoulder, then bursting out and leaving a jagged hole, leaping chasms and spinning violently around the curve, trailing a far silken call. Near her father's store flowed a little woven river full of garishly dyed rocks. Here next spring she would wander alone, alone, and carry her jaded heart to the proper tree. There were no stately assertive trees here in the Delta, only dolorous oaks and willows, and the corpulent oranges dwarfed by procreation, squatting in the sun like fat tropical wives.

There was a willow behind the orchard. She saw it now, and in her fancy she straightened its sagging limbs and deepened its green, until it stood forth a tall athletic fir, utterly possessing the imagined rocks. How often had she stood at the clothesline and wrought that hilly dream!

The baby beat his all-day-sucker against the porch screen and crowed to her. Olga reached out, flapping her sunny hand.

"Bye-bye! Make bye-bye for mama!"

Minus returned from the river. He threw himself under a tangelo tree near his stepmother. He took out his scout knife and pecked disconsolately at the ground, not comprehending Olga's equanimity after the news of the inspectors—resenting it. For the child of an impoverished father, Minus was incongruously fat. His head was enormous, with a high proud brow, and practically no neck, so that he seemed always in the act of drawing his head into his fat shoulders.

"Why don't you go play, son, and blow your nose?"

Minus's mouth, sunken deeply between his great red cheeks, rounded into a pout. He sniffled glumly, and dug his knife blade into and into a place on the ground where a sun ray lay like a tarnished coin.

"Them gubment mens comin' here to-morrow, I think," he said, lifting his eyes to hers.

Olga rammed the last clothespin home. She went to Minus and impatiently threw her weight on one hip. "Minus, why do you keep saying that? We've got nothing to fear from the inspectors, son!"

But when she walked towards the house, Minus saw her turn and look back at him, her face momentarily shadowed. Minus's eyes brightened.

At supper, Nick was uncommonly cheerful. The summer ducks were tender and succulent. Olga knew how to cook game, with Creole seasoning. Nick was cheerful because he had a prospect of a job that would last a week, caulking and installing new lignum-vitae in one of the pilot boats at the ship repair yard. During the meal Olga comported herself as gaily as she could. Nick noticed her blithe mood. He said nothing, but he perceived all; and she was glad, relishing the rich calm security of living with a strong man who had so little to say with his mouth. It was only with his hands that Nick expressed his true self. A born mender, he loved a good tool. The new oaken fish-board on the sink was as neat and solid as a proverb; and about the baby's willow crib which Nick had woven, there was something of the cunning finality of an epigram. Watching him now hunched over his meal, she wondered from what secret source Nick drew his tranquil strength.

"Pa, you seen them gubment mens?" asked Minus.

A delicate breath of cold air seemed to wash over Olga. In the silence, she kept her eyes on her plate, picking a bit of shell from the oyster dressing.

"What men?" Nick asked absently. "What government men?"

"He means the state tree inspectors," said Olga lightly, looking deeply into Nick's secure blue eyes. "They're going over the groves. Minus seems worried or concerned or something."

"If that's all we've got to worry about—" said Nick.

Olga smiled at Minus. The boy gravely devoured his bread and guava paste. He ate with stolid, grub-like tenacity, the avid child eyes set in his square fat face roaming about the table disgruntledly.

After the dishes, in the cool twilight they put the baby to bed, donned their suits and went for a swim. Under a barbarously flaming sky, the clean bare river lay stained to its farthest verges, a slick pane of magic color. Nick talked a few minutes on the levee with a returning Cajin hunter, whose torso was draped with limp alligator hides; and Olga, wading out, felt the alert and lonely hunter-eyes follow her tallness. She gripped Minus's fat hand and hummed something. In the water she knelt as if in supplication on the cold firm silt, inviting buoyancy and peace, until the baby shrimp began exploring her limbs with timid feelers that barely grazed the hairs of calf and thigh. The strong blond river laved her pores, and was gentle.

"Mama, I'm all over goose-bumps!" Minus piped.

She gathered the boy to her, the strange soft body, the other woman's child that she had tried to love. "Do I feel warm?"

"Only up here." He cupped his hands behind her neck.

"Do you love your Olga?" she whispered.

"Bounce me!"

"What do you want Olga to fix you for lunch tomorrow?"

"Sossage! Poke sossage!"

"You mustn't try to worry Olga, son."

"I ain't worryin' ya. Bounce me!"

"About those inspectors. Of course, you were trying to worry me."

Minus left her and made a somersault in the water. He reached for a handful of mud and threw at the levee. She felt a bright pang of hostility cleave her chest. Minus saw her face.

"Our trees got the canker," he said, reaching for more mud.

He stood pouring mud from hand to hand, and watching Olga's face, the pale wet oval, faintly netted with bygone wiles and yearnings, the eyes clouded by a fear of fear. She fought a sense of hatred for the child that rose within her like a fanged thing. The horrid little beast!

"Tell your father that! Tell him that, do you hear?"

"I *know* they got the canker. Might be pretty, but they got the canker. You wait to-morrow!"

Olga splashed him with water and vented a trill of laughter, desperately striving to be playful. "Well, we don't care if they have! Who cares?" But her eyes kept searching his that gave no hint of truth or guile, and into her voice a half hysterical rasping had crept.

"You wait!" said Minus.

In the night, Nick sat in the kitchen carving orangewood sticks. He had an order for six gross of the sticks. Olga rocked on the front porch—bothered about something again, he supposed. The rocker had been croaking steadily for an hour. She was a case, Olga. His big problem child, he often called her in an effort to make her take herself less seriously.

Olga came in presently, pale and somewhat haggard, and stood in the doorway, and fixed her fevered eyes upon her husband, his capable relaxed legs and rather burly shoulders. She wanted to say something. Her eyes were big with question. But she did not speak, because Nick would look at her. She felt that if he should look at her now with his brown calm smile, she would screech. She went into the kids' room and lay beside Minus, and passed her hand over his clean warm face.

"Minus!" she whispered. "Wake up, son! Tell Olga—listen, son, how do you know our trees have canker?"

The boy stirred in his sleep. His eyes opened. "Huh?"

"How do you know our trees have canker? Who told you? Tell Olga the truth, because if it's true we can go out early in the morning and break off the sick leaves. Were you just joking? Minus! Tell Olga, who says our trees have canker!"

"Alfred," the child murmured. "Nigger Alfred."

Olga smiled in the dark. She chided herself for being silly, and went in and kissed Nick good-night.

After they were in bed a while, Nick noticed that Olga was lying too still, but he asked no questions. Any attempt to comfort her would bring on a scene. She would be all right to-morrow. Olga lay awake, vexed by some annoying idea hovering about her mind which she could not grasp.

Nick left at midnight to go fishing in Spanish Pass. Her husband had not been gone ten minutes when the idea which had been bothering Olga took shape in her mind. Little nigger Alfred's uncle had worked in their orchard in the spring. Nick had discharged him for sleeping on the job.

At three o'clock, Olga took some hot milk, but sleep would not come. Her tongue seemed to be swollen to an enormous size. In the silence that brimmed over from the river, some nocturnal marsh creature was uttering over and over a maddening sound, like a clock being wound. And Olga lay piecing together to-morrow's disaster, justifying her fears.

She saw them chopping down the fruitful trees, dragging them to a huge bonfire in the rear marsh, around which a gang of Cajin boys danced like demons, playing with the fallen green fruit.

They would start chopping near the levee. The first tree would be the large one in the corner of the property, which they called Thelma. This fine tree had shaded hundreds of city picnickers. It was thirty years old, carefully tended, and invariably it bore a bounteous crop. She heard the first gluttonous grunt of the descending ax. The tree seemed surprised!—Nick had once thrashed

Minus for driving a tack into its trunk. Nick was walking among the workers, quietly looking on, thoughtfully pulling at his lower lip. Nick was taking it philosophically, of course. He must show her that disaster is meaningless, that it does no good to worry or oppose fate.

"The little ones, too?" she heard herself ask the inspectors. "The ones we budded last year?"

"The little ones, too," was the answer.

When they had finished, the fire was gigantic. The house stood strangely huge and conspicuous in a great barren space surrounded by stumps with white jagged fangs. There was no shade anywhere, no reason for a house to be there. The mystified hens walked about in the bitter sunlight, cocking their heads this way and that.

Olga left her bed and went to the screened porch. Outside the mosquitoes were inanely jubilant. Olga could feel her blood laboring past her joints. There seemed to be sand in her blood. She wrapped her robe about her and crossed the wet crisp grass to the levee. The depthless firmament hovered softly purple, without cause or meaning, the enormous earth glowed profoundly, bringing her the sly trivial accents of the dark, the knowing whisper of stirring boughs, the faint glassy clinking of a shattered wave. Nick's skiff lay on the levee, bottom up. Lying on the skiff confronting the stars, she did not feel the mosquitoes, but her body seemed unusually long and hollow and wasted, save for the sandy blood pulling heavily past her brain and bones. On the levee road, sauntering footsteps thudded.

The dark shape of the man went past her uncertainly, then returned and stood near, smelling faintly of wine—solid and palpable, yet appearing as a mere curved void among the stars, bowed and timid.

"Hoddoo." The voice was high in pitch as a woman's, soft and courteous and discordant. "Are you—uh—hurt?" She had never heard before the voice or the soft decorous cough. "In trouble, lady?"

"I don't think you can help, thanks," she said.

"I see. Don't be excited. Maybe—" He glanced at the house.

"Excited! You are the state inspector?"

"Yes, mam. One of them. I'm not in charge. Mr. Quarella—"

"I live here. Our trees have canker. You'll find out when—do you inspect the trees?"

"Yes, mam. I help Mr. Quarella. How do you know? You say—"

"The boy said so."

"What boy?"

Olga looked down the empty road.

"What boy said so?"

"His uncle worked for us, pruning and spraying. He told my little stepson."

The man looked at the house, and sighed deeply through his nostrils. He had been walking alone in the night a long time. "You can't always believe these boys," he said.

"You don't understand. Minus—there are other things."

"I see. Still—"

"We're going to lose our trees, our livelihood. We have nothing else. Nothing. We've lived like animals all year, counting the days. So I thought perhaps—"

The man rubbed his chin. She could tell by the sound. He was a nice man. "Of course, if the place is shonuff infected—"

"You couldn't pass us by, until my husband has a chance to take off the sick leaves? He'll be back—"

"No, mam. Not that." Now the voice was dim with official solicitude. Close at hand, like some sort of subterranean applause, came the sound of the marsh creature winding its clock.

"And you're not corruptible," said Olga, to herself.

"How's that?"

"Corruptible."

"No, mam. At least not me. You—uh—we—"

"Thanks."

He went off quickly, with dusty thudding steps. Between the sepia trunks of the willows, the east had gone ashen.

At daylight the trees came forth all bathed in black dew, serried against a sky glowing with great resinous streaks of varied red, and the river bore many tinted vapors. It was such a soft virginal morning that Olga's fears were partly allayed. Yet she went into the orchard with a ladder, and passed from tree to tree, parting the boughs and peering between the wet fruit for canker.

Minus awoke fully an hour earlier than usual. Discovering his stepmother's absence, he tiptoed out and stole in among the trees, cocking his ears, glancing furtively about. Olga crouched behind a tree trunk, secretly watching the boy with his rumpled hair and the red rabbit embroidered on his pyjama jacket. She held her breath when he passed a few yards from her. He returned to the backyard, played a while with a fiddler crab, and went back inside. Olga climbed another tree, searching. It was getting late. She did not know what the canker looked like. Three young birds stuck their ugly heads from a nest and offered her their gaping throats; and the mother cardinal flashed redly past her face, chirping angrily. Olga found one branch stained with mild silvery fungi growing in fine geometric patterns; and on some leaves there appeared what she recognized as beneficial parasites, but—there was no use. She did not know the canker.

At breakfast the baby crowed rapturously, putting buttons in a tin can and taking them out. Minus gulped the last of his oatmeal. It was after seven, and the inspectors had not yet come. Olga sat among the unwashed dishes, pallid and motionless. When Minus left the room, her eyes came to life and followed him out to the glittering blue-and-gold portal of the orchard. Minus ran down the levee. Around the bend he saw the two inspectors coming. He faced about and ran back home, talking to himself joyously.

"Mama, here they come!" he announced radiantly. Olga stared at his round live eyes, then she turned and went into the front room, and began pacing from window to window. When the inspectors came, she greeted them at the back door.

"We're from the Depawtment," said the taller of the two. "Comin' to take a little look around, if you don't mind."

"It's quite all right," said Olga.

"A nice place you've got here, I must say. Look at that fine grapefruit, Gram. A pinkmeat. Looka here! A chicken with a blue bill! Say, sonny, what's that on the chicken's bill, anyhow?"

"Wash bluing and starch," said Minus. "For chicken pox."

"Well, well, well! I never knew *chickens* get chicken pox! Come on, Gram. Let's get going. A chicken with chicken pox!"

As they moved off, Mr. Quarella asked in a low voice: "Is she the one?"

"I don't know. I think she is."

"It's the only place with a skiff in front. Well, she'd never corrupt me, all I got to say. Too tall and lanky. Kinda sick and peevish looking. Like she's got a hang-over, eh? Her husband used to run the filling station in Lacroix. He set it afire with a cigarette. The Cajins don't like him because he's a Protestant and works too hard. You like her look, Gram?"

"She looks like a nice woman. I feel sorry for her."

"If we find canker, I'll let her corrupt you. Wouldn't you like that, Gram? Give 'em a clear report?"

"I wouldn't say that."

"Trim the sick leaves and go away and let her corrupt you, eh Gram? Her husband's not—"

"She doesn't mean corrupt that way. She means by appealing to our sympathy, I reckon."

"You got a lot to learn, Gram."

Mr. Quarella stopped and gazed up into a Creole Sweet tree over Gramercy's head. "Well, there it is," he announced briskly, pointing.

Gramercy swung about and lifted his mild eyes. The tree was a noble creature, smooth and venerable and solidly rooted with years of good growth, lambent with tremulous light and generously freighted with fruit.

"There's your canker," said Mr. Quarella.

The two inspectors walked from the orchard to the house. There was no one about. Mr. Quarella closed his fist and rapped several times on the weatherboards. The impact of his bones on the wood sounded inordinately loud and hollow, as though the house had been secretly emptied of its contents. Slow footsteps then sounded inside, and Olga stood in the doorway. The baby whom she had left on the bed began screaming. The child was cross because Olga's milk had no nourishment to-day. Mr. Quarella offered Olga a little spray of orange leaves, and said: "I'm sorry, but your place seems to be infected, madam. This came from the first tree we inspected."

"I understand," said Olga quietly. Mr. Gramercy could not believe this was the same woman he had spoken to the night before. Olga stood twirling the diseased twig in her fingers. The fearful mottling on the leaves had a sinister beauty, iridescent jewels clustered on a field of green. "We knew nothing about this," she said.

"That certainly is a pity, madam."

"And our trees must be burned."

"I'm afraid so. That's the law, you know. The canker's spreading fast, and other folks have got to be protected."

Olga's eyes glowed like fanned coals, and around her lips was a margin, paler than they. "You can't do a thing like that," she said. "I wouldn't advise you to start yet. There'll be trouble."

"When could we see your husband?"

"This afternoon. And I warn you—"

"We'll be back," said Quarella. "Come on, Gram."

Minus turned and ran out to find Alfred.

Nick returned about one o'clock with two large bunches of fine speckled trout. He pushed his way through the little crowd gathered before his home. The two inspectors met him in the yard and told him. They were very polite. Nick stood looking from one to the other of their faces with bulging, incredulous eyes, his own features grown suddenly old, and drained of blood. The levee bystanders were silent, waiting for Nick to talk. He compressed his lips and gazed at the ground, then walked quietly to the house, dropping the fish on the back steps. Three Negroes whom the inspectors had hired were waiting against the chicken house with axes. When Nick disappeared, the crowd on the levee burst into French. Minus came back, and followed his father inside, hopping eagerly. Olga was in the front room rocking in the chair.

"Of all tough luck," said Nick. "What do you think of that!" He sat on a chair and took one of his knees into his folded fingers. "Go outside, son," he told Minus. The boy backed out, eyeing his stepmother. Olga's head was bowed sideways, with her hand pressed over her mouth to keep back the shrill cry waiting behind her larynx.

"If this isn't the very limit!" said Nick softly. He got up and straightened a scarf on the table. He began shifting his eyes about helplessly, to the ceiling, the phonograph, the sleeping baby. He tugged at his belt, passed his foot over a bulge in the rug. "A fine howdy-do this is! Well—" He turned to go.

"What are you going to do?" Olga asked.

"What can I do, sweetheart? Plant some more trees, I guess."

"No!" Her cry was like the last yelp of an animal. "I *won't* suffer in silence! They're going to burn us up! Burn our trees!"

"For God's sake, Olga, brace up! What can we do about it?"

"Something's *got* to be done! Our crop! Our trees! I've got to go home in the spring! Don't we own the place? Aren't you a man? Can't you—can't you do something? I'm dependent on you, down here in the swamps without—can't you resist them? Run them off your place! This is our property!"

"Listen, sweetheart, you've got to quit talking like a child, and be a help and a comfort to me. Why, this is the state government. What do you expect me to do?"

Olga leapt from her chair, wild-eyed and snarling. "Fight!" she screamed. "Fight the government! Get your gun and do something! Chase them away! This is *our* property, don't you understand? They want to burn our trees!"

Nick took her by the arms and spoke soothingly: "Shh! Now listen to me, Olga. This thing is nobody's fault. Who are you going to hold responsible? It just happened, that's all. It's childish to talk about fighting. It's tough luck, that's all. A little trick of fate. Be quiet, now! Olga! For the love of—"

They wrestled and overturned a fern that scattered mud and bits of pottery underfoot. "Fight fate!" Olga screeched. "Fight fate! You're always giving up to fate! If it's childish, I'll do it myself! I'll get a gun and chase them off! They'll *not* touch my trees! I'll fight until they kill me. You're a coward! Coward! You *never* do anything! I'll go take your part!"

"Olga! Let go, now, or I'll have to hurt you. Listen—"

Minus stood on a soap box outside, peering into the room through a place where a blind was missing, watching Olga threshing around the floor, writhing her long white legs, beating her heels on the carpet. Minus was biting his fingernails and blinking his eyes excitedly. Little nigger Alfred was with him. Alfred tugged at Minus's sleeve, pleading: "Minus, le' *me* see a lil bit. You been up there a long time."

"Wait a minute, can't you?"

"Minus, Ah'm going' on home, you don' le' me see a lil bit befo' it's all ovah."

"He's holding her down! She's kickin' at him! She wants to shoot the gubment mens! Now he's lockin' her in the room! He done went out and locked her in!"

"Come on, Minus, Ah'm go' be mad at you."

Minus jumped down and Alfred climbed on the box; but peering in, he saw only Mrs. Dobravich alone in the room, crouched before the locked door, whimpering and clawing at the door weakly.

Alfred jumped down in disgust. "She ain' doin' nuthin' now. You wouldn't le' me see nuthin' an' Ah'm mad at you, ole white trash!"

"Well," said Minus, "she ain't your stepmaw!"

Minus climbed on the box and looked in, then dismounted and skipped excitedly into the orchard, where interesting things were beginning to happen. Behind the new toilet, his father was mopping his brow, and gravely talking to the inspectors, breathing rapidly with his thin hair still in disarray. A few timid Cajins were loafing about, gaping. A yellow Negro laborer went off towards the rear of the orchards with his gleaming ax on his shoulder. Minus started alertly behind him. Then he heard over his shoulder the grunt of an ax driven into a tree, and several thuds of dislodged fruit striking the ground. His mouth fell apart, and he stopped uncertainly. At the same moment, a noiseless gray cat slunk past him with one of the large purple-and-silver trout between its teeth, stopped and glanced at Minus over its shoulder, then crept towards the bushes with a soft growl. A sharp icy thread of panic went through the boy.

He scampered over and stood close beside his father's firmly planted legs, not knowing what to do or say.

Shirley Ann Grau

Shirley Ann Grau (1929–   )

Born in New Orleans, Grau lived there and in Alabama during her childhood. She attended Sophie Newcomb College in New Orleans where she received her B.A. in 1950. She now lives in Metairie, and spends part of each year in Martha's Vineyard. Among her books are The Black Prince and Other Stories *(1954),* The Hard Blue Sky *(1958),* The House on Coliseum Street *(1961),* The Keepers of the House *(1964),* Winner of the 1965 Pulitzer Prize, The Condor Passes *(1971),* The Winding Shifting West *(1973),* Evidence of Love *(1977), and* Nine Women *(1986). "Joshua" is taken from* The Black Prince and Other Stories.

JOSHUA

South of New Orleans, down along the stretch that is called the Lower Coast, the land trails off to a narrow strip between river and marsh. Solid ground here is maybe only a couple of hundred feet across, and there is a dirt road that runs along the foot of the green, carefully sodded levee. It once had state highway markers, but people used the white painted signs for shotgun targets, until they were so riddled they crumbled away. The highway commission has never got around to replacing them. Maybe it doesn't even know the signs are gone; highway inspectors hardly ever come down this way. To the east is the expanse of shifting swamp grass, and beyond that is the little, sheltered Bay Cardoux, and farther still, beyond the string of protecting islands, is the Gulf. To the west is the Mississippi, broad and slow and yellow.

At intervals along the road there are towns—scattered collections of rough, unpainted board houses with tin roofs, stores that are like the houses except that they have crooked painted signs, and long, flat, windowless warehouses to store the skins of the muskrats that are taken every year from the marsh. Each building perches on stilts two or three feet high; in the spring the bayous rise. The waters always reach up to the roadbed and sometimes even cover it with a couple of inches of water. There is no winter to speak of. Sometimes there is a little scum of ice on the pools and backwaters of the bayous and a thin coating over the ruts in the road. But the temperature never stays below freezing more than a day or two, and the little gray film of ice soon disappears under the rain.

For it rains almost constantly from October to March. Not hard; not a storm; there is never any lightning. There is just a steady, cold rain.

The river is high. The trees that grow out on the *batture*—on the land between the river's usual bed and the levee, on the land that all summer and fall has been dry and fertile—are half-covered with water.

The inside walls of the houses drip moisture in tiny beads like sweat, and bread turns moldy in a single day. Roofs begin to leak, and the pans put under the leaks have to be emptied twice a day. From the bayous and the swamps to the east come heavy, choking odors of musk and rotting grasses.

259

It is mostly all colored people here in the lower reaches. Poor people, who live on what they find in the river and the swamps and the Gulf beyond them.

Joshua Samuel Watkin sat at the kitchen table in one of the dozen-odd houses that make up Bon Secour, Good Hope, the farthest of the towns along the dirt highway, which ends there, and the nearest town to the river's mouth.

Joshua Samuel Watkin leaned both elbows on the table and watched the way his mother used her hands when she talked. She swung them from her wrist, limply, while the fingers twisted and poked, way off by themselves.

His small, quick, black eyes shifted from her hands to her lips, which were moving rapidly. Joshua stared at them for a moment and then went back to the hands. He had the ability to shut out sounds he did not wish to hear. His mother's flaming, noisy temper he could shut out easily now; it had taken the practice of most of his eleven years.

He glanced at the doorway, where his father was standing. He had just come in. The shoulders of his light-gray jacket were stained black by the rain, and the tan of his cap had turned almost brown. Joshua glanced briefly down at his father's hands. They were empty; he would have dropped the string of fish outside on the porch. Pretty soon, Joshua knew, one of his parents was going to remember those fish and send him outside to clean them for supper. It was a job he had never liked. No reason, really. He would have to squat outside, working carefully, so that most of the mess fell over the side into the yard, where the cats could fight for it.

His father yanked one of the wooden chairs from under the table and sat down on it heavily. He was answering now, Joshua noticed, and his face was beginning to get the straight-down-the-cheek lines of anger. He tilted his chair back against the wall and jammed both hands down deep into his pockets.

From the way things were beginning to look, Josh thought, it might be just as well if he got out for a while. But he'd better stay long enough to see if there was going to be any supper. He still hadn't bothered to listen to them, to either of them; he knew what they were saying. He balanced his spoon across the top of his coffee cup and then tapped it with his finger gently, swinging it.

He miscalculated, and the spoon hit the oilcloth with a sharp crack.

His father's chair crashed down and with an extra rattle one of the rungs came loose. "Christ Almighty," his father said. "Ain't I told you a million times not to do nothing like that?"

"He ain't done nothing," his mother said, and, reaching out her limp black hand, balanced the spoon across the cup again.

Joshua smiled to himself, though his face did not move. It was one sure way to get his mother on his side—just let his father say a word against him. It worked the other way, too; let his mother fuss at him and his father would be sure to take his part. It was as if they couldn't ever be together.

His father let his breath out with a high-pitched hiss.

"He ain't done nothing," his mother repeated. "Just drop his spoon a little."

His father kept on staring at her, his head bent a little, the dark eyes in his dark face glaring.

"Leastways he ain't just sitting around the house on his tail end, scared to stick his nose outside."

"Woman," his father said, "iffen you ain't the naggingest—"

"Scared." His mother stuck out her underlip. "You just plain scared."

"I ain't scared of nothing a man ain't got cause to be scared of."

"I hear you talking," his mother said. "Only I plain don't see you moving nohow."

"Nagging bitch," his father said, almost gently, under his breath.

His mother's underlip stuck out even farther, and she whistled sharply, derisively, through her teeth.

His father bent forward, slapping a hand down, one on each knee. "Sure I scared!" he shouted in her face. She did not even blink. "Everybody scared!"

Joshua turned his eyes toward the window. All he could see was gray sky. Raining, solid, gray sky in all four directions—east over the swamps and west over the river and north to the city and south to the Gulf, where the fishing boats went, and the U-boats were hiding.

His father was saying: "Like Jesse Baxter, you want me to plain get blown to bits."

Joshua did not take his eyes off the square of gray sky, but he was seeing something else. The fishing boats from Bon Secour, three of them, had come on the two U-boats, surfaced in the fog and together, exchanging supplies. And one of the ships had lobbed a couple of shots from its deck gun square into Baxter's boat. There wasn't anything but pieces left, and the two other fishing boats hadn't even time to look for them, they were so busy running. All they'd heard, just for a second or so, was the men around the gun laughing. The two surviving boats had not gone out again. Nobody would take them out.

Joshua had heard the story and he had dreamed about it often enough. He would wake up sweating even in the cold and shaking with fear. He couldn't quite imagine a U-boat, so its outline and shape changed with each dream. But the action was always the same—the gun pointing at him and the laughing.

With a little shudder, Joshua turned his eyes back to his parents. "That been a week and a half," his mother was saying, "and how you think we gonna eat? How you think we gonna eat iffen you don't find a boat?"

"We been eating." His father had his chin pressed down against the rolled collar of his gray wool sweatshirt. "Ain't we been eating?"

His mother snorted. "Why, sure," she said. "You man enough to go sneaking out in the little old back bayous and catch us a couple of fish."

"Fish ain't bad," his father said. "Ask *him* iffen he going hungry."

Joshua felt their eyes focused on him, and he squirmed.

"Don't go putting words in the boy's mouth," his mother said. "Just you ask him."

"Ask him iffen there ain't things you got to have money to buy. Ask him iffen he don't got no coat to wear with the cold. Ask him iffen he don't need a new coat." She turned to Joshua. "You tell him what you want. You tell him what you plain got to have." Her voice ended in a kind of ragged shriek.

"I get him a coat," his father said.

"When that gonna be? He plain gonna freeze first."

"Ain't no son of mine gonna freeze," his father said.

"You plain scared," his mother taunted. "You just plain scared."

Joshua got to his feet and slipped around the edge of the table and outside. On the porch he found a square of black canvas and wrapped it around himself, letting it make a cowl above his head. It had been used to cover an engine, and it smelled of grease and was slippery to the touch, but it would keep him dry and very warm.

He noticed the string of fish that his father had brought home. With the toe of one blue canvas sneaker, he kicked the string down into the yard. It hit the soggy ground with a little splash. The cats would be coming around at dark.

He walked down the road, stepping carefully, watching for the biggest puddles, keeping to the levee side, where the ground was highest. The rain was falling noisily on his square of tarpaulin. With the steady, quick, clicking sound of drops all around him, falling on his head but not touching him, tapping on his shoulders but not really being there, after a while he wouldn't be sure of his balance any more, or his direction, there would be such an echo in his head. He kept blinking to steady himself, but that didn't seem to do much good. He had heard men say they would rather get drenched to the skin and maybe get the fever than spend hours under a tarpaulin with a slow, steady winter rain falling.

The wind blew in swirling eddies—like puffs of smoke, almost, the drops were so fine. Joshua rubbed the wet from his eyes. Over the noise of the rain he heard the faint sound of the river against the levee, a sound that went on day and night, winter and spring, until you got so used to it you had to make a special effort to hear it. Squinting, he looked up. The tops of water aspens on the other side of the levee shuddered under the rain, showing the frightened white underside of their leaves.

Joshua hunched the tarpaulin higher over his head and walked faster. Over to the right now he could see the landings where Goose Bayou swung in close and deep. And there were the boats, moored and wet under the rain, and empty, just where they'd been for the last week or more, and, at the far end of one of the landings, the empty space where Jesse Baxter's boat belonged.

Joshua stopped and stared at the empty space, at the muddy, rain-specked water and Baxter's mooring posts with the ropes still around them but dragging down into the water. Like it was in his dreams, he thought, when, cold and sweating, he saw the shape of a ship in the fog and heard the sound of a deck gun.

He reached the shelter of the overhang of a building and let the tarpaulin drop from his head. He still kept it wrapped around his shoulders, because he was shivering. In the middle of the board platform in front of the building, a yellow dog with black-marked flanks was scratching behind one ear, slowly, limply, and overhead a double-board sign hung upside down at a sharp angle. On one side of it was painted, in white letters: "Bourgeois Store." Years ago the wind had lifted it and turned it on its hook, and it had jammed that way, with only the blank side showing. Nobody ever seemed to notice. Maybe because nobody ever looked up.

Joshua peeped in through the window. A single electric-light bulb way up against the ceiling in the center of the room was burning, because the day was so dark. It was a little bulb and almost worn out—you could see the red, glowing coils of wire inside it; and it wasn't much brighter inside the store than out.

Joshua rubbed his fingers against the glass and stared harder. There were two tables set together lengthwise across the front of the room, and behind them two more. They were covered with clothes in neat little piles, according to size and color. There were wall shelves, too, filled with a clutter of hardware. There were so many things in the room that you couldn't find any single object quickly, even if the thing you were looking for was as big as a man.

Joshua finally located Claude Bourgeois at the side of the room, over by the stove, almost hidden behind small crab nets that were hanging by long cords from the ceiling. There were two men sitting with him. Joshua could have known he would be there; he hardly ever moved from that spot during the winter, his bones ached so. Now that he was old, he'd stopped fighting the rain and the cold; he just let them have their way outside the store. He didn't move outside at all. His wife, Kastka, who was part Indian, rubbed his arms and legs with liniment and kept the fire going full away in the silver-painted potbellied stove.

Joshua opened the door. Just inside he let his tarpaulin fall in a heap. Claude and the two men with him turned and looked, and Claude said: "Close that there door quick, boy," and they went back to their talking.

Joshua recognized the two other men: Oscar Lavie and Stanley Phillips. Lavie ran Claude's fishing boat for him now that he was too old to go out, and Phillips was never very far away from Lavie. They always worked together; it had been that way since they were kids.

Joshua walked over to the small glass case that stood against the left wall, the case that was filled with knives. He stood looking down at them, at one in particular, one in the middle of the case. It had a blade at least six inches long, and its handle was of some white stuff, white and iridescent and shining as the inside of an oyster shell that is wet and fresh. Someday, he told himself, when he had money of his own, he would buy that. If just nobody got to it first.

Not that he needed a knife; his father had bought him one a month or less ago, with the money from the last haul the men had made. He remembered how angry his mother had been. "God Almighty," she'd said. "Iffen you ain't plain crazy, you. Buying that there trash when the boy needs a coat."

His father had just winked at him and said: "You don't hear him complaining none."

"Maybe he ain't got no more sense than you," his mother had said, "but he gonna be mighty cold this winter without no coat."

"Woman," his father had said, "ain't you got but one idea in you head?"

Little Henry Bourgeois came and stood alongside of Joshua. He was Claude's son, the son of his old age, the son of the woman who was part Indian. Henry had the round Negro features of his father and the skin color of his mother, a glowing red, deep and far down, so deep that it wasn't so much a skin color as a color under that. It was almost like seeing the blood.

"You heard the news?" Henry asked. His father had a radio in the store, a small one in a square green case. It was the only radio in Bon Secour.

"No," Joshua said.

"They came almost up the river," Henry said. "They sink one of the freighter ships again."

The war and the shooting and the submarines. And just a little way off. Joshua felt his breath catch in the middle of his chest, catch on the lump that was so big and cold that it hurt. And he remembered all his dreams: the fog, and the other ship, and himself in the gray, rain-speckled water, dying, in a million pieces for the fish to chew. His face did not change. He kept on looking at the knife. "That right?" he said.

"Josh," old Claude Bourgeois called to him. "You come over here."

He turned and crossed through the maze of tables and ducked under the hanging skeins of nets.

"Boy," Claude Bourgeois said, "iffen you don't quit leaning on that there glass it gonna crack through, sure as anything."

Joshua looked down at his feet in the blue canvas sneakers, blue stained darker by the water he had been walking through. He wiggled his toes, and they made little bumps on the outside of the canvas.

"You papa home?" Claude Bourgeois asked.

Joshua nodded.

"He wanting to go out fishing?"

"I reckon—it Ma wanting him to go out."

Oscar Lavie shifted in his chair, lifted one bare foot, and hooked it between his cupped hands. "Iffen you want you boat out," he told Claude Bourgeois, "I reckon you plain better take it out yourself."

Claude opened his mouth, and then, thinking better of whatever he was about to say, closed it again.

"I seen that there ship popping up out of the fog," Oscar went on, "and it ain't nobody's fault it ain't blown me up, place of Jesse Baxter."

Stanley Phillips nodded his head slowly. He stuttered badly, and when he talked people hardly ever understood him. So he let others do the talking. But his lack of speech had given him an air of confidence. Sometimes when he stood leaning against the corner of a building, his hands jammed down in his pockets, his slight body arched back and braced for balance, he seemed to own everything he looked at—the streets and the houses and the people. All the women liked him; some of them got a dreamy look in their eyes when he passed. "He don't have to talk, him," they would say. Only last year Stanley Phillips had married—all proper, in the church over at Petit Bayou—a wife, by far the prettiest colored girl anywhere along the river. And when he'd been out fishing, gone for maybe a couple of days or a week, he'd always head straight home, and when he got within fifty yards of his house, he'd stop and give a long, loud whistle and then walk on slowly, counting his steps, and every fifth step giving another whistle, so his wife would have time to get ready for what was coming.

"Iffen you was in the army," Claude Bourgeois said softly, "you wouldn't have no chance to say no."

Neither Stanley nor Oscar had bothered registering for the army. They just disappeared whenever any stranger came around asking questions, which wasn't very often.

"You figure on anything there?" Oscar asked, his eyes resting on the fat, lumpy body of the old man.

"Not me," Claude Bourgeois said hastily. "Not me."

"That real fine of you," Oscar said. "Then I reckon I ain't gonna have to slice up all you fat and feed it to the gators."

"Me?" Claude rolled his eyes around so that they almost disappeared. "I ain't gonna do nothing like that."

"That nice of you," Oscar said.

"Why, man," Claude said, changing the subject quickly, "you plain got to go out eventually."

"That ain't yet," Oscar said, and Stanley nodded. "It ain't worth nothing going out to get blown to pieces."

"How they gonna find you in all that water out there?"

"It ain't worth the chance," Oscar said.

Joshua stared over at the pot of coffee on the stove top, where it always stood to keep warm. Nobody offered him any, so he looked away.

"Why, man"—Claude was holding his hand outspread in front of him—"you can't go on living on bayou fish forever; there other things you got to have money for." He nodded at Joshua. "This here boy need a coat, only his daddy ain't working to give him none."

"Leastways his daddy ain't lying in pieces all over the bottom of the Gulf, with the fishes eating on him," Oscar said. "Leastways, iffen you are so concerned, you plain can give him a coat. Just you give him one on credit now."

"You gonna do that?" Joshua asked.

Claude coughed. "There ain't no cause to do nothing like that," he said. "This here a matter of business, and this ain't good business, any way you looks at it. There all sort of money waiting for his daddy out there, iffen you wasn't too scared to go get it."

Joshua drifted away toward the door. He picked up the tarpaulin, studied it for a minute, then flipped it around himself and went outside. Little Henry Bourgeois followed right behind him. The low gray sky was thickening with the evening. In the branches of a chinaberry tree a hawk and a catbird were fighting. "Where you going?" Henry asked.

Joshua went down the steps and out into the road. The mud was soft and gummy, and stuck to the bottom of his shoes in heavy cakes. Each step was a sucking sound.

"Damn gumbo mud," he said. He could hear Henry's steps behind him.

They walked about a block, with their heads bent way down, so they really couldn't see where they were going. Henry gave a quick little squishing skip and came abreast of Joshua. "Where you going?" he asked again. "You going there?"

Joshua nodded.

They came to the warehouse. The fur-trading company had put it up maybe ten years ago, when they first discovered all the muskrat around here. There'd been need for extra space then. But things had changed; a couple of hurricanes had drowned out the animals, and they were coming back slowly. It hardly paid for a man to set his traps during the season, since he had to take the skins up to Petit Bayou now to sell them.

But the old warehouse still stood, at the north end of the string of houses. It was a rough building with plain, unpainted wood sides that time and rain and fogs had stained to an almost uniform black. On the far side, behind some low bushes—barberry bushes, with thick thorns and pronged leaves—Joshua had discovered a loose board. It had taken him nearly three hours to work it loose.

The two boys wiggled through the bushes, pried down the board, and slipped inside. They shook themselves like wet puppies and kicked off their shoes. The building was unheated, but somehow it always seemed warm, maybe only because it was dry. The floor boards were double thickness and carefully waterproofed with tar. It was a single room, big and almost empty. There were no windows, and when Henry put the board back in place, the only light came from the thin cracks between the boards. The two boys had been here so often that they knew their way around the room; they did not need to see.

They both walked straight out into the center of the room, until their bare feet felt the familiar rough texture of burlap. There had been a big heap of old bags in the warehouse, and the boys had carefully piled them in a circle, leaving a clear place about four feet across in the middle. When they sat there, the bags were higher than their heads and kept off drafts and cold. In the corners of the warehouse they had found a few furs—tattered, mangy things, too poor to be sold—and they used these as seats or beds, for sometimes they slept here, too. Their families did not miss them; after all, a boy should be able to look out for himself.

Joshua and Henry settled themselves, and Joshua lit the kerosene lantern he had brought a couple of days before. His mother had stomped and raged for a whole day after she discovered it was missing. Joshua did not even have to lie about it; before she had thought to ask him, his father came home and her anger turned on him, and they argued long and hard, and ended as they always did, going in their room to make love.

"I done brought something this time," Henry said. He pulled a paper-wrapped package from under his jacket. The greasy stains of food were already smearing the brown paper. "This here is our supper."

They divided the cold fried fish and the bread, and then Joshua put out the lamp—it was hard to get kerosene for it—and they ate in the darkness, with just the sound of rain on the tar-paper roof and the sound of their own chewing and the occasional scurry of a rat or maybe a lizard or a big roach.

"Man," Joshua said slowly. "This is fine, no?"

"Sure," Henry agreed, with his mouth full. "Sure is."

"Look like they gonna be a fog tonight."

"Sure do," Henry said. "It a good night to be right in here. It a fine night to be in here."

Joshua's fingers brushed the surface of one of the moldy-smelling pelts with a faint scratching sound. "You might even could make a coat outa these here, iffen you had enough," he said.

"No," Henry said scornfully.

Joshua did not argue.

They fell asleep then, because it was dark and warm and they weren't hungry any longer. And Joshua dreamed the same dream he dreamed almost every night. There was a thing that he knew was a submarine. Even the way its shape kept changing—from long, like a racing boat only a hundred times bigger, to narrow and tall, like the picture postcards of the buildings in New Orleans. But it was always fog-colored. At times it slipped back into the fog, and when it came out again, it was a different shape. And he was always there, too, in a boat sometimes, a pirogue or a skiff, hunched down, trying not to be seen, or on foot in the marsh, in knee-high water, crouched down behind some few, almost transparent grasses. Hiding where he knew there was no hiding place.

Joshua shook himself, turned over, bent his other arm and pillowed his head on it, and went back to the dream. He did not wake again, but from time to time he whimpered.

That night one of the submarines was destroyed. The patrol boats found it almost a quarter mile inside the pass, headed for the shipping upriver. The heavy, cold, raining night exploded and then exploded again. Joshua woke up and couldn't be sure he wasn't still in his dream, for the waking was like a dream. Alongside him, Henry was whispering: "Sweet Jesus. Sweet Jesus." With fumbling fingers and a quick sharp scratch of matches, Joshua lit the lantern. The light raced to the roof and stayed there, holding back the darkness. Quickly, afraid, he glanced around the room. He was almost surprised to find it empty.

"What that?" Henry asked. His eyes caught the light and reflected it—bright, flat animal eyes.

Joshua did not answer. His throat was quivering too much. He looked around the empty room again and shook his head slowly.

"What that?" Henry repeated.

Joshua turned up the wick high as it would go. The top of the glass chimney began to cloud with smoke, but he did not lower the flame.

Henry jiggled his elbow persistently. "What that go up out there?" he asked.

"Ain't nothing."

Outside, people were yelling, their voices frightened and sleepy. Their words were muffled and garbled by the walls.

"You reckon maybe we ought to go out and see?" Henry asked.

"I reckon not," Joshua said, and there was a flat note of decision in his voice. "I reckon we best stay right here."

A plane flew by, close overhead. The building shook and the lamp flame wavered.

"I reckon the war come plain close," Joshua said.

"It quiet now," Henry said, and even managed to smile.

Joshua moved his lips but no sound came out. His tongue fluttered around in his throat.

The shouting outside was stopping. There were now just two voices, calling back and forth to each other, slower and slower, like a clock running down. Finally they stopped, too.

Henry said: "It smoking some."

Joshua turned the lampwick down. The circle of light around them contracted. He watched it out of the corner of his eye and quickly turned the wick back up again.

"Ain't you better put that out?" Henry said. "We ain't got all that much kerosene."

"We got enough," Joshua said.

"You scared."

"Me?" Joshua said. "Me? No." Even he did not believe this. He tried hard to stay awake, knowing that just as soon as he fell asleep, just as soon as he stepped over that line, the indistinct shape, gray like fog, would be waiting to kill him.

Suddenly it was broad daylight. The lamp had burned out; its chimney was solid black. Henry pointed to it. Joshua nodded. "You left the lamp burning till it run out of oil," Henry said.

Joshua walked slowly across the room. "Me?" he said. "No."

"I heard you talking in you sleep."

"I don't talk in my sleep, me." Joshua put his shoulder to the loose board and pushed. He felt the cold, damp air in his face. He blinked and looked out at the gray day.

"You was crying," Henry said. "You was crying and saying 'Don't.' That what you was doing."

Joshua wriggled through the opening without answering.

Henry stuck his head out after him. "You was scared," he shouted.

Joshua kept going steadily. He could feel a trembling behind his knees, and he had to concentrate with all his might to keep his walk straight.

As he went up the splintered wooden steps of his house, he could hear his father singing:

> *"Mo parle Simon, Simon, Simon,*
> *Li parle Ramon, Ramon, Ramon,*
> *Li parle Didine,*
> *Li tombe dans chagrin."*

Sober, his father wouldn't even admit to understanding the downriver version of French. He'd near killed a man once who'd called him a Cajun. Drunk, he would remember that he knew hundreds of Cajun songs.

Joshua opened the door and went inside. His father and Oscar Lavie were in the kitchen, sitting at opposite ends of the table. Stanley Phillips was not around; he wasn't ever one for leaving his wife before afternoon.

In the middle of the green-checked oilcloth table cover were two gallon jugs of light-colored orange wine. One was already half empty. And on the table, too, next to the big wine bottles, was the

small, round bottle of white lightning. Just in case they should
need it.

They were so busy with their song they did not notice Joshua.
He looked at them, wondering where his mother was. Then he
went looking for his food. He found some beans on a plate at the
back of the stove, and a piece of bread in the wall cupboard. He
ate them, standing up in a corner.

Slowly his father swung his head around to him and said: "Look
who come in."

Oscar Lavie said: "We celebrating way they blow up everything
last night."

"You ma gone rushing out of here like the devils of hell
hanging on her petticoat."

"I ain't done nothing of the kind." His mother popped her head
in through the narrow little door that led to the lean-to at the
back of the house. "I just went to get some kindling wood, so you
crazy fool drunks ain't gonna freeze to death."

Oscar began singing, almost to himself:

> *"Cher, mo l'aime toi.*
> *Oui, mo l'aime toi.*
> *Vec tou mo coeur*
> *Comme cochon l'aime la bou."*

"Ain't I told you to get out?" his father said softly to his mother.
"Ain't I told you I sick and tired of looking at you?"

Joshua finished eating silently. Oscar gave a deep sigh. "Us all
gonna starve to death," he said. "Us all."

His father poured himself another glass of the wine. Joshua's
mother did not move. She stood in the doorway holding the
kindling in her arms.

His father's heavy-lidded eyes focused on Joshua and lifted a
little. "What you gonna eat tonight?" his father asked.

The boy turned and put the dish back where he had found it,
on the stove. "I don't know, me," he said.

His father began to laugh. He laughed so hard that he had to
put his head down on the tabletop, and the table shook, and the
wine in the bottle swished back and forth. When he spoke, it was
from under his arms. "You hear him, Oscar, man," he said. "He
don't know what he going to eat. He don't know."

Oscar did not even smile as he stared off into space. The black
of his skin seemed almost blue under the morning light.

"He don't know what he going to eat. I don't know either, me."
Joshua stood watching them.

"I ain't going out today, me, to look for nothing," his father
said. "I plain sick of catching a couple of fish or shrimp with a
hand net."

"Han Oliver, he got a pig," Lavie said, with a dreamy look on
his face.

"Man," Joshua's father said, "Han plain swears he gonna kill
anybody what tried to touch his pig, and he been sitting guard on
it."

"I seen a dog out front there."

"I just ain't that hungry yet."

Lavie sighed deeply. "It ain't gonna hurt us none not to eat for
one day."

"No," his father said, and was silent for so long that Joshua
began walking toward the door. He had no clear idea what he
would do outside; he only felt he had to leave. His father's head
jerked up. "Unless *he* go out."

Joshua stopped short. "Me?" he said.

Oscar looked at him. His eyes faltered, focused again, and held.
"He a fine little boy," he said. "He can go run my lines."

"No," Joshua said.

"He ain't gonna do that," his mother said. She came into the
room now and dumped her armload of kindling alongside the
stove.

"That kindling plain all wet," Oscar said vaguely, scowling.

"You ain't never found nothing dry in winter," his mother
snapped.

"It gonna smoke," Oscar said plaintively.

"No skin off my nose," his mother said.

"Ain't I told you to get out?" his father said.

"You done told me a lot of things," his mother said.

"I tired of hearing you—"

"You ain't sending that little old boy out where you scared to
go."

"Ain't scared," Oscar corrected. "Drunk."

"Woman," his father said, "I plain gonna twist you head around
till you sees where you been."

He stood up, a little uncertain on his feet, and his chair fell
over. His mother turned and ran out. They could see her through
the window, scurrying over to the Delattes' house, next door. She

was yelling something over her shoulder; they couldn't make out what.

His father looked at Joshua, his eyes traveling up and down every inch of his body. "You going out," he said.

"I ain't," Josh whispered.

"You going out and save you poor old papa some work," his father said. "Or I gonna twist up every bone in you body till you feels just like a shrimp."

Joshua edged his way carefully to the door.

"You know I mean what I done said."

Joshua ducked out the door. Behind him he heard his father laugh.

Henry was down at the landing, leaning against one of the black tar-coated pilings and teasing a big yellow tomcat with a long piece of rope. Joshua walked past without a word, and righted his father's pirogue and pushed it into the water.

"You going out?" Henry asked, and his voice quivered with interest.

"Reckon so." Josh bent down to tie the lace of one of his sneakers.

"Why you going out?"

"Reckon somebody got to see about getting something to eat."

"Oh," Henry said.

"My papa, he gonna stay drunk today."

"I heard."

"I reckon I could let you come along."

"That okay. We ain't needing no fish at my house."

"You afraid." Joshua looked at him and lifted his eyebrows. "You plain afraid."

"No-o-o," Henry said, and scowled.

"Why ain't you come along with me, then?"

"I ain't said I ain't coming." Henry tossed the piece of rope away. The cat pounced on it in spitting fury. "I ain't said nothing like that."

"Let's get started, then."

"I tell you what," Henry said. "I gonna go borrow my daddy's shotgun. Maybe we see something worth shooting at. I seen a couple of ducks yesterday or so."

Joshua nodded. It would feel better, having a shotgun with

them. Wasn't much good, maybe, but it was something. In his nightmares, he'd wished often enough that he had one with him.

While he waited, he got down in the pirogue and took his place in the stern. Carefully he wrapped the grease-stained black tarpaulin around him. "It cold, all right, man," he said aloud. The yellow tomcat turned his head and watched him. For a minute Joshua stared into the bright yellow eyes and at the straggling broken tufts of whiskers.

Joshua made the sign of the cross quickly. "If you a evil spirit, you can't touch me now," he said. The cat continued to look at him, its black pupils widening slightly and then contracting. Joshua began to wonder if maybe this wasn't one of his nightmares, if this wasn't all part of something he was dreaming. Maybe when he woke up he'd just be back in his bed, and maybe his mother would be shaking him and telling him to stop yelling and his father would be laughing at him for a coward. He took one of his fingers, cracked and almost blue with the cold, between his teeth. He bit it so hard the tears came to his eyes. But he'd done that before in dreams and still he hadn't waked up. No matter how scared he was, he had to finish it out, right to the end.

He held the lightly moving pirogue in place with his paddle and waited for Henry, impatiently, humming a little tune under his breath—the one he'd heard his father singing:

> *Mo Parle Simon, Simon, Simon,*
> *Li parle Ramon, Ramon, Ramon . . .*

and told himself that the cold in his stomach was the weather outside.

He noticed something different. He lifted his head, sniffing the air; it had stopped raining. The sky had not cleared or lifted, and the air was still so heavy you could feel it brushing your face. Everything was soaked through; the whole world was floating, drenched, on water. But for a little while there was not the sound of rain.

And he missed that sound. He felt lonesome without it, the way he always did in spring—suspended and floating. For there isn't any real spring here—just a couple of weeks of hesitation and indecision between the rainy winter and the long, dry summer. There are always more fights and knifings then.

Henry came running back, a shotgun in one hand and four or five shells in the other. "I done got it," he said.

"Don't you point that there thing at me," Joshua said, and jerked his head aside.

"Us can go now," Henry said. He laid the gun in the bottom of the boat and then quickly got in the bow and wrapped a narrow blanket around his shoulders and knees. "I feel better with that along, me."

Joshua shrugged. "It don't matter to me."

They paddled out, following the curve of Goose Bayou, grinning to themselves with the fine feel of the pirogue—the tight, delicate, nervous quiver of the wood shell, the feel of walking across the water the way a long-legged fly does.

A couple of hundred yards down Goose Bayou they turned south, into a small bayou, which, for all anybody knew, had no name. It circled on the edge of a thick swamp, which nobody had bothered to name, either, though most people at one time or other had gone exploring in the tangle of old cypress and vines and water aspens and sudden bright hibiscus plants. Way back in the center somewhere, so that people hardly ever saw them, some cats lived—plain house cats gone wild and grown to almost the size of a panther, living up in the tangled branches of the trees, breeding there. Some nights you could hear their screaming— pleasure or maybe pain; you couldn't tell.

Nobody had ever had the courage to go all the way through the swamp. It wasn't all that big; people simply went around it. Except for one man, and that was an old story, maybe true, maybe not. Anyhow, it had been on to fifty years past. There'd been a white man with yellow hair, the story said, and he'd jumped ship out there in the river. He'd had a long swim in from the channel to the levee, but by the time he climbed up the muddy *batture*, he wasn't as tired as he should have been. Maybe he was hopped up on dope of some sort. Anyhow, when he came walking out of the river, just a little above Bon Secour, his clothes dripping and sticking to his body, his yellow hair all matted and hanging down over his face, there was a girl walking on the levee top. She stopped, watched him stumbling and slipping on the wet, slimy river mud, waved to the people she was with to wait a little, and went down to help him, making her way carefully through the tangle of aspens and hackberries, so that her dress wouldn't get torn.

It was torn clear off her, almost, when they found her half an hour later—those people she'd been walking with. They'd finally got tired waiting for her and gone down to see. They'd have killed him, white man or not, if they'd found him. For nearly two days the men hunted for him while the women went ahead with the funeral. They trailed him at last to the small stretch of swamp, and then they stopped, because none of them wanted to go in there themselves and they couldn't ever have found him in there, in a stretch about four miles long and maybe a mile wide. They did look in the outer fringes—in the part they knew. They could see the signs of where he'd been; they could see that he was heading right straight for the middle of the swamp. Nobody ever saw him again. Maybe he fought his way out and went on like he intended to, though the way he went crashing around, he didn't seem to know where he was going. Or maybe he kept on living in there; it wouldn't have been hard. He had a knife; he'd killed the girl with it. Or maybe he just died, and the fish and the ants and the little animals cleaned his bones until they were left shining white and the shreds of his hair shining yellow.

Joshua and Henry paddled past the thick swamp and remembered the story, and listened for the screaming of the cats, but since it was daylight, they heard nothing.

"It good to get out, man," Joshua said.

Henry did not answer, but then nobody talked much in the swamps. People got suddenly embarrassed and shy of their words and spoke only in whispers when they said anything at all, because the swamp was like a person listening. The grasses and bushes and trees and water were like a person holding his breath, listening, and ready to laugh at whatever you said.

Joshua and Henry found the trotlines that Oscar Lavie had set out the day before across a little cove that the bayou made in the swampy island. Oscar had tied a red strip of handkerchief to the end of a vine to mark the place. Henry reached up and unknotted the cloth. "Man," he said, "this wet through." He squeezed the rag over the side of the pirogue.

"It been raining," Joshua said. He gave the pirogue a quick shove up among the cypress knees to the one the line was tied to. "Iffen you loose that, we see what all we got." A sudden swinging vine hit his cheek. He jumped slightly, then grinned.

They worked their way back across the little cove, checking each of the seven single lines. The first three were empty, the bait gone. The next two held only the heads of catfish; the bodies were eaten clean away. "That plain must have been a gar," Henry said, and Joshua nodded.

They could tell by the drag of the lines that the last two were full. Joshua coaxed the lines slowly to the surface—two catfish with dripping whiskers, and gigs, sharp and pointed and set.

"Watch 'em," Josh said. "They slice you up good."

"You ain't gonna worry about me," Henry said. "You just bring 'em up where I can get at 'em." He picked up the steel-pointed gaff from the bottom of the boat and jabbed it through the whiskered bottom jaw of one of the fish. While Joshua steadied the boat, Henry held the fish until its convulsive movements had all but stopped.

When they had finished, Joshua coiled up the trotline and dropped it in the center of the boat with the fish. "Granddaddies, them, all right," he said.

Henry nodded, breathless from exertion.

Joshua turned the pirogue back out into the bayou and paddled rapidly. Soon they passed the swampy island and were in the salt marshes, miles of grasses rustling lightly and stretching off flat on both sides, with just a few *chênières*—shell ridges with dwarfed, twisted water oaks—scattered on the trembling, shifting surface.

"Man, it cold!" Joshua said. "Sure wish I had me a old heavy coat."

"Look there," Henry said. From a *chênière* away to the left, four or five shapes pumped heavily up into the air.

"Too far away to do us no good."

"Leastways they still got some duck around."

"That a bunch of pintails," Joshua said.

"How you tell?"

"I just plain know, man. I just plain can tell, that all."

Henry was staring over where the indistinct shapes had faded into the low sky. "It mighty late for them to be around."

Joshua dug his paddle deeper in the water. The pirogue shuddered and shot ahead.

"You can't tell what they are from way over here," Henry said.

"I plain can."

Henry turned his head and studied him. "What the matter with you?"

"I hope to God that that there moccasin chew out you wagging tongue," Joshua said.

Henry jerked around; the pirogue swayed wildly. "Where a moccasin?"

"There." Joshua pointed to a long, dark form that was disappearing among the reeds and the Spanish-fern bushes. "And, man, you plain better stop jumping or you have us in this here water."

"I ain't liked snakes."

"You plain scared," Joshua said softly.

"Maybe we get in shooting range of some ducks," Henry said.

Joshua snorted.

Henry said: "Wonder why they all afraid to come out. Ain't nothing out here."

After a moment Joshua said: "I aim to have a look at where all the trouble was. I aim to keep on going till I can plain see the river." He had been afraid last night; and Henry had seen him. Now there was something he had to prove.

For a while Henry was quiet. Then he said: "Man, I'm colding stiff. Let's go back."

"Ain't no use to yet," Josh said.

"I'm freezing up."

"Me, too," Josh said. "But there ain't no use to turn back yet."

They moved steadily south, in a twisting line through the narrow waterways, following the pattern of a curve that would bring them to the river, far down where it met the Gulf.

In about an hour they were there, in a narrow passage of water sheltered by a curve of reeds from the full force of the river, but where they could see into the broad stream and across to the faint, low line of grasses on the other side. Here the river was just a yellow-brown pass flowing between banks of sifting mud and reeds and tough, tangled bushes and twisted, dead trees brought down years ago and left far up out of the usual channel by the flood waters.

The wind was high. The grasses all around bent with a small screaming sound. The water was swift and almost rough. The pirogue shuddered and bounced. They let their bodies move with it, balancing gently. "Watch that old alligator grass there," Henry said as the craft swung over near the tall reeds. "They plain cut you up like a knife."

Joshua turned the pirogue crosswise in the channel. Behind them a pair of ducks rose, hung for a minute, and then began a quick climb up the strips of wind.

"God Almighty!" Henry said. "There more duck!"

Joshua stood up in the pirogue, following the sweep of their flight. They disappeared almost at once in the low sky. He sat down.

"You reckon we ever gonna get close enough for a shot?" Henry said.

Joshua did not answer. Out of the corner of his eye he had seen something—something blue-colored. And that was one color you did not see down here in the marsh, ever. There were browns and greens and yellows, but never blue—not even the sky in winter. Still, when he had stood up in the pirogue, so that he was taller than the surrounding reeds, and had followed the flight of the ducks, his eyes had passed over a bright blue. He stood up again, balancing himself gently in the moving boat, and let his eyes swing back—carefully this time.

He found it. Down a way, on the other side of the stretch of reeds, right by the open stream of river. There must be a little shell mound there, he thought, a little solid ground, because bushes grew there, and there was one bare, twisted dead chinaberry tree. The river was always throwing up little heaps like that and then in a couple of years lifting them away. His eyes found the spot of blue color again. "Look there," he said.

Henry got to his feet slowly, carefully. The wooden shell rocked and then steadied. Henry squinted along the line of the pointing finger. "Sweet Jesus God!" he whispered. "That a man there!"

They were still for a long time. The pirogue drifted over to one side of the channel and nudged gently against the reeds. They took hold of the tops of the grasses, steadying themselves. The water got too rough; they had to sit down quickly.

Joshua found a small channel opening through the grass. He pushed the pirogue through it until there was only a dozen yards or so of low oyster grass ahead of them. The river there was full of driftwood, turning and washing down with the slow force of a truck.

"We plain can't get around the other side," Joshua said.

"Ain't no need to get closer," Henry said.

"I plain wonder who he is."

They could see so clearly now: bright-blue pants and a leather jacket.

They were bent forward, staring. "He got yellow hair," Henry said. The water made a sucking sound against the hull, and he looked down at it with a quick, nervous movement. "Water sound like it talking, times," he said.

"I plain wonder who he is."

"Ain't been here long, that for sure," Henry said. "Ain't puffed up none."

"That right," Joshua said.

"Remember the way it was with the people after the hurricane? And they only out two days?" Henry's voice trailed off to a whisper.

"I remember," Joshua said.

The man had been washed up high into the tough grasses. He was lying face down. He would stay here until the spring floods lifted him away—if there was anything left then.

"He got his hands stuck out up over his head," Henry said. They could not see the hands, but the brown, leather-clad arms were lifted straight ahead and pointing into the tangle of hackberries.

"His fingers is hanging down so the fishes nibble on them," Joshua said, and felt his shoulders twitch.

"I done felt fish nibble on my fingers," Henry said.

"Not when you was dead."

They were quiet again. All around them the sound of the miles of moving water was like breathing.

Suddenly Henry remembered. "I bet I know who he is."

"Who?" Joshua did not turn his eyes.

"I bet he off that there submarine that got sunk out in the river."

"Maybe," Joshua said.

"Or maybe he off one of the ships that got sunk."

"It don't make no difference, none."

"It ain't no use to hang around here," Henry said finally. "What we hanging around here for?"

Joshua did not answer. Henry turned and looked at him. Joshua was rubbing his chin slowly. "He got a mighty nice jacket there," he said.

"Ain't no use hanging around admiring a dead man's clothes, none."

"I might could like that jacket, me," Joshua said.

Henry stared back over his shoulder.

"You think I scared," Joshua said.

"No," Henry said. "I ain't thinking that."

"I ain't scared of going over there and getting that coat that I like," Joshua bragged.

Henry shook his head.

"Him there—he ain't gonna need it no more," Joshua said.

"You ain't gonna do that."

"You think I afraid. I reckon I just gonna do that."

"You plain could get killed going on that riverside, with all the driftwood coming down."

"Ain't going on that side," Joshua said. "I gonna climb over from this here side."

"Iffen you ain't drown yourself," Henry said, "you gonna get cut to pieces by swordgrass or get bit by one of them snakes we seen a little while ago."

"I ain't afraid," Joshua said.

He handed Henry the paddle. "You steady it now, man," he said. He got to his feet, and the pirogue did not even tremble with his movement. He took a firm grasp on the top of the toughest grasses and jumped over the side. The boat dipped heavily and the yellow, cold water splashed in.

"God Almighty," Henry said. "You like to upset us for sure."

Joshua fought his way through the twenty feet or so of matted oyster grass and waist-high water until he reached the little shell mound. The water was shallower there; it came only a little above his ankles. He began to move slowly along through the tangle of bushes, working his way across to the riverside. A heavy branch snapped away from his shoulders and clipped him in the face. He jerked his head back and clapped his hand to the cut spot.

"What that?" Henry called. "A snake ain't got you?"

"No," Joshua said. "I ain't afraid of no snakes when I sees something I want, me."

He could feel a quivering deep down inside himself. But he said aloud: "That just the cold, just the cold water, boy. I can just think how warm and fine it gonna be with a nice coat, me."

He took his hand away and looked at it. There was blood all over the palm. The branch must have cut his cheek deeply.

"It beginning to rain again," Henry called.

"I ain't afraid of no little rain," Joshua called back.

The ground under his feet must have been covered with moss, for it was slippery walking. He lost his balance once and almost fell. He felt the water splash cold up to his shoulders.

"That a gator got you?" Henry's voice was thin and ragged.

"I ain't afraid of no gators," Joshua called back. He had reached the man now. He bent down and touched the soft brown leather of the jacket. From the feel, he knew that it was buttoned across the chest. He'd have to turn the body over. He tugged at one shoulder, but the arms were caught somehow.

"You come help me," he told Henry, and, getting no answer, he looked around quickly. "Iffen you got any ideas of getting scared and running off, I just gonna peel you hide off."

He spread his legs and braced himself and pulled harder and harder. The body turned over stiffly, with a swish of water. Joshua did not look at the face. He stared at the two buttons, and then his cold fingers fumbled with them. They would not loosen.

"What you doing?" Henry called.

Joshua took out his knife, the one his father had given him, and cut off the buttons. One fell in the water. The other he caught between two fingers and dropped in his own pocket.

"Ain't you near got it?"

Joshua looked up and over at Henry when he pulled the jacket off.

"Come on," Henry said, and waved the paddle in the air.

Joshua, still without looking down, turned and worked his way back, dragging the jacket from one hand, in the water.

By the time they got home, it was almost dark and the rain was falling heavily. All the color had washed out of the country, leaving it gray and streaked and blurry, like the clouds overhead. The marshes off a little way looked just like the lower part of the sky.

Joshua picked up the fish with one hand, and with the other he tossed the jacket over his right shoulder.

He could feel the leather pressing cold against his neck. It had a smell, too. He crinkled his nose. A slight smell, one you wouldn't notice unless you were taking particular notice of such things. Faint, but distinct, too—like the way the swamp smelled, because it had so many dead things in it.

There was a cold wind coming up with the night; you could hear its angry murmuring out in the marshes. Wet as he was, and shivering, Joshua stopped for just one moment and turned and looked back the way they had come, down Goose Bayou, across the gray grasses, and he blinked and shook his head, because he couldn't quite see clear. It had gotten that dark.

Ernest Gaines

Ernest Gaines (1933–   )

Ernest J. Gaines was born in Oscar, Louisiana. At the age of 15 he moved to California with his mother. After receiving a B.A. from San Francisco State College, Gaines returned to Louisiana and began publishing his first stories. All of his writing centers on black Americans living in the rural Louisiana where he was born and raised. Recently, he was appointed professor of creative writing at the University of Southwestern Louisiana. Among his books are Catherine Carmier *(1964),* Of Love and Dust *(1967),* The Autobiography of Miss Jane Pittman *(1971),* In My Father's House *(1978), and* A Gathering of Old Men *(1983), all novels. His collection of short stories,* Bloodline, *was published in 1968. "The Sky is Gray" is taken from* Bloodline.

THE SKY IS GRAY

I

GO'N BE COMING IN A FEW minutes. Coming round that bend down there full speed. And I'm go'n get out my handkerchief and wave it down, and we go'n get on it and go.

I keep on looking for it, but Mama don't look that way no more. She's looking down the road where we just come from. It's a long old road, and far's you can see you don't see nothing but gravel. You got dry weeds on both sides, and you got trees on both sides, and fences on both sides, too. And you got cows in the pastures and they standing close together. And when we was coming out here to catch the bus I seen the smoke coming out of the cows's noses.

I look at my mama and I know what she's thinking. I been with Mama so much, just me and her, I know what she's thinking all the time. Right now it's home—Auntie and them. She's thinking if they got enough wood—if she left enough there to keep them warm till we get back. She's thinking if it go'n rain and if any of them go'n have to go out in the rain. She's thinking 'bout the hog—if he go'n get out, and if Ty and Val be able to get him back in. She always worry like that when she leaves the house. She don't worry too much if she leave me there with the smaller ones, 'cause she know I'm go'n look after them and look after Auntie and everything else. I'm the oldest and she say I'm the man.

I look at my mama and I love my mama. She's wearing that black coat and that black hat and she's looking sad. I love my mama and I want put my arm round her and tell her. But I'm not supposed to do that. She say that's weakness and that's crybaby stuff, and she don't want no crybaby round her. She don't want you to be scared, either. 'Cause Ty's scared of ghosts and she's always whipping him. I'm scared of the dark, too, but I make 'tend I ain't. I make 'tend I ain't 'cause I'm the oldest, and I got to set a good sample for the rest. I can't ever be scared and I can't ever cry. And that's why I never said nothing 'bout my teeth. It's been hurting me and hurting me close to a month now, but I never said it. I didn't say it 'cause I didn't want act like a crybaby, and 'cause I know we didn't have enough money to go have it pulled. But, Lord, it been hurting me. And look like it wouldn't start till at night when you was trying to get yourself little sleep.

Then soon 's you shut your eyes—ummm-ummm, Lord, look like it go right down to your heartstring.

"Hurting, hanh?" Ty'd say.

I'd shake my head, but I wouldn't open my mouth for nothing. You open your mouth and let that wind in, and it almost kill you.

I'd just lay there and listen to them snore. Ty there, right 'side me, and Auntie and Val over by the fireplace. Val younger than me and Ty, and he sleeps with Auntie. Mama sleeps round the other side with Louis and Walker.

I'd just lay there and listen to them, and listen to that wind out there, and listen to that fire in the fireplace. Sometimes it'd stop long enough to let me get little rest. Sometimes it just hurt, hurt, hurt. Lord, have mercy.

II

Auntie knowed it was hurting me. I didn't tell nobody but Ty, 'cause we buddies and he ain't go'n tell nobody. But some kind of way Auntie found out. When she asked me, I told her no, nothing was wrong. But she knowed it all the time. She told me to mash up a piece of aspirin and wrap it in some cotton and jugg it down in that hole. I did it, but it didn't do no good. It stopped for a little while, and started right back again. Auntie wanted to tell Mama, but I told her, "Uh-uh." 'Cause I knowed we didn't have any money, and it just was go'n make her mad again. So Auntie told Monsieur Bayonne, and Monsieur Bayonne came over to the house and told me to kneel down 'side him on the fireplace. He put his finger in his mouth and made the Sign of the Cross on my jaw. The tip of Monsieur Bayonne's finger is some hard, 'cause he's always playing on that guitar. If we sit outside at night we can always hear Monsieur Bayonne playing on his guitar. Sometimes we leave him out there playing on the guitar.

Monsieur Bayonne made the Sign of the Cross over and over on my jaw, but that didn't do no good. Even when he prayed and told me to pray some, too, that tooth still hurt me.

"How you feeling?" he say.

"Same," I say.

He kept on praying and making the Sign of the Cross and I kept on praying, too.

"Still hurting?" he say.

"Yes, sir."

Monsieur Bayonne mashed harder and harder on my jaw. He mashed so hard he almost pushed me over on Ty. But then he stopped.

"What kind of prayers you praying, boy?" he say.

"Baptist," I say.

"Well, I'll be—no wonder that tooth still killing him. I'm going one way and he pulling the other. Boy, don't you know any Catholic prayers?"

"I know 'Hail Mary,'" I say.

"Then you better start saying it."

"Yes, sir."

He started mashing on my jaw again, and I could hear him praying at the same time. And, sure enough, after while it stopped hurting me.

Me and Ty went outside where Monsieur Bayonne's two hounds was and we started playing with them. "Let's go hunting," Ty say. "All right," I say; and we went on back in the pasture. Soon the hounds got on a trail, and me and Ty followed them all 'cross the pasture and then back in the woods, too. And then they cornered this little old rabbit and killed him, and me and Ty made them get back, and we picked up the rabbit and started on back home. But my tooth had started hurting me again. It was hurting me plenty now, but I wouldn't tell Monsieur Bayonne. That night I didn't sleep a bit, and first thing in the morning Auntie told me to go back and let Monsieur Bayonne pray over me some more. Monsieur Bayonne was in his kitchen making coffee when I got there. Soon's he seen me he knowed what was wrong.

"All right, kneel down there 'side that stove," he say. "And this time make sure you pray Catholic. I don't know nothing 'bout that Baptist, and I don't want know nothing 'bout him."

III

Last night Mama say, "Tomorrow we going to town."

"It ain't hurting me no more," I say. "I can eat anything on it."

"Tomorrow we going to town," she say.

And after she finished eating, she got up and went to bed. She always go to bed early now. 'Fore Daddy went in the Army, she used to stay up late. All of us sitting out on the gallery or round the fire. But now, look like soon 's she finish eating she go to bed.

This morning when I woke up, her and Auntie was standing

'fore the fireplace. She say, "Enough to get there and get back. Dollar and a half to have it pulled. Twenty-five for me to go, twenty-five for him. Twenty-five for me to come back, twenty-five for him. Fifty cents left. Guess I get little piece of salt meat with that."

"Sure can use it," Auntie say. "White beans and no salt meat ain't white beans."

"I do the best I can," Mama say.

They was quiet after that, and I made 'tend I was still asleep.

"James, hit the floor," Auntie say.

I still made 'tend I was asleep. I didn't want them to know I was listening.

"All right," Auntie say, shaking me by the shoulder. "Come on. Today's the day."

I pushed the cover down to get out, and Ty grabbed it and pulled it back.

"You, too, Ty," Auntie say.

"I ain't getting no teef pulled," Ty say.

"Don't mean it ain't time to get up," Auntie say. "Hit it, Ty."

Ty got up grumbling.

"James, you hurry up and get in your clothes and eat your food," Auntie say. "What time y'all coming back?" she say to Mama.

"That 'leven o'clock bus," Mama say. "Got to get back in that field this evening."

"Get a move on you, James," Auntie say.

I went in the kitchen and washed my face, then I ate my breakfast. I was having bread and syrup. The bread was warm and hard and tasted good. And I tried to make it last a long time.

Ty came back there grumbling and mad at me.

"Got to get up," he say. "I ain't having no teefes pulled. What I got to be getting up for?"

Ty poured some syrup in his pan and got a piece of bread. He didn't wash his hands, neither his face, and I could see that white stuff in his eyes.

"You the one getting your teef pulled," he say. "What I got to get up for. I bet if I was getting a teef pulled, you wouldn't be getting up. Shucks; syrup again. I'm getting tired of this old syrup. Syrup, syrup, syrup. I'm go'n take with the sugar diabetes. I want me some bacon sometime."

"Go out in the field and work and you can have your bacon,"

Auntie say. She stood in the middle door looking at Ty. "You better be glad you got syrup. Some people ain't got that—hard 's time is."

"Shucks," Ty say. "How can I be strong."

"I don't know too much 'bout your strength," Auntie say; "but I know where you go'n be hot at, you keep that grumbling up. James, get a move on you; your mama waiting."

I ate my last piece of bread and went in the front room. Mama was standing 'fore the fireplace warming her hands. I put on my coat and my cap, and we left the house.

IV

I looked down there again, but it still ain't coming. I almost say, "It ain't coming yet," but I keep my mouth shut. 'Cause that's something else she don't like. She don't like for you to say something just for nothing. She can see it ain't coming, I can see it ain't coming, so why say it ain't coming. I don't say it, I turn and look at the river that's back of us. It's so cold the smoke's just raising up from the water. I see a bunch of pool-doos not too far out—just on the other side the lilies. I'm wondering if you can eat pool-doos. I ain't too sure, 'cause I ain't never ate none. But I done ate owls and black birds, and I done ate redbirds, too. I didn't want kill the redbirds, but she made me kill them. They had two of them back there. One in my trap, one in Ty's trap. Me and Ty was go'n play with them and let them go, but she made me kill them 'cause we needed the food.

"I can't," I say. "I can't."

"Here," she say. "Take it."

"I can't," I say. "I can't. I can't kill him, Mama, please."

"Here," she say. "Take this fork, James."

"Please, Mama, I can't kill him," I say.

I could tell she was go'n hit me. I jerked back, but I didn't jerk back soon enough.

"Take it," she say.

I took it and reached in for him, but he kept on hopping to the back.

"I can't, Mama," I say. The water just kept on running down my face. "I can't," I say.

"Get him out of there," she say.

I reached in for him and he kept on hopping to the back. Then I reached in farther, and he pecked me on the hand.

"I can't, Mama," I say.

She slapped me again.

I reached in again, but he kept on hopping out my way. Then he hopped to one side and I reached there. The fork got him on the leg and I heard his leg pop. I pulled my hand out 'cause I had hurt him.

"Give it here," she say, and jerked the fork out my hand.

She reached in and got the little bird right in the neck. I heard the fork go in his neck, and I heard it go in the ground. She brought him out and helt him right in front of me.

"That's one," she say. She shook him off and gived me the fork. "Get the other one."

"I can't, Mama," I say. "I'll do anything, but don't make me do that."

She went to the corner of the fence and broke the biggest switch over there she could find. I knelt 'side the trap, crying.

"Get him out of there," she say.

"I can't, Mama."

She started hitting me 'cross the back. I went down on the ground, crying.

"Get him," she say.

"Octavia?" Auntie say.

'Cause she had come out of the house and she was standing by the tree looking at us.

"Get him out of there," Mama say.

"Octavia," Auntie say, "explain to him. Explain to him. Just don't beat him. Explain to him."

But she hit me and hit me and hit me.

I'm still young—I ain't no more than eight; but I know now; I know why I had to do it. (They was so little, though. They was so little. I 'member how I picked the feathers off them and cleaned them and helt them over the fire. Then we all ate them. Ain't had but a little bitty piece each, but we all had a little bitty piece, and everybody just looked at me 'cause they was so proud.) Suppose she had to go away? That's why I had to do it. Suppose she had to go away like Daddy went away? Then who was go'n look after us? They had to be somebody left to carry on. I didn't know it then, but I know it now. Auntie and Monsieur Bayonne talked to me and made me see.

V

Time I see it I get out my handkerchief and start waving. It's still 'way down there, but I keep waving anyhow. Then it come up and stop and me and Mama get on. Mama tell me go sit in the back while she pay. I do like she say, and the people look at me. When I pass the little sign that say "White" and "Colored," I start looking for a seat. I just see one of them back there, but I don't take it, 'cause I want my mama to sit down herself. She comes in the back and sit down, and I lean on the seat. They got seats in the front, but I know I can't sit there, 'cause I have to sit back of the sign. Anyhow, I don't want sit there if my mama go'n sit back here.

They got a lady sitting 'side my mama and she looks at me and smiles little bit. I smile back, but I don't open my mouth, 'cause the wind'll get in and make that tooth ache. The lady take out a pack of gum and reach me a slice, but I shake my head. The lady just can't understand why a little boy'll turn down gum, and she reach me a slice again. This time I point to my jaw. The lady understands and smiles little bit, and I smiles little bit, but I don't open my mouth, though.

They got a girl sitting 'cross from me. She got on a red overcoat and her hair's plaited in one big plait. First, I make 'tend I don't see her over there, but then I start looking at her little bit. She make 'tend she don't see me, either, but I catch her looking that way. She got a cold, and every now and then she h'ist that little handkerchief to her nose. She ought to blow it, but she don't. Must think she's too much a lady or something.

Every time she h'ist that little handkerchief, the lady 'side her say something in her ear. She shakes her head and lays her hands in her lap again. Then I catch her kind of looking where I'm at. I smile at her little bit. But think she'll smile back? Uh-uh. She just turn up her little old nose and turn her head. Well, I show her both of us can turn us head. I turn mine too and look out at the river.

The river is gray. The sky is gray. They have pool-doos on the water. The water is wavy, and the pool-doos go up and down. The bus go round a turn, and you got plenty trees hiding the river. Then the bus go round another turn, and I can see the river again.

I look toward the front where all the white people sitting. Then

I look at that little old gal again. I don't look right at her, 'cause I don't want all them people to know I love her. I just look at her little bit, like I'm looking out that window over there. But she knows I'm looking that way, and she kind of look at me, too. The lady sitting 'side her catch her this time, and she leans over and says something in her ear.

"I don't love him nothing," that little old gal says out loud.

Everybody back there hear her mouth, and all of them look at us and laugh.

"I don't love you, either," I say. "So you don't have to turn up your nose, Miss."

"You the one looking," she say.

"I wasn't looking at you," I say. "I was looking out that window, there."

"Out that window, my foot," she say. "I seen you. Everytime I turned round you was looking at me."

"You must of been looking yourself if you seen me all them times," I say.

"Shucks," she say, "I got me all kind of boyfriends."

"I got girlfriends, too," I say.

"Well, I just don't want you getting your hopes up," she say.

I don't say no more to that little old gal 'cause I don't want have to bust her in the mouth. I lean on the seat where Mama sitting, and I don't even look that way no more. When we get to Bayonne, she jugg her little old tongue out at me. I make 'tend I'm go'n hit her, and she duck down 'side her mama. And all the people laugh at us again.

VI

Me and Mama get off and start walking in town. Bayonne is a little bitty town. Baton Rouge is a hundred times bigger than Bayonne. I went to Baton Rouge once—me, Ty, Mama, and Daddy. But that was 'way back yonder, 'fore Daddy went in the Army. I wonder when we go'n see him again. I wonder when. Look like he ain't ever coming back home.... Even the pavement all cracked in Bayonne. Got grass shooting right out the sidewalk. Got weeds in the ditch, too; just like they got at home.

It's some cold in Bayonne. Look like it's colder than it is home. The wind blows in my face, and I feel that stuff running down my nose. I sniff. Mama says use that handkerchief. I blow my nose and put it back.

We pass a school and I see them white children playing in the yard. Big old red school, and them children just running and playing. Then we pass a café, and I see a bunch of people in there eating. I wish I was in there 'cause I'm cold. Mama tells me keep my eyes in front where they belong.

We pass stores that's got dummies, and we pass another café, and then we pass a shoe shop, and that bald-head man in there fixing on a shoe. I look at him and I butt into that white lady, and Mama jerks me in front and tells me to stay there.

We come up to the courthouse, and I see the flag waving there. This flag ain't like the one we got at school. This one here ain't got but a handful of stars. One at school got a big pile of stars—one for every state. We pass it and we turn and there it is—the dentist office. Me and Mama go in, and they got people sitting everywhere you look. They even got a little boy in there younger than me.

Me and Mama sit on that bench, and a white lady come in there and ask me what my name is. Mama tells her and the white lady goes on back. Then I hear somebody hollering in there. Soon's that little boy hear him hollering, he starts hollering, too. His mama pats him and pats him, trying to make him hush up, but he ain't thinking 'bout his mama.

The man that was hollering in there comes out holding his jaw. He is a big old man and he's wearing overalls and a jumper.

"Got it, hanh?" another man asks him.

The man shakes his head—don't want to open his mouth.

"Man, I thought they was killing you in there," the other man says. "Hollering like a pig under a gate."

The man don't say nothing. He just heads for the door, and the other man follows him.

"John Lee," the white lady says. "John Lee Williams."

The little boy juggs his head down in his mama's lap and holler more now. His mama tells him go with the nurse, but he ain't thinking 'bout his mama. His mama tells him again, but he don't even hear her. His mama picks him up and takes him in there, and even when the white lady shuts the door I can still hear little old John Lee.

"I often wonder why the Lord let a child like that suffer," a lady says to my mama. The lady's sitting right in front of us on another bench. She's got on a white dress and a black sweater. She must be a nurse or something herself, I reckon.

"Not us to question," a man says.

"Sometimes I don't know if we shouldn't," the lady says.

"I know definitely we shouldn't," the man says. The man looks like a preacher. He's big and fat and he's got on a black suit. He's got a gold chain, too.

"Why?" the lady says.

"Why anything?" the preacher says.

"Yes," the lady says. "Why anything?"

"Not us to question," the preacher says.

The lady looks at the preacher a little while and looks at Mama again.

"And look like it's the poor who suffers the most," she says. "I don't understand it."

"Best not to even try," the preacher says. "He works in mysterious ways—wonders to perform."

Right then little John Lee bust out hollering, and everybody turn they head to listen.

"He's not a good dentist," the lady says. "Dr. Robillard is much better. But more expensive. That's why most of the colored people come here. The white people go to Dr. Robillard. Y'all from Bayonne?"

"Down the river," my mama says. And that's all she go'n say, 'cause she don't talk much. But the lady keeps on looking at her, and so she says, "Near Morgan."

"I see," the lady says.

VII

"That's the trouble with the black people in this country today," somebody else says. This one here's sitting on the same side me and Mama's sitting, and he is kind of sitting in front of that preacher. He looks like a teacher or somebody that goes to college. He's got on a suit, and he's got a book that he's been reading. "We don't question is exactly our problem," he says. "We should question and question and question—question everything."

The preacher just looks at him a long time. He done put a toothpick or something in his mouth, and he just keeps on turning it and turning it. You can see he don't like that boy with that book.

"Maybe you can explain what you mean," he says.

"I said what I meant," the boy says. "Question everything. Every stripe, every star, every word spoken. Everything."

"It 'pears to me that this young lady and I was talking 'bout God, young man," the preacher says.

"Question Him, too," the boy says.

"Wait," the preacher says. "Wait now."

"You heard me right," the boy says. "His existence as well as everything else. Everything."

The preacher just looks across the room at the boy. You can see he's getting madder and madder. But mad or no mad, the boy ain't thinking 'bout him. He looks at that preacher just 's hard 's the preacher looks at him.

"Is this what they coming to?" the preacher says. "Is this what we educating them for?"

"You're not educating me," the boy says. "I wash dishes at night so that I can go to school in the day. So even the words you spoke need questioning."

The preacher just looks at him and shakes his head.

"When I come in this room and seen you there with your book, I said to myself, 'There's an intelligent man.' How wrong a person can be."

"Show me one reason to believe in the existence of a God," the boy says.

"My heart tells me," the preacher says.

"'My heart tells me,'" the boy says. "'My heart tells me.' Sure, 'My heart tells me.' And as long as you listen to what your heart tells you, you will have only what the white man gives you and nothing more. Me, I don't listen to my heart. The purpose of the heart is to pump blood throughout the body, and nothing else."

"Who's your paw, boy?" the preacher says.

"Why?"

"Who is he?"

"He's dead."

"And your mom?"

"She's in Charity Hospital with pneumonia. Half killed herself, working for nothing."

"And 'cause he's dead and she's sick, you mad at the world?"

"I'm not mad at the world. I'm questioning the world. I'm questioning it with cold logic, sir. What do words like Freedom, Liberty, God, White, Colored mean? I want to know. That's why *you* are sending us to school, to read and to ask questions. And because we ask these questions, you call us mad. No, sir, it is not us who are mad."

"You keep saying 'us'?"

"'Us.' Yes—us. I'm not alone."

The preacher just shakes his head. Then he looks at everybody in the room—everybody. Some of the people look down at the floor, keep from looking at him. I kind of look 'way myself, but soon 's I know he done turn his head, I look that way again.

"I'm sorry for you," he says to the boy.

"Why?" the boy says. "Why not be sorry for yourself? Why are you so much better off than I am? Why aren't you sorry for these other people in here? Why not be sorry for the lady who had to drag her child into the dentist office? Why not be sorry for the lady sitting on that bench over there? Be sorry for them. Not for me. Some way or the other I'm going to make it."

"No, I'm sorry for you," the preacher says.

"Of course, of course," the boy says, nodding his head. "You're sorry for me because I rock that pillar you're leaning on."

"You can't ever rock the pillar I'm leaning on, young man. It's stronger than anything man can ever do."

"You believe in God because a man told you to believe in God," the boy says. "A white man told you to believe in God. And why? To keep you ignorant so he can keep his feet on your neck."

"So now we the ignorant?" the preacher says.

"Yes," the boy says. "Yes." And he opens his book again.

The preacher just looks at him sitting there. The boy done forgot all about him. Everybody else make 'tend they done forgot the squabble, too.

Then I see that preacher getting up real slow. Preacher's a great big old man and he got to brace himself to get up. He comes over where the boy is sitting. He just stands there a little while looking down at him, but the boy don't raise his head.

"Get up, boy," preacher says.

The boy looks up at him, then he shuts his book real slow and stands up. Preacher just hauls back and hit him in the face. The boy falls back 'gainst the wall, but he straightens himself up and looks right back at that preacher.

"You forgot the other cheek," he says.

The preacher hauls back and hit him again on the other side. But this time the boy braces himself and don't fall.

"That hasn't changed a thing," he says.

The preacher just looks at the boy. The preacher's breathing real hard like he just run up a big hill. The boy sits down and opens his book again.

"I feel sorry for you," the preacher says. "I never felt so sorry for a man before."

The boy makes 'tend he don't even hear that preacher. He keeps on reading his book. The preacher goes back and gets his hat off the chair.

"Excuse me," he says to us. "I'll come back some other time. Y'all, please excuse me."

And he looks at the boy and goes out of the room. The boy h'ist his hand up to his mouth one time to wipe 'way some blood. All the rest of the time he keeps on reading. And nobody else in there say a word.

VIII

Little John Lee and his mama come out the dentist office, and the nurse calls somebody else in. Then little bit later they come out, and the nurse calls another name. But fast 's she calls somebody in there, somebody else comes in the place where we sitting, and the room stays full.

The people coming in now, all of them wearing big coats. One of them says something 'bout sleeting, another one says he hope not. Another one says he think it ain't nothing but rain. 'Cause, he says, rain can get awful cold this time of year.

All round the room they talking. Some of them talking to people right by them, some of them talking to people clear 'cross the room, some of them talking to anybody'll listen. It's a little bitty room, no bigger than us kitchen, and I can see everybody in there. The little old room's full of smoke, 'cause you got two old men smoking pipes over by that side door. I think I feel my tooth thumping me some, and I hold my breath and wait. I wait and wait, but it don't thump me no more. Thank God for that.

I feel like going to sleep, and I lean back 'gainst the wall. But I'm scared to go to sleep. Scared 'cause the nurse might call my name and I won't hear her. And Mama might go to sleep, too, and she'll be mad if neither one of us heard the nurse.

I look up at Mama. I love my mama. I love my mama. And

when cotton come I'm go'n get her a new coat. And I ain't go'n get a black one, either. I think I'm go'n get her a red one.

"They got some books over there," I say. "Want read one of them?"

Mama looks at the books, but she don't answer me.

"You got yourself a little man there," the lady says.

Mama don't say nothing to the lady, but she must've smiled, 'cause I seen the lady smiling back. The lady looks at me a little while, like she's feeling sorry for me.

"You sure got that preacher out here in a hurry," she says to that boy.

The boy looks up at her and looks in his book again. When I grow up I want be just like him. I want clothes like that and I want keep a book with me, too.

"You really don't believe in God?" the lady says.

"No," he says.

"But why?" the lady says.

"Because the wind is pink," he says.

"What?" the lady says.

The boy don't answer her no more. He just reads in his book.

"Talking 'bout the wind is pink," that old lady says. She's sitting on the same bench with the boy and she's trying to look in his face. The boy makes 'tend the old lady ain't even there. He just keeps on reading. "Wind is pink," she says again. "Eh, Lord, what children go'n be saying next?"

The lady 'cross from us bust out laughing.

"That's a good one," she says. "The wind is pink. Yes, sir, that's a good one."

"Don't you believe the wind is pink?" the boy says. He keeps his head down in the book.

"Course I believe it, honey," the lady says. "Course I do." She looks at us and winks her eye. "And what color is grass, honey?"

"Grass? Grass is black."

She bust out laughing again. The boy looks at her.

"Don't you believe grass is black?" he says.

The lady quits her laughing and looks at him. Everybody else looking at him, too. The place quiet, quiet.

"Grass is green, honey," the lady says. "It was green yesterday, it's green today, and it's go'n be green tomorrow."

"How do you know it's green?"

"I know because I know."

"You don't know it's green," the boy says. "You believe it's green because someone told you it was green. If someone had told you it was black you'd believe it was black."

"It's green," the lady says. "I know green when I see green."

"Prove it's green," the boy says.

"Sure, now," the lady says. "Don't tell me it's coming to that."

"It's coming to just that," the boy says. "Words mean nothing. One means no more than the other."

"That's what it all coming to?" that old lady says. That old lady got on a turban and she got on two sweaters. She got a green sweater under a black sweater. I can see the green sweater 'cause some of the buttons on the other sweater's missing.

"Yes, ma'am," the boy says. "Words mean nothing. Action is the only thing. Doing. That's the only thing."

"Other words, you want the Lord to come down here and show Hisself to you?" she says.

"Exactly, ma'am," he says.

"You don't mean that, I'm sure?" she says.

"I do, ma'am," he says.

"Done, Jesus," the old lady says, shaking her head.

"I didn't go 'long with that preacher at first," the other lady says; "but now—I don't know. When a person say the grass is black, he's either a lunatic or something's wrong."

"Prove to me that it's green," the boy says.

"It's green because the people say it's green."

"Those same people say we're citizens of these United States," the boy says.

"I think I'm a citizen," the lady says. "Citizens have certain rights," the boy says. "Name me one right that you have. One right, granted by the constitution, that you can exercise in Bayonne."

The lady don't answer him. She just looks at him like she don't know what he's talking 'bout. I know I don't.

"Things changing," she says.

"Things are changing because some black men have begun to think with their brains and not their hearts," the boy says.

"You trying to say these people don't believe in God?"

"I'm sure some of them do. Maybe most of them do. But they don't believe that God is going to touch these white people's hearts and change things tomorrow. Things change through action. By no other way."

Everybody sit quiet and look at the boy. Nobody says a thing.

Then the lady 'cross the room from me and Mama just shakes her head.

"Let's hope that not all your generation feel the same way you do," she says.

"Think what you please, it doesn't matter," the boy says. "But it will be men who listen to their heads and not their hearts who will see that your children have a better chance than you had."

"Let's hope they ain't all like you, though," the old lady says. "Done forgot the heart absolutely."

"Yes, ma'am, I hope they aren't all like me," the boy says. "Unfortunately, I was born too late to believe in your God. Let's hope that the ones who come after will have your faith—if not in your God, then in something else, something definitely that they can lean on. I haven't anything. For me, the wind is pink, the grass is black."

IX

The nurse comes in the room where we all sitting and waiting and says the doctor won't take no more patients till one o'clock this evening. My mama jumps up off the bench and goes up to the white lady.

"Nurse, I have to go back in the field this evening," she says.

"The doctor is treating his last patient now," the nurse says. "One o'clock this evening."

"Can I at least speak to the doctor?" my mama asks.

"I'm his nurse," the lady says.

"My little boy's sick," my mama says. "Right now his tooth almost killing him."

The nurse looks at me. She's trying to make up her mind if to let me come in. I look at her real pitiful. The tooth ain't hurting me at all, but Mama says it is, so I make 'tend for her sake.

"This evening," the nurse says, and goes on back in the office.

"Don't feel 'jected, honey," the lady says to Mama. "I been round them a long time—they take you when they want to. If you was white, that's something else; but we the wrong color."

Mama don't say nothing to the lady, and me and her go outside and stand 'gainst the wall. It's cold out there. I can feel that wind going through my coat. Some of the other people come out of the room and go up the street. Me and Mama stand there a little while and we start walking. I don't know where we going. When we come to the other street we just stand there.

"You don't have to make water, do you?" Mama says.

"No, ma'am," I say.

We go on up the street. Walking real slow. I can tell Mama don't know where she's going. When we come to a store we stand there and look at the dummies. I look at a little boy wearing a brown overcoat. He's got on brown shoes, too. I look at my old shoes and look at his'n again. You wait till summer, I say.

Me and Mama walk away. We come up to another store and we stop and look at them dummies, too. Then we go on again. We pass a café where the white people in there eating. Mama tells me keep my eyes in front where they belong, but I can't help from seeing them people eat. My stomach starts to growling 'cause I'm hungry. When I see people eating, I get hungry; when I see a coat, I get cold.

A man whistles at my mama when we go by a filling station. She makes 'tend she don't even see him. I look back and I feel like hitting him in the mouth. If I was bigger, I say; if I was bigger, you'd see.

We keep on going. I'm getting colder and colder, but I don't say nothing. I feel that stuff running down my nose and I sniff.

"That rag," Mama says.

I get it out and wipe my nose. I'm getting cold all over now—my face, my hands, my feet, everything. We pass another little café, but this'n for white people, too, and we can't go in there, either. So we just walk. I'm so cold now I'm 'bout ready to say it. If I knowed where we was going I wouldn't be so cold, but I don't know where we going. We go, we go, we go. We walk clean out of Bayonne. Then we cross the street and we come back. Same thing I seen when I got off the bus this morning. Same old trees, same old walk, same old weeds, same old cracked pave—same old everything.

I sniff again.

"That rag," Mama says.

I wipe my nose real fast and jugg that handkerchief back in my pocket 'fore my hand gets too cold. I raise my head and I can see David's hardware store. When we come up to it, we go in. I don't know why, but I'm glad.

It's warm in there. It's so warm in there you don't ever want to leave. I look for the heater, and I see it over by them barrels.

Three white men standing round the heater talking in Creole. One of them comes over to see what my mama want.

"Got any axe handles?" she says.

Me, Mama, and the white man start to the back, but Mama stops me when we come up to the heater. She and the white man go on. I hold my hands over the heater and look at them. They go all the way to the back, and I see the white man pointing to the axe handles 'gainst the wall. Mama takes one of them and shakes it like she's trying to figure how much it weighs. Then she rubs her hand over it from one end to the other end. She turns it over and looks at the other side, then she shakes it again, and shakes her head and puts it back. She gets another one and she does it just like she did the first one, then she shakes her head. Then she gets a brown one and do it that, too. But she don't like this one, either. Then she gets another one, but 'fore she shakes it or anything, she looks at me. Look like she's trying to say something to me, but I don't know what it is. All I know is I done got warm now and I'm feeling right smart better. Mama shakes this axe handle just like she did the others, and shakes her head and says something to the white man. The white man just looks at his pile of axe handles, and when Mama pass him to come to the front, the white man just scratch his head and follows her. She tells me come on and we go on out and start walking again.

We walk and walk, and no time at all I'm cold again. Look like I'm colder now 'cause I can still remember how good it was back there. My stomach growls and I suck it in to keep Mama from hearing it. She's walking right 'side me, and it growls so loud you can hear it a mile. But Mama don't say a word.

X

When we come up to the courthouse, I look at the clock. It's got quarter to twelve. Mean we got another hour and a quarter to be out here in the cold. We go and stand 'side a building. Something hits my cap and I look up at the sky. Sleet's falling.

I look at Mama standing there. I want stand close 'side her, but she don't like that. She says that's crybaby stuff. She say you got to stand for yourself, by yourself.

"Let's go back to that office," she says.

We cross the street. When we get to the dentist office I try to open the door, but I can't. I twist and twist, but I can't. Mama pushes me to the side and she twist the knob, but she can't open the door, either. She turns 'way from the door. I look at her, but I don't move and I don't say nothing. I done seen her like this before and I'm scared of her.

"You hungry?" she says. She says it like she's mad at me, like I'm the cause of everything.

"No, ma'am," I say.

"You want eat and walk back, or you rather don't eat and ride?"

"I ain't hungry," I say.

I ain't just hungry, but I'm cold, too. I'm so hungry and cold I want to cry. And look like I'm getting colder and colder. My feet done got numb. I try to work my toes, but I don't even feel them. Look like I'm go'n die. Look like I'm go'n stand right here and freeze to death. I think 'bout home. I think 'bout Val and Auntie and Ty and Louis and Walker. It's 'bout twelve o'clock and I know they eating dinner now. I can hear Ty making jokes. He done forgot 'bout getting up early this morning and right now he's probably making jokes. Always trying to make somebody laugh. I wish I was right there listening to him. Give anything in the world if I was home round the fire.

"Come on," Mama says.

We start walking again. My feet so numb I can't hardly feel them. We turn the corner and go on back up the street. The clock on the courthouse starts hitting for twelve.

The sleet's coming down plenty now. They hit the pave and bounce like rice. Oh, Lord; oh, Lord, I pray. Don't let me die, don't let me die, don't let me die, Lord.

XI

Now I know where we going. We going back of town where the colored people eat. I don't care if I don't eat. I been hungry before. I can stand it. But I can't stand the cold.

I can see we go'n have a long walk. It's 'bout a mile down there. But I don't mind. I know when I get there I'm go'n warm myself. I think I can hold out. My hands numb in my pockets and my feet numb, too, but if I keep moving I can hold out. Just don't stop no more, that's all.

The sky's gray. The sleet keeps on falling. Falling like rain now—plenty, plenty. You can hear it hitting the pave. You can see it bouncing. Sometimes it bounces two times 'fore it settles.

We keep on going. We don't say nothing. We just keep on going, keep on going.

I wonder what Mama's thinking. I hope she ain't mad at me. When summer come I'm go'n pick plenty cotton and get her a coat. I'm go'n get her a red one.

I hope they'd make it summer all the time. I'd be glad if it was summer all the time—but it ain't. We got to have winter, too. Lord, I hate the winter. I guess everybody hate the winter.

I don't sniff this time. I get out my handkerchief and wipe my nose. My hands's so cold I can hardly hold the handkerchief.

I think we getting close, but we ain't there yet. I wonder where everybody is. Can't see a soul but us. Look like we the only two people moving round today. Must be too cold for the rest of the people to move round in.

I can hear my teeth. I hope they don't knock together too hard and make that bad one hurt. Lord, that's all I need, for that bad one to start off.

I hear a church bell somewhere. But today ain't Sunday. They must be ringing for a funeral or something.

I wonder what they doing at home. They must be eating. Monsieur Bayonne might be there with his guitar. One day Ty played with Monsieur Bayonne's guitar and broke one of the strings. Monsieur Bayonne was some mad with Ty. He say Ty wasn't go'n ever 'mount to nothing. Ty can make everybody laugh when he starts to mocking Monsieur Bayonne.

I used to like to be with Mama and Daddy. We used to be happy. But they took him in the Army. Now, nobody happy no more.... I be glad when Daddy comes home.

Monsieur Bayonne say it wasn't fair for them to take Daddy and give Mama nothing and give us nothing. Auntie say, "Shhh, Etienne. Don't let them hear you talk like that." Monsieur Bayonne say, "It's God truth. What they giving his children? They have to walk three and a half miles to school hot or cold. That's anything to give for a paw? She's got to work in the field rain or shine just to make ends meet. That's anything to give for a husband?" Auntie say, "Shhh, Etienne, shhh." "Yes, you right," Monsieur Bayonne say. "Best don't say it in front of them now. But one day they go'n find out. One day." "Yes, I suppose so," Auntie say. "Then what, Rose Mary?" Monsieur Bayonne say. "I don't know, Etienne," Auntie say. "All we can do is us job, and leave everything else in His hand..."

We getting closer, now. We getting closer. I can even see the railroad tracks.

We cross the tracks, and now I see the café. Just to get in there, I say. Just to get in there. Already I'm starting to feel little better.

XII

We go in. Ahh, it's good. I look for the heater; there 'gainst the wall. One of them little brown ones. I just stand there and hold my hands over it. I can't open my hands too wide 'cause they almost froze.

Mama's standing right 'side me. She done unbuttoned her coat. Smoke rises out of the coat, and the coat smells like a wet dog.

I move to the side so Mama can have more room. She opens out her hands and rubs them together. I rub mine together, too, 'cause this keep them from hurting. If you let them warm too fast, they hurt you sure. But if you let them warm just little bit at a time, and you keep rubbing them, they be all right every time.

They got just two more people in the café. A lady back of the counter, and a man on this side the counter. They been watching us ever since we come in.

Mama gets out the handkerchief and count up the money. Both of us know how much money she's got there. Three dollars. No, she ain't got three dollars, 'cause she had to pay us way up here. She ain't got but two dollars and a half left. Dollar and a half to get my tooth pulled, and fifty cents for us to go back on, and fifty cents worth of salt meat.

She stirs the money round with her finger. Most of the money is change 'cause I can hear it rubbing together. She stirs it and stirs it. Then she looks at the door. It's still sleeting. I can hear it hitting 'gainst the wall like rice.

"I ain't hungry, Mama," I say.

"Got to pay them something for they heat," she says.

She takes a quarter out the handkerchief and ties the handkerchief up again. She looks over her shoulder at the people, but she still don't move. I hope she don't spend the money. I don't want her spending it on me. I'm hungry, I'm almost starving I'm so hungry, but I don't want her spending the money on me.

She flips the quarter over like she's thinking. She's must be thinking 'bout us walking back home. Lord, I sure don't want walk home. If I thought it'd do any good to say something, I'd say it. But Mama makes up her own mind 'bout things.

She turns 'way from the heater right fast, like she better hurry up and spend the quarter 'fore she change her mind. I watch her go toward the counter. The man and the lady look at her, too. She tells the lady something and the lady walks away. The man keeps on looking at her. Her back's turned to the man, and she don't even know he's standing there.

The lady puts some cakes and a glass of milk on the counter. Then she pours up a cup of coffee and set it 'side the other stuff. Mama pays her for the things and comes on back where I'm standing. She tells me sit down at the table 'gainst the wall.

The milk and the cakes's for me; the coffee's for Mama. I eat slow and I look at her. She's looking outside at the sleet. She's looking real sad. I say to myself, I'm go'n make all this up one day. You see, one day, I'm go'n make all this up. I want say it now; I want tell her how I feel right now; but Mama don't like for us to talk like that.

"I can't eat all this," I say.

They ain't got but just three little old cakes there. I'm so hungry right now, the Lord knows I can eat a hundred times three, but I want my mama to have one.

Mama don't even look my way. She knows I'm hungry, she knows I want it. I let it stay there a little while, then I get it and eat it. I eat just on my front teeth, though, 'cause if cake touch that back tooth I know what'll happen. Thank God it ain't hurt me at all today.

After I finish eating I see the man go to the juke box. He drops a nickel in it, then he just stand there a little while looking at the record. Mama tells me keep my eyes in front where they belong. I turn my head like she say, but then I hear the man coming toward us.

"Dance, pretty?" he says.

Mama gets up to dance with him. But 'fore you know it, she done grabbed the little man in the collar and done heave him 'side the wall. He hit the wall so hard he stop the juke box from playing.

"Some pimp," the lady back of the counter says. "Some pimp."

The little man jumps up off the floor and starts toward my

mama. 'Fore you know it, Mama done sprung open her knife and she's waiting for him.

"Come on," she says. "Come on. I'll gut you from your neighbo to your throat. Come on."

I go up to the little man to hit him, but Mama makes me come and stand 'side her. The little man looks at me and Mama and goes on back to the counter.

"Some pimp," the lady back of the counter says. "Some pimp." She starts laughing and pointing at the little man. "Yes, sir, you a pimp, all right. Yes sir-ree."

XIII

"Fasten that coat, let's go," Mama says.

"You don't have to leave," the lady says.

Mama don't answer the lady, and we right out in the cold again. I'm warm right now—my hands, my ears, my feet—but I know this ain't go'n last too long. It done sleet so much now you got ice everywhere you look.

We cross the railroad tracks, and soon's we do, I get cold. That wind goes through this little old coat like it ain't even there. I got on a shirt and a sweater under the coat, but that wind won't pay them no mind. I look up and I can see we got a long way to go. I wonder if we go'n make it 'fore I get too cold.

We cross over to walk on the sidewalk. They got just one sidewalk back here, and it's over there.

After we go just a little piece, I smell bread cooking. I look, then I see a baker shop. When we get closer, I can smell it more better. I shut my eyes and make 'tend I'm eating. But I keep them shut too long and I butt up 'gainst a telephone post. Mama grabs me and see if I'm hurt. I ain't bleeding or nothing and she turns me loose.

I can feel I'm getting colder and colder, and I looked up to see how far we still got to go. Uptown is 'way up yonder. A half mile more, I reckon. I try to think of something. They say think and you won't get cold. I think of that poem, "Annabel Lee." I ain't been to school in so long—this bad weather—I reckon they done passed "Annabel Lee" by now. But passed it or not, I'm sure Miss Walker go'n make me recite it when I get there. That woman don't never forget nothing. I ain't never seen nobody like that in my life.

I'm still getting cold. "Annabel Lee" or no "Annabel Lee," I'm still getting cold. But I can see we getting closer. We getting there gradually.

Soon 's we turn the corner, I see a little old white lady up in front of us. She's the only lady on the street. She's all in black and she's got a long black rag over her head.

"Stop," she says.

Me and Mama stop and look at her. She must be crazy to be out in all this bad weather. Ain't got but a few other people out there, and all of them's men.

"Y'all done ate?" she says.

"Just finished," Mama says.

"Y'all must be cold then?" she says.

"We headed for the dentist," Mama says. "We'll warm up when we get there."

"What dentist?" the old lady says. "Mr. Bassett?"

"Yes, ma'am," Mama says.

"Come on in," the old lady says. "I'll telephone him and tell him y'all coming."

Me and Mama follow the lady in the store. It's a little bitty store, and it don't have much in there. The old lady takes off her head rag and folds it up.

"Helena?" somebody calls from the back.

"Yes, Alnest?" the old lady says.

"Did you see them?"

"They're here. Standing beside me."

"Good. Now you can stay inside."

The old lady looks at Mama. Mama's waiting to hear what she brought us in here for. I'm waiting for that, too.

"I saw y'all each time you went by," she says. "I came out to catch you, but you were gone."

"We went back to town," Mama says.

"Did you eat?"

"Yes, ma'am."

The old lady looks at Mama a long time, like she's thinking Mama might be just saying that. Mama looks right back at her. The old lady looks at me to see what I have to say. I don't say nothing. I sure ain't going 'gainst my mama.

"There's food in the kitchen," she says to Mama. "I've been keeping it warm."

Mama turns right around and starts for the door.

"Just a minute," the old lady says. Mama stops. "The boy'll have to work for it. It ain't free."

"We don't take no handout," Mama says.

"I'm not handing out anything," the old lady says. "I need my garbage moved to the front. Ernest has a bad cold and can't go out there."

"James'll move it for you," Mama says.

"Not unless you eat," the old lady says. "I'm old, but I have my pride, too, you know."

Mama can see she ain't go'n beat this lady down, so she just shakes her head.

"All right," the old lady says. "Come into the kitchen."

She leads the way with that rag in her hand. The kitchen is a little bitty little old thing, too. The table and the stove just 'bout fill it up. They got a little room to the side. Somebody in there laying 'cross the bed—'cause I can see one of his feet. Must be the person she was talking to: Ernest or Alnest—something like that.

"Sit down," the old lady says to Mama. "Not you," she says to me. "You have to move the cans."

"Helena?" the man says in the other room.

"Yes, Alnest?" the old lady says.

"Are you going out there again?"

"I must show the boy where the garbage is, Alnest," the old lady says.

"Keep that shawl over your head," the old man says.

"You don't have to remind me, Alnest. Come, boy," the old lady says.

We go out in the yard. Little old back yard ain't no bigger than the store or the kitchen. But it can sleet here just like it can sleet in any big back yard. And 'fore you know it, I'm trembling.

"There," the old lady says, pointing to the cans. I pick up one of the cans and set it right back down. The can's so light, I'm go'n see what's inside of it.

"Here," the old lady says. "Leave that can alone."

I look back at her standing there in the door. She's got that black rag wrapped round her shoulders, and she's pointing one of her little fingers at me.

"Pick it up and carry it to the front," she says. I go by her with the can, and she's looking at me all the time. I'm sure the can's empty. I'm sure she could've carried it herself—maybe both of them at the same time. "Set it on the sidewalk by the door and come back for the other one," she says.

I go and come back, and Mama looks at me when I pass her. I get the other can and take it to the front. It don't feel a bit heavier than that first one. I tell myself I ain't go'n be nobody's fool, and I'm go'n look inside this can to see just what I been hauling. First, I look up the street, then down the street. Nobody coming. Then I look over my shoulder toward the door. That little lady done slipped up there quiet 's mouse, watching me again. Look like she knowed what I was go'n do.

"Ehh, Lord," she says. "Children, children. Come in here, boy, and go wash your hands."

I follow her in the kitchen. She points toward the bathroom, and I go in there and wash up. Little bitty old bathroom, but it's clean, clean. I don't use any of her towels; I wipe my hands on my pants legs.

When I come back in the kitchen, the old lady done dished up the food. Rice, gravy, meat—and she even got some lettuce and tomato in a saucer. She even got a glass of milk and a piece of cake there, too. It looks so good, I almost start eating 'fore I say my blessing.

"Helena?" the old man says.

"Yes, Alnest?"

"Are they eating?"

"Yes," she says.

"Good," he says. "Now you'll stay inside."

The old lady goes in there where he is and I can hear them talking. I look at Mama. She's eating slow like she's thinking. I wonder what's the matter now. I reckon she's thinking 'bout home.

The old lady comes back in the kitchen.

"I talked to Dr. Bassett's nurse," she says. "Dr. Bassett will take you as soon as you get there."

"Thank you, ma'am," Mama says.

"Perfectly all right," the old lady says. "Which one is it?"

Mama nods toward me. The old lady looks at me real sad. I look sad, too.

"You're not afraid, are you?" she says.

"No, ma'am," I say.

"That's a good boy," the old lady says. "Nothing to be afraid of. Dr. Bassett will not hurt you."

When me and Mama get through eating, we thank the old lady
again.

"Helena, are they leaving?" the old man says.

"Yes, Alnest."

"Tell them I say good-bye."

"They can hear you, Alnest."

"Good-bye both mother and son," the old man says. "And may
God be with you."

Me and Mama tell the old man good-bye, and we follow the old
lady in the front room. Mama opens the door to go out, but she
stops and comes back in the store.

"You sell salt meat?" she says.

"Yes."

"Give me two bits worth."

"That isn't very much salt meat," the old lady says.

"That's all I have," Mama says.

The old lady goes back of the counter and cuts a big piece off
the chunk. Then she wraps it up and puts it in a paper bag.

"Two bits," she says.

"That looks like awful lot of meat for a quarter," Mama says.

"Two bits," the old lady says. "I've been selling salt meat behind
this counter twenty-five years. I think I know what I'm doing."

"You got a scale there," Mama says.

"What?" the old lady says.

"Weigh it," Mama says.

"What?" the old lady says. "Are you telling me how to run my
business?"

"Thanks very much for the food," Mama says.

"Just a minute," the old lady says.

"James," Mama says to me. I move toward the door.

"Just one minute, I said," the old lady says.

Me and Mama stop again and look at her. The old lady takes
the meat out of the bag and unwraps it and cuts 'bout half
of it off. Then she wraps it up again and juggs it back in the
bag and gives the bag to Mama. Mama lays the quarter on the
counter.

"Your kindness will never be forgotten," she says. "James," she
says to me.

We go out, and the old lady comes to the door to look at us.
After we go a little piece I look back, and she's still there watching
us.

The sleet's coming down heavy, heavy now, and I turn up my coat collar to keep my neck warm. My mama tells me turn it right back down.

"You not a bum," she says. "You a man."

Andre Dubus

Andre Dubus (1936–   )

Dubus was born in Lake Charles, Louisiana. He served five years in peacetime Marine Corps before entering the Writers' Workshop at the University of Iowa. Widely acclaimed as one of the best short story writers of his generation, Dubus now resides in New England. Among his many collections of stories are Separate Flights *(1975),* Adultery and Other Choices *(1978),* Finding a Girl in America *(1980),* The Times Are Never So Bad *(1983), and* We Don't Live Here Anymore *(1984). "Goodbye" is taken from* The Times Are Never So Bad.

GOODBYE

On a Sunday morning in June, Paul and Judith finished cleaning their apartment, left the key in the mailbox, and drove across town to the house Paul had left on a grey and windy day last March. It was the first house his father had ever bought: a small yellow one with a green door, a picture window, a car port. His father had bought it four years ago, when they moved from Lafayette to Lake Charles; it was a new house, built for selling in a residential section where at first there were half a dozen houses and wide, uncut fields where cottontails and meadowlarks lived. There were few trees. *My prairie*, Paul's mother called it. Now the fields were lawns and everywhere you looked there was a house, but still she said to friends: *Come out to the prairie and see us.* She said this in front of Paul's father too, her tone joking on the surface, yet no one could fail to hear the caverns of shame and bitterness beneath it. *Come to my little yellow house on the prairie*, she said.

Now, with hangered dresses lying on the back seat, and his new Marine uniform with the new gold bars hanging in a plastic bag from the hook above the window, he came in sight of the house, rectangular and yellow against the pale blue of the hot afternoon, and he felt a sense of dread, as though he were a child who had done something foolish and disobedient, and now must go home and pay the price. But he was also in luck (though he couldn't actually call it that, for he had planned it, and left enough cleaning and packing for after Mass so they wouldn't arrive in time to have lunch with his father): his mother's Chevrolet stood alone in the car port, his father's company car was gone, and glancing at his watch, Paul imagined him about now within sight of the oaks, the fairways, the limp red flags. He reached across the overnight bag and took Judith's hand, this nineteen-year-old blond girl who he knew had saved him from something as intangible as love and fear. He held her hand until he had to release it to turn left at what he still thought of as his street, then right into the driveway where, as though in echo of his incompetent boyhood, he depressed the clutch too late, and the Ford stopped with a shudder.

When he had unloaded what they needed for the night, he went to the kitchen. In the refrigerator were two six-packs of

Busch-Bavarian beer. There were also cantaloupes, which he and Judith could not afford, and for a moment he allowed himself to believe his last day and night at home would be a series of simple, tangible exchanges of love: his father, who rarely drank beer, had bought some for him; he would drink it, as he would eat the roast tonight and the cantaloupes tomorrow. But when he took a beer into the living room, where his mother and Judith sat with demitasses poised steady and graceful above their pastel laps, his mother said: "Oh, you found your beer." Then to Judith: "His Daddy brought two six-packs home yesterday and I said those children will never drink all that, but all he said was Paul likes his beer. And I got some cantaloupes, for your breakfast tomorrow."

"Good," he said, and sat in his father's easy chair.

After a while his mother went to her room for a nap. Judith got a magazine from the rack and sat on the couch, under a large watercolor of magnolias, painted long ago by a friend of his parents. Paul was looking at *Sports Illustrated* when his mother called him to the bedroom. She stood at the foot of her bed, wearing a slip and summer robe.

"Would you get my pen from under the bed?" she said loudly, motioning with her head toward the living room and Judith. "Your young body can bend better than mine."

"Your pen?" He even started to bend over, to look; he would have crawled under the bed if she hadn't stopped him with a hand on his arm, a finger to her lips.

"I went to see Monsignor," she whispered. "To see if you and Judith were bad. I—"

"You did *what?*"

Her hand quickly tightened on his arm, her fingers rose to her lips; he whispered: "You did *what?*"

"I had to know, Paul, and it's good I went, he was very nice, he said you were both very good young people, that the bad ones don't get into trouble—"

"You mean pregnant?"

Nodding quickly, her finger to her lips again: "—that only the innocent ones did because they didn't plan things."

"Mother—Mother, why did you have to ask him that? Why didn't you *know* that?"

"Well, because—"

"What's *wrong* with you?"

But he did not want to know, not ever—turning from her,

leaving the room, down the hall past the photographs of him and his sisters, Amy and Barbara; he had only this afternoon and tonight to be at home, and he did not want to know anything more. Judith was looking at him.

"I think I'll go run," he said.

"In this heat? After drinking a beer?"

"Yes."

"But your things are packed. And they're clean."

"I'll unpack them and you can throw them in the washer when I finish."

Under the early afternoon sun he ran two miles on hot black-top; for a while he ran in anger, then it left him when he was too hot to think of anything but being hot. When he got back his mother was sleeping. He took a beer into the shower and stayed a long time.

At six-thirty his mother began watching the clock, her eyes quick and trapped. She was in the pale green kitchen, moving through the smell of roast; Paul and Judith sat at the table, drinking beer.

"Don't y'all want to go to the living room instead of this hot old kitchen? You don't have to stay in here with me."

Paul told her no, he didn't like the smell of air-conditioned rooms, he wanted to smell cooking. He was watching the clock too. Certainly she must remember the meals after Amy and Barbara had gone: if she didn't talk, the three of them ate to the sounds of silverware on china. There was nothing else her memory could give her, unless she had dreamed this night of goodbyes out of some memory of her own childhood, with the five brothers and four sisters, the loud meals at that long table where he too had sat as a child and watched black hands lowering bowls and platters, and had daydreamed beneath the voices, the laughter of the Kelleys, who had once had money and perhaps dignity and now believed they had lost both because they had lost the first. The lawyer father had died in debt, with his insurance lapsed, and the sons had sold their house, whose grounds were so big that, when Paul played there, he had not needed to imagine size: it seemed as large as Sherwood Forest. Jews bought the house, tore the vines from its brick walls, and painted the first story pink. Maybe they had got around to painting the top story; he didn't know. He hadn't been to New Iberia in years, and when his mother went she refused to pass the house.

He watched her at the stove. If his father missed the cocktail hour, Paul would be spared while she suffered; and more: he knew by now, after those nights—one or two a month—that when his father came home late for dinner, drunk (she called it tight), gentle, and guilty, Paul sided with him; and in the face of his mother's pique they played a winking, grinning game of two men who by their natures were bound to keep the sober women waiting at their stoves. He even drew pleasure from it, though as a boy he had loved his mother more than anyone on earth, he loved her still, he had always been able to talk with her, although now he had things to say that she didn't want to hear: hardly reason enough to make her the sheep he offered for a few warm and easy (not really: faked, strained) moments with his father. But he would probably do it again. Since waking from her nap, she had not tried to speak to him alone; she had kept them with Judith; and her voice and eyes asked his forgiveness.

By seven-thirty, when the roast was done, they had moved with their drinks to the living room: Paul in his father's chair, his head resting on the doily, on the same spot (from Vaseline hair tonic, two drops a day, and Paul used it too) faintly soiled by his father's head. His mother, sitting with Judith on the couch, was not wearing a watch; but at exactly seven-thirty, she asked Paul the time.

"All right, he'd rather drink out there with his friends than with his own family. All right: I'm used to that. I've lived with it. But not the dinner. He can't do this to the dinner. Call him, Paul. I'm sorry, Judith: families should be quiet about these things. Paul, call your father."

"Not me." He shook his head. "No: not me."

When he was a boy in Lafayette she had sometimes told him to call the golf course and ask his father how long before he'd be home. He did it, feeling he was an ally against his father, whose irritation—*All right: tell her I'm coming*—was not, he knew, directed at him; was even in collusion with him; but that knowledge didn't help. Also, at thirteen and fourteen and then fifteen his voice hadn't changed yet, so he was doubly humiliated: when he asked for his father the clerk always said: *Yes ma'am, just a second—*

"Then I'll call," his mother said. "Should I call him, Judith, or should we just go ahead and eat without him?"

"Maybe we could wait another few minutes."

"All right. Fifteen. I'll wait until quarter to eight. Paul, fix your mother a drink. I might as well get tight, then. That's what they say: join your husband in his vices."

"Drinking isn't Daddy's vice."

"No, who said it was? It's that *golf* that's his vice. I might as well have married a sea captain, Judith, at least then I wouldn't be out here on my prairie—"

"You could live by the sea," Judith said, "and have a widow's walk."

Paul took his mother's glass and pushed through the swinging kitchen door, out of the sound and smell of air-conditioning, into the heat, and the fragrance of roast.

At twenty before ten, they sat down to dinner. His mother set Paul's place at the head of the table, but Paul said no, Daddy might come home while we're eating. He sat opposite Judith. His mother said they should have eaten at eight-fifteen. It took fifteen minutes to drive home from the club, and at eight o'clock she had gone to her room, and slid the door shut in a futile attempt at privacy in a house too small to contain what it had to. They heard her voice: hurt, bitter, whining. And at once—though his mother was right, his father wrong by something as simple as an hour and a half—he was against her. Maybe if she didn't whine, if she had served dinner at seven-thirty and said the hell with him, the old bastard can eat it cold when he gets home, maybe then he would have joined her. But he knew that wasn't true either, that it wasn't her style he resented so much as her vision—or lack of it—which allowed her to have that style and feel it was her due. When perhaps all the time his father, by staying away, was telling her: *You shouldn't have planned this, you are not helping us all but failing us all, and I choose not to bear the pain of it.* But it that were true, then his father's method was cowardly, and his cowardice added to or even created the problem he couldn't face.

For nearly three hours after the call his mother went on with the recitation of betrayal which was her attack. It was not continuous. Often enough, with the voice of someone waiting for a phone call that will change her life, she was able to talk of other things: guesses about what their new life would be like, what sort of people they would meet at Quantico (all educated, I'm sure; a lot of Northerners too; I hope y'all get along); and it was a blessing there wasn't a war, Paul was lucky, too young for Korea and now it

looked like there would be peace for a long time unless those
Russians did something crazy; she said his father had been saved
from war too, he had grown up between them, so Paul was the
first Clement to be in the service; there had been three Kelleys,
her nephews, in World War II, they had all fought and all come
home; but no one in the family had ever been a Marine lieutenant. And she spoke to Judith of food prices and ways to save; she
offered recipes; and once she mentioned the child: she said she
hoped Judith would be able to go back to college after the baby
came. Always, though, she returned to the incredible and unpre-
dictable violation of her evening; again and again she told them,
with anger posing as amazement, how his father had said they
were playing gin and time had slipped up on him, had taken him
by surprise, had passed him by. And he had said he was coming.
Thirty minutes ago, and the way he drives it only takes ten
minutes. An hour ago. With all that drinking from—from four,
four-thirty on, that's when they finish—maybe he was in an
accident.

"Paul, you'd better call and see if he's left, maybe he's—"

Around a mouthful of mayonnaised pineapple, Paul said no.

"Well, all right, youth is callous, you know he was in an accident
before, he was lucky it was so clearly the other man's fault,
because he had been drinking, he had played golf that day, and
then we went out to eat with the Bertrands. He's a wonderful
driver, Judith. But how could—oh, that *miserable* man, we'll have
to go get him. He won't be able to drive."

Paul thought they wouldn't have to, that surely his father would
weave in, blinking, flirting with Judith in his deep, mellow drinking voice, averting his eyes from the woman whose face showed
years of waiting not only for him but for all that she wanted—
money, prominence, perhaps even love: or perhaps only that, and
was it impossible, and if so, who had made it impossible?—and
dealing her a series of bourbon-thickened apologies, renuncia-
tions, promises. But it didn't happen. At ten-forty the dishwasher
was doing its work, the women had wiped and swept every crumb
from the table and floor, sponged every spot of grease from the
stove, and drunk second cups of coffee. Then his mother said:
"Oh that *man*. I'm going to bed, I've had a lovely evening with you
two anyway; Paul, give me a kiss, and you and your wife go get
him."

"Why don't we just leave him alone?"

"He's been drinking for seven *hours*, he's got to come *home*."

"He can handle it."

"All right, I won't go to bed, I'll go alone, and we'll leave his car at the club all night for everyone to see in the morning, if he doesn't have any pride, why should I care, his friends would think it's funny, oh look there's old Paul's car; I wish that damn company had never got him into the club, I don't know if Paul told you this, Judith, but his company pays the dues, we don't have that kind of money; when they transferred him from Lafayette he said he wouldn't come unless they got him into the club and paid his dues, because there's no golf course here, and they did it, it's all they've ever done for him all these years, and I wish they'd never done that—"

Paul was about to say *But think how unhappy he'd be*, when he realized that was precisely what she meant, and perhaps not only for vengeance but also to cut off all his avenues of escape and force him to find happiness for her and with her, or find none at all.

"—well, I'm used to it, I don't care, I'm past caring now—"

"Mother."

"—in Lafayette he left me and married the golf course, and now he's married to his old country club, he might as well bring a bed—"

"Mother, we'll go."

"No, you don't have to, I can—"

"Go to bed, if you want. We'll go."

The shells of the parking lot were white in the moonlight. Paul stopped beside his father's car in the shadow of palmettos and told Judith she might as well wait outside, because his father would be in the locker room. She said she'd wait at the wharf, and he touched her hand, then slid out of the car and went slowly to the front door, where he paused and looked out at the lake; on that wharf he had first kissed Judith. Then he went in, past loud men with their wives at tables in the bar, into the locker room. The four men sat at a card table between rows of tall green wall lockers; his father's back was turned. Mr. Clay looked up and said: "Young man you know, Paul."

His father turned, the reddening of his already sun-red face starting up at once, with his grin; then as he beckoned to a chair he began to cough, that deep, liquid body-wrenching cough that

Paul had heard for years, a cough from about four hundred thousand cigarettes and two or three lies his father told himself: *a holder helps, filters make a difference, sometimes switching brands.* Now he came out of it, patted his chest and swallowed while his eyes watered; his voice was weak: "Hi, Son. Have a seat and we'll get you a drink."

"Judith's waiting outside."

"Oh? Did your momma come out too? We could buy 'em a drink, couple of good-looking women, we could handle that—"

"She's home."

"Oh." He looked at the cards on the table, took a drink from his bourbon and water. "Did you drink all that beer?"

"Just about."

"You all packed and ready?"

"Yep."

"This boy would like to be called Lieutenant by you old bastards. Second lieutenant, United States Marine Corps. He'll do my *fight*in' for me."

"He can do something else for you too, you old hoss."

"When do you leave, son?" Mr. Clay said.

"Tomorrow."

"Tomorrow?" He looked at Paul's father. Then he stood up. "Well, I'm going home and boil me an egg."

"Me too," another said. "Before y'all win my house and bird dog too."

His father rose, grinning, lighting a cigarette, and Paul tensed for the cough, but it didn't come; it was down there, waiting.

They walked through the bar, his father weaving some, his shoulders forward in a subtle effort to balance his velocity and weight.

"Judith's down at the wharf."

"Oh?" Then the cough came. Paul stood watching him; he thought of his father collapsing: he would catch him before his face struck the shells, carry him to the car. His father brought up something from deep in his body and spit. "Okay, good. We'll go see Judith at the wharf."

They crunched over shells, then walked quietly on damp earth sloping to the wharf, then onto it, walking the length of it, their footsteps loud, over the lapping of waves on the pilings and the shore. Ahead of them, at the wharf's end, Judith's moonlit hair was silver.

"Hi, darling," his father said, and put his arm around her; Paul moved to the other side, and the three of them stood arm in arm, looking out at the black water shimmering under the moon.

"I wanted to see it before we left," Judith said.

"Is this where y'all did it?"

He felt Judith stiffen then relax, and then he felt her hugging his father.

"No," he said. "No, it's where we first kissed."

They started back, still arm in arm; holding Judith, Paul was guiding his father. Judith said: "Will you be all right?"

"That car responds to me, darling. You can come with me, though, for company; one of y'all."

They left the wharf and started up the gentle slope. When they reached the shells Judith said: "Okay." Paul was looking straight ahead, at the palmettos before the shadowed colonial front of the club. He felt his father looking at Judith.

"How come my bride doesn't know I got to get drunk to tell my boy goodbye? We had our first kiss on a porch swing, his momma and me. That's where we courted in those days. Maybe that's why nothing happened."

"What *did* happen?" Paul said.

They crossed the deep shells. He thought his father had not heard, or, hearing, hadn't understood. But when they reached the company car, his father said: "God knows, Son." They he opened the door and got in.

Judith waited, looking up at Paul. His father started the engine. Then Paul turned quickly away, toward his own car, Judith got in with his father, and he followed them home, watching their heads moving as they talked. The house was quiet, and they crept in and went to bed.

In the morning they were together for about an hour. The talk was of the details of departure, and their four voices called from room to room, from house to car, and filled the kitchen as they ate cantaloupes and bacon and eggs. No one mentioned last night; it showed on no one's face. At the door he kissed and embraced his quietly weeping mother. "There goes our last one," she said. "We should have had more." He looked through tears into his father's damp eyes, and they hugged fiercely, without a word. He did not look at them again until he had backed out of the driveway: they stood in their summer robes, his father's hand resting on his mother's shoulder. They waved. His father coughed, his lifted arm faltering, dropping; then he recovered, and waved again. Paul waved back, and drove down the road.

James Lee Burke

James Lee Burke (1936-   )

James Lee Burke was born in Houston, Texas, and moved as a child to Louisiana, where he was raised. Before turning to university teaching he worked in the oil industry: on the pipeline and in the field. He has also held jobs as a social worker, a land surveyor, and a newspaper reporter. He has published several novels and many short stories. Among his novels are the two most recent, Heaven Prisoners *(1988) and* Neon Rain *(1988). "The Convict" is taken from his 1985 collection of short stories,* The Convict. *It first appeared in the Spring 1985 issue of the* Kenyon Review.

THE CONVICT

(for Lyle Williams)

My father was a popular man in New Iberia, even though his ideas were different from most people's and his attitudes were uncompromising. On Friday afternoon he and my mother and I would drive down the long, yellow, dirt road through the sugarcane fields until it became a blacktop and followed the Bayou Teche into town, where my father would drop my mother off at Musemeche's Produce Market and take me with him to the bar at the Frederic Hotel. The Frederic was a wonderful old place with slot machines and potted palms and marble columns in the lobby and a gleaming, mahogany-and-brass barroom that was cooled by long-bladed wooden fans. I always sat at a table with a Dr. Nut and a glass of ice and watched with fascination the drinking rituals of my father and his friends: the warm handshakes, the pats on the shoulder, the laughter that was genuine but never uncontrolled. In the summer, which seemed like the only season in south Louisiana, the men wore seersucker suits and straw hats, and the amber light in their glasses of whiskey and ice and their Havana cigars and Picayune cigarettes held between their ringed fingers made them seem everything gentlemen and my father's friends should be.

But sometimes I would suddenly realize that there was not only a fundamental difference between my father and other men but that his presence would eventually expose that difference, and a flaw, a deep one that existed in him or them, would surface like an aching wisdom tooth.

"Do you fellows really believe we should close the schools because of a few little Negro children?" my father said.

"My Lord, Will. We've lived one way here all our lives," one man said. He owned a restaurant in town and a farm with oil on it near St. Martinville.

My father took the cigar out of his teeth, smiled, sipped out of his whiskey, and looked with his bright, green eyes at the restaurant owner. My father was a real farmer, not an absentee landlord, and his skin was brown and his body straight and hard. He could pick up a washtub full of bricks and throw it over a fence.

"That's the point," he said. "We've lived among Negroes all our lives. They work in our homes, take care of our children, drive

329

our wives on errands. Where are you going to send our own children if you close the school? Did you think of that?"

The bartender looked at the Negro porter who ran the shoe-shine stand in the bar. He was bald and wore an apron and was quietly brushing a pair of shoes left him by a hotel guest.

"Alcide, go down to the corner and pick up the newspapers," the bartender said.

"Yes suh."

"It's not ever going to come to that," another man said. "Our darkies don't want it."

"It's coming, all right," my father said. His face was composed now, his eyes looking through the opened wood shutters at the oak tree in the courtyard outside. "Harry Truman is integrating the army, and those Negro soldiers aren't going to come home and walk around to the back door anymore."

"Charlie, give Mr. Broussard another manhattan," the restaurant owner said. "In fact, give everybody one. This conversation puts me in mind of the town council."

Everyone laughed, including my father, who put his cigar in his teeth and smiled good-naturedly with his hands folded on the bar. But I knew that he wasn't laughing inside, that he would finish his drink quietly and then wink at me and we'd wave good-bye to everyone and leave their Friday-afternoon good humor intact.

On the way home he didn't talk and instead pretended that he was interested in mother's conversation about the New Iberia ladies' book club. The sun was red on the bayou, and the cypress and oaks along the bank were a dark green in the gathering dusk. Families of Negroes were cane fishing in the shallows for goggle-eye perch and bullheads.

"Why do you drink with them, Daddy? Y'all always have a argument," I said.

His eyes flicked sideways at my mother.

"That's not an argument, just a gentleman's disagreement," he said.

"I agree with him," my mother said. "Why provoke them?"

"They're good fellows. They just don't see things clearly sometimes."

My mother looked at me in the back seat, her eyes smiling so he could see them. She was beautiful when she looked like that.

"You should be aware that your father is the foremost authority in Louisiana on the subject of colored people."

"It isn't a joke, Margaret. We've kept them poor and uneducated and we're going to have to settle accounts for it one day."

"Well, you haven't underpaid them," she said. "I don't believe there's a darkie in town you haven't lent money to."

I wished I hadn't said anything. I knew he was feeling the same pain now that he had felt in the bar. Nobody understood him— not my mother, not me, none of the men he drank with.

The air suddenly became cool, the twilight turned a yellowish green, and it started to rain. Up the blacktop we saw a blockade and men in raincoats with flashlights in their hands. They wore flat campaign hats and water was dancing on the brims. My father stopped at the blockade and rolled down the window. A state policeman leaned his head down and moved his eyes around the inside of the car.

"We got a nigger and a white convict out on the ground. Don't pick up no hitchhikers," he said.

"Where were they last seen?" my father said.

"They got loose from a prison truck just east of the four-corners," he said.

We drove on in the rain. My father turned on the headlights, and I saw the anxiety in my mother's face in the glow from the dashboard.

"Will, that's only a mile from us," she said.

"They're probably gone by now or hid out under a bridge somewhere," he said.

"They must be dangerous or they wouldn't have so many police officers out," she said.

"If they were really dangerous, they'd be in Angola, not riding around in a truck. Besides, I bet when we get home and turn on the radio we'll find out they're back in jail."

"I don't like it. It's like when all those Germans were here."

During the war there was a POW camp outside New Iberia. We used to see them chopping in the sugar cane with a big white P on their backs. Mother kept the doors locked until they were sent back to Germany. My father always said they were harmless and they wouldn't escape from their camp if they were pushed out the front door at gunpoint.

The wind was blowing hard when we got home, and leaves from the pecan orchard were scattered across the lawn. My pirogue, which was tied to a small dock on the bayou behind the house, was knocking loudly against a piling. Mother waited for my father to open the front door, even though she had her own key, then she turned on all the lights in the house and closed the curtains. She began to peel crawfish in the sink for our supper, then turned on the radio in the window as though she were bored for something to listen to. Outside, the door on the tractor shed began to bang violently in the wind. My father went to the closet for his hat and raincoat.

"Let it go, Will. It's raining too hard," she said.

"Turn on the outside light. You'll be able to see me from the window," he said.

He ran through the rain, stopped at the barn for a hammer and a wood stob, then bent over in front of the tractor shed and drove the stob securely against the door.

He walked back into the kitchen, hitting his hat against his pants leg.

"I've got to get a new latch for that door. But at least the wind won't be banging it for a while," he said.

"There was a news story on the radio about the convicts," my mother said. "They had been taken from Angola to Franklin for a trial. One of them is a murderer."

"Angola?" For the first time my father's face looked concerned.

"The truck wrecked, and they got out the back and then made a man cut their handcuffs."

He picked up a shelled crawfish, bit it in half, and looked out the window at the rain slanting in the light. His face was empty now.

"Well, if I was in Angola I'd try to get out, too," he said. "Do we have some beer? I can't eat crawfish without beer."

"Call the sheriff's department and ask where they think they are."

"I can't do that, Margaret. Now, let's put a stop to all this." He walked out of the kitchen, and I saw my mother's jawbone flex under the skin.

It was about three in the morning when I heard the shed door begin slamming in the wind again. A moment later I saw my father walk past my bedroom door buttoning his denim coat over his undershirt. I followed him halfway down the stairs and watched him take a flashlight from the kitchen drawer and lift the twelve-gauge pump out of the rack on the dining-room wall. He saw me, then paused for a moment as though he were caught between two thoughts.

Then he said, "Come on down a minute, Son. I guess I didn't get that stob hammered in as well as I thought. But bolt the door behind me, will you?"

"Did you see something, Daddy?"

"No, no. I'm just taking this to satisfy your mother. Those men are probably all the way to New Orleans by now."

He turned on the outside light and went out the back door. Through the kitchen window I watched him cross the lawn. He had the flashlight pointed in front of him, and as he approached the tractor shed, he raised the shotgun and held it with one hand against his waist. He pushed the swinging door all the way back against the wall with his foot, shined the light over the tractor and the rolls of chicken wire, then stepped inside the darkness.

I could hear my own breathing as I watched the flashlight beam bounce through the cracks in the shed. Then I saw the light steady in the far corner where we hung the tools and tack. I waited for something awful to happen—the shotgun to streak fire through the boards, a pick in murderous hands to rake downward in a tangle of harness. Instead, my father appeared in the doorway a moment later, waved the flashlight at me, then replaced the stob and pressed it into the wet earth with his boot. I unbolted the back door and went up to bed, relieved that the convicts were far away and that my father was my father, a truly brave man who kept my mother's and my world a secure place.

But he didn't go back to bed. I heard him first in the upstairs hall cabinet, then in the icebox, and finally on the back porch. I went to my window and looked down into the moonlit yard and saw him walking with the shotgun under one arm and a lunch pail and folded towels in the other.

Just at false dawn, when the mist from the marsh hung thick on the lawn and the gray light began to define the black trees along the bayou, I heard my parents arguing in the next room. Then my father snapped: "Damn it, Margaret. The man's hurt."

Mother didn't come out of her room that morning. My father banged out the back door, was gone a half hour, then returned and cooked a breakfast of *couche-couche* and sausages for us.

"You want to go to a picture show today?" he said.

"I was going fishing with Tee Batiste." He was a little Negro boy whose father worked for us sometimes.

"It won't be any good after all that rain. Your mother doesn't want you tracking mud in from the bank, either."

"Is something going on, Daddy?"

"Oh, Mother and I have our little discussions sometimes. It's nothing." He smiled at me over his coffee cup.

I almost always obeyed my father, but that morning I found ways to put myself among the trees on the bank of the bayou. First, I went down on the dock to empty the rainwater out of my pirogue, then I threw dirt clods at the heads of water moccasins on the far side, then I made a game of jumping from cypress root to cypress root along the water's edge without actually touching the bank, and finally I was near what I knew my father wanted me away from that day: the old houseboat that had been washed up and left stranded among the oak trees in the great flood of 1927. Wild morning glories grew over the rotting deck, kids had riddled the cabin walls with .22 holes, and a slender oak had rooted in the collapsed floor and grown up through one window. Two sets of sharply etched footprints, side by side, led down from the levee, on the other side of which was the tractor shed, to a sawed-off cypress stump that someone had used to climb up on the deck.

The air among the trees was still and humid and dappled with broken shards of sunlight. I wished I had brought my .22, and then I wondered at my own foolishness in involving myself in something my father had been willing to lie about in order to protect me from. But I had to know what he was hiding, what or who it was that would make him choose the welfare of another over my mother's anxiety and fear.

I stepped up on the cypress stump and leaned forward until I could see into the doorless cabin. There were an empty dynamite box and a half-dozen beer bottles moted with dust in one corner, and I remembered the seismograph company that had used the houseboat as a storage shack for their explosives two years ago. I stepped up on the deck more bravely now, sure that I would find nothing else in the cabin other than possibly a possum's nest or a squirrel's cache of acorns. Then I saw the booted pants leg in the gloom just as I smelled his odor. It was like a slap in the face, a mixture of dried sweat and blood and the sour stench of swamp mud. He was sleeping on his side, his knees drawn up before him, his green-and-white, pin-striped uniform streaked black, his bald, brown head tucked under one arm. On each wrist was a silver manacle and a short length of broken chain. Someone had slipped a narrow piece of cable through one manacle and had nailed both looped ends to an oak floor beam with a twelve-inch iron spike. In that heart-pounding moment the length of cable and the long spike leaped at my eye even more than the convict did, because both of them came from the back of my father's pickup truck.

I wanted to run but I was transfixed. There was a bloody tear across the front of his shirt, as though he had run through barbed wire, and even in sleep his round, hard body seemed to radiate a primitive energy and power. He breathed hoarsely through his open mouth, and I could see the stumps of his teeth and the snuff stains on his soft, pink gums. A deerfly hummed in the heat and settled on his forehead, and when his face twitched like a snapping rubber band, I jumped backward involuntarily. Then I felt my father's strong hands grab me like vice grips on each arm.

My father was seldom angry with me, but this time his eyes were hot and his mouth was a tight line as we walked back through the trees toward the house. Finally I heard him blow out his breath and slow his step next to me. I looked up at him and his face had gone soft again.

"You ought to listen to me, Son. I had a reason not to want you back there," he said.

"What are you going to do with him?"

"I haven't decided. I need to talk with your mother a little bit."

"What did he do to go to prison?"

"He says he robbed a laundromat. For that they gave him fifty-six years."

A few minutes later he was talking to mother again in their room. This time the door was open and neither one of them cared what I heard.

"You should see his back. There are whip scars on it as thick as my finger," my father said.

"You don't have an obligation to every person in the world. He's an escaped convict. He could come in here and cut our throats for all you know."

"He's a human being who happens to be a convict. They do things up in that penitentiary that ought to make every civilized man in this state ashamed."

"I won't have this, Will."

"He's going tonight. I promise. And he's no danger to us."

"You're breaking the law. Don't you know that?"

"You have to make choices in this world, and right now I choose not to be responsible for any more suffering in this man's life."

They avoided speaking to each other the rest of the day. My mother fixed lunch for us, then pretended she wasn't hungry and washed the dishes while my father and I ate at the kitchen table. I saw him looking at her back, his eyelids blinking for a moment, and just when I thought he was going to speak, she dropped a pan loudly in the dish rack and walked out of the room. I hated to see them like that. But I particularly hated to see the loneliness that was in his eyes. He tried to hide it but I knew how miserable he was.

"They all respect you. Even though they argue with you, all those men look up to you," I said.

"What's that, Son?" he said, and turned his gaze away from the window. He was smiling, but his mind was still out there on the bayou and the houseboat.

"I heard some men from Lafayette talking about you in the bank. One of them said, 'Will Broussard's word is better than any damned signature on a contract.'"

"Oh, well, that's good of you to say, Son. You're a good boy."

"Daddy, it'll be over soon. He'll be gone and everything will be just the same as before."

"That's right. So how about you and I take our poles and see if we can't catch us a few goggle-eye?"

We fished until almost dinnertime, then cleaned and scraped our stringer of bluegill, goggle-eye perch, and sacalait in the sluice of water from the windmill. Mother had left plates of cold fried chicken and potato salad covered with wax paper for us on the kitchen table. She listened to the radio in the living room while we ate, then picked up our dishes and washed them without ever speaking to my father. The western sky was aflame with the sunset, fireflies spun circles of light in the darkening oaks on the lawn, and at eight o'clock, when I usually listened to "Gangbusters," I heard my father get up out of his straw chair on the porch and walk around the side of the house toward the bayou.

I watched him pick up a gunny sack weighted heavily at the bottom from inside the barn door and walk through the trees and up the levee. I felt guilty when I followed him, but he hadn't taken the shotgun, and he would be alone and unarmed when he freed the convict, whose odor still reached up and struck at my face. I was probably only fifty feet behind him, my face prepared to smile instantly if he turned around, but the weighted gunny sack rattled dully against his leg and he never heard me. He stepped up on the cypress stump and stooped inside the door of the houseboat cabin, then I heard the convict's voice: "What game you playing, white man?"

"I'm going to give you a choice. I'll drive you to the sheriff's office in New Iberia or I'll cut you loose. It's up to you."

"What you doing this for?"

"Make up your mind."

"I done that when I went out the back of that truck. What you doing this for?"

I was standing behind a tree on a small rise, and I saw my father take a flashlight and a hand ax out of the gunny sack. He squatted on one knee, raised the ax over his head, and whipped it down into the floor of the cabin.

"You're on your own now. There's some canned goods and an opener in the sack, and you can have the flashlight. If you follow the levee you'll come out on a dirt road that'll lead you to a railway track. That's the Southern Pacific and it'll take you to Texas."

"Gimmie the ax."

"Nope. You already have everything you're going to get."

"You got a reason you don't want the law here, ain't you? Maybe a still in that barn."

"You're a lucky man today. Don't undo it."

"What you does is your business, white man."

The convict wrapped the gunny sack around his wrist and dropped off the deck onto the ground. He looked backward with his cannonball head, then walked away through the darkening oaks that grew beside the levee. I wondered if he would make that freight train or if he would be run to ground by dogs and state police and maybe blown apart with shotguns in a cane field before he ever got out of the parish. But mostly I wondered at the incredible behavior of my father, who had turned Mother against him and broken the law himself for a man who didn't even care enough to say thank you.

It was hot and still all day Sunday, then a thundershower blew in from the Gulf and cooled everything off just before supper-time. The sky was violet and pink, and the cranes flying over the cypress in the marsh were touched with fire from the red sun on the horizon. I could smell the sweetness of the fields in the cooling wind and the wild four-o'clocks that grew in a gold-and-crimson spray by the swamp. My father said it was a perfect evening to drive down to Cypremort Point for boiled crabs. Mother didn't answer, but a moment later she said she had promised her sister to go to a movie in Lafayette. My father lit a cigar and looked at her directly through the flame.

"It's all right, Margaret. I don't blame you," he said.

Her face colored, and she had trouble finding her hat and her car keys before she left.

The moon was bright over the marsh that night, and I decided to walk down the road to Tee Batiste's cabin and go frog gigging with him. I was on the back porch sharpening the point of my gig with a file when I saw the flashlight wink out of the trees behind the house. I ran into the living room, my heart racing, the file still in my hand, my face evidently so alarmed that my father's mouth opened when he saw me.

"He's back. He's flashing your light in the trees," I said.

"It's probably somebody running a trotline."

"It's him, Daddy."

He pressed his lips together, then folded his newspaper and set it on the table next to him.

"Lock up the house while I'm outside," he said. "If I don't come back in ten minutes, call the sheriff's office."

He walked through the dining room toward the kitchen, peeling the wrapper off a fresh cigar.

"I want to go, too. I don't want to stay here by myself," I said.

"It's better that you do."

"He won't do anything if two of us are there."

He smiled and winked at me. "Maybe you're right," he said, then took the shotgun out of the wall rack.

We saw the flashlight again as soon as we stepped off of the back porch. We walked past the tractor shed and the barn and into the trees. The light flashed once more from the top of the levee. Then it went off, and I saw him outlined against the moon's reflection off the bayou. Then I heard his breathing—heated, constricted, like a cornered animal's.

"There's a roadblock just before that railway track. You didn't tell me about that," he said.

"I didn't know about it. You shouldn't have come back here," my father said.

"They run me four hours through a woods. I could hear them yelling to each other, like they was driving a deer."

His prison uniform was gone. He wore a brown, short-sleeved shirt and a pair of slacks that wouldn't button at the top. A butcher knife stuck through one of the belt loops.

"Where did you get that?" my father said.

"I taken it. What do you care? You got a bird gun there, ain't you?"

"Who did you take the clothes from?"

"I didn't bother no white people. Listen, I need to stay here two or three days. I'll work for you. There ain't no kind of work I can't do. I can make whiskey, too."

"Throw the knife in the bayou."

"What 'chu talking about?"

"I said throw it away."

"The old man I taken it from put an inch of it in my side. I don't throw it in no bayou. I ain't no threat to you, nohow. I can't go nowhere else. Why I'm going to hurt you or the boy?"

"You're the murderer, aren't you? The other convict is the robber. That's right, isn't it?"

The convict's eyes narrowed. I could see his tongue on his teeth.

"In Angola that means I won't steal from you," he said.

I saw my father's jaw work. His right hand was tight on the stock of the shotgun.

"Did you kill somebody after you left here?" he said.

"I done told you, it was me they was trying to kill. All them people out there, they'd like me drug behind a car. But that don't make no nevermind, do it? You worried about some no-good nigger that put a dirk in my neck and cost me eight years."

"You get out of here," my father said.

"I ain't going nowhere. You done already broke the law. You got to help me."

"Go back to the house, Son."

I was frightened by the sound in my father's voice.

"What you doing?" the convict said.

"Do what I say. I'll be along in a minute," my father said.

"Listen, I ain't did you no harm," the convict said.

"Avery!" my father said.

I backed away through the trees, my eyes fixed on the shotgun that my father now leveled at the convict's chest. In the moonlight I could see the sweat running down the Negro's face.

"I'm throwing away the knife," he said.

"Avery, you run to the house and stay there. You hear me?"

I turned and ran through the dark, the tree limbs slapping against my face, the morning-glory vines on the ground tangling around my ankles like snakes. Then I heard the twelve-gauge explode, and by the time I ran through the back screen into the house I was crying uncontrollably.

A moment later I heard my father's boot on the back step. Then he stopped, pumped the spent casing out of the breech, and walked inside with the shotgun over his shoulder and the red shells visible in the magazine. He was breathing hard and his face was darker than I had ever seen it. I knew then that neither he, my mother, nor I would ever know happiness again.

He took his bottle of Four Roses out of the cabinet and poured a jelly glass half full. He drank from it, then took a cigar stub out of his shirt pocket, put it between his teeth, and leaned on his arms against the drainboard. The muscles in his back stood out as though a nail were driven between his shoulder blades. Then he seemed to realize for the first time that I was in the room.

"Hey there, little fellow. What are you carrying on about?" he said.

"You killed a man, Daddy."

"Oh no, no. I just scared him and made him run back in the marsh. But I have to call the sheriff now, and I'm not happy about what I have to tell him."

I didn't think I had ever heard more joyous words. I felt as though my breast, my head, were filled with light, that a wind had blown through my soul. I could smell the bayou on the night air, the watermelons and strawberries growing beside the barn, the endlessly youthful scent of summer itself.

Two hours later my father and mother stood on the front lawn with the sheriff and watched four mud-streaked deputies lead the convict in manacles to a squad car. The convict's arms were pulled behind him, and he smoked a cigarette with his head tilted to one side. A deputy took it out of his mouth and flipped it away just before they locked him in the back of the car behind the wire screen.

"Now, tell me this again, Will. You say he was here yesterday and you gave him some canned goods?" the sheriff said. He was a thick-bodied man who wore blue suits, a pearl-gray Stetson, and a fat watch in his vest pocket.

"That's right. I cleaned up the cut on his chest and I gave him a flashlight, too," my father said. Mother put her arm in his.

"What was that fellow wearing when you did all this?"

"A green-and-white work uniform of some kind."

"Well, it must have been somebody else because I think this man stole that shirt and pants soon as he got out of the prison van. You probably run into one of them niggers that's been setting traps out of season."

"I appreciate what you're trying to do, but I helped the fellow in that car to get away."

"The same man who turned him in also helped him escape? Who's going to believe a story like that, Will?" The sheriff tipped his hat to my mother. "Good night, Mrs. Broussard. You drop by and say hello to my wife when you have a chance. Good night, Will. And you, too, Avery."

We walked back up on the porch as they drove down the dirt road through the sugar-cane fields. Heat lightning flickered across the blue-black sky.

"I'm afraid you're fated to be disbelieved," Mother said, and kissed my father on the cheek.

"It's the battered innocence in us," he said.

I didn't understand what he meant, but I didn't care, either. Mother fixed strawberries and plums and hand-cranked ice cream, and I fell asleep under the big fan in the living room with the spoon still in my hand. I heard the heat thunder roll once more, like a hard apple rattling in the bottom of a barrel, and then die somewhere out over the Gulf. In my dream I prayed for my mother and father, the men in the bar at the Frederic Hotel, the sheriff and his deputies, and finally for myself and the Negro convict. Many years would pass before I would learn that it is our collective helplessness, the frailty and imperfection of our vision that ennobles us and saves us from ourselves; but that night, when I awoke while my father was carrying me up to bed, I knew from the beat of his heart that he and I had taken pause in our contention with the world.

Robb Forman Dew

Robb Forman Dew (1946–   )

Robb Forman Dew moved to Baton Rouge, Louisiana, from Ohio when she was four years old. She began writing in her late twenties, and published her first work with The Southern Review *in the 1970s. Since then she has published two novels,* Dale Loves Sophie to Death *(1981), winner of the American Book Award for the Best First Novel of 1982, and* The Time of Her Life *(1984). Her stories have appeared in* The New Yorker *and* The Virginia Quarterly. *"Two Girls Wearing Perfume in the Summer" is taken from* Selected Stories From The Southern Review: 1955-1985 *(1988).*

"Two Girls Wearing Perfume in the Summer," by Robb Forman Dew. Reprinted by permission of the author.

TWO GIRLS
WEARING PERFUME
IN THE SUMMER

THOSE NATCHEZ GIRLS WERE STILL young enough so that they could drink coffee all day long. They had coffee at breakfast and again at lunch. They often had coffee as they worked in the early afternoon, and they always made some fresh when Lucy got home and then even had one more cup each after dinner. At night they slept easily despite a gentle trembling of their nerves, not because they were especially untroubled but because they were unencumbered. And when they had drunk so much coffee that they became giddy, they merely regarded this thin energy as one more barrier against the lethargy that threatened to engulf them in the heat. And now as Lucy leaned back against the cooling bricks and sipped her mug of sweetened coffee, she felt lightheaded and altogether less substantial than she knew she was by rights as the humid weight of the air lifted in the New Orleans twilight. Sarah was tapping the ash of her cigarette into her saucer with an agitated rustle of her long fingers against the paper. She sat with her head tilted to one side and her chin tucked in, as she often did when she was repressing irritation; she was so good-natured. But at last she leaned back in her chair and abruptly flicked her cigarette over the railing. "I don't know why you want to go," she said to Lucy, but with her eyes on the street. "There's something wrong about him. Is it that he's...coarse? Oh, there's a pretense I don't like somehow. You know, Lucy, *you* don't have a coarse bone in your body!"

Lucy's blouse lay across her back in damp streaks, and she had been thinking that it would be hard to go anywhere this evening because of the effort it would entail, but she didn't say so. "It's what I've thought I've always needed," she said to Sarah, "just one coarse bone in my body." The dark interior of their rooms lay in serene disarray beyond the French windows, and she was in no hurry to leave. In the living room the morning newspapers still lay in sections across the couch, and the sandals she had just stepped out of stood together right inside the door. She yearned half-heartedly to do nothing more right now than lie on her cool sheets and rest, simply allowing herself to settle into the disor-

345

dered sensuality of the bedroom. Sarah's helmeted hair dryer always stood open on the desk; it sat perched there like a sated pelican. And on the floor in the vicinity of the mirror were strewn shoe boxes of hair rollers, a handheld blow dryer, powder, make-up, nail polish, shoes, and various pieces of clothing, so that the way in which the room was furnished without these things could no longer be determined. Lucy always left that room with a feeling of regret, lingering over one last cigarette while her dates waited in the living room. But she went on anyway with what she had meant to say, "Besides, *coarse* isn't the word you want. You might say Dan is *brash*. No, not that either, exactly. Well, I know what you have in mind. Just because he doesn't seem like someone who would write, though . . . his *wife* said for us to come, you know! I'm not interested in him, Sarah, but I do like working with him at the *Review*. And you must think he's attractive, at least?"

Sarah was beginning to feel the solace of the evening, and her expression remained so placid that it gave no hint of an opinion as she sat gazing out into the street, hardly following Lucy's voice. She knew, though, that *brash* was not what she thought about Dan—*arrogant* came closer. "Oh well, it's been so hot today . . . I'm really tired. And, you know, I've been thinking all day that we could probably have gotten by on a cocktail party education. Do you know what I mean? A few interesting facts to fill the spaces, good manners. It seems to me we worked too hard to have ended up doing what we're doing."

Lucy turned her head to consider Sarah. "You could have gotten by, I think. You have just the right kind of looks. Well, but then it depends on the kind of cocktail party, too, doesn't it?" They smiled at each other and out at the street, which was beginning to appear shadowed. On their balcony they were caught in the last shaft of light before the sun disappeared behind the building across the street. "I'm going to get dressed," Lucy said. "Do you want to bathe first?"

"Oh, he's your poet! I'm not even going to look in the mirror before we go!" Sarah was so at ease that when Lucy went in she made no attempt to pull herself away. She remained on the balcony seated close up against the wall on the pretext of watching Lucy's cat, but the cat, who had not yet reconciled himself to Sarah, had turned his back and was carefully washing his paws. In order to keep his company Sarah chose not to mind his air of condescension, and she was coming, in any case, to respect the sort of animal he was. Lucy said he was an unusual sort of cat in that he would live within a fence. Only, of course, if the fence were built around the yard to which he was already accustomed. Sarah was prepared to believe this, although the cat did not live within the wrought-iron railings that enclosed their courtyard. She gathered from this that the move to New Orleans had emboldened him, but she thought that it had not served his appearance well. He had been a Natchez cat with a glistening coat, and he had been so much a part of his household that he was missed now in that vicinity. He had become lean and hollow-sided from his new street adventures.

Lucy and Sarah were missed as well, even though there are always so many young girls in Natchez just waiting in the wings. No one said—perhaps no one really thought—"Ah, now, those two girls...too bad they've gone!" In Natchez, events continued as they always had, celebration after celebration and births and deaths. But for all their lives Lucy and Sarah had been the focus of a great deal of attention as their stars ascended in the dense familial atmosphere of Natchez. One can't presume anything about such girls. They weren't beauties by any means, not really, but all of Natchez could see in Sarah's face, for instance, as it narrowed toward the chin, the line of her father's jaw and her mother's gentle, down-turned mouth. And Lucy, well, her head at a certain angle was so like both her uncle's and her father's that it was uncanny. This strong resemblance was often taken for beauty, and Lucy and Sarah themselves took it so as they looked in the mirror at faces so keenly stamped with their own lineage. But over the years they had come to understand that something was expected in return for so much sympathetic scrutiny, and each of them had developed a ferocious charm, even guile, that was, at least, tempered a little by compassion. But they always came out ahead, it seemed to Sarah, who even this moment was relaxing in the same self-congratulation exhibited by the cat now that he was well-groomed and sitting neatly in the last spot of sun. The cat, in fact, was a case in point. No pets were allowed in this apartment, and yet these two girls were blessed with such good fortune that they possessed a cat with charm and cunning of his own, a cat who fled the rooms to the farthest corners of the closet when the landlord visited. What luck they had!

And yet, Sarah's mind tick-ticked with restlessness, as though she had ambitions, or as though she ought, at least, to have some plans. And charm or no, here she was in this city on her own balcony, and yet she stayed well out of the air, against the wall, because to lean out against the balustrade was to indicate solidarity with the street community just below. Sometimes, to her surprise, she was mistaken for someone else, or greeted, at any rate, as though she were known to some person on the street, and that assumption by a stranger made her feel peculiarly vulnerable. And it made her lonely as well, watching all those people going in and out of each other's doorways and nodding and speaking to one another as they passed. She often saw a tall woman enter the storefront Italian restaurant directly across the street and settle at a table by the window, where she would draw out a book from her straw bag and read. She always had one glass of wine before dinner and a second with her meal. It was not the woman who so beguiled Sarah; it was the woman's self-sustenance—she seemed to feel no need to beguile anyone. Thinking of this Sarah leaned out from the wall and lightly stroked the cat, who slunk down and away from her hand, affronted by such a liberty.

And to have found this apartment, that had been such good luck too. It was a series of huge rooms strung out railway fashion, and it had bookshelves and a fireplace. But today the bedroom at the rear of the apartment had received the sun all day, and now it was hot and still, and humid too, so that although Lucy had said she was going to dress she was still just sitting in her slip on the edge of the bed, waiting for the window air conditioner to make some impression on the temperature. She was thinking that she must change her clothes, and that she needed to refresh herself somehow after the wilting day. And she was wondering what Dan's wife could be like. One afternoon in the *Review* office he and Lucy had been sitting at their desks with sandwiches and coffee for a quick lunch. Dan had been self-contained all morning, much like her own cat, Lucy had thought, when he's not hungry.

"Such a strange thing happened last night," he said all of a sudden, and Lucy had turned full around with attention, looking at him more intently than she would have meant. It wasn't often in her experience that she had come across a man so absolutely handsome, and she meant not to notice this; it must be an embarrassment to him sometimes.

"Lilah and I went out for a beer. Just to a little neighborhood place. We were sitting in the front room and people were coming in and going through to the back." He was eating all the while between sentences, so Lucy had nodded her continued attention as he chewed. "Well, it's not a fancy place, or anything—no waiters—and I went back to get us another beer. I heard this guy talking about some beautiful woman sitting out front, so when I took our drinks back I looked all around; I didn't see *anybody!*" He looked at Lucy expectantly, and she could see that he was ready to laugh with her, so she began a smile. "It was *Lilah*, you see!" he said. "He was talking about Lilah!" He was so plainly delighted that Lucy had smiled at him.

"Oh, I see," she said. "But, you know, I haven't met her yet." At that moment all that she had recognized was that depression was overtaking her at the thought of Dan's having such a beautiful wife. In fact, all that afternoon she had felt dragged out, though not forlorn. She had her own life, after all; this was just her job! But as she had walked from her bus stop down Royal Street, it had suddenly struck Lucy that *he* hadn't known; he hadn't thought it could be Lilah who was sitting in the front room of that bar being so beautiful. Well, perhaps Dan had only been trying to tell her something about the nature of his marriage, how little he and his wife really saw each other anymore, that sort of thing. So now, thinking back on it with deliberation, she forced herself to take heart, and she roused herself long enough to call through the vast rooms to Sarah to, for God's sake, remember to call the landlord about this air conditioner! Then she bathed in tepid water, and when she stepped out of the tub she carefully dried herself and dusted her whole body with cool, dry powder, so that now in the general fog of the bathroom she almost felt a chill along her wrists and ankles. She had read somewhere that if immediately upon stepping from a bath one rubs one's hands over a steamy mirror the glass will clear, and she tried this, but the effect was that the mirror remained streaked with stubborn condensation. It was getting late, though, so standing still damp and nude she brushed her teeth and strapped on her slender watch, but after a moment she took it right off again to step on the scales. She stepped on and off again several times just to make sure, and then she felt even better. So with very little consideration she chose her clothes and dressed with pleasure, and finally sprayed her throat and wrists and the backs of her knees with Blue Grass perfume.

Lucy always wore Blue Grass in the summer, but Sarah wore Chanel No. 5 the year round. Oh, these girls walked in an effusion of scent, the two of them. And as they left their apartment and walked down Dumaine Street to catch their bus, Lucy idly reached out her hand to brush a mimosa branch that flowered along the brick wall they passed. Her hand jumped away all of itself when the bloom disintegrated even at that light touch. Just—poof—it became a drift of silken wisps and powder in the heavy New Orleans air. It had so surprised her expectations that it made her smile, and a lady sitting in a city bus parked along the curb smiled as well. The perfumes of these two girls had drifted through her open window just as the mimosa fell into so many parts, and the lady thought, "Oh, my, what girls! What pretty girls! Imagine, wearing perfume on such a hot day in summer!"

When Sarah and Lucy transferred on Canal Street and boarded the trolley, they could not speak to each other any longer because of the tremendous roar of the metal wheels on the track. Quaint as it was, and picturesque too, neither of them liked to ride it at all. The trolley set up a terrible swaying once it gathered speed, and so they sat gripping their seats grimly and pondering their separate thoughts. Lucy was growing more and more apprehensive, hating herself for sweating where the hair curled onto the back of her neck, and so sweating more.

But it was adventure they were setting off to. Everything was adventure these days in this city. "Look, Sarah," Lucy had said when they had first moved into the Quarter. "They put their garbage in these sorts of holes! They aren't manhole covers at all! I wondered why there were so many of them." They had stood struck with admiration, gazing along a sidewalk dotted with numerous metal discs which enclosed sunken cans. They were enchanted! Such ingenuity! But then at two o'clock in the morning they had been awakened by the clanking all down the street of the heavy lids being thrown roughly off as the trash was taken away. Nonetheless, they were pleased every morning when they awoke and found themselves where they were. "I don't think there could be any other city quite like New Orleans," they said to each other now and then. These girls, though, had never been to any of the other cities to which people go on purpose. Or, at least, the cities to which they had gone had been visited with some specific purpose in mind: shopping, or a doctor's appointment. Even so, they had not made their way through a childhood in Natchez and emerged naïve. No—in fact the intensity of relationships in such close quarters had left them at once languid and on edge. There was nothing left to surprise them except, perhaps, their own feelings, so they were left on the brink of what might happen to them in all their lives. They had come to New Orleans, and they were pleased with it, because new possibilities still seemed to open before them like morning glories.

In the mornings they ate beignets and drank café au lait alongside the truckers who made early deliveries to the French Market. They would never tire of this; how could they? And being the girls they were, they, too, left an impression wherever they went in the city. Waiters remembered them; the truck drivers took note of those two girls, so easy-limbed somehow, all at home with their own bodies though neither of them possessed extraordinary grace. But they were so clearly not awkward. A social life had blossomed around them immediately; they had only to be there. And as the trolley reeled down St. Charles, Sarah was wondering if perhaps they had plunged in without enough discretion. She knew she would have to approach Robert Leland about the broken air conditioner sooner or later, because it turned out that it was she who dealt best with businessmen—privately she was wary of them, but only because they made no pretense of altruism in their various dealings. This seemed to Sarah a social gaffe, and she had no method of dealing with it. These men were mysterious, she thought: they had wealth disproportionate to their vaguely suspicious origins. Well, she didn't know what to make of them. And it was through one of these men that she had met Mr. Leland and finally rented their apartment.

At first he had shown them a number of small efficiencies, scarcely taking any notice of them and seeming to them almost handsome, but sleek, too, like a beetle in his black suit. Finally Sarah had said again, but with more apparent despair, "But, you see, I need a whole separate room just for my sewing!" He had looked around at her sharply while he fitted the key of another small apartment and led the way inside. He sat down wearily on the fold-down couch and stretched his arms along its back. "Why don't you girls look for another apartment out around Metairie? There are lots of bigger places out there. Do you know how hard it is to find a decent apartment in the Quarter?"

Sarah had felt so dejected; Metairie was no different than a suburb of Natchez. She turned from the window to see his face. "But we haven't got a car," she said. "And neither of us likes to be out so far." Mr. Leland appeared to be staring off into space, so Sarah sat down on the far end of the couch and watched his face for some hint. In the small, musty room he seemed large and heavily fleshed, though not fat. He frowned, finally, to himself, and nodded at them absently.

"All right, girls, come with me, but there are no pets allowed in this one."

Sarah and Lucy had both begun to feel relief as they had followed him through the one-way streets; they felt this might be it, and they had been looking for so long that they had been about to give up the search. "Are all these yours?" Sarah had asked as they walked. "Do you own all these? I mean the entire buildings of each of the apartments we've seen? How does this sort of thing work?"

He had given her a quick look of interest. "Oh well, it's pretty complicated." When he had shown them the huge apartment on Dumaine Street with the courtyard and the goldfish pond downstairs, they had been overwhelmed and had walked all around it looking into closets while he sat in the kitchen noting down something on one of his pads. Eventually he had followed them into the living room. "I'm glad you like it," he said, looking around vaguely. "So you sew," he said to Sarah, looking at her bluntly. "I wouldn't have guessed it. You look like you own the place."

Fleetingly she had pictured herself among her fabrics, and she had thought of explaining that what she did was not exactly "sewing"; it was almost like architecture; it was design—her job! But she had no idea what good luck had gotten them this apartment, so she just nodded while Mr. Leland explained all the details of renting.

One evening a month or so after they had moved in, Sarah had happened to meet him on the street, and they had gone to have a drink together, so now she must call him Bob, at least in person. And one weekend when Lucy had gone home to Natchez, Sarah had locked herself out, and she and her date had had to locate Mr. Leland and get a second key. First she had had to telephone a central office and explain the situation to the night operator. "Well, isn't there anywhere else you could spend the night?" the operator had asked irritably and to Sarah's astonishment. But out of force of habit Sarah always tried to oblige, and she duly cast her eye over the man waiting for her at the table in the little bar from which she was phoning.

"No, I'm afraid not," she had said at last.

It had been nearly one o'clock in the morning, but Mr. Leland's apartment was very near her own as it turned out, and he had met them in the lobby wearing a dark green silk robe and pajamas. She saw that he was amused; perhaps he had only been watching television and had not really had to disturb himself on her account. At least that was what she had found herself hoping. All the way from his building to her own, however, as she went along the sidewalk, she had had a slight queasy feeling; it might have left her far less unsettled if he had shown some sign of irritation.

He had dropped by in the middle of that next week to retrieve his key, and Sarah had felt that she must offer him a drink. He had sat contentedly in the living room still seeming amused, and he had relaxed into an attitude so peculiarly sedentary it was as though he might never move from his chair. And he did stay some time, so that eventually the cat crouching in the bedroom on the upper shelf of the closet let out a low guttural yowl of impatience, but it went unnoticed, or at least unremarked upon.

Thinking back on it, Sarah thought that it was only that she had been a victim of that particular day which had been so mild. The lighter, unoppressive air had seemed to demand an expansion of the spirit, and Sarah had felt herself to be beautifully displayed, like a butterfly on a page, by the flat, dry rectangle of sun that lay across the brown rug and all over the couch where they sat. The rest of the room lay in shadow and surrounded them like a curtain. She had felt... well, gaiety she called it now, but it had stemmed from a sudden realization of her own perfect balance and control. Just as if she *had* looked down and discovered corresponding spots on her translucent wings. It had filled her with sensuality, this momentary assurance, and there she had finally been, not only kissing Robert Leland on that pale afternoon, but finding it pleasant to have his heavy torso leaning over her. Eventually he had stood up and gone to hang his coat carefully in the closet and then to make a drink, rolling back his sleeves fastidiously to run the water and shake the ice from the trays. He came to sit beside her again, clasping his hands around his drink, which he held between his knees. She was feeling an affection for all that was excessive about him—the weight of him and even the abundance of dark, wiry hair that grew thickly along his arms and across the backs of his hands. And then she noticed on the inside of his arm, a little above his wrist, a delicately traced tattoo of a flowering vine which spiraled its way up at least to the bend of his elbow, and perhaps beneath his rolled sleeve it continued beyond that. Her stomach felt leaden with distaste. She almost sighed with relief just sitting there, because at least she had not gotten herself into even deeper water. When he once again laid his arm along the back of the couch and brushed her cheek, she arose and withdrew. "I've got to go out in a few minutes, I hadn't noticed the time," she had said. "Why don't I walk down with you?"

But now that she must get in touch with him, how could she ask a favor without some sort of consequence? And if Robert Leland himself came to look at the air conditioner, what would she do this time about the cat? She gave it up, finally, tired of mulling it over, and just sat in the swaying trolley staring out at the houses as they lurched by.

Lucy and Sarah could walk from the trolley's terminus to Dan's house, and they had little to say to each other in the early dark. Sarah was hoping that they would have a good meal, and Lucy, wishing for a chance to comb her hair before they got there, was distressed by her own agitation. She felt even less at ease when they arrived and were seated amidst strangers in a cream-colored room filled with massive furniture decorated only by its own wood grains. She had an impression of large, floating planes of soft color. She had never been in a room like this in the whole of her social life, and the statement these surroundings made to her was that they possessed no history; the atmosphere was brittle with an air of immediacy. Her perspective was thrown off kilter, and she felt her neck beneath her hair grow damp with sweat once again.

But Sarah sat bemused, since she had nothing to lose and had already decided that these people wouldn't interest her. She, too, was perplexed by this environment, but it had occurred to her right away that it was for the people who would live in these rooms that she designed the dresses she sold to the little boutiques in the Quarter. Not for herself, with her full body which was better suited to gentle prints and such. No, she made neat, quick slips of dresses like flexible arrows of color. Brilliant and clean. She had never seen anyone wearing one; she made them for sizes 6, 8, and 10, when she herself wore a 12, but she was delighted to have found, at least, the proper place for them, and she simply sat still trying to absorb it all. She didn't think to come to Lucy's aid; she didn't even notice whether aid was required.

Lucy was sitting next to a small, slender man with glasses and such a pale, dusty look that she might not have seen him at all if she hadn't been sitting right there. No one had told her who he was, and he gave no sign of being interested in conversation, but she was beginning to feel uncomfortable just sitting silent. "I feel I've used up a whole evening's energy already, just getting here," she said, though he remained seated as he was, with his head lolled back against the wall and his eyes closed. Then all at once he turned just his head and looked at her sharply, like a sparrow. "We came on the trolley," she explained, "and it's exhausting."

She thought he was regarding her impassively, but suddenly he spoke with a surprising passion. "The trolley is *filthy*; it's just filthy! If they're going to go in for that sort of nostalgia, for God's sake, they ought to do a decent job of it. Like the cable cars!"

Lucy was amazed at how drunk this man was beneath his gray facade. "Are you from California?" she asked softly, hoping to persuade him by her example to lower his voice.

"Yes," he said, and once more leaned back in his chair and closed his eyes.

"I've never been to California," Lucy said. "I don't think I even know anyone in California, but I've heard that parts of it are lovely."

He began to giggle in a strange, choked manner as though, with his head tilted back as it was, he were strangling on his own laughter. Lucy looked at him with dismay. "Don't *know* anybody in California," he repeated with the same rasping giggle. "My God!" he announced loudly. "Here is a girl—right here—who knows *no one* in California!"

A general silence fell over the room as everyone looked their way and paused for a moment to take his drunkenness into account. When conversation in the room resumed, he roused himself and moved away to leave Lucy to herself. He crossed the room and hung over Lilah's chair as she earnestly listened to a pretty woman in a caftan. Lucy was relieved that no one was noticing her for the moment, because she needed the time to get her bearings. She especially wanted a moment to study Lilah, whom she had scarcely even seen. She was trying to interpret Lilah's attraction, because it was plainly apparent, but her looks were not of Lucy's experience. Lilah had greeted them at the door wearing red velour shorts and a man's shirt tied at the waist. "We swam earlier," she had said, gesturing at herself with a hint of apology, but still Lucy had been very nearly insulted by the lack of formality. Lilah's hair was long and very curly, a light brown, and she had simply clasped it at the back of her neck with a wide, tortoise-shell barrette. But she was devastating anyway; Lucy could see that in spite of herself. Thinking of her own soft face with its blunt features, she envied Lilah above all else the precise and elegant lines of her face, almost sharp. When she spoke, her small, even teeth put one in mind of some quick animal. She certainly gave one pause, Lucy thought, but still, she hardly seemed the type to be noticed in a New Orleans bar.

Dinner was nowhere apparent. There was no hint of it in the air or anywhere in the dining room, but Lilah was making frequent trips to the kitchen to see about something, and both girls hoped it was food. Lucy was now sipping her third glass of pale yellow wine, which was too sweet, she thought, but was all that had been offered to her, and Sarah was just hungry. Lilah approached from across the room, but not with a smile as hostesses do; instead she looked grave, so that Lucy was expecting their first exchange to be of some import. But Lilah simply hesitated in front of them for a moment uncertainly and then sat down right there with a sigh. "Maybe you girls would help me with the lettuce," she said with a very delicate reluctance and a slight frown. "I hate to do lettuce, you know. Would you mind?"

Neither Lucy nor Sarah had ever thought about whether they liked to do lettuce or not—they had salads sometimes, but who usually fixed them? They couldn't think, and as they followed Lilah to the kitchen they were both uncertain about their ability to do lettuce at all.

"I hear you're a huge help at the *Review*, Lucy," Lilah said as she handed them the colander. "You're Lucy, aren't you? Dan's described you, of course—soft and southern and pretty—but both of you are that." Lucy was watching as Lilah bent to retrieve a pan from beneath the sink, and it seemed to Lucy that Lilah's face at that angle was the most delicate of triangles, a fragile wedge, with so little of laxity about it that, whatever her expression, there was always an inherent tension implied. Lilah smiled up at them, and it became clear that a smile from Lilah was a statement; she smiled apart from her speaking. "Oh—charming—I should say that about both of you," she said as she considered them with a quiet pleasure. "So charming!"

The girls were surprised and smiled back at her. "Well," said Lucy, "the *Review* fascinates me. I'm getting a chance to read a lot of things I never would have come across on my own. And it still leaves me time to work on my own writing in the evenings."

"Do you write?" Lilah appeared to be even more interested. "Dan didn't say so. Oh, I wrote too once, when I was younger." She looked down into the colander, into which Sarah had begun to tear pieces of lettuce. "Be sure not to put the stems in! I'm going to get one more glass of wine and see how everyone's doing, then I'll slice the mushrooms." And she headed out toward the makeshift bar on the buffet.

"Well," Sarah said finally, "busy hands, you know." Lucy put down the lettuce and took another sip of wine.

At last the party was seated wherever there was room. Everyone settled their plates on their laps to eat however they could manage and drink more wine. Dan sat down next to Lucy on the rug, and they braced themselves one against the other companionably. Lilah sat above them on the couch between Sarah and the same persistent pale moth of a man who despised the trolley. He had pursued Lilah all evening, so this was the first time he had sat down in several hours, as far as Lucy could remember.

"You'd better eat, Jimmy," Lilah said to him with concern.

"Eat! Oh God, Lilah!" And for a moment he looked alarmingly distressed as he passed a hand briefly across his eyes. But then he looked down and studied his food with surprise. "There are too many distractions. Where did you get these girls?" And he bent forward, almost folding himself onto his own plate as he leaned around Lilah to indicate Sarah and Lucy. "These pretty, pretty girls?"

Dan grinned just in general, which he did sometimes, and which, Lucy thought, erased from his face its look of ponderous responsibility, which could occasionally be so dampening to the spirit. "Now, Jimmy," he said, "these are my girls, you know. I discovered them. And how do you think you'll make Lilah feel, letting your eye rove like that?"

Lilah smiled her detached smile and looked vaguely around the room, not seeming to pay anyone much heed. But all of a sudden she turned back to them. "No, that's right, Jimmy," she said. "Don't ever fall in love with anyone else! I think I would be . . . well, distraught. Unless she were just the right person. You're too innocent, you know, to look after your own interests."

Lucy had a twinge of severe uneasiness, just as though she were sitting with grownups whose conversation had risen above her head. Dan was grinning now with even greater pleasure, which seemed an odd thing to her.

"Lilah couldn't do without you, Jimmy!" he said between bites. "I think that's the truth. She needs to have people in love with her, not just loving her."

Lilah smiled directly down at him, and it was a peculiar look they exchanged, their faces were so barren of pretense. Dan went back to finishing his meal, and Lilah reached out and massaged his shoulder with a light pressure. "You know," she said lazily, "I think you're right, Love. I suppose you and I know each other so well we've become like one sex. Do you see what I mean? We've been married almost seventeen years." She sat with her hand just resting now on Dan's shoulder, apparently considering this thought for the first time, but Dan only laughed.

"Well, which sex is it, Lilah?" he said.

Lilah settled back on the couch and smiled a very slow, almost disappointed smile, as though her point had been missed. "Oh, a little of each, I guess. But, Jimmy, don't take up with girls like these! In case you were thinking of it." She linked her arm through Sarah's and pressed it to her side fondly. "As charming as these two are . . . they still could be eaten alive. Or else they'll become pretty fierce." She smiled around at Lucy and Sarah to show that she was teasing them. "You're too vulnerable, Jimmy. I don't know what might happen to you. And," she added, "it might not be so good for them either. Bad all the way around."

Sarah and Lucy exchanged a glance, each thinking how drunk everyone had become in such short order.

It was late when the girls boarded the trolley once more for the return trip, and there were only one or two people aboard, none of whom seemed interested in them or in the least threatening. Besides, those two girls had no idea of real fear. They walked around the streets of the Quarter any time of day or night to do their laundry or go to the drugstore. They couldn't have been called brave; it was just that they had assimilated such a powerful sense of identity through all their lives in Natchez that in their minds it would simply be too much of a coincidence to be *who* they were and still have something terrible happen to them. So it never occurred to them to dread the long ride home other than for the discomfort of it. They sat together on a bench along the side and gave themselves up to the swaying of the trolley.

"Do you remember that song we sang at summer camp the last

year we went?" Sarah asked over the roar of the wheels, and then she began to sing it:

> We are the Natchez girls
> We wear our hair in curls
> We wear our dungarees
> Way up above our knees
> We wear our daddy's shirts
> And boy are we big flirts
> We saw the boys today
> That's why we feel this way
> Ta rah rah boom te ay
> We saw the boys today
> Ta rah rah boom te ay
> That's why we feel this way.

Lucy looked around at the other passengers with embarrassment, but these people riding the trolley so late at night had taken no notice of them. They barely saw two pretty girls who were only two more people, slightly drunk, having to get from one place to another.

The next few days were lost to the girls for so many reasons. It took all of Saturday to recover from the night before, and they stayed out of each other's way in the big apartment. Sunday, Monday, and Tuesday were consumed by the terrible heat. Tuesday morning, as she walked from her bus stop to the *Review* office, Lucy reflected bitterly that there was no breathing in this heavy air. At least in Natchez, as hot as it often got, there had always been the possibility that the season would change. But here, this was endless; she was sure it would continue this way forever. She had not been able to think, so absorbed had she been by the heat, and even the Quarter had been less rowdy throughout the last few oppressive nights. She envisioned all the inhabitants sitting by their windows, soporific with the warm weight of the atmosphere. What could there be to talk about or to celebrate when one's skin was lightly slick and damp with a film of sweat? Before she began to sort the mail she tried to phone Sarah to remind her to get in touch with Mr. Leland about the air conditioner, even though in the huge bedroom it would probably have no more effect than the pleated paper fans the girls fashioned for themselves from magazine covers.

Sarah had already called Robert Leland that morning, but she had been made so uneasy by a slight pause in his voice, a slight change in tone, that immediately after hanging up she had left the apartment. She was sitting in Walgreens with a glass of iced tea while she waited for the cool air to stop her from sweating. She looked around her with a little interest and decided that no one can be hot and look good at the same time, so she felt a little better about her own dishevelment.

She had arranged for Mr. Leland to come in the evening so Lucy would be there, but she hoped he wouldn't come at all, that he would send some repairman. "It's not working at all?" he had asked. "Hard to keep a curl in your hair, I bet." She sipped her tea and put him out of her mind for the moment, but on the way out she bought a small toy for the cat as reparation for the time he would spend in seclusion that evening. When she got home she wandered around the rooms, unable to settle to serious sewing, and finally she opened the cat's gift and proffered it. But the cat inspected it with disdain—it was only a small plastic ball containing a bell—and almost as an afterthought he gave it a casual bat as he was walking by. When the bell tinkled he flicked his back in irritation. Well, she thought desultorily, he is not to be placated.

By the time Lucy had come home, Sarah was depressed and had eaten too many chocolate cookies, but she had taken the time to change her clothes. The cat was asleep on Lucy's bed, and they weren't sure what to do with him. The closet was no refuge this time, because it was in the same room as the air conditioner. Finally they closed him outside on the balcony and decided that if he were noticed they could claim he belonged to somebody else.

Mr. Leland arrived just as they finished dinner, and Lucy had begun washing up. He was brisk and in a hurry tonight and showed no inclination to linger. But checking the air conditioner took some time. After flipping various switches in the apartment, he had to make several trips back and forth down the stairs to the basement, and on the third trip he arrived back at their door red-faced and sweating so that his shirt clung wetly to his chest and back. Sarah gave him some iced tea, which he drank in one long swallow while standing in the doorway. Sweat had dampened the hair above his ears, and he made her think of a seal.

"Thanks," he said when he handed her back the glass. "I'm not sure what's wrong with that thing. We may have to get you a new one. I imagine we can turn one up somewhere." They were all three standing in the doorway of the kitchen, which was the only entrance to the apartment, and he was leaning against the door-frame looking worn out, but suddenly he began to smile, and then he laughed. "I've got to get going," he said, not looking directly at either of them. "I'll see if we can't get this fixed or replaced at least by the first of the week." He turned to go and shook his head ruefully. "I'll tell you," he said with a quick glance at them, "with apartments as hard to find as they are these days, you've really got to be something special to get away with drinking your milk off the floor!" And he smiled with unnerving satisfaction as he headed toward the stairs, still shaking his head. Sarah closed the door behind him and turned to look at Lucy, and they both looked down to see the cat's bowl full of milk in plain sight under the kitchen table. They simply stood there for a moment, and then Sarah looked at Lucy apologetically. "I took his food out to the balcony," she said, "but I forgot about his milk."

Lucy left the room, though Sarah couldn't tell if she were angry or tired, or perhaps both. After all, she reminded herself, it is Lucy's cat! Sarah slowly went about the business of straightening up where Lucy had left off, and then she mixed two very tall gin and tonics, though she supposed in the long run the drinks would make them even warmer. "I've fixed you a drink," she called through the rooms to Lucy. And when Lucy came in they both sat exactly in their places at the table, sipping their drinks through straws Sarah had found in the cupboard.

"At the very least," Lucy said, "really, the least we can do . . . we've got to get rid of that cat!" She sat tracing rings around her glass with her index finger, thinking that she could take him home this weekend if she made a special trip, or perhaps when she went up on the 24th. Of course, she supposed, there was no real hurry.

John William Corrington

John William Corrington (1932-1988)

John William Corrington was born in Memphis, Tennessee, and moved as a child to Shreveport, Louisiana, where he attended Centenary College. He later received an M.A. from Rice University, a Ph.D. from Sussex University, and a J.D. from Tulane Law School. He taught at several universities, including Louisiana State University and Loyola University of the South, and he later practiced law in New Orleans. Among his numerous publications are eight novels and three collections of short stories. His most recent books are All My Trials *(1987) and* A Civil Death *(1987), written in collaboration with his wife Joyce H. Corrington.* "Pleadings" *is taken from* Selected Stories From The Southern Review: 1965-1985 *(1988).*

PLEADINGS

I

DINNER WAS ON THE TABLE WHEN the phone rang, and Joan just stared at me.

—Go ahead, answer it. Maybe they need you in Washington.

—I don't want to get disbarred, I said.—More likely they need me at the Parish Prison.

I was closer than she was. It was Bertram Bijou, a deputy out in Jefferson Parish. He had a friend. With troubles. Being a lawyer, you find out that nobody has trouble, really. It's always a friend.

—Naw, on the level, Bert said.—You know Howard Bedlow?

No, I didn't know Howard Bedlow, but I would pretty soon.

They came to the house after supper. As a rule, I put people off when they want to come to the house. They've got eight hours a day to find out how to incorporate, write a will, pull their taxes down, or whatever. In the evening I like to sit quiet with Joan. We read and listen to Haydn or Boccherini and watch the light fade over uptown New Orleans. Sometimes, though I do not tell her, I like to imagine we are a late Roman couple sitting in our atrium in the countryside of England, not far from Londinium. It is always summer, and Septimus Severus has not yet begun to tax Britain out of existence. Still, it is twilight now, and there is nothing before us. We are young, but the world is old, and that is all right because the drive and the hysteria of destiny is past now, and we can sit and enjoy our garden, the twisted ivy, the huge caladiums, and if it is April, the daffodils that plunder our weak sun and sparkle across the land. It is always cool in my fantasy, and Joan crochets something for the center of our table, and I refuse to think of the burdens of administration that I will have to lift again tomorrow. They will wait, and Rome will never even know. It is always a hushed single moment, ageless and serene, and I am with her, and only the hopeless are still ambitious. Everything we will do has been done, and for the moment there is peace.

It is a silly fantasy, dreamed here in the heart of booming America, but it makes me happy, and so I was likely showing my mild irritation when Bert and his friend Howard Bedlow turned up. I tried to be kind. For several reasons. Bert is a nice man. An honest deputy, a politician in a small way, and perhaps what the Civil Law likes to call *un bon pere du famille*—though I think at

365

Common Law Bert would be "an officious intermeddler." He seems prone to get involved with people. Partly because he would like very much to be on the Kenner City Council one day, but, I like to imagine, as much because there lingers in the Bijou blood some tincture of piety brought here and nurtured by his French sires and his Sicilian and Spanish maternal ascendants. New Orleans has people like that. A certain kindness, a certain sympathy left over from the days when one person's anguish or that of a family was the business of all their neighbors. Perhaps that fine and profound Catholic certainty of death and judgment which makes us all one.

And beyond approving Bert as a type, I have found that most people who come for law are in one way or another distressed: the distress of loss or fear, of humiliation or sudden realization. Or the more terrible distress of greed, appetite gone wild, the very biggest of deals in the offing, and O, my God, don't let me muff it.

Howard Bedlow was in his late forties. He might have been the Celtic gardener in my imaginary Roman garden. Taller than average, hair a peculiar reddish gold more suited to a surfing king than to an unsuccessful car salesman, he had that appearance of a man scarce half made up that I had always associated with European workmen and small tradesmen. His cuffs were frayed and too short. His collar seemed wrong; it fit neither his neck nor the thin stringy tie he wore knotted more or less under it. Once, some years ago, I found, he had tried to make a go of his own Rambler franchise, only to see it go down like a gunshot animal, month by month, week by week, until at last no one, not even the manager of the taco place next door, would cash his checks or give him a nickel for a local phone call.

Now he worked, mostly on commission, for one used car lot or another, as Bert told it. He had not gone bankrupt in the collapse of the Rambler business, but had sold his small house on the west bank and had paid off his debts, almost all of them dollar for dollar, fifty here, ten there. When I heard that, I decided against offering them coffee. I got out whiskey. You serve a man what he's worth, even if he invades your fantasies.

As Bert talked on, only pausing to sip his bourbon, Bedlow sat staring into his glass, his large hands cupping it, his fingers moving restlessly around its rim, listening to Bert as if he himself had no stake in all that was passing. I had once known a musician who had sat that way when people caught him in a situation where talk was inevitable. Like Bedlow, he was not resentful, only elsewhere, and his hands, trained to a mystical perfection, worked over and over certain passages in some silent score.

Bedlow looked up as Bert told about the house trailer he, Bedlow, lived in now—or had lived in until a week or so before. Bedlow frowned almost sympathetically, as if he could find some measure of compassion for a poor man who had come down so far.

—Now I got to be honest, Bert said at last, drawing a deep breath.—Howard, he didn't want to come. Bad times with lawyers.

—I can see that, I said.

—He can't put all that car franchise mess out of mind. Bitter, you know. Gone down hard. Lawyers like vultures, all over the place.

Bedlow nodded, frowning. Not in agreement with Bert on his own behalf, but as if he, indifferent to all this, could appreciate a man being bitter, untrusting after so much. I almost wondered if the trouble wasn't Bert's, so distant from it Bedlow seemed.

—I got to be honest, Bert said again. Then he paused, looking down at his whiskey. Howard studied his drink, too.

—I told Howard he could come along with me to see you, or I had to take him up to Judge Talley. DWI, property damage, foul and abusive, resisting, public obscenity. You could pave the river with charges. I mean it.

All right. You could. And sometimes did. Some wise-ass tries to take apart Millie's Bar, the only place for four blocks where a working man can sit back and sip one without a lot of hassle. You take and let him consider the adamantine justice of Jefferson Parish for thirty days or six months before you turn him loose at the causeway and let him drag back to St. Tammany Parish with what's left of his tail tucked between his legs. Discretion of the Officer. That's the way it is, the way it's always been, the way it'll be till the whole human race learns how to handle itself in Millie's Bar.

But you don't do that with a friend. Makes no sense. You don't cart him off to Judge Elmer Talley who is the scourge of the working class if the working class indulges in what others call the curse of the working class. No, Bert was clubbing his buddy. To get him to an Officer of the Court. All right.

—He says he wants a divorce, Bert said.—Drinks like a three-legged hog and goes to low rating his wife in public and so on. Ain't that fine?

No, Bedlow acknowledged, frowning, shaking his head. It was *not* fine. He agreed with Bert, you could tell. It was sorry, too damned bad.

—I'm not going to tell you what he called his wife over to Sammie's Lounge last night. Sammie almost hit him. You know what I mean?

Yes I did. Maybe, here and there, the fire is not entirely out. I have known a man to beat another very nearly to death because the first spoke slightingly of his own mother. One does not talk that way about women folk, not even one's own. The lowly, the ignored, and the abused remember what the high-born and the wealthy have forgotten.

—Are you separated, I asked Bedlow.

—I ain't livin with the woman, he said laconically. It was the first time he had spoken since he came into my house.

—What's the trouble?

He told me. Told me in detail while Bert listened and made faces of astonishment and disbelief at me. Bert could still be astonished after seventeen years on the Jefferson Parish Sheriff's squad. You wonder that I like him?

It seemed that there had been adultery. A clear and flagrant act of faithlessness resulting in a child. A child that was not his, not a Bedlow. He had been away, in the wash of his financial troubles, watching the Rambler franchise expire, trying hard to do right. And she did it, swore to Christ and the Virgin she never did it, and went to confinement carrying another man's child.

—When," I asked. "How old is...?

—Nine," Bedlow said firmly.—He's...it's nine...

I stared at Bert. He shrugged. It seemed to be no surprise to him. Oh, hell, I thought. Maybe what this draggle-assed country needs is an emperor. Even if he taxes us to death and declares war on Guatemala. This is absurd.

—Mr. Bedlow, I said.—You can't get a divorce for adultery with a situation like that.

—How come?

—You've been living with her all that...nine years?

—Yeah.

—They...call it reconciliation. No way. If you stay on, you are presumed...what the hell. How long have you lived apart?

—Two weeks and two days, he answered. I suspected he could have told me the hours and minutes.

—I couldn't take it any more. Knowing what I know...

Bedlow began to cry. Bert looked away, and I suppose I did. I have not seen many grown men cry cold sober. I have seen them mangled past any hope of life, twisting, screaming, cursing. I have seen them standing by a wrecked car while police and firemen tried to saw loose the bodies of their wives and children. I have seen men, told of the death of their one son, stand hard-jawed with tears running down their slabby sunburned cheeks, but that was not crying. Bedlow was crying, and he did not seem the kind of man who cries.

I motioned Bert back into the kitchen.—What the hell...

—This man, Bert said, spreading his hands,—is in trouble.

—All right, I said, hearing Bedlow out in the parlor, still sobbing as if something more than his life might be lost.—All right. But I don't think it's a lawyer he needs.

Bert frowned, outraged.—Well, he sure don't need one of...them.

I could not be sure whether he was referring to priests or psychiatrists. Or both. Bert trusted the law. Even working with it, knowing better than I its open sores and ugly fissures, he believed in it, and for some reason saw me as one of its dependable functionaries. I guess I was pleased by that.

—Fill me in on this whole business, will you?

Yes, he would, and would have earlier over the phone, but he had been busy mollifying Sammie and some of his customers who wanted to lay charges that Bert could not have sidestepped.

It was short and ugly, and I was hooked. Bedlow's wife was a good woman. The child was a hopeless defective. It was kept up at Pineville, at the Louisiana hospital for the feebleminded, or whatever the social scientists are calling imbeciles this year. A vegetating thing that its mother had named Albert Sidney Bedlow before they had taken it away, hooked it up for a lifetime of intravenous feeding, and added it to the schedule of cleaning up filth and washing, and all the things they do for human beings who can do nothing whatever for themselves. But Irma Bedlow couldn't let it go at that. The state is equipped, albeit poorly, for this kind of thing. It happens. You let the thing go, and they see to it, and one day, usually not long hence, it dies of pneumonia or a virus, or one of the myriad diseases that float and sift through the air of a place like that. This is the way these things are done, and all of us at the law have drawn up papers for things call "Baby So-and-so," sometimes, mercifully, without their parents' having laid eyes on them.

Irma Bedlow saw it otherwise. During that first year, while the Rambler franchise was bleeding to death, while Bedlow was going half crazy, she had spent most of her time up in Alexandria, a few miles from the hospital, at her cousin's. So that she could visit Albert Sidney every day.

She would go there, Bert told me—as Bedlow had told him—and sit in the drafty ward on a hard chair next to Albert Sidney's chipped institutional crib, with her rosary, praying to Jesus Christ that He would send down His grace on her baby, make him whole, and let her suffer in his place. She would kneel in the twilight beside the bed stiff with urine, and stinking of such excrement as a child might produce who has never tasted food, amidst the bedlam of chattering and choking and animal sounds from bed-ridden idiots, cretins, declining mongoloids, microcephalics, and assorted other exiles from the great altarpiece of Hieronymus Bosch. Somehow, the chief psychologist had told Howard, her praying upset the other inmates of the ward, and at last he had to forbid Irma coming more than once a month. He told her that the praying was out altogether.

After trying to change the chief psychologist's mind, and failing, Irma had come home. The franchise was gone by then, and they had a secondhand trailer parked in a run-down court where they got water, electricity, and gas from pipes in the ground and a sullen old man in a prewar De Soto station wagon picked up garbage once a week. She said the rosary there, and talked about Albert Sidney to her husband who, cursed now with freedom by the ruin of his affairs, doggedly looking for some kind of a job, had nothing much to do or think about but his wife's abstracted words and the son he had almost had. Indeed, did have, but had in such a way that the having was more terrible than the lack.

It had taken no time to get into liquor, which his wife never touched, she fasting and praying, determined that no small imperfection in herself should stay His hand who could set things right with Albert Sidney in the flash of a moment's passing.

—And in that line, Bert said,—she ain't...they...never been man and wife since then. You know what I mean?

—Ummm.

—And she runs off on him. Couple or three times a year. They always find her at the cousin's. At least till last year. Her cousin won't have her around any more. Seems Irma wanted her to fast for Albert Sidney, too. Wanted the cousin's whole family to do it, and there was words, and now she just takes a room at the tourist court by the hospital and tries to get in as often as that chief psychologist will let her. But no praying, he holds to that.

—What does Bedlow believe?

—Claims he believes she got Albert Sidney with some other man.

—No, I mean... does he believe in praying?

—Naw. Too honest, I guess. Says he don't hold with beads and saying the same thing over and over. Says God stands on His own feet, and expects the same of us. Says we ain't here to s... around. What's done is done.

—Do you think he wants a divorce?

—Could he get one...?

—Yes.

—Well, how do I know?

—You brought him here. He's not shopping for religious relics, is he?

Bert looked hurt. As if I were blaming him unfairly for some situation beyond his control or prevention.

—You want him in jail?

—No, I said.—I just don't know what to do about him. Where's he living?

—Got a cabin at the Bo-Peep Motel. Over off Veterans Highway. He puts in his time at the car lot and then goes to drinking and telling people his wife has done bastardized him.

—Why did he wait so long to come up with that line?

—It just come on him, what she must of done, he told me.

—That's right, Bedlow said, his voice raspy, aggressive.—I ain't educated or anything. I studies on it and after so long it come to me. I saw it wasn't *mine*, that... thing of hers. Look, how come she can't just get done mourning and say, well, that's how it falls out sometimes and I'm sorry as all hell, but you got to keep going. That's what your ordinary woman would say, ain't it?

He had come to the kitchen where Bert and I were standing, his face still wet with tears. He came in talking, and the flow went on as if he were as compulsive with his tongue as he was with a bottle. The words tumbled out so fast that you felt he must have practiced, this country man, to speak so rapidly, to say so much.

—But no. I tell you what: she's mourning for what she done to that...thing's real father, that's what she's been doing. He likely lives in Alex, and she can't get over what she done him when she got that...thing. And I tell you this, I said, look, honey, don't give it no name, 'cause if you give it a name, you're gonna think that name over and over and make like it was the name of a person and it ain't, and it'll ruin us just as sure as creaking hell. And she went and named it my father's name, who got it after Albert Sidney Johnston at Shiloh...look, I ain't laid a hand on that woman in God knows how many years, I tell you that. So you see, that's what these trips is about. She goes up and begs his pardon for not giving him a fine boy like he wanted, and she goes to see...the thing, and mourns...and g......t to hell, I got to get shut of this...whole *thing*.

It came in a rush, as if, even talking, saying more words in the space of a moment than he had ever said before, Bedlow was enlarging, perfecting his suspicions—no, his certainty of what had been done to him.

We were silent for a moment.

—Well, it's hard, Bert said at last.

—Hard, Bedlow glared at him as if Bert had insulted him. —You don't even know hard...

—All right, I said.—We'll go down to the office in the morning and draw up and file.

—Huh?

—We'll file for legal separation. Will your wife contest it?

—Huh?

—I'm going to get you what you want. Will your wife go along?

—Well, I don't know. She don't...think about...things. If you was to tell her, I don't know.

Bert looked at him, his large dark face settled and serious. —That woman's a...Catholic, he said at last, and Bedlow stared back at him as if he had named a new name, and things needed thinking again.

A little while later they left, with Bedlow promising me and promising Bertram Bijou that he'd be in my office the next morning. For a long time after I closed the door behind them, I sat looking at the empty whiskey glasses and considered the course of living in the material world. Then I went and fixed me a shaker of martinis, and became quickly wiser. I considered that it was time to take Zeno seriously, give over the illusion of motion, of sequence. There are only a few moments in any life and when they arrive, they are fixed forever and we play through them, pretending to go on, but coming back to them over and over, again and again. If it is true that we can only approach a place but never reach it as the Philosopher claims, it must be corollary that we may almost leave a moment, but never quite. And so, as Dr. Freud so clearly saw, one moment, one vision, one thing come upon us, becomes the whole time and single theme of all we will ever do or know. We are invaded by our own one thing, and going on is a dream we have while lying still.

I thought, too, mixing one last shaker, that of the little wisdom in this failing age, Alcoholics Anonymous must possess more than its share. I am an alcoholic, they say. I have not had a drink in nine years, but I am an alcoholic, and the shadow, the motif of my living is liquor bubbling into a glass over and over, again and again. That is all I really want, and I will never have it again because I will not take it, and I know that I will never really know why not.

—It's bedtime, Joan said, taking my drink and sipping it.

—What did they want?

—A man wants a divorce because nine years ago his wife had a feebleminded baby. He says it's not his. Wants me to claim adultery and unclaim the child.

—Nice man.

—Actually, I began. Then no. Bedlow did not seem a nice man or not a nice man. He seemed a driven man, outside whatever might be his element. So I said that.

—Who isn't, Joan sniffed. She is not the soul of charity at two-thirty in the morning.

—What? Isn't what?

—Driven. Out of her...his...element?

I looked at her. Is it the commonest of things for men in their forties to consider whether their women are satisfied? Is it a sign of the spirit's collapse when you wonder how and with whom she spends her days? What is the term for less than suspicion: a tiny circlet of thought that touches your mind at lunch with clients or on the way to the office, almost enough to make you turn back home, and then disappears like smoke when you try to fix it, search for a word or an act that might have stirred it to life?

—Are you...driven, I asked much too casually.

—Me? No, she sighed, kissing me.—I'm different, she said. Was she too casual, too?

—Bedlow isn't different. I think he wants it all never to have happened. He had a little car franchise and a pregnant wife ten years ago. Clover. He had it made. Then it all went away.

Joan lit a cigarette, crossed her legs and sat down on the floor with my drink. Her wrapper fell open, and I saw the shadow of her breasts.—It always goes away. If you know anything, you know that. Hang on as long as you can. 'Cause it's going away. If you know anything...

I looked at her as she talked. She was as beautiful as the first time I had seen her. It was an article of faith: nothing had changed. Her body was still as soft and warm in my arms, and I wait for summer to see her in a bathing suit, and to see her take it off, water running out of her blond hair, between her breasts that I love better than whatever it is that I love next best.

—Sometimes it doesn't go away, I said. Ponderously, I'm sure.

She cocked her head, almost said something, and sipped the drink instead.

What made me think then of the pictures there in the parlor? I went over them in the silence, the flush of gin, remembering where and when we had bought each one. That one in San Francisco, in a Japanese gallery, I thinking that I would not like it long, but thinking too that it didn't matter, since we were at the end of a long difficult case with a fee to match. So if I didn't like it later, well...

And the Danish ship, painted on wood in the seventeenth century. I still liked it very much. But why did I think of these things? Was it that they stood on the walls, amidst our lives, adding some measure of substance and solidity to them, making it seem that the convention of living together, holding lovely things in common, added reality to the lives themselves. Then, or was it later, I saw us sitting not in a Roman garden in Britain, but in a battered house trailer in imperial America, the walls overspread with invisible pictures in the image of a baby's twisted unfinished face. And how would that be? How would we do then?

Joan smiled, lightly sardonic.—Ignore it, and it'll go away.

—Was there...something I was supposed to do, I asked.

The smile deepened, then faded.—Not a thing, she said.

II

The next morning, a will was made, two houses changed hands, a corporation, closely held, was born, seven suits were filed and a deposition was taken from a whore who claimed that her right of privacy was invaded when the vice squad caught her performing an act against nature on one of their members in a French Quarter alley. Howard Bedlow did not turn up. Joan called just after lunch.

—I think I'll go over to the beach house for a day or two, she said, her voice flat and uncommunicative as only a woman's can be.

I guess there was a long pause. It crossed my mind that once I had wanted to be a musician, perhaps even learn to compose.—I can't get off till the day after tomorrow, I said, knowing that my words were inapposite to anything she might have in mind.—I could come Friday.

—That would be nice.

—Are you . . . taking the children?

—Louise will take care of them.

—You'll be . . . by yourself?

A pause on her side this time.

—Yes. Sometimes . . . things get out of hand.

—Anything you want to talk about?

She laughed.—You're the talker in the family.

—And you're what? The actor. Or the thinker?

—That's it. I don't know.

My voice went cold then. I couldn't help it.—Let me know if you figure it out. Then I hung up. And thought at once that I shouldn't have and yet glad of the miniscule gesture because however puny, it was an act, and acts in law are almost always merely words. I live in a storm of words: words substituting for actions, words to evade actions, words hinting of actions, words pretending actions. I looked down at the deposition on my desk and wondered if they had caught the whore *talking* to the vice squad man in the alley. Give her ten years: the utterance of words is an act against nature, an authentic act against nature. I had read somewhere that in Chicago they have opened establishments wherein neither massage nor sex is offered: only a woman who, for a sum certain in money, will talk to you. She will say anything you want her to say: filth, word-pictures of every possible abomination, fantasies of domination and degradation, sadistic orgies strewn out in detail, oaths, descriptions of rape and castration. For a few dollars you can be told how you molested a small child, how you have murdered your parents and covered the carcasses with excrement, assisted in the gang rape of your second grade teacher. All words.

The authentic crime against nature has finally arrived. It is available somewhere in Chicago. There is no penalty, for after all, it is protected by the first amendment. Scoff on, Voltaire, Rousseau, scoff on.

My secretary, who would like to speak filth to me, buzzed.

—Mr. Bijou.

—Good. Send him in.

—On the phone.

Bert sounded far away.—You ain't seen Howard, have you?

—No, I said.—Have you?

—Drunk somewhere. Called coughing and moaning something about a plot to shame him. Talking like last night. I think you ought to see Irma. You're supposed to seek reconciliation, ain't you?

—I think you're ripe for law school, Bert. Yes, that's what they say do.

—Well, he said.—Lemme see what I can do.

I was afraid of that. When I got home there was a note from Louise, the childrens' nurse. She had taken them to her place up in Livingston Parish for a day or two. They would like that. The house was deserted, and I liked that. Not really. I wondered what a fast trip to the Gulf coast would turn up, or a call to a friend of mine in Biloxi who specializes in that kind of thing. But worse, I wasn't sure I cared. Was it that I didn't love Joan anymore, that somewhere along the way I had become insulated against her acts? Could it be that the practice of law had slowly made me responsive only to words? Did I need to go to Chicago to feel real again?

I was restless and drank too many martinis and was involved so much in my own musings that time passed quickly. I played some Beethoven, God knows why. I am almost never so distraught that I enjoy spiritual posturing. Usually, his music makes me grin.

I tried very hard to reckon where I was and what I should do. I was in the twentieth century after Christ, and it felt all of that long since anything on earth had mattered. I was in a democratic empire called America, an officer of its courts, and surely a day in those courts is as a thousand years. I was an artisan in words, shaping destinies, allocating money and blame by my work. I was past the midpoint of my life and could not make out what it had meant so far.

Now amidst this time and place, I could do almost as I chose. Should it be the islands of the Pacific with a box of paints? To the Colorado mountains with a pack, beans, a guitar, pencils, and much paper? Or, like an anchorite, declare the longest of nonterminal hunger strikes, this one against God Almighty, hoping that public opinion forces Him to reveal that for which I was made and put in this place and time.

Or why not throw over these ambiguities, this wife doing whatever she might be doing on the coast of the Gulf, these anonymous children content with Louise up the country, contemplating chickens, ducks, and guinea-fowl. Begin again. Say every word you have ever said, to new people: hello, new woman, I love you. I have good teeth and most of my mind. I can do well on a good night in a happy bed. Hello, new colleagues, what do we do this time? Is this a trucking firm or a telephone exchange? What is the desiderata? Profit or prophecy?

Bert shook my arm.—Are you okay? You didn't answer the door.

I studied him for a moment, my head soft and uncentered. I was nicely drunk, but coming back.—Yeah, I said.—I'm fine. What have you got tonight?

—Huh? Listen, can I turn down that music?

—Sure.

He doused the Second Symphony, and I found I was relieved, could breathe more deeply.—I brought her, he said.—She's kinda spaced out, like the kids say.

He frowned, watched me.—You sure you're all right?

I smiled.—All I needed was some company, Bert.

He smiled back.—All right, fine. You're probably in the best kind of shape for Irma.

—Huh?

He looked at the empty martini pitcher.—Nothing. She's just...

His voice trailed off and I watched him drift out of my line of sight. In the foyer, I could hear his voice, soft and distant, as if he were talking to a child.

I sobered up. Yes, I have that power. I discovered it in law school. However drunk, I can gather back in the purposely loosed strands of personality or whatever of us liquor casts apart. It is as if one were never truly sober, and hence one could claim back from liquor what it had never truly loosed. Either drunkenness or sobriety is an illusion.

Irma Bedlow was a surprise. I had reckoned on a woman well gone from womanhood. One of those shapeless bun-haired middle-aged creatures wearing bifocals, smiling out from behind the secrecy of knowing that they are at last safe from any but the most psychotic menaces from unbalanced males. But it was not that way. If I had been dead drunk on the one hand, or shuffling up to the communion rail on the other, she would have turned me around.

She was vivid. Dark hair and eyes, a complexion almost pale, a lovely body made more so by the thoughtless pride with which she inhabited it. She sat down opposite me, and our eyes held for a long moment.

I am used to a certain deference from people who come to me in legal situations. God knows we have worked long and hard enough to establish the mandarin tradition of the law, that circle of mysteries that swallows up laymen and all they possess like a vast desert or a hidden sea. People come to the law on tiptoe, watching, wishing they could know which words, what expressions and turns of phrase are *the ones* which bear their fate. I have smiled remembering that those who claim or avoid the law with such awe have themselves in their collectivity created it. But they are so far apart from one another in the sleep of their present lives that they cannot remember what they did together when they were awake.

But Irma Bedlow looked at me as if she were the counselor, her dark eyes fixed on mine to hold me to whatever I might say. Would I lie, and put both our cases in jeopardy? Would I say the best I knew, or had I wandered so long amidst the stunted shrubs of language, making unnatural acts in the name of my law, that words had turned from stones with which to build into ropy clinging undergrowth in which to become enmeshed?

I asked her if she would have a drink. I was surprised when she said yes. Fasts for the sake of an idiot child, trying to get others to do it, praying on her knees to Jesus beside the bed of Albert Sidney who did not know about the prayers, and who could know about Jesus only through infused knowledge there within the mansions of his imbecility. But yes, she said, and I went to fix it.

Of course Bert followed me over to the bar.—I don't know. I think maybe I ought to take care of Howard and let *her* be your client.

—Don't do that, I said, and wondered why I'd said it.

—She's fine, Bert was saying, and I knew he meant nothing to do with her looks. He was not a carnal man, Bert. He was a social man. Once he had told me he wanted either to be mayor of Kenner or a comedian. He did not mean it humorously and I did not take it so. He was the least funny of men. Rather he understood with his nerves the pathos of living and would have liked to divert us from it with comedy. But it would not be so, and Bert would end up mayor trying to come to grips with our common anguish instead of belittling it.

—I never talked to anyone like her. You'll see.

I think then I envisioned the most beautiful and desirable Jehovah's Witness in the world. Would we try conclusions over Isaiah? I warn you, Irma, I know the Book and other books beyond number. I am a prince in the kingdom of words, and I have seen raw respect flushed up unwillingly in the eye of other lawmongers, and have had my work mentioned favorably in appellate decisions which, in their small way, rule all this land.

—Here you are, I said.

She smiled at me as if I were a child who had brought his mother a cool drink unasked.

—Howard came to see you, she said, sipping the martini as if gin bruised with vermouth were her common fare.—Can you help me...help him?

—He wants a divorce, I said, confused, trying to get things in focus.

—No, she said. Not aggressively, only firmly. Her information was better than mine. I have used the same tone of voice with other attorneys many times. When you know, you know.

—He only wants it over with, done with. That's what he wants.

Bert nodded. He had heard this before. There goes Bert's value as a checkpoint with reality. He believes her. Lordy.

—You mean...the marriage?

—No, not that. He knows what I know. If it *was* a marriage, you can't make it be over. You can only desert it. He wouldn't do that.

I shrugged, noticing that she had made no use of her beauty at all so far. She did not disguise it or deny it. She allowed it to exist and simply ignored it. Her femininity washed over me, and yet I knew that it was not directed toward me. It had some other focus, and she saw me as a moment, a crossing in her life, an occasion to stop and turn back for an instant before going on. I wondered what I would be doing for her.

—He *says* he wants a divorce.

She looked down at her drink. Her lashes were incredibly long, though it was obvious she used no makeup at all. Her lips were deep red, a color not used in lipsticks since the forties. I understood why Bedlow drank. Nine years with a beautiful woman you love and cannot touch. Is that your best idea?

—He told you... I'd been unfaithful.

Bert was shaking his head, blushing. Not negating what Howard had said, or deprecating it.

—He said that, I told her.

—And that our baby... that Albert Sidney wasn't... his?

—Yes, I said. Bert looked as if he would cry from shame.

She had not looked up while we talked. Her eyes stayed down, and while I waited, I heard the Beethoven tape, turned down but not off, running out at the end of the—Appassionata. It was a good moment to get up and change to something decent. I found a Vivaldi Chamber Mass, and the singers were very happy. The music was for God in the first instance, not for the spirit of fraternity or Napoleon or some other rubbish.

—What else, she asked across the room. I flipped the tape on, and eighteenth-century Venice came at us from four sides. I cut back the volume.

—He said you... hadn't been man and wife for nine years.

—All right.

I walked back and sat down again. I felt peculiar, neither drunk nor sober, so I poured another one. The first I'd had since they came.—Howard didn't seem to think so. He said... you wouldn't let him touch you.

She raised her eyes then. Not angrily, only that same firmness again.—That's not true, she said, no, whispered, and Bert nodded as though he had been an abiding presence in the marriage chamber for all those nine long years. He could contain himself no more. He fumbled in his coat pocket and handed me a crumpled and folded sheet of paper. It was a notice from American Motors canceling Howard Bedlow's franchise. Much boilerplate saying he hadn't delivered and so on. Enclosed find copy of agency contract with relevant revocation clauses underlined. Arrangements will be made for stock on hand, etc.

It was dated 9 May 1966. Bert was watching me. I nodded.

—Eight years ago, I said.

—Not ten, Bert was going on.—You see...

—He lost the business . . . six months after . . . the . . . Albert Sidney.
We sat looking at the paper.

—I never denied him, Irma was saying.—After the baby . . . he
couldn't. At first, we didn't think of it. What had we done? What
had gone wrong? What were we . . . supposed to do? Was there
something we were supposed to do?

—Genes were wrong . . . hormones, who knows, I said.

Irma smiled at me. Her eyes were black, not brown.—Do you
believe that?

—Sure, I said, startled as one must be when he has uttered what
passes for a common truth and it is questioned.—What else?

—Nothing, she said.—It's only . . .

She and Bert were both staring at me as if I had missed
something. Then Irma leaned forward.—Will you go somewhere
with me?

I was thinking of the Gulf coast, staring down at the face of my
watch. It was almost one-thirty. There was a moon and the tide
was in, and the moon would be rolling through soft beds of cloud.

—Yes, I said.—Yes I will. Yes.

III

It was early in the morning when we reached Alexandria. The
bus trip had been long and strange. We had talked about east
Texas where Irma had grown up. Her mother had been from
Evangeline Parish, her father a tool-pusher in the Kilgore fields
until he lost both hands to a wild length of chain. She had been
keeping things together working as a waitress when she met
Howard.

On the bus, as if planted there, had been a huge black woman
with a little boy whose head was tiny and pointed. It was so
distorted that his eyes were pulled almost vertical. He made
inarticulate noises and rooted about on the floor of the bus. The
other passengers tried to ignore him, but the stench was very bad,
and his mother took him to an empty seat in back and changed
him several times. Irma helped once. The woman had been loud,
aggressive, unfriendly when Irma approached her, but Irma
whispered something, and the woman began to cry, her sobs loud
and terrible. When they had gotten the child cleaned up, the
black woman put her arms around Irma and kissed her.

—I tried hard as I could, miss, but I can't manage . . . oh, sweet

Jesus knows I wisht I was dead first. But I can't manage the other four ... I *got* to ...

The two of them sat together on the rear seat for a long time, holding hands, talking so softly that I couldn't hear. Once, the boy crawled up and stopped at my seat. He looked up at me like some invertebrate given the power to be quizzical. I wondered which of us was in hell. He must have been about twelve years old.

In the station, Irma made a phone call while I had coffee. People moved through the twilit terminal, meeting, parting. One elderly woman in a thin print dress thirty years out of date even among country people kissed a young man in an army uniform good-bye. Her lips trembled as he shouldered his dufflebag and moved away.—Stop, she cried out, and then realized that he could not stop, because the dispatcher was calling the Houston bus. —Have you ... forgotten anything? The soldier paused, smiled, and shook his head. Then he vanished behind some people trying to gather up clothes which had fallen from a cardboard suitcase with a broken clasp. Somewhere a small child cried as if it had awakened to find itself suddenly, utterly lost.

Irma came back and drank her coffee, and when we walked outside it was daylight in Alexandria, even as on the Gulf coast. An old station wagon with a broken muffler pulled up, and a thin man wearing glasses got out and kissed Irma as if it were a ritual and shook hands with me in that peculiar limp and diffident way of country people meeting someone from the city who might represent threat or advantage.

We drove for twenty minutes or so, and slowed down in front of a small white frame place on a blacktop road not quite in or out of town. The yard was large and littered with wrecked and cannibalized autos. The metal bones of an old Hudson canted into the rubble of a '42 Ford convertible. Super deluxe. There was a shed which must have been an enlarged garage. Inside I could see tools, a lathe, work benches. A young man in overalls without a shirt looked out at us and waved casually. He had a piece of drive shaft in his hand. Chickens ambled stupidly in the grassless yard, pecking at oil patches and clumps of rust.

We had eggs and sausage and biscuits and talked quietly. They were not curious about me. They had seen a great deal during the years and there was nothing to be had from curiosity. You come to learn that things have to be taken as they come and it is no use to probe the gestations of tomorrows before they come. There is very little you can do to prepare.

It turned out there had been no quarrel between Irma and her sister's family. Her sister, plain as Irma was beautiful, who wore thick glasses and walked slowly because of her varicose veins, talked almost without expression, but with some lingering touch of her mother's French accent. She talked on as if she had saved everything she had seen and come to know, saved it all in exhaustive detail, knowing that someone would one day come for her report.

—It wasn't never any quarrel, and Howard had got to know better. Oh, we fussed, sure. My daddy always favored Irma and so I used to take after her over anything, you know. Jesus spare me, I guess I hated my own little sister. Till the baby come, and the Lord lifted the scales from my eyes. I dreamed He come down just for me. He looked like Mr. Denver, the station agent down to the L & N depot, and He said, "Elenor, I had enough stuff out of you, you hear? You see Albert Sidney? You satisfied now? Huh? Is that enough for you? You tell me that, 'cause I got to be getting on. I don't make nobody more beautiful or more smart or anything in this world, but I do sometimes take away their looks or ruin their minds or put blindness on 'em, or send 'em a trouble to break their hearts. Don't ask why 'cause it's not for you to know, but that's what I do. Now what else you want for Irma, huh?"

Tears were flowing down Elenor's face now, but her expression didn't change.—So I saw it was my doing, and I begged Him to set it right, told Him to strike me dead and set it right with that helpless baby. But He just shook His head and pushed up his sleeves like he could hear a through-freight coming. "It's not how it's done. It ain't like changing your mind about a hat or a new dress. You see that?"

—Well, I didn't, but what could I say? I said yes, and he started off and the place where we was began getting kind of fuzzy, then He turned and looked back at me and smiled. "How you know it *ain't* all right with Albert Sidney," he asked. And I saw then that He loved me after all. Then, when I could hardly see Him, I heard Him say, "Anything you forgot, Elly," but I never said nothing at all, only crossed myself the way Momma used to do.

Elenor touched her sister's shoulder shyly. Irma was watching me, something close to a smile on her lips.—Well, Elenor said,

—We've prayed together since then, ain't we, hon? Irma took her sister's hand and pressed it against her cheek.

—We been close since then, Charlie, Elenor's husband said.
—Done us all good. Except for poor Howard.

It seemed Howard had hardened his heart from the first. Charlie had worked for him in the Rambler franchise, manager of the service department. One day they had had words and Charlie quit, left New Orleans which was a plague to him anyway, and set up this little backyard place in Alex.

Why the fight, I asked Charlie. He was getting up to go out to work.—Never mind that, he said.—It...didn't have nothing to do with...this.

Elenor watched him go.—Yes it did, she began.

—Elenor, Irma stopped her.—Maybe you ought not...Charlie's...

Elenor was wiping her cheeks with her apron.—This man's a lawyer, ain't he? He knows what's right and wrong.

I winced and felt tired all at once, but you cannot ask for a pitcher of martinis at seven-thirty in the morning in a Louisiana country house. That was the extent of my knowledge of right and wrong.

—A couple of months after Albert Sidney was born, I was at their place, Elenor went on.—Trying to help out. I was making the beds when Howard come in. It was early, but Howard was drunk and he talked funny, and before I knew, he pulled me down on the bed, and...I couldn't scream, I couldn't. Irma had the baby in the kitchen...and he couldn't. He tried to...make me...help him, but he couldn't anyhow. And I told Charlie, because a man ought to know. And they had words, and after that Charlie whipped him, and we moved up here...

Elenor sat looking out of the window where the sun was beginning to show over the trees.—And we come on up here.

Irma looked at her sister tenderly.—Elly we got to go on over to the hospital now.

As we reached the door, Elenor called out.—Irma...

—Yes...?

—Honey, you know how much I love you, don't you?

—I always did know, silly. You were the one didn't know.

We took the old station wagon and huffed slowly out of the yard. Charlie waved at us and his eyes followed us out of sight down the blacktop.

IV

Irma was smiling at me as we coughed along the road.—I feel kind of good, she said.

—I'm glad. Why?

—Like some kind of washday. It's long and hard, but comes the end, and you've got everything hanging out in the fresh air. Clean.

—It'll be dirty again, I said, and wished I could swallow the words almost before they were out.

Her hand touched my arm, and I almost lost control of the car. I kept my eyes on the road to Pineville. I was here to help her, not the other way around. There was too much contact between us already, too much emptiness in me, and what the hell I was doing halfway up the state with the wife of a man who could make out a showing that he was my client was more than I could figure out. Something to do with the Gulf.—There's another washday coming, she whispered, her lips close to my ear.

Will I be ready for washday, I wondered. Lord, how is it that we get ready for washday?

The Louisiana State Hospital is divided into several parts. There is one section for the criminally insane, and another for the feebleminded. This second section is, in turn, divided into what are called "tidy" and "untidy" wards. The difference is vast in terms of logistics and care. The difference in the moral realm is simply that between the seventh and the first circles. Hell is where we are.

Dr. Tumulty met us outside his office. He was a small man with a large nose and glasses which looked rather like those you can buy in a novelty shop—outsized nose attached. Behind the glasses, his eyes were weak and watery. His mouth was very small, and his hair thin, the color of corn shucks. I remember wondering then, at the start of our visit, whether one of the inmates had been promoted. It was a very bad idea, but only one of many.

—Hello, Irma, he said. He did not seem unhappy to see her.

—Hello, Monte, she said.

—He had a little respiratory trouble last week. It seems cleared up now.

Irma introduced us and Dr. Tumulty studied me quizzically.—A lawyer...?

—Counselor, she said.—A good listener. Do you have time to show him around?

He looked at me, Charon sizing up a strange passenger, one who it seemed would be making a round trip.—Sure, all right. You coming?

—No, Irma said softly.—You can bring him to me afterward.

So Dr. Tumulty took me through the wards alone. I will not say everything I saw. There were mysteries in that initiation that will not go down into words. It is all the soul is worth and more to say less than all when you have come back from that place where, if only they knew, what men live and do asleep is done waking and in truth each endless day.

Yes, there were extreme cases of mongolism, cretins and imbeciles, dwarfs and things with enormous heads and bulging eyes, ears like tubes, mouths placed on the sides of their heads. There was an albino without nose or eyes or lips, and it sat in a chair, teeth exposed in a grin that could not be erased, its hands making a series of extremely complicated gestures over and over again, each lengthy sequence a perfect reproduction of the preceding one. The gestures were perfectly symmetrical and the repetition exact and made without pause, a formalism of mindlessness worthy of a Balinese dancer or a penance—performance of a secret prayer—played out before the catatonic admiration of three small blacks who sat on the floor before the albino watching its art with a concentration unknown among those who imagine themselves without defect.

This was the tidy ward, and all these inventions of a Bosch whose medium is flesh wore coveralls of dark gray cloth with a name patch on the left breast. This is Paul whose tongue, abnormally long and almost black and dry, hangs down his chin, and that, the hairless one with the enormous head and tiny face, who coughs and pets a filthy toy elephant, that is Larry. The dead-white one, the maker of rituals, is Anthony. Watching him are Edward and Joseph and Michael, microcephalics all, looking almost identical in their shared malady.

—Does... Anthony, I began.

—All day. Every day, Dr. Tumulty said.—And the others watch. We give him tranquilizers at night. It used to be... all night, too.

In another ward they kept the females. It was much the same

there, except that wandering from one chair to another, watching the others, was a young girl, perhaps sixteen. She would have been pretty—no, she was pretty, despite the gray coverall and the pallor of her skin.—Hello, doctor, she said. Her voice sounded as if it had been recorded—cracked and scratchy. But her body seemed sound, her face normal except for small patches of what looked like eczema on her face. That, and her eyes were a little out of focus. She was carrying a small book covered in imitation red leather. My Diary, it said on the cover.

—Does she belong here, I asked Tumulty.

He nodded.—She's been here over a year.

The girl cuddled against him, and I could see that she was trying to press her breasts against him. Her hand wandered down toward his leg. He took her hand gently and stroked her hair.

—Hello, doctor, she croaked again.—Hi, Nancy, he answered.

—Are you keeping up your diary?

She smiled.—For home. Hello, doctor.

—For home, sure, he said, and sat her down in a chair opposite an ancient television locked in a wire cage and tuned, I remember, to "Underdog". She seemed to lose interest in us, to find her way quickly into the role of Sweet Polly, awaiting the inevitable rescue. Around her on the floor were scattered others of the less desperate cases. They watched the animated comedy on the snow-flecked, badly focused screen with absolute concentration. As we moved on, I heard Nancy whisper,—There's no need to fear...

—Congenital syphilis, Tumulty said.—It incubates for years, sometimes. She was in high school. Now she's here. It's easier for her now than at first. Most of her mind is gone. In a year she'll be dead.

He paused by a barred window, and looked out on the rolling Louisiana countryside beyond the distant fence.—About graduation time.

—There's no treatment...?

—The cure is dying.

What I can remember of the untidy wards is fragmentary. The stench was very bad, the sounds were nonhuman, and the inmates, divided by sex, were naked in large concrete rooms, sitting on the damp floors, unable to control their bodily functions, obese mostly, and utterly asexual with tiny misshappen heads. There were benches along the sides of the concrete rooms, and the floors sloped down to a central caged drain in the center. One of the things—I mean inmates—was down trying slowly, in a fashion almost reptilian, to lick up filthy moisture from the drain. Another was chewing on a plastic bracelet by which it was identified. Most of the rest, young and older, sat on the benches or the floor staring at nothing, blubbering once in a while, scratching occasionally.

—Once, Dr. Tumulty said thoughtfully,—a legislator came. A budgetary inspection. We didn't get any more money. But he complained that we identified the untidy patients by number. He came and saw everything, and that's...what bothered him.

By then we were outside again, walking in the cool Louisiana summer morning. We had been inside less than an hour. I had thought it longer.

—It's the same everywhere. Massachusetts, Wyoming, Texas. Don't think badly of us. There's no money, no personnel, and even if there were...

—Then you could only...cover it.

—Cosmetics, yes. I've been in this work for eighteen years. I've never forgotten anything I saw. Not anything. You know what I think? What I really *know?*

—...?

Tumulty paused and rubbed his hands together. He shivered a little, that sudden inexplicable thrill of cold inside that has no relationship to the temperature in the world, that represents, according to the old story, someone walking across the ground where your grave will one day be. A mockingbird flashed past us, a dark blur of gray, touched with the white of its wings. Tumulty started to say something, then shrugged and pointed at a small building a little way off.

—They're over there. One of the attendants will show you.

He looked from one building to another, shaking his head.

—There's so much to do. So many of them...

—Yes, I said.—Thank you. Then I began walking toward the building he had indicated.

—Do...whatever you can...for her, Dr. Tumulty called after me.—I wish...

I turned back toward him. We stood perhaps thirty yards apart then.—Was there...something else you wanted to say, I asked.

He looked at me for a long moment, then away.—No, he said. —Nothing.

I stood there as he walked back into the clutter of central

buildings, and finally vanished into one of them. Then, before I walked back to join Irma, I found a bench under an old magnolia and sat down for a few minutes. It was on the way to becoming warm now, and the sun's softness and the morning breeze were both going rapidly. The sky was absolutely clear, and by noon it would be very hot indeed. A few people were moving across the grounds. A nurse carrying something on a tray, two attendants talking animatedly to each other, one gesturing madly. Another attendant was herding a patient toward the medical building. It was a black inmate, male or female I could not say, since all the patients' heads were close-cropped for hygienic purposes, and the coverall obscured any other sign of sex. It staggered from one side of the cinder path to the other, swaying as if it were negotiating the deck of a ship in heavy weather out on the Gulf. Its arms flailed, seeking a balance it could never attain, and its eyes seemed to be seeking some point of reference in a world awash. But there was no point, the trees whirling and the buildings losing their way, and so the thing looked skyward, squinted terribly at the sun, pointed upward toward that brazen glory, almost fell down, its contorted black face now fixed undeviatingly toward that burning place in the sky which did not shift and whirl. But the attendant took its shoulder and urged it along, since it could not make its way on earth staring into the sky.

As it passed by my bench, it saw me, gestured at me, leaned in my direction amidst its stumblings, its dark face twinkling with sweat.

—No, Hollis, I heard the attendant say as the thing and I exchanged a long glance amidst the swirling trees, the spinning buildings, out there on the stormy Gulf. Then it grinned, its white teeth sparkling, its eyes almost pulled shut from the effort of grimace, its twisted fingers spieling a language both of us could grasp.

—Come on, Hollis, the attendant said impatiently, and the thing reared its head and turned away. No more time for me. It took a step or two, fell, and rolled in the grass, grunting, making sounds like I had never heard.—Hollis, I swear to God, the attendant said mildly, and helped the messenger to its feet once more.

The nurse in the building Tumulty had pointed out looked at me questioningly.—I'm looking for . . . Mrs. Bedlow.

—You'll have to wait . . . she began, and then her expression changed.—Oh, you must be the one. I knew I'd forgotten something. All right, straight back and to the left. Ward Three.

I walked down a long corridor with lights on the ceiling, each behind its wire cover. I wondered if Hollis might have been the reason for the precaution. Had he or she or it once leaped upward at the light, clawing, grasping, attempting to touch the sun? The walls were covered with an ugly pale yellow enamel which had begun peeling long ago, and the smell of cheap pine-scented deodorizer did not cover the deep ingrained stench of urine, much older than the blistered paint. Ward Three was a narrow dormitory filled with small beds. My eyes scanned the beds and I almost turned back, ready for the untidy wards again. Because here were the small children—what had been intended as children.

Down almost at the end of the ward, I saw Irma. She was seated in a visitor's chair, and in her arms was a child with a head larger than hers. It was gesticulating frantically, and I could hear its sounds the length of the ward. She held it close and whispered to it, kissed it, held it close, and as she drew it to her, the sounds became almost frantic. They were not human sounds. They were Hollis' sounds, and as I walked the length of the ward, I thought I knew what Tumulty had been about to say before he had thought better of it.

—Hello, Irma said. The child in her arms paused in its snufflings and looked up at me from huge unfocused eyes. Its tongue stood out, and it appeared that its lower jaw was congenitally dislocated. Saliva ran down the flap of flesh where you and I have lips, and Irma paid no mind as it dripped on her dress. It would have been pointless to wipe the child's mouth because the flow did not stop, nor did the discharge from its bulging, unblinking eyes. I looked at Irma. Her smile was genuine.

—This is... I began.

—Albert Sidney, she finished.—Oh, no. I wish it were. This is Barry. Say hello.

The child grunted and buried its head in her lap, sliding down to the floor and crawling behind her chair.

—You... wish...?

—This is Albert Sidney, she said, turning to the bed next to her chair.

He lay there motionless, the sheet drawn up to what might have been the region of his chin. His head was very large, and bulged out to one side in a way that I would never have supposed could support life. Where his eyes should have been, two blank white surfaces of solid cataract seemed to float lidless and intent. He had no nose, only a small hole surgically created, I think, and ringed with discharge. His mouth was a slash in the right side of his cheek, at least two inches over and up from where mouths belong. Irma stepped over beside him, and as she reached down and kissed him, rearranged the sheets, I saw one of his hands. It was a fingerless club of flesh dotted almost randomly with bits of fingernail.

I closed my eyes and then looked once more. I saw again what I must have seen at first and ignored, the thing I had come to see. On Albert Sidney's deformed and earless head, almost covering the awful disarray of his humanity, he had a wealth of reddish golden hair, rich and curly, proper aureole of a Celtic deity. Or a surfing king.

V

We had dinner at some anonymous restaurant in Alexandria, and then found a room at a motel not far from Pineville. I had bought a bottle of whiskey. Inside, I filled a glass after peeling away its sticky plastic cover that pretended to guard it from the world for my better health.

—Should I have brought you, Irma asked, sitting down on the bed.

—Yes, I said.—Sure. Nobody should...nobody ought to be shielded from this.

—But it...hasn't got anything to do with...us. What Howard wants to do, does it?

—No, I said.—I don't think so.

—Howard was all right. If things had gone...the way they do mostly. He wasn't...isn't...a weak man. He's brave, and he used to work...sometimes sixteen hours a day. He was very...steady. Do you know, I loved him...

I poured her a drink.—Sometimes, I said, and heard that my voice was unsteady.—None of us know...what we can...stand.

—If Howard had had just any kind of belief...but...

—...He just had himself...?

—Just that. He...his two hands and a strong back, and he was quick with figures. He always...came out...

—...ahead.

She breathed deeply, and sipped the whiskey.—Every time. He...liked hard times. To work his way through. You couldn't stop him. And very honest. An honest man.

I finished the glass and poured another one. I couldn't get rid of the smells and the images. The whiskey was doing no good. It would only dull my senses prospectively. The smells and the images were inside for keeps.

—He's not honest about...

—Albert Sidney? No, but I...it doesn't matter. I release him of that. Which is why...

—You want me to go ahead with the divorce?

—I think. We can't help each other, don't you see?

—I see that. But...what will you do?

Irma laughed and slipped off her shoes, curled her feet under her. Somewhere back in the mechanical reaches of my mind, where I was listening to Vivaldi and watching a thin British rain fall into my garden, neither happy nor sad, preserved by my indifference from the Gulf, I saw that she was very beautiful and that she cared for me, had brought me to Alexandria as much for myself as for her sake, though she did not know it.

—...do what needs to be done for the baby, she was saying.

—I've asked for strength to do the best...thing.

—What do you want me to do?

—About the divorce? I don't know about...the legal stuff. I want to...how do you say it...? Not to contest it?

—There's a way. When the other person makes life insupport-able...

Irma looked at me strangely, as if I were not understanding.

—No, no. The other...what he says.

—Adultery?

—And the rest. About Albert Sidney...

—No. You can't...

—Why can't I? I told you, Howard is all right. I mean, he could be all right. I want to let him go. Can't you say some way or other what he claims is true?

I set my glass down.—In the pleadings. You can always accept what he says in your...answer.

—Pleadings?

—That's what they call...what we file in a suit. But I can't state an outright...lie...

—But you're his counsel. You have to say what he wants you to say.

—No, only in good faith. The Code of Civil Practice...if I pleaded a lie...anyhow, Jesus, after all this...I couldn't...Plead adultery...? No way.

—Yes, Irma said firmly, lovingly. She rose from the bed and came to me.

—Yes, she whispered.—You'll be able to.

VI

The next evening the plane was late getting into New Orleans. There was a storm line along the Gulf, a series of separate systems, thin monotonous driving rain that fell all over the city and the southern part of the state. The house was cool and humid when I got home, and my head hurt. The house was empty, and that was all right. I had a bowl of soup and turned on something very beautiful. *La Stravaganza.* As I listened, I thought of that strange medieval custom of putting the mad and the demented on a boat, and keeping it moving from one port to another. A ship full of lunacy and witlessness and rage and subhumanity with no destination in view. *Furiosi,* the mad were called. What did they call those who came into this world like Irma's baby, scarce half made up? Those driven beyond the human by the world were given names and a status. But what of those who came damaged from the first? Did even the wisdom of the Church have no name for those who did not scream or curse or style themselves Emperor Frederic II or Gregory come again? What of those with bulbous heads and protruding tongues and those who stared all day at the blazing sun, all night at the cool distant moon? I listened and drank, and opened the door onto the patio so that the music was leavened with the sound of the falling rain.

It was early the next morning when Bert called me at home. He did not bother apologizing. I think he knew that we were both too much in it now. The amenities are for before. Or afterward.

—Listen, you're back.

—Yes.

—I got Howard straightened up. You want to talk to him?

—What's he saying?

—Well, he's cleared up, you see? I got him to shower and drink a pot of coffee. It ain't what he says is different, but he *is* himself and he wants to get them papers started. You know? You want to drop by Bo-Peep for a minute?

—No, I said,—but I will. I want to talk to that stupid bastard.

—Ah, Bert said slowly.—Un-huh. Well, fine, counselor. It's cabin 10. On the street to the right as you come in. Can't miss it.

I thought somebody ought to take a baseball bat and use it on Howard Bedlow until he came to understand. I was very tight about this thing now, no distance at all. I had thought about other things only once since I had been back. When a little phrase of Vivaldi's had shimmered like a waterfall, and, still drunk, I had followed that billow down to the Gulf in my mind.

There were fantasies, of course. In one, I took Irma away. We left New Orleans and headed across America toward California, and she was quickly pregnant. The child was whole and healthy and strong, and what had befallen each of us back in Louisiana faded and receded faster and faster, became of smaller and smaller concern until we found ourselves in a place near the Russian River, above the glut and spew of people down below.

Acres apart and miles away, we had a tiny place carved from the natural wood of the hills. We labored under the sun and scarcely talked, and what there was, was ours. She would stand near a forest pool, nude, our child in her arms, and the rest was all forgotten as I watched them there, glistening, with beads of fresh water standing on their skin, the way things ought to be, under the sun.

Then I was driving toward Metairie amidst the dust and squalor of Airline Highway. Filling stations, hamburger joints, cut-rate liquor, tacos, wholesale carpeting, rent-a-car, people driving a little above the speed limit, sealed in air-conditioned cars, others standing at bus stops staring vacantly, some gesticulating in repetitive patterns, trying to be understood. No sign of life anywhere.

The sign above the Bo-Peep Motel pictured a girl in a bonnet with a shepherd's crook and a vast crinoline skirt. In her lap she held what looked from a distance like a child. Close, you could see that it was intended to be a lamb curled in her arms, eyes closed, hoofs tucked into its fleece, peacefully asleep. Bo-Peep's face, outlined in neon tubing, had been painted once, but most of the paint had chipped away, and now, during the day, she wore a faded leer of unparalleled perversity, red lips and china blue eyes flawed by missing chips of color.

Bert sat in a chair outside the door. He was in uniform. His car was parked in front of cabin 10. The door was open, and just inside Howard Bedlow sat in an identical chair, staring out like a prisoner who knows there must be bars even though he cannot see them. He leaned forward, hands hanging down before him, and even from a distance he looked much older than I had remembered him.

Bert walked out as I parked.—How was the trip?

We stared at each other.—A revelation, I said.—He's sober?

—Oh, yeah. He had a little trouble last night down at the Kit-Kat Klub. Bert pointed down the road to a huddled cinderblock building beside a trailer court.

—They sent for somebody to see to him, and luck had it be me.

Howard looked like an old man up close. His eyes were crusted, squinting up at the weak morning sun, still misted at that hour. His hands hung down between his legs, almost touching the floor, and his forefingers moved involuntarily as if they were tracing a precise and repetitious pattern on the dust of the floor. He looked up at me, licking his lips. He had not shaved in a couple of days, and the light beard had the same tawny reddish color as his hair. He did not seem to recognize me for a moment. Then his expression came together. He looked almost frightened.

—You seen her, huh?

—That's right.

—What'd she say?

—It's all right with her.

—What's all right?

—The divorce. Just the way you want it.

—You mean...like everything I said...all that...?

—She said maybe she owes you that much. For what she did.

—What she did?

—You know...

—What I said, told you?

—Wonder what the hell that is, Bert put in. He walked out into the driveway and stared down the street.

Bedlow shook his head slowly.—She owned up, told you everything?

—There was...a confirmation. Look, I said.—Bert will line you up a lawyer. I'm going to represent Ir...your wife.

—Oh? I was the one come to you...

I took a piece of motel stationery out of my pocket. There was a five-dollar bill held to it with a dark bobby pin. I remembered her hair cascading down, flowing about her face.—You never gave me a retainer. I did not act on your behalf.

I held out the paper and the bill.—This is my retainer. From her. It doesn't matter. She won't contest. I'll talk to your lawyer. It'll be easy.

—I never asked for nothing to be easy, Bedlow murmured.

—If you want to back off the adultery thing, which is silly, which even if it is true you cannot prove, you can go for rendering life insupportable...

—Life insupportable...? I never asked things be easy...

—Yes you did, I said brutally.—You just didn't know you did.

I wanted to tell him there was something rotten and weak and collapsed in him. His heart, his guts, his genes. That he had taken a woman better than he had any right to, and that Albert Sidney...but how could I? Who was I to...and then Bert stepped back toward us, his face grim.

—S..., he was saying,—I think they've got a fire down to the trailer court. You all reckon we ought to...

—If it's mine, let it burn. Ain't nothing there I care about. I need a drink.

But Bert was looking at me, his face twisted with some pointless apprehension that made so little sense that both of us piled into his car, revved the siren and fishtailed out into Airline Highway almost smashing into traffic coming from both directions as he humped across the neutral ground and laid thirty yards of rubber getting to the trailer court.

The trailer was in flames from one end to the other. Of course it was Bedlow's. Bert's face was working, and he tried to edge the car close to the end of it where there were the least flames.

—She's back in Alex, I yelled at him.—She's staying in a motel back in Alex. There's nothing in there.

But my eyes snapped from the burning trailer to a stunted and dusty cottonwood tree behind it. Which was where the old station wagon was parked. I could see the tail pipe hanging down behind as I vaulted out of the car and pulled the flimsy screen door off the searing skin of the trailer with my bare hands. I was working on the inside door, kicking it, screaming at the pliant aluminum to give way, to let me pass, when Bert pulled me back.—You g......d fool, you can't...

But I had smashed the door open by then and would have been

into the gulf of flame and smoke inside if Bert had not clipped me alongside the head with the barrel of his .38.

Which was just the moment when Bedlow passed him. Bert had hold of me, my eyes watching the trees, the nearby trailers whirling, spinning furiously. Bert yelled at Bedlow to stop, that there was no one inside, an inspired and desperate lie—or was it a final testing.

—She is, I know she is, Bedlow screamed back at Bert.

I was down on the ground now, dazed, passing in and out of consciousness not simply from Bert's blow, but from exhaustion, too long on the line beyond the boundaries of good sense. But I looked up as Bedlow shouted, and I saw him standing for a split second where I had been, his hair the color of the flames behind. He looked very young and strong, and I remember musing in my semiconsciousness, maybe he can do it. Maybe he can.

—...And she's got my boy in there, we heard him yell as he vanished into the smoke. Bert let me fall all the way then, and I passed out for good.

VII

It was late afternoon when I got home. It dawned on me that I hadn't slept in over twenty-four hours. Huge white thunderheads stood over the city, white and pure as cotton. The sun was diminished, and the heat had fallen away. It seemed that everything was very quiet, that a waiting had set in. The evening news said there was a probability of rain, even small-craft warnings on the Gulf. Then, as if there were an electronic connection between the station and the clouds, rain began to fall just as I pulled into the drive. It fell softly at first, as if it feared to come too quickly on the scorched town below. Around me, as I cut off the engine, there rose that indescribable odor that comes from the coincidence of fresh rain with parched earth and concrete. I sat in the car for a long time, pressing Bert's handkerchief full of crushed ice against the lump on the side of my head. The ice kept trying to fall out because I was clumsy. I had not gotten used to the thick bandages on my hands, and each time I tried to adjust the handkerchief, the pain in my hands made me lose fine control. My head did not hurt so badly, but I felt weak, and so I stayed there through all the news, not wanting to pass out for the second time in one day, or to lay unconscious in an empty house.

—Are you just going to sit out here, Joan asked me softly.

I opened my eyes and looked up at her. She looked very different. As if I had not see her in years, as if we had lived separate lives, heights and depths in each that we could never tell the other. —No, I said.—I was just tired.

She frowned when I got out of the car.—What's the lump? And the hands? Can't I go away for a few days?

—Sure you can, I said a little too loudly, forcefully.—Anytime at all. I ran into a hot door.

She was looking at my suit. One knee was torn, and an elbow was out. She sniffed.—Been to a fire-sale, she asked as we reached the door.

—That's not funny, I said.

—Sorry, she answered.

The children were there, and I tried very hard for the grace to see them anew, but it was just old Bart and tiny Nan trying to tell me about their holiday. Bart was still sifting sand on everything he touched, and Nan's fair skin was lightly burned. Beyond their prattle, I was trying to focus on something just beyond my reach.

Their mother came in with a pitcher of martinis and ran the kids back to the television room. She was a very beautiful woman, deep, in her thirties, who seemed to have hold of something— besides the martinis. I thought that if I were not married and she happened by, I would likely start a conversation with her.

—I ended up taking the kids with me, she said, sighing and dropping into her chair.

—Huh?

—They cried and said they'd rather come with me than stay with Louise. Even considering the ducks and chickens and things.

Hence the sand and sunburn. I poured two drinks as the phone rang.—That's quite a compliment, I said, getting up for it.

—You bet. We waited for you. We thought you'd be coming.

No, I thought as I picked up the phone. I had a gulf of my own. It was Bert. His voice was low, subdued.

—You know what, he was saying,—he made it. So help me Christ, he made it all the way to the back where...they were. Can you believe that?

—Did they find...

Bert's voice broke a little.—Yeah, he was right. You know how bad the fire was...but they called down from the state hospital and said she's taken the baby, child...out. Said must have had somebody help...

—No, I said.—I didn't, and as I said it I could see Dr. Tumulty rubbing his hands over nineteen years of a certain hell.

—Never mind, listen...when the fire boys got back there, it was...everything fused. They all formed this one thing. Said she was in a metal chair, and he was like kneeling in front, his arms...and they...you couldn't tell, but it had got to be...

I waited while he got himself back together.—It had got to be the baby she was holding, with Howard reaching out, his arms around...both...

—Bert, I started to say, tears running down my face.—Bert...

—It's all right, he said at last, clearing his throat. There was an empty silence on the line for a long moment, and I could hear the resonance of the line itself, that tiny lilting bleep of distant signals that you sometimes hear. It sounded like waves along the coast.

—It really is. All right, he said.—It was like...they had, they was...

—Reconciled, I said.

Another silence.—Oh, s..., he said.—I'll be talking to you sometimes.

Then the line was empty, and after a moment I hung up.

Joan stared at me, at the moisture on my face, glanced at my hands, the lump on my head, the ruined suit.—What happened while I was gone? Did I miss anything?

—No, I smiled at her.—Not a thing.

I walked out onto the patio with my drink. There was still a small rain falling, but even as I stood there, it faded and the clouds began to break. Up there, the moon rode serenely from one cloud to the next, and far down the sky in the direction of the coast, I could see pulses of heat lightning above the rigolets where the lake flows into the Gulf.

About the Editor

Ben Forkner is the Director of the English Department at the University of Angers in France, where he teaches American and Irish literature. A graduate of Stetson University in Florida, he received his M.A. and his Ph.D. from the University of North Carolina in Chapel Hill. He has published articles on writers from Ireland and the American South and has edited two anthologies of Irish short stories: *Modern Irish Short Stories* (Penguin) and *A New Book of Dubliners* (Methuen). He has also co-edited (with Patrick Samway) three anthologies of Southern literature: *Stories of the Modern South* (Penguin), *A Modern Southern Reader* (Peachtree), and *Stories of the Old South* (Penguin). He currently edits the *Journal of the Short Story in English*, published biannually by the University of Angers Press.